THE LAW OF SEIZURE OF GOODS

Debtor's Rights and Remedies

THE LAW OF SEIZURE OF GOODS

Debtor's Rights and Remedies

JOHN KRUSE

BARRY ROSE LAW PUBLISHERS LTD
CHICHESTER, ENGLAND

British Library Cataloguing in Publication Data
Data available

ISBN 1 902 681 10 X

Printed in Great Britain

CONTENTS

PREFACE vii
INTRODUCTION ix
GLOSSARY OF CASE REPORTS xi
TABLE OF CASES xvii
TABLE OF STATUTES lvii
STATUTORY INSTRUMENTS lxi

PART ONE – LEGAL CONTEXT
1 HISTORY AND DEVELOPMENT 1
2 CURRENT REGIME 5

PART TWO – PRE-LEVY TACTICS
3 PREVENTING SEIZURE 13
4 INSOLVENCY 45

PART THREE – LEVY PROCEDURE
5 WRONGFUL DISTRESS: FORMS AND REMEDIES 65
6 COMMENCING LEVIES: ISSUE 77
7 COMMENCING LEVIES: INITIAL VISITS 95
8 CONDUCTING LEVIES: PROCEDURE 116
9 CONDUCTING LEVIES: GOODS 139
10 CONCLUDING LEVIES: REMOVAL AND SALE 194
11 CONCLUDING LEVIES: CHARGES 216

PART FOUR – GENERAL REMEDIES AND CONCLUSIONS
12 COMPLAINTS TO CREDITORS AND BAILIFFS 231

FURTHER READING 241

INDEX 243

PREFACE

The law as stated in this text is correct as of March 31, 1999. However enforcement law is on the threshold of a period of reform, the pace of which will gradually accelerate over the next five to 10 years, as the effects of the civil justice reforms are extended through English civil law.

In the short term a number of minor changes have been implemented since the text was completed. Their impact on certain sections of the book must be noted:

- *6.2.10 Certification:* The Distress for Rent (Amendment) Rules 1999 (SI 1999/2360) have made various changes to the process of certification of private bailiffs by county courts. Special certificates have been abolished and the detail of the application procedure altered. The complaints procedure has also been changed slightly: a standard complaints form has been introduced (Form 4) and a new form is provided to enable creditors who uphold a complaint against their own bailiff to feed that decision into the county court complaints process. Provision is also made for complaints to be transferred on written request to the complainant's nearest issuing court. Such a request should be made not less than 14 days before a hearing (r.8(4A) & (4B)).
- *7.2.2 Day of levy:* In the changes engendered by the Civil Procedure Rules 1998, the previous county court and High Court restrictions upon levies upon Sundays were lost. However the author understands from LCD (by personal communication) that a practice direction will be issued (November 1999) stating that, unless the court orders otherwise, a writ or warrant of execution must not be executed on a Sunday, Good Friday or Christmas Day.
- *9.6 Statutory exemptions - magistrates' court distraint:* By the Magistrates' Court (Miscellaneous Amendments) Rules 1999 (SI 1999/2756) r.54(4) of the 1981 Rules have been amended to require that the following shall not be taken in distraint - "the clothing or bedding of any person or his family or the tools, books, vehicles or other equipment which he personally needs to use in his employment, business or vocation, provided that in this paragraph the word "person" shall not include a corporation."
- *11.3.1 Taxation of bailiffs' fees:* The previous power of a county court District Judge to tax bailiffs' fees expressly referred to in CCR O.38 r.22 has been lost in the transition to the CPR. However LCD have confirmed (by personal communication) that the power continues as the main enabling provisions are to be found in the various statutory fee scales applicable to bailiffs which permit taxation by the court. The process of reviewing bills will now be by 'detailed assessment' under CPR Part 47. This is confirmed by the recently revised Distress for Rent Rules 1988 r.11.

- *10.8.1 Irregular levies:* Finally, please note that county court provisions on irregular execution (s.125 County Courts Act 1984) are extended to execution for road traffic penalties by article 4 ERTDO 1993.

As mentioned above, broader reform of bailiffs' law may be contemplated in the longer term. The current initiatives are:

- *Civil enforcement review:* The author has been involved with this as part of the 'warrants and writs expert panel' convened by LCD to draft proposals for the harmonisation of the powers of county court bailiffs and sheriffs' officers. It is anticipated that after further consultation these will form the basis of a new Part of the CPR.
- *Bailiff's law review:* Professor Jack Beatson of Cambridge University has been commissioned to review the whole of bailiffs' law, with a view to recommending reform and harmonisation. The initial report is due in summer 2000.
- *Distress for rent:* The LCD has promised that at a later stage of the enforcement review the Law Commission report of 1991, recommending the abolition of distress for rent, will be given final consideration.
- *Private security industry regulation:* In its White Paper on the private security industry, the Home Office has proposed a new system of licencing and regulating private security staff. This includes court contracted enforcement officers (i.e. magistrates' court bailiffs) so that this new system may provide the basis for a new comprehensive regulatory regime for bailiffs.

A body of enforcement law that has for too long lain neglected and confused may at last have a prospect of modernisation and simplification. It will not be an easy process, however, due to the complexity into which it has been allowed to slip.

The author would like to thank the following for their patience and assistance: his publisher his family and the long-suffering librarians at the Royal Courts of Justice and Institute of Advanced Legal Studies.

John Kruse
January 2000

INTRODUCTION

This book is written for the use of legal practitioners advising those facing enforcement of debts by bailiffs. It describes the rights of the bailiff, the "distrainor", and of the debtor/ the distrainee. It then proceeds to examine the practical remedies available to the distrainee, whether by negotiation, less formal non-judicial pressure or by litigation. The practical elements of each remedy will be reviewed.

The reasons for writing this book are fivefold:

- the use of distress as a remedy continues to grow. This is due both to its extension in existing regimes, such as the encouragement of magistrates' courts to employ it more frequently, and also due to the development of new forms by Parliament (and the resurrection of an old form, in one case);
- it is an area of which few legal practitioners have much knowledge. A few specialising in the field of commercial property leasing will have employed the remedy of distress for rent and have expert knowledge of that one rather unique form, but on the whole it is a neglected field. With the growth in legal aid franchising and the community legal service, particularly into such areas as welfare and debt advice, more and more practitioners will encounter the day to day realities of enforcement by seizure of goods and will require information upon the subject;
- the information currently available to practitioners is often outdated, relatively inaccessible and not aimed at practical problem resolution. Appendix Three reviews the existing material, amongst which "Halsbury's Laws" inevitably features prominently. The relevant volumes are however very outdated and are academic discussions of the subject;
- much of the interest that does exist considers only the immediate parties to the process- that is, the creditor and debtor. This book specifically aims to take a broader approach, as by its nature seizure of goods can have an impact on many more interests than just those of the debtor; and,
- the area of enforcement of debt by bailiffs is sadly one where there is scope for, and, not infrequently, evidence of abuse. This is partly because the law is so unclear, partly because the enforcement agents are relatively poorly regulated and partly because the debtor- bailiff relationship is one which is liable to exploitation, taking place as it does in the privacy of a person's premises, with a large imbalance in power between enforcer and the subject of the levy.

In response to all these matters this text aims to provide an effective aid to assist those confronted with enforcement by seizure of goods. It appropriately explores each stage of the levy process and recommends remedies at every point. The first part of the book puts the process of distress in its current political and legal context. The second part examines how the bailiff may be avoided, whether by negotiation etc. or by the more extreme solution of insolvency. The third part goes through the procedure blow by blow, from the issue of a warrant to sale. At each stage the parties' rights and responsibilities are described, both in respect of the general principles of the law of distress and in light of the particular form of distress being levied; remedies are discussed and issues of legal controversy are explored. Finally in the fourth part of the book general remedies such as creditors' or professional associations' complaints procedures are outlined.

The book is designed for practitioners assisting the following groups:

- debtors: whether they are individuals, members of partnerships or limited companies;
- the debtor's relatives: whether spouses, cohabitees, children or other family members who might find themselves involved in enforcement;
- tenants and lodgers of debtors (or their families); or,
- third parties with an interest in property on the debtor's premises, whether they are holders of bills of sale or debentures, trustees or liquidators in an insolvency, finance companies who have let property on lease or hire purchase, manufacturers with claims under retention of title clauses, other creditors of the distrainee or any other third party whose goods might be threatened.

GLOSSARY OF CASE REPORTS

This glossary lists the case citations used in the text. The older English reports, if not available directly, will be found in the English Reports or in the Digest (Butterworths). The latter also contains most of the commonwealth cases cited. The mediaeval Year Book cases may be found either in the sixteenth century editions of the Year Book, or in parallel translation in editions by the Seldon Society, the Ames Foundation, or the Rolls Series. Year Book citations are generally by term, regnal year of the monarch and page and plea number. More modern reports are listed by reporter(s), court(s) covered, and year of publication.

A&E	Adolphus & Ellis, King's Bench & Queen's Bench, 1834–42
ABC	Australian Bankruptcy Cases, 1928–64
AC	Law Reports, Appeal Courts, 1865–present
Ad & El	see A&E
Adviser	The Adviser, 1986–present
All ER	All England Reports, 1936–present
Amb	Ambler, Chancery, 1716–83
And	Anderson, Common Pleas, sixteenth century
Anst	Anstruther, Exchequer, 1792–7
App Cas	Law Reports, Appeal Cases, House of Lords, 1875–90
AR	Ontario Appeal Reports, 1876–1900
Atk	Atkyns, Chancery, 1736–54
B & Ald	Barnewell & Alderson, King's Bench, 1817–22
B & Ad	Barnewall & Adolphus, King's Bench, 1830–34
B&A	either of above
B&C	Best & Smith, Queen's Bench, 1861–70
Barn KB	Barnardiston, King's Bench, 1726–34
Barnes	Barnes' Notes of Cases, Common Pleas, 1732–60
BCC	British Company Cases
BCLC	Butterworth's Company Law Cases
BCR	British Columbia Reports, 1867–1947
Beav	Beavan, Rolls, 1838–66
Bing	Bingham, Common Pleas, 1822–34
Bing NC	Bingham New Cases, Common Pleas, 1834–40
Bl Rep	Blackstone (either Henry or Sir William – see later under initial)
Bligh NS	Bligh's New Series, House of Lords, 1827–37
Bom Cr Cas	Bombay Reports, Crown Cases
Bos & Pul	Bosanquet & Puller, Common Pleas, 1796–1804
Bos & P NR	Bosanquet & Puller New Reports, Common Pleas, 1804–7
Bro CC	Brown's Reports of Cases in Chancery, 1778–94

Brod & Bing	Broderip & Bingham, Common Pleas, 1819–22
Bull NP	Buller's Nisi Prius (see Appendix 3)
Burr	Burrow's King's Bench, 1756–72
C M & R	Crompton, Meeson & Roscoe, Exchequer, 1834–5
C&K	Carrington & Kirwan, Nisi Prius & Criminal, 1834–53 (also Car & Kir)
C&P	Carrington & Payne, Nisi Prius & Criminal, 1823–41
Cab & El	Cababé & Ellis, Queen's Bench, 1882–85
Cab & E	as above
Cald	Caldecott's Settlement Cases, King's Bench, 1776–1885
Camp	Campbell, Nisi Prius, 1807–16
Car & Kir	see above
CBNS	Common Bench, New Series, Common Pleas, 1856–65
CCC	Canadian Criminal Cases Annotated, 1892–present
CCR	Law Reports, Crown Cases Reserved, 1865–75
Ch	Law Reports, Chancery Division, 1890–present
Ch D	Law Reports, Chancery Division, 1875–90
Ch App	Law Reports, Chancery Appeals, 1865–75
Chitt	Chitty, King's Bench, 1770–1822
Cl & Fin	Clark & Finnelly, House of Lords, 1831–46
CL	Current Law (monthly), 1947–present
CLY	Current Law Yearbook, 1947–present
Co Rep	Coke, Common Law, 1572–1616
Com Dig	Comyn's Digest, Common Law, 1695–1740
Comb	Comberbatch, King's Bench, 1685–98
Coop	George Cooper, Chancery, 1792–1815
Cowp	Cowper, King's Bench, 1774–8
Cox CC	Cox's Criminal Court Reports, 1843–1945
CP	Upper Canada Common Pleas, 1850–81
CPD	Law Reports, Common Pleas Division, 1875–80
Cr App R	Cohen's Criminal Appeal Reports, 1908–present
Cr & M	Crompton & Meeson, Exchequer, 1832–4
Cr M & R	see C M & R earlier
Cr & J	Crompton & Jervis, Exchequer, 1830–32
Cr & Ph	Craig & Philips, Chancery, 1840–41
Crim LR	Criminal Law Review, 1954–present
Cro Eli/ Jac/Car	Croke, Common Law, in reigns of Elizabeth I, James I & Charles I
Cun	Cunningham, King's Bench, 1734–5
D M & G	De Gex, Macnaghten & Gordon, Chancery Appeals, 1851–7
D&E	Durnford & East (see TR)
D&L	Dowling & Lowndes, Bail Court, 1843–49
De G & J	De Gex & Jones, Chancery Appeals, 1857–9
De G & Sm	De Gex & Smale, Chancery, 1846–52
De G M & G	see above D M & G

Deac	Deacon, Bankruptcy, 1834–40
Diprose's	Diprose & Gammon, 1897 Friendly Society Reports
DLR	Dominion Law Reports (Canada), 1912–55, 2nd series 1956– present
Doug KB	Douglas' King's Bench Reports, 1778–85
Dow & Ry	Dowling & Ryland, King's Bench, 1822–27
Dow & L	see above D&L
Dowl PC	Dowling's Practice Reports, Bail Court, 1830–41
Dowl	as above
Drew	Drewry, Chancery, 1852–59
Dyer	Dyer, Common Law, 1513–81
E&B	Ellis & Blackburn, Queen's Bench, 1852–4
East	East, King's Bench, 1800–12
EB&E	Ellis, Blackburn & Ellis, Queen's Bench, 1858–60
EG	Estates Gazette, 1858–present
EGCS	Estates Gazette Cases Summaries
EGLR	Estates Gazette Law Reports, 1985–present
El & Bl	as above E&B
Eq	Law Reports, Equity, 1865–75
Eq Cas Abr	Equity Cases Abridged, Chancery, 1664–1744
ER	English Reports, 1220–1865
Esp	Espinasse, Nisi Prius, 1793–1810
Ex D	Law Reports, Exchequer Division, 1875–80
Exch D	Law Reports, Exchequer Division, 1865–75
F&F	Foster & Finlayson, Nisi Prius & Criminal Courts, 1856–67
FLR	Family Law Reports, 1980–present
Gale	Gale, Exchequer, 1835–6
H Bl	Henry Blackstone, Common Pleas, 1788–96
H&C	Hurlstone & Coltman, Exchequer, 1862–66
H&N	Hurlstone & Norman, Exchequer, 1856–62
Hard	Hardres, Exchequer, 1655–69
Hardr	as above
HBR	Hansell's Bankruptcy Reports, 1915–17
Het	Hetley, Common Pleas, 1627–31
HL Cas	Clark's House of Lords Reports, 1847–66
Hob	Hobart, Common Law, 1613–25
Holt KB	Holt, King's Bench, 1688–1710
ICLR	Irish Common Law Reports, 1849–66
ILT	Irish Law Times, 1867–present
Ir CL	Irish Reports Common Law, 1866–77
Ir L Rec	Law Recorder (Ireland), 1827–38
IR CL	as above Ir CL

ILR	Irish Law Reports, 1838–50
Jeb & Sy	Jebb & Symes, Queen's Bench Ireland, 1838–41
Jac	Jacob, Chancery, 1821–23
Jo	Johnson, Chancery, 1858–60; or either Sir T or Sir W Jones later
JP	Justice of the Peace, 1837–present
Jur	The Jurist, all courts, 1837–54, new series, 1855–67
K&J	Kay & Johnson, Chancery, 1854–8
KB	Law Reports, King's Bench, 1901–52
Keb	Keble, King's Bench, 1661–77
Keble	as above
Keny	Kenyon's Notes of Cases, King's Bench, 1753–9
Lat	Latch, King's Bench, 1625–8
Ld Raym	Lord Raymond, Common Law, 1694–1732
Leon	Leonard, Common Law, 1552–1615
Lev	Levinz, Common Law, 1660–96
LGR	Local Government Reports, 1902–present
LJ (NS)	Law Journal, New Series, all courts, 1832–1949
LJ (OS)	Law Journal, Old Series, all courts, 1822–31
Lofft	Lofft, King's Bench, 1772–4
LR Ir	Law Reports, Ireland, Chancery & Common Law, 1877–93
LT	Law Times Reports, 1859–1947
Legal Action	Journal of Legal Action Group
LT(os)	Law Times Old Series, 1843–59
LT Jo	Law Times Newspapers, 1843–1965
Lutw	Lutwyche, Common Pleas, 1682–1704
M'Clel	M'Cleland, Exchequer & Equity, 1824
M&G	Manning & Granger, Common Pleas, 1840–45
M&S	Maule & Selwyn, King's Bench, 1813–17
M&W	Meeson & Welsby, Exchequer, 1836–47
Madd	Maddock, Chancery, 1815–21
Man LR	Manitoba Law Reports, 1883–present
Man & G	as above M&G
Mans	Manson, bankruptcy, 1893–1914
Mod Rep	Modern Reports (Leach's), all courts, 1669–1775
Moo	Moore, Common Pleas, 1817–27
Moo & S	Moore & Scott, Common Pleas, 1831–34
Moo PC	see below Moo PCC
Mood Ind App	Moore's Indian Appeal Cases, Privy Council, 1836–72
Moo PCC	Moore's Privy Council Cases, 1836–63
Moo & R	Moody & Robinson, Nisi Prius, 1830–44
Mood & R	as above
Mood & M	Moody & Malkin, Nisi Prius, 1826–30
Moore CP	as above Moo

Morr	Morrell's Bankruptcy Cases, 1884–93
MR	see Mod Rep
NB Eq Rep	New Brunswick Equity Reports, 1894–1912
NBR	New Brunswick Reports, 1883–1929, 2nd series 1949–present
Nev & M KB	Neville & Manning, King's Bench, 1832–36
Nfld LR	Newfoundland Law Reports, 1817–1940
Noy	Noy, King's Bench, 1558–1649
NPC	New Practice Cases, 1844–48
NSR	Nova Scotia Reports, 1834–1929
NSWLR	New South Wales Law Reports, 1971–present
NZ Recent Law	New Zealand Recent Law
NZLR	New Zealand Law Reports, 1883–present
OLR	Ontario Law Reports, 1901–30
OR	Ontario Reports, 1882–1900
P	Law Reports, Probate, Divorce & Admiralty, 1890–1971
Park	Parker, Exchequer, 1743–67; Appeal Court 1678–1717
PEI	Prince Edward Island Reports, 1850–82
Ph	Phillip, Chancery, 1841–49
Poll	Pollexfen, King's Bench, 1670–82
PR	Ontario Practice Reports, 1848–1900
Price	Price, Exchequer, 1814–24
QB	Adolphus & Ellis New Series Queen's Bench Reports, 1841–52
QB	Law Reports, Queen's Bench, 1891–1901, 1952–present
QBD	Law Reports, Queen's Bench, 1875–1890
QSCR	Queensland Supreme Court Reports, 1860–1881
R&G	Nova Scotia Reports (Russell & Geldert), 1879–95
RA	Rating Appeals, 1965–present
Roll Rep	Rolle, King's Bench, 1614–25
RTR	Road Traffic Reports, 1970–present
Russ & Ry	Russell & Ryan's Crown Cases Reserved, 1800–23
RVR	Rating & Valuation Reports, 1960–present
Ry &	Ryan & Moody, Nisi Prius, 1823–26
Salk	Salkeid, King's Bench, 1689–1712
Saund	Saunders, King's Bench, 1666–1672
Say	Sayer, King's Bench, 1751–56
Scott NR	Scott's New Reports, Common Pleas, 1840–45
Sel Soc	Selden Society series
Show	Shower, King's Bench, 1678–95
Sid	Siderfin, King's Bench, Common Pleas & Exchequer, 1657–70
Sir W Jones	Sir William Jones, Common Law, 1620–40

Sir T Jones	Sir Thomas Jones, Common Law, 1667–85
Sm & G	Smale & Giffard, Chancery, 1852–57
Smith LC	Smith's Leading Cases, Common Law Courts
Sol Jo	Solicitor's Journal, all courts, 1857–present
SRQ	Queensland Reports, Supreme Court, 1860–81
Stra	Strange Nisi Prius, 1814–23
Swa	Swabey, Admiralty, 1855–59
Taunt	Taunton, Common Pleas, 1807–19
Tax Cases	Tax Case Reports, all courts, 1875–present
TLR	Times Law Reports, all courts, 1884–1950
TR	Term Reports (Durnford & East), King's Bench, 1785–1800
UCR	Upper Canada Reports; King's Bench, 1831–44; Queen's Bench 1844–81; Common Pleas, 1850–82
Vent	Ventris, all courts, 1668–91
Vern	Vernon, Chancery, 1680–1719
Ves Jen/Jnr	Vesey Senior, Chancery, 1747–56; Junior, Chancery, 1789–1817
Vin Abr	Viner's Abridgment, see Appendix 3
VLR	Victorian Law Reports, 1875–1956
VR(L)	Victorian Reports (Law)
W&T	White & Tudor's Leading Cases in Equity
W&W	Wyatt & Webb, Australian courts, 1861–63
WALR	Western Australian Law Reports, 1898–1959
Will Woll & Dav	Willmore, Wollaston & Davison, Queen's Bench & Bail Ct, 1837
Willes	Willes, Common Pleas, 1737–58
Wils	George Wilson, Common Law, 1742–74
Win	Winch, Common Pleas, 1621–25
WLR	Weekly Law Reports, 1953–present
WM BI	Sir William Blackstone, Common Law, 1746–79
Wms Saunds	William's Notes to Saunder's Reports, 1871
WN	Weekly Notes, all courts, 1866–1952
WR	Weekly Reporter, all courts, 1852–1906
WRTLB	Wilkinson's Road Traffic Law Bulletin
WWR	Western Weekly Reports (Canada), 1912–70
Y&J	Younge & Jervis, Exchequer, 1826–30
YB	Year Books, Common Law, 1273–1535
Yelv	Yelverton, King's Bench, 1602–13

TABLE OF CASES

A W Garnage Ltd *v.* Payne [1925] 134 LT 222 169
A W Ltd *v.* Cooper & Hall Ltd [1925] 2 KB 816 218
Abbot *v.* Smith (1774) 2 Wm Bl 947 95
Abbott *v.* Parfitt [1871] 6 QB 346 151
Abingdon RDC *v.* O'Gorman [1968] 3 All ER 79 CA 32, 34
Absolon *v.* Knight & Barker (1743) 94 ER 998 22
Ackland *v.* Paynter (1820) 8 Price 95 128
Ackworth *v.* Kempe [1778] 99 ER 30 72
Adams *v.* Grane (1833) 1 Cr & M 380 168
Addison *v.* Shepherd [1908] 2 KB 118 149
Aga Kurboolie Mahomed *v.* The Queen (1843) 4 Moo PC 239 104, 201
Aireton *v.* Davis (1833) 9 Bing 740 203
Aitkenhead *v.* Blades (1813) 5 Taunt 198 194, 212
Alchin *v.* Wells [1793] 5 Term Rep 470 218
Aldenburgh *v.* Peaple (1834) 6 C & P 212 96
Aldred *v.* Constable [1844] 6 QB 370 66, 205
Allan *v.* Lavine (1942) 1 DLR 731 144
Allan *v.* Overseers of Liverpool [1874] 9 QB 180 171
Allan *v.* Place (1908) 15 DLR 476 80
Allen *v.* Sharp (1848) 2 Exch 352 23, 187
Aluminium Industrie Vaassen *v.* Romalpa Aluminium Ltd [1976] 2 All ER 552 162
Alwayes *v.* Broom 2 Lutw 1262 34
Ambergate, Nottingham & Boston & Eastern Junction Co. *v.* Midland Railway Co [1853] 2 El & Bl 792 9, 137
American Concentrated Must *v.* Hendry (1893) 57 JP 521; (1893) 68 LT 742; (1893) WN 67 1, 99, 100, 104
American Express *v.* Hurley [1985] 3 All ER 564 204
Ancona *v.* Rogers (1876) 1 Ex D 285 119
Anderson *v.* Henry (1898) 29 OR 719 128
Andrew, *In Re* [1937] 1 Ch 122 56
Andrews *v.* Dixon (1820) 3 B & Ald 645 90
Andrews *v.* Morris [1841] 1 QB 3 70, 74
Andrews *v.* Russel [1786] BNP 81d 203
Anglehart *v.* Rathier (1876) 27 CP 97 101
Anglo-Baltic & Mediterranean Bank *v.* Barber [1924] 2 KB 410 60
Annot Lyle, The [1886] 11 P 114 14
Anon Cro Eliz 13 210
Anon Dyer 312 191
Anon 3 Leon Rep 15 185

Anon Loyt 253 218
Anon Moore 7 209, 210
Anon [1314] YB 8 E 2 202
Anon [1412/13] YB 14 Hen 4 13a p12 104
Anon (1495) YB 11 Hen 7 fo 5 pl 18 96
Anon (1535) 1 And 31 32
Anon (1568) 3 Dyer 280 211
Anon (1700) 12 MR 397 211
Anon (1702) 7 Mod Rep 118 187
Anon (1705) 11 Mod Rep 64 32
Anon (1758) 2 Keny 372/96 ER 1214 102
Anon *ex parte* Descharmes 1 Atk 102 49
Anscombe *v.* Shore [1808] 1 Camp 285 200
Antoniadi *v.* Smith [1907] 2 KB 589 159
Arminer *v.* Spotwood (1773) Loft 114 54
Armoduct Manufacturing Co Ltd *v.* General Incandescent Co Ltd [1911] 2 KB 143 61
Armstrong *v.* Terry (1967) 1 OR 588 153
Armytage, *Re* [1880] 14 Ch D 379 145
Arnison *ex parte* (1868) LR 3 Exch 56 220
Aro Co Ltd, *Re* [1980] 1 All ER 1067 60
Arthur *v.* Anker [1996] 3 All ER 783 136, 137
Artistic Color Printing, *ex parte* Fourdrinie, *In Re* [1882] 21 Ch D 510 48
Arundell *v.* Trevell (1662) 1 Sid 81 186
Ash *v.* Dawnay (1852) 8 Exch 237 194
Ash *v.* Wood (1587) Cro Eliz 59 188
Ashowle *v.* Wainwright (1842) 2 QB 837 200
Aspey *v.* Jones (1884) 54 LJQB 98 74
Aspinall, *Re* [1961] Ch 526 36
Assiniboia Land Co *v.* Acres (1915) 25 DLR 439 143
Astley *v.* Pinder (1760) 99
Atkins *v.* Kilby (1840) 11 Ad & El 777 75
Atkinson *v.* Jamieson (1792) 5 TR 25 96
Atlee *v.* Backhouse (1838) 3 M & W 633 227
Attack *v.* Bramwell (1863) 3 B & S 520 65, 100, 183, 185
Attorney General *v.* Bradlaugh [1885] 14 QBD 667 79
Attorney General *v.* Dakin [1820] 4 HL 338 97
Attorney General *v.* Leonard [1888] 38 Ch D 622 92
Augustien *v.* Challis (1847) 1 Exch 279 90
Austin *v.* Davey (1844) 4 LTOS 160 70
Avenell *v.* Coker [1828] Mood & M 172 66
Averill *v.* Caswell & Co (1915) 31 WLR 953 120
Axford *v.* Perret (1828) 4 Bing 586 187
Ayshford, *ex parte* Lovering, *Re* [1887] 4 Morr 164 50
Ayshford *v.* Murray (1870) 23 LT 470 45, 203

B (BPM) *v.* B (MM) [1969] 2 WLR 862 16

Baber *v.* Harris (1839) 9 Ad & El 532 190
Bach *v.* Meaks [1816] 5 M & S 200 37
Bagge *v.* Mawby (1853) 8 Exch 641 85, 209, 211
Bagge *v.* Whitehead [1892] 2 QB 355 CA 73
Bagshaw *v.* Farnsworth (1860) 2 LT 390 156
Bagshaw *v.* Goward (1609) Yelv 96 202
Bagshawes *v.* Deacon [1898] 2 QB 173 137
Bailey *v.* Bailey (1665) 1 Lev 174 45
Bailey (C H) *v.* Memorial Enterprises [1974] 1 All ER 1003 19
Baker *v.* Leathes [1810] Wight 113 17
Baker *v.* Wicks [1904] 1 KB 743 66
Baldwin, *Re* (1858) 2 Deg & J 230 141
Bales *v.* Wingfield (1843) 4 A & E 580 205
Balls *v.* Pink (1845) 4 LTOS 356 128
Balme *v.* Hutton (1833) 9 Bing 471 54
Bank of Nova Scotia *v.* Jordison (1963) 40 DLR 790 153
Bank of Toronto *v.* Adames, Sheriff of Acadia (1923) 1 DLR 432 132
Bannister *v.* Hyde (1860) 2 E & E 627 104, 128
Barclay *ex parte* 5 DM & G 410 142
Barclays Bank *v.* Roberts [1954] 1 WLR 1212 67
Barff *v.* Probyn (1895) 64 LJQB 557 185
Barker *v.* Dynes (1832) 1 Dowl 169 217
Barker *v.* Furlong [1891] 2 Ch 172 41
Barnard *v.* Leigh (1815) 1 Stark 43 146
Barons *v.* Luscombe [1835] 3 Ad & El 589 17
Barrow *v.* Bell (1855) 5 E & B 540 152
Barrow *v.* Poile (1830) 1 B & Ad 629 58
Bashall *v.* Bashall (1894) 11 TLR 152 41
Basham, *Re* (1881) WN 161 125
Bastow, *Re* (1867) LR 4 Eq 689 59
Batchelor *v.* Vyse (1834) 4 Moo & S 552 205
Bates *v.* Northampton City Council [1990] Legal Action 3/91 113
Bavin *v.* Hutchinson (1862) 6 LT 504 77
Bayliss *v.* Fisher (1830) 7 Bing 153 184
Baynes *v.* Smith [1794] 1 Esp 206 151, 167
Bealy *v.* Sampson (1688) 2 Vent 93 203
Beanland *v.* Bradley [1854] 2 Sm & G 339 158
Beard *v.* Knight (1858) 8 E & B 865 91
Beaufort, Duke of *v.* Bates [1862] 6 LT 82 145
Beavan *v.* Delahey [1788] 1 Hy Bl 5 20
Beck *v.* Denbigh (1860) 29 LJCP 273 66, 144, 196
Becker *v.* Riebold (1913) 30 TLR 142 233
Beckett *v.* Corporation of Leeds [1871] 7 Ch App 421 98
Bedford (Sheriff of) & Toseland Building Supplies Ltd *v.* Bishop [1993] CA unreported 149
Beeche's Case (1608) 77 ER 559 32
Beeston, *Re* [1899] 1 QB 626 221, 226

Belair *v.* Banque d'Hochelaga (1923) 2 WWR 771 156
Belcher *v.* Patten (1848) 6 CB 608 152
Bell, *Re* (1938) 2 DLR 754 153
Bell *v.* Hutchinson (1844) 8 Jur 895 140
Bell *v.* Oakley (1814) 2 M & S 259 100, 110
Bellaglade, *Re* [1977] 1 All ER 319 58
Bellyse *v.* M'Ginn [1891] 2 QB 227 53
Belshaw *v.* Bush (1851) 11 CB 191 198
Belshaw *v.* Chapman Marshall (1832) 4 B & A 336 68, 73
Bennet's Case (1727) 2 Stra 787 89
Bennet *v.* Bayes (1860) 5 H & N 391 198, 219, 233
Bennett *v.* Powell (1855) 3 Drew 326 74
Bent *v.* McDougall (1881) 2 R & G 468 168
Berkley *v.* Poulett (1976) 241 EG 911 142
Berliner Industriebank Aktiengesellschaft *v.* Jost [1971] 1 QB 278 78
Berry (Herbert), *Re* [1977] 1 WLR 617 58
Berry *v.* Farrow [1914] 1 KB 632 23, 89, 122, 174
Bessey *v.* Windham (1844) 6 QB 166 207
Bevill's Case (1585) 4 Co Rep 6a; 4 Rep 116 31, 198
Bhatnagar & Elanrent *v.* Whitehall Investments (1996) 5 CL 166 183
Biggins *v.* Goode (1832) 2 C & J 364 213
Bignell *v.* Clarke [1860] 5 H & N 485 132
Bikker *v.* Beeston (1860) 29 LJ Exch 121 69
Billing *v.* Pill [1954] 1 QB 70 143
Binns, *Re* [1875] 1 Ch D 285 51
Birch *v.* Dawson (1834) 2 A & E 37 146
Bird *v.* Bass (1843) 6 Scotts NR 928 127
Bird *v.* Hildage [1948] 1 KB 91 19-20
Birmingham Gaslight & Coke Co, *ex parte, In Re*: Adams (1870) 11 Eq 204 62
Birstall Candle Co *v.* Daniels [1908] 2 KB 254 79
Biscop *v.* White (1600) 78 ER 991 98
Bishop (deceased), *Re* [1965] Ch 450 160
Bishop *v.* Bryant (1834) 6 C & P 484 201
Bishop *v.* Elliot (1885) 11 Exch 113 146
Bishop of Rochester *v.* Le Fanu [1906] 1 Ch 513 49
Bissett *v.* Caldwell (1791) Peake 50; 1 Esp 206 151, 194
Bissicks *v.* Bath Colliery (1877) 2 Ex D 459 67
Black *v.* Coleman (1878) 29 CP 507 123, 128
Blackburn *v.* Bowering [1994] OC 3 All ER 380 CA 30
Blades *v.* Arundale (1813) 1 M & S 711 91, 132, 152
Blades *v.* Higgs (1861) 10 CBNS 713 31
Blake *v.* Newburn (1848) 17 LJQB 216 227, 229
Blankenstein *v.* Robertson [1890] 24 QBD 543 42
Blanket *v.* Palmer [1940] 1 All ER 524 89
Blenkhorn, *ex parte* Jay, *Re* [1874] LR 9 Ch App 697 120
Blue Bird Mines, *Re* [1942] 44 WLR 85 63

Bluston & Bramley Ltd *v.* Leigh [1950] 2 KB 554 55
Boden *v.* Roscoe [1894] 1 QB 608 18
Bolt & Nut Co (Tipton) Ltd *v.* Rowlands, Nicholls & Co [1964] 2 QB 10 198
Bolton *v.* Canham (1670) Pollexfen 20 85
Bond Worth, *Re* [1979] 3 All ER 919 CA 163
Booth *v.* Macfarlane (1831) 1 B & Ad 904 19
Booth *v.* Walkden Spinning & Manufacturing Co Ltd [1909] 2 KB 368 60
Borden (UK) *v.* Scottish Timber Products Ltd [1979] 3 All ER 961 CA 163
Boswell *v.* Crucible Steel Co [1925] 1 KB 119 142
Bott *v.* Ackroyd [1859] 23 JP 661 74
Botten *v.* Tomlinson (1847) 16 LJCP 138 73
Boucher *v.* Wiseman (1595) Cro Eliz 440 80
Boulton *v.* Reynolds [1859] 2 E & E 369 197
Bourgoin SA *v.* Ministry of Agriculure [1986] 1 QB 716 235
Bower & Co *v.* Hett [1895] 2 QB 51 57, 129
Bowkett *v.* Fullers United Electrical Works [1923] 1 KB 160 60
Boyd *v.* Profaze (1867) 16 LT 431 103
Boyd *v.* Shorrock (1867) 5 Eq 72 142, 143
Bradford MBC *v.* Arora [1991] 2 WLR 1377 CA 109
Bradley *v.* Bayliss [1881] 8 QBD 195 171
Bradshawe's Case [1597] Cro Eliz 570 186
Bradyll *v.* Ball (1785) 1 Bro CC 427 51
Braithwaite *v.* Cooksey & Another 1 H Bl 465 85
Braithwaite *v.* Marriott (1862) 1 H & C 591 222, 229
Branscomb *v.* Bridges (1823) 1 B & C 145 198, 219
Branscombe *v.* Scarborough [1844] 6 QB 13 188
Brelsford, *Re* [1932] 1 Ch 24 54
Brenner, *ex parte* Saffery, *In Re* [1881] 16 Ch D 668 120
Breton *v.* Mockett [1878] 9 Ch D 95 41
Bretton's Estate, *In Re* [1881] 17 Ch D 416 41
Brewer *v.* Drew (1843) 11 M & W 625 183, 188
Brice *v.* Hare (1824) 2 LJOSKB 194 96
Bridge *v.* Cage (1605) Cro Jac 103 225
Bridges *v.* Smyth (1829) 5 Bing 410 21
Brigg's Case 1 Roll Rep 336 12
Briggs *v.* Sowry [1841] 8 M & W 729 52
Brintons *v.* Wyre Forest DC [1976] 3 WLR 749 118, 119
Bristol, Earl of, *v.* Wilsmore (1823) 2 Dow & Ry 755 39
Bristol Airport *v.* Powdrill [1990] Ch 744 63
British Economical Lamp Co *v.* Empire, Mile End (1913) 29 TLR 386 143
British Mutoscope & Biograph Co Ltd *v.* Homer [1901] 1 Ch 671 141, 166
British Salicylates Ltd, *Re* [1919] 2 Ch 155 90
Brocklehurst *v.* Lawe (1857) 7 E & B 176 51-2
Brooke, *In Re* [1894] 2 Ch 600 152
Brooke *v.* Noakes [1828] 8 B & C 537 36, 37
Brookes *v.* Harris [1995] *The Times*, April 22 150
Broome *v.* Cassell & Co [1972] AC 1027 109, 183

Broomhall *v.* Norton (1690) 2 Jo 193 17, 192
Broster, *Re* [1897] 2 QB 429 91
Brough *v.* Wallace & Affleck (1863) 2 W & W 195 173
Broughton *v.* Wilkerson (1880) 44 JP 781 28
Brown, *Re* [1878] 3 QBD 545 86
Brown *v.* Arundell (1850) 10 CB 54 169
Brown *v.* Cooper (1870) 1 VR(L) 210 141
Brown *v.* Copley (1844) 8 Scott NR 350 72
Brown *v.* Crowley [1963] 3 All ER 655 30
Brown *v.* Glenn [1851] 16 QB 254 96, 99
Brown *v.* LB Haringey [1986] noted at [1992] 2 All ER 704 113, 132
Brown *v.* Shevill (1834) 2 Ad & El 138 168
Brown *v.* Watson (1871) 23 LT 745 67
Brown Bayley & Dixon, *ex parte* Roberts & Wright, *In Re* [1881] 18 Ch D 649 52
Browne *v.* Powell (1827) 4 Bing 230 199
Browning *v.* Dann [1735] Bullers NP 81c 117
Bruce *v.* Smith (1923) 3 DLR 887 143
Brun *v.* Hutchinson [1844] 2 D & L 43 199, 218
Brunswick, Duke of *v.* Sloman (1849) 3 CB 317 69
Bryant, *Re* (1876) 4 Ch D 98 45
Buckingham *v.* Pembroke (1672) 3 Keb 74 146
Buckland *v.* Butterfield (1820) 2 Brod & B 58 146
Buckle *v.* Bewes 91825) 4 B & C 154 217
Budd *v.* Pyle (1846) 10 JP 203 100
Buist *v.* McCombe [1883] 8 AR 598 18
Bull, *ex parte*, Bew, *In Re* [1887] 18 QBD 642 86
Bullen *v.* Ansley & Smith (1807) 6 Esp 111 218
Buller's Case 29 Eliz CB 77
Bumpus, *ex parte* White, *Re* [1908] 2 KB 330 49
Bunch *v.* Kennington [1841] 1 QB 679 173
Burdett, *Re* [1888] 20 QBD 310 43
Burdett *v.* Abbot [1811] 14 East 1 12, 103
Burns *v.* Christianson (1921) 60 DLR 173 147
Burrell *v.* Jones 3 B & A 47 52
Burton *v.* Le Gros [1864] 34 LJQB 91 73
Bushell *v.* Timson [1934] 2 KB 79 207
Butler *v.* Smith (1895) 39 SJ 406 226
Button, *ex parte* Haviside, *In Re* [1907] 2 KB 180 192
Byford *v.* Russell [1907] 2 KB 522 161
Bygus *v.* Goode (1832) 2 Cr & J 364 212

Caidan, *Re* (1942) Ch 90 80, 232
Cain *v.* Moon [1896] 2 QB 283 40
Cameron *v.* Gibson (1889) 17 OR 233 156
Cameron *v.* Lightfoot (1778) 2 Wm Bl 1190 68
Canadian National Railways *v.* Norwegian (1971) 1 WWR 766 149

Canadian Pacific Wine Co *v.* Tuley [1921] 2 AC 417 110
Capel *v.* Buszard [1829] 6 Bing 150 18, 97
Caribbean Products (Yam Importers), *In Re* [1966] Ch 331 56
Carr *v.* Goslington (1727) 11 MR 414 89
Carratt *v.* Morley [1841] 1 QB 18 70
Carriage Co-operative Supply Association, *ex parte* Clemence, *Re* [1883] 23 Ch D 154 51
Carrington *v.* Saldin (1925) 133 LT 432 21
Carter *v.* St Mary Abbot's Vestry (1900) 64 JP 548 160, 232
Carter *v.* Salmon (1880) 43 LT 490 112
Cartwright *v.* Comber 2 Ld Raym 1427 194
Cartwright *v.* Smith & Batty (1833) 1 Mood & R 284 37
Cash *v.* Wells (1830) 1 B & Ad 375 68
Castle *v.* Ruttan (1854) 4 CP 252 209
Cave *v.* Capel [1954] 1 QB 367 177, 180
Cawthorne *v.* Campbell [1790] 1 Anst 205 186
Central Printing Works *v.* Walter (1907) 24 LT 88 119
Challoner *v.* Robinson [1908] 1 Ch 490 168
Chamberlain *v.* Greenfield (1772) 3 Wils 292 108
Chamberlayn's Case (1590) 74 ER 202 202
Chamberlayne *v.* Collins (1894) 70 LT 217 143
Chancellor *v.* Webster [1893] TLR 568 22, 191
Chandler *v.* Doulton (1865) 3 H & C 553 214
Chapman, *ex parte* Goodyear, *Re* (1894) 10 TLR 449 51
Chapman *v.* Bowlby (1841) 8 M & W 249 211
Chappell *v.* Harrison [1910] 103 LT 594 170
Chesterfield *v.* Farringdon 11 Ann CB 196
Chiandetti, *Re* (1921) 91 LJKB 70 55
Chic Fashions *v.* Jones [1968] 2 QB 299 109
Chidley, *In Re* and *In Re*: Leonard [1875] 1 Ch D 177 62
Child *v.* Chamberlain (1834) 5 B & A 1049 116
Child *v.* Edwards [1909] 2 KB 753 20
Childrens *v.* Saxby (1683) 1 Vern 207 69
China *v.* Harrow UDC [1954] 1 QB 178 78
Chinn, *In Re* [1881] 17 Ch D 839 55
Christie *v.* Winnington (1853) 8 Exch 287 55
Chubb Cash Ltd *v.* John Crilley & Son (1983) 2 All ER 294 182, 184
Churchill *v.* Siggers (1854) 3 E & B 929 68
Churchward *v.* Johnson (1889) 54 JP 326 167
Clark *v.* Clement (1796) 6 TR 525 154
Clark *v.* Cullen [1882] 9 QBD 355 154
Clark *v.* Gaskarth (1818) 8 Taunt 431 173
Clark *v.* Woods [1848] 2 Ex 395 75
Clarke *v.* Clement & English (1796) 6 TR 525 95
Clarke *v.* Davey (1820) 4 Moo 465 75
Clarke *v.* Dickenson [1858] EB & E 148 228
Clarke *v.* Grant [1950] 1 KB 104 21

Clarke *v.* Holford (1848) 2 C & K 540 185
Clarke *v.* Millwall Dock [1886] 17 QBD 494 168
Clarke *v.* Nicholson [1835] 4 LJNS Exch 66 217
Cleaver, *ex parte* Rawlings, *Re* [1887] 18 QBD 489 42
Clement *v.* Milner (1800) 3 Esp 95 98, 172
Clerk *v.* Withers (1704) 6 Mod Rep 290 120
Cliffe, *ex parte* Eatough & Co Ltd, *Re* (1880) 42 LT 95 51
Climie *v.* Wood [1868] 3 Exch 257 144
Clissold *v.* Cratchley [1910] 2 KB 244 68
Clowes *v.* Hughes (1870) 5 Exch 160 182
Clun's Case [1613] 10 Co Rep 127a 18
Coal Consumers Association, *Re* (1876) 4 Ch D 625 51
Cobbett, *Re* (1861) 10 WR 40 70
Cobbold *v.* Chilver (1842) 4 Man & G 62 70
Cochrane *v.* Entwistle [1890] 25 QBD 116 43
Cockburn *v.* Jeanette (1942) 3 DLR 216 80
Codd *v.* Cabe (1876) 1 Ex D 352 78
Coffin *v.* Dyke (1884) 48 JP 757 128
Cohen *v.* Das Rivas (1891) 64 LT 661 218
Cole, *ex parte* Mutton, *Re* (1872) LR 14 Eq 178 120
Cole, *ex parte* Trustee of Bankrupt's Property, *Re* [1964] 1 Ch 175 40
Cole *v.* Davies (1968) 1 Ld Raym 624 55, 118
Colegrave *v.* Dias Santos (1823) 2 B & C 76 146
Collingridge *v.* Paxton (1851) 11 CB 683 140
Collins, *Re* (1888) 21 LR Ir 508 50
Collins *v.* Renison [1754] Say 138/96 ER 830 29, 173
Collins *v.* Rose (1839) 5 M & W 194 75
Colls *v.* Coates (1840) 11 Ad & El 826 218
Colyer *v.* Speed (1820) 2 Brod & Bing 67 91, 92
Combe *v.* De La Bere [1882] 22 Ch D 316 97
Company of Proprietors of Parrett Navigation *v.* Stower, Trott & Munckton (1840) 6 M & W 564 32
Concorde Graphics *v.* Andromeda Investments (1983) 265 EG 386 85
Condon, *ex parte* James, *Re* [1874] 9 Ch App 609 53
Condy *v.* Blaiberg [1891] 55 JP 580 43
Constellation, The (1966) 1 WLR 272 60
Controlled Parking Systems *v.* Sedgewick (1980) 4 WWR 425 136
Cook *v.* Allen [1833] 2 LJ Ex 199 176
Cook *v.* Cook Andr 219 89
Cook *v.* Corbett (1875) 24 WR 181 CA 203
Cook *v.* Palmer (1827) 6 B & C 739 73, 205
Cook *v.* Plaskett [1882] 47 JP 265 216
Cooke *v.* Birt (1814) 5 Taunt 765 98, 194
Cooper, *Re* [1958] Ch 922 126
Cooper *v.* Willomatt (1845) 1 CB 72 160
Cotsworth *v.* Betison (1696) 1 Ld Raym 104; (1696) 1 Salk 247 31, 32
Cotton *v.* Bull (1857) CP 118

Cotton *v.* Kaldwell (1833) 2 Nev & M KB 391 27, 76, 219
Courtoy *v.* Vincent (1852) 15 Beav 486 140
Cox *v.* Liddell (1895) 2 Mans 212 51
Crabtree *v.* Robinson [1885] 15 QBD 812 100
Craig *v.* Kannsen [1943] KB 256 CA 70
Craig & Sons, *ex parte* Hinchcliffe, *In Re* [1916] 2 KB 497 50
Cramer & Co *v.* Mott (1870) LR 5 QB 357 118
Crane & Sons *v.* Ormerod [1903] 2 KB 37 206
Cranley *v.* Kingswell (1617) Hob 207 20, 197
Crawshaw *v.* Harrison [1894] 1 QB 79 204
Craycraft, *Re* (1878) 8 Ch D 596 217
Cresswell *v.* Jeffreys (1912) 28 TLR 413 102
Crew *v.* Terry (1877) 2 CPD 403 211
Cripps, Ross & Co, *Re* [1888] 21 QBD 472 57
Crook *ex parte* Collins, *Re* (1891) 66 LT 29 49
Crook, *ex parte* Southampton Sheriff, *Re* (1894) 63 LJQB 756 203
Crosby *v.* Wandsworth LBC [1991] Legal Action 3/91 175
Crosier *v.* Tomkinson (1759) 2 Keny 439 172
Crossland *v.* Crossland [1993] 1 FLR 175 17
Crossley Bros Ltd *v.* Lee [1908] 1 KB 86 165, 167
Crowder *v.* Self [1839] 2 Mood & Ry 190 214
Crowther *v.* Long (1828) 8 B & C 598 73, 152
Crowther *v.* Ramsbottom 7 TR 658 214
Croyer *v.* Pilling 4 B & C 26 69
Cubitt *v.* Gamble [1919] 3 TLR 223 68
Culling *v.* Tufnal (1694) Bull NP (5th edn) 147
Cunliffe Engineering *v.* English Industrial Estates [1994] BCC 974 164
Curlewis *v.* Lawrie [1848] 12 QB 640 69, 99
Curtis *v.* Maloney [1951] 1 KB 736 207
Curtis *v.* Mayne (1842) 2 Dowl NS 37 217
Curtis *v.* Wainbrook Iron Co [1884] Cab & E 351 53
Cuthbertson, *ex parte* Edey, *In Re* [1875] LR 19 Eq 264 43, 152
Cyril Morgan (Holdings) *v.* Dyer (1995) 11 CLY 193 33

D S Paterson & Co Ltd, *Re* (1931) OR 777 63
D Wilson (Birmingham) Ltd *v.* Metropolitan Property Development Ltd [1975] 2 All ER 814 59
Dalton, *ex parte* Herrington & Carmichael *v.* Trustee, *Re* [1963] Ch 336 124, 137
Dalton *v.* Whittem [1842] 3 QB 961 143
Daniel *v.* Gracie [1844] 6 QB 145 86
Daniel *v.* Stepney [1874] 9 Exch 185 20, 22
Darby *v.* Harris [1841] 1 QB 895 146, 147
Darlye's Case (1631) 124 ER 433 225
Davey & Co *v.* Williamson & Son [1898] 2 QB 194 163
Davidson *v.* Carlton Bank [1893] 1 QB 82 42
Davidson *v.* Roach & Co (1991) Bristol CC (Legal Action) May 30th 129

Davies, *In Re* (1872) LR 7 Ch 314 80
Davies, *ex parte* Williams, *Re* [1872] 7 Ch App 314 54, 119
Davies *v.* Edmunds (1843) 12 M & W 31 217, 223
Davies *v.* Harris [1900] 1 QB 729 147
Davies *v.* Powell Willes 46 166
Davies *v.* Property & Reversionary Co Ltd [1929] 2 KB 222 196
Davies *v.* Rees [1886] 17 QBD 408 42
Davis, *Re* (1885) 55 LJQB 217 92
Davis, *ex parte* Pollen's Trustees, *Re* (1885) 55 LJQB 217 50
Davis *v.* Bromley UDC (1903) 67 JP 275 CA 108
Davis *v.* Gyde (1835) 2 A & E 623 198
Davis *v.* Hyman & Co [1903] 1 KB 854 155
Davis *v.* Lisle [1936] 2 KB 434 28
Davis *v.* Shapley [1830] 1 B & Ad 54 54, 70
Dawe *v.* Cloud & Dunning (1849) 14 LTOS 155 227, 232
Dawes *ex parte, In Re:* Husband [1875] 19 Eq 438 54
Dawson *v.* Cropp (1845) 1 CB 961 209
Dawson *v.* Wood (1810) 3 Taunt 256 157
Day *v.* Bisbitch (1595) 78 ER 622 145
Day *v.* Carr (1852) 7 Exch 883 176
Day *v.* Davies [1938] 2 KB 74; [1938] 1 All ER 686 218, 223
De Busscher *v.* Alt (1878) 8 CLD 286 232
De Coppet *v.* Barnet [1901] 17 TLR 273 179
De Costa Small *v.* Kirkpatrick [1979] 68 Cr App R 186 78
De Falbe, *Re* [1901] 1 Ch 523 143
De Gondouin *v.* Lewis [1839] 10 Ad & E 117 68, 185
De Grouchy *v.* Sivret (1890) 30 NBR 104 125
De La Rue *v.* Hernu, Peron & Stockwell Ltd [1936] 2 KB 164 175-6
De Medina *v.* Grove [1847] 10 QB 172 69
De Mesnil, Baron *v.* Dakin [1867] 3 QB 18 72
Dean *v.* Allalley (1799) 3 Esp 11 147
Dean *v.* Whittaker (1823) 1 C & P 347 160
Death *v.* Harrison (1871) 6 Exch 15 180
Debtor (No. 2 of 1977), *Re* A (1979) 1 WLR 956 72
Debtor (No. 10 of 1992), *Re* A (1995) *The Times*, February 1 62
Debtor (No. 340 of 1992), *Re* A [1994] 3 All ER 269 CA 38
Debtor (Nos. 13A & 14A-IO-1995), *In Re* A (1995) 1 WLR 1127 46
Debtor, *ex parte* Smith, *Re* A [1902] 2 KB 260 211
Dennis *v.* Whetham (1874) LR 9 QB 345 72, 139, 208
Dering *v.* Winchelsea 1 WLR 106 193
Devoe *v.* Long & Long (1951) 1 DLR 203 31
Dew *v.* Parsons (1819) 2 B & Ald 562 223, 227
Dews *v.* Riley (1851) 11 CB 434 74
Dibb *v.* Brooke & Son [1894] 2 QB 338 53
Dibble *v.* Bowater [1853] 2 E & B 564 18, 36
Dicas *v.* Warne (1833) 10 Bing 341 152, 211
Dickenson, *ex parte* Charrington & Co, *In Re* [1888] 22 QBD 187 55

Diggles *v.* Austin [1868] 18 LT 890 53
Dimock *v.* Miller (1897) 30 NSR 74 122
Dimsons Estate Fire Clay Co, *In Re* [1874] 19 Eq 202 59
Discount Banking Company of England & Wales *v.* Lambarde [1893] 2 QB 329 179
Dix *v.* Groom (1880) 5 Ex D 91 188, 189
Dixon *v.* Blackpool and Fleetwood Tranroad Co [1909] 1 KB 860 27
Dixon *v.* Calcraft [1892] 1 QB 458 183, 188
Dixon *v.* McKay (1903)[1912] 21 Man LR 762 35
D'Jan *v.* Bond St Estates [1993] NPC 36 197
Dod *v.* Monger (1704) 6 Mod 215 34, 110, 130
Dod *v.* Saxby (1735) 2 Stra 1024 90
Dodd *v.* Vail (1913) 9 DLR 534 34
Dodds *v.* Thompson [1866] 1 CP 133 8
Doe d Cox *v.* Roe (1847) 5 Dow & L 272 37, 106
Doe d Davy *v.* Oxenham (1840) 7 M & W 131 79
Doe d Elney *v.* Benham [1845] 7 QB 976 20
Doe d Haverson *v.* Franks (1847) 2 Car & Kir 678 37, 106
Doker *v.* Hader [1825] 2 Bing 479 208
Domine *v.* Grimsdall [1937] 2 All ER 119 74
Donaghue *v.* Campbell [1901] 2 OLR 124 43
Dorton *v.* Pickup Selw NP 670 202
Dougal *v.* McCarthy [1893] 1 QB 736 20
Dowse *v.* Gorton [1891] AC 190 152
Drages Ltd *v.* Owen [1935] All ER Rep 342 170
Drake *v.* Sikes (1797) 7 TR 113 73
Drear *v.* Warren (1833) 10 Bing 341 210
Driver, *Re* (1899) 43 Sol Jo 705 50
Druce & Co Ltd *v.* Beaumont Property Trust Ltd [1935] 2 KB 257 190
Dry Docks Corporation of London, *In Re* [1888] 39 Ch 306 58-9
Duck *v.* Braddyll (1824) M'Clel 217 91
Duck *v.* Tower Galvanising Co Ltd [1901] 2 KB 314 163
Lord Dudley *v.* Lord Ward (1751) Amb 113 145
Duffil *v.* Spottiswoode [1828] 3 C & P 435 160
Dumergue *v.* Rumsey (1863) 2 H & C 777 145
Duncan *v.* Cashin (1875) 1 Cp 554 151
Duncan *v.* Garrett (1824) 1 C & P 169 161
Dundas *v.* Dutens (1790) 1 Ves Jnr 196 141
Dunk *v.* Hunter (1822) 5 B & Ald 322 21, 86
Dunstan *v.* Paterson (1857) 2 CBNS 495 72, 157, 174
Duppa *v.* Mayo 1 Saund 287 18
Dyal Singh *v.* Kenyan Insurance Ltd [1954] AC 287 207
Dye *v.* Leatherdale [1769] 3 Wils 20 109, 110
Dyer *v.* Munday & Price [1895] 1 QB 742 232

E India Co *v.* Skinner (1695) 1 Botts PL 259; (1695) 90 ER 516 140, 206
Eagleton *v.* Gutteridge (1843) 11 M & W 465 103

Eastcheap Alimentary Products Ltd, *Re* [1936] 3 All ER 276 89
Eastern Holdings Establishment of Valduz *v.* Singer & Friedlander Ltd [1967] 2 All ER 1192 48
Easton Estate & Mining Co *v.* Western Waggon & Property Co (1886) 50 JP 790 156
Eaton *v.* Southby (1738) 7 Mod Rep 251 168
Eddowes *v.* Argentine Loan & Mercantile Agency Co Ltd (1890) 62 LT 602 95
Edge *v.* Kavanagh (1884) 24 LR Ir 1 204, 205
Edgson *v.* Caldwell (1873) 8 CP 647 188
Edmondson *v.* Nuttall (1864) 17 CBNS 280 183
Edmunds *v.* Ross (1821) 9 Price 5 210
Edmunds *v.* Wallingford [1885] 14 QBD 811 44, 192
Edwards *v.* Edwards [1875] 1 Ch D 454; [1876] 2 Ch 291 124, 164
Edwards *v.* Kelly 6 M & S 204 22
Edwards *v.* Marston [1891] 1 QB 225 42
Ehlers, Seel & Co *v.* Kauffman & Gates (1883) 49 LT 806 80
Eldridge *v.* Stacy (1863) 15 CBNS 458 103, 129
Electricity Supply Nominees *v.* IAF Group (1993) 2 EGLR 95 22
Elias *v.* Pasmore [1934] 2 KB 164 110
Elitestone *v.* Morris [1997] 1 WLR 687 142, 147
Eller *v.* Grovecrest [1995] QB 272; [1995] 2 WLR 278 4, 22
Elliot *v.* Yates [1900] 2 QB 370 79, 94
Elliott *v.* Bishop (1854) 10 Exch 496 145
Ellis *v.* Wadeson [1899] 1 QB 714 154
ELS, *Re* [1995] Ch 11 4, 164
Endrizzi *v.* Peto & Beckley (1917) 1 WWR 1439 149
Engelbach *v.* Dixon (1875) 10 CP 645 176
Engineering Industry Training Board *v.* Samuel Talbot (Engineers) Ltd [1969] 2 QB 270 53
England *v.* Cowley (1873) 28 LT 67; (1873) LR 8 Exch 126 96, 182
England *v.* Marsden 1 CP 529 193
English & Ayling, *ex parte*Murray & Co, *In Re* [1903] 1 KB 680 57
Erskine, Oxenford & Co *v.* Sachs [1901] 2 KB 504 232
Escalus Properties *v.* Robinson (1995) 31 EG 71 85
Essex Sheriff, Terrell *v.* Fisher, *Re* (1862) 10 WR 796 72
Etherton *v.* Popplewell (1801) 1 East 139 107, 212
Evans, *In Re* [1887] 34 Ch D 597 151
Evans, *Re* (1916) 2 HBR 111 54
Evans *v.* Bowen (1850) 19 LJQB 8 187, 189
Evans *v.* Elliot (1836) 5 Ad & El 142 199
Evans *v.* Hallam [1871] 6 QB 713 53
Evans *v.* Manero (1841) 7 M & W 463 70
Evans *v.* Rival Granite Quarries [1910] 2 KB 979 163
Evans *v.* Roberts (1826) 5 B & C 829 156
Evans *v.* South Ribble BC [1992] 2 All ER 695 116, 129, 132, 133, 135, 192
Evans *v.* Stephen (1882) 3 NSWLR 154 141

Evans *v.* Wright (1857) 2 H & N 527 44, 206
Everett *v.* Griffiths [1921] AC 631 74
Exall *v.* Partridge (1799) 8 TR 308 192
Exhall Mining Co Ltd, *In Re* (1864) 33 LJ Ch NS 595 50, 58

Fairley, *Re* [1922] 2 Ch 791 55
Farr *v.* Newman (1792) 4 TR 621 151
Farrance *v.* Elkington (1811) 2 Camp 591 19
Farrant *v.* Thompson (1822) 5 B & Ald 826; (1822) 2 Dow & Ry KB 1 146, 207
Farrar *v.* Beswick (1836) 1 M & W 682 141
Farrer *v.* Brooks (1673) 1 MR 188 80
Federal Bank *v.* Kretschmann [1886] 7 NSWLR 183 122, 134
Fell *v.* Whittaker [1871] 7 QB 120 186, 214, 228
Fenton *v.* Blythe [1890] 25 QBD 417 43
Fenton *v.* Boyle [1807] 2 Bos & Pul NP 391 186
Ferrier, *Re* [1944] Ch 295 162
Field *v.* Adams (1840) 2 Ad & El 649 173
Field *v.* Mitchell [1806] 6 Esp 71 66, 215
Figg *v.* Moore [1894] 2 QB 690 54
Finch, *ex parte* Sheriff of Essex, *Re* (1891) 65 LT 466 132, 203, 221
Finch *v.* Miller (1848) 5 CB 428 197
Findon *v.* M'Laren [1845] 6 QB 891 168
Finn *v.* Morrison (1856) 13 UCR 568 CAN 126
Firth *v.* Purvis (1793) 5 TR 432 33, 118, 125, 199
Fisher *v.* Magnay (1843) 6 Scott NR 588; (1843) 12 LJCP 276 70, 72
Flanagan *v.* Crilley (1987) unreported 220
Fletcher *v.* Manning (1844) 12 M & W 571 120
Fletcher *v.* Williams (1805) 6 East 283 75
Flint, Coal & Cannel Co Ltd, *Re* The (1887) 56 LJ Ch 232 48
Florence, *ex parte* Wingfield, *Re* [1878] 10 Ch D 591 168, 172
Flude Ltd *v.* Goldberg [1916] 1 KB 662 155
Foakes *v.* Beer (1884) 9 App Cas 610 HL 225
Follows, *ex parte* Follows, *In Re* [1895] 1 QB 521 211
Ford, *Re* [1886] 18 QBD 369 178
Ford, *Re* [1900] 1 QB 264 54, 57
Ford *v.* Baynton (1832) 1 Dowl 359 160
Fordham *v.* Akers (1863) 4 B & S 578 187
Forhan & Read Estates *v.* Hallet & Vancouver Auto Towing Service (1959) 19 DLR 756 136
Forrest *v.* Brighton JJ [1981] 2 All ER 711 88
Forster *v.* Baker [1910] 2 KB 636 210
Forster *v.* Clowser [1897] 2 QB 362 179
Forster *v.* Cookson [1841] 1 QB 419 91
Fort Frances Pulp & Paper Co *v.* Telegram Printing Co, *Re* (1923) 4 DLR 204 140
Foss *v.* Racine (1838) 8 C & P 699 103

Fouldes *v.* Willoughby (1841) 8 M & W 540 184
Foulger *v.* Taylor (1860) WN 220 91
Fowkes *v.* Joice 2 Vern 131 173
Fox, *Re* [1948] Ch 407 171
France *v.* Campbell (1841) 9 Dowl 914 140
Francis *v.* Nash (1734) 95 ER 32 139
Francome *v.* Pinche [1766] Esp NP (3rd edn) 382 103
Fredericks and Palhams Timber Buildings *v.* Wilkins
[1971] 1 WLR 1197; [1971] 3 All ER 545 178, 180
Freeman *v.* Cooke (1849) 4 Exch 654 159
Freeman *v.* Rosher (1849) 13 QB 780 232
French *v.* Getling [1922] 1 KB 236 42, 159
Frisch *v.* Gateshead MBC (1992) 25 Adviser 17 220
Furneaux *v.* Fotherby (1815) 4 Camp 136 36

G Winterbottom Ltd, *In Re* [1937] 2 All ER 232 61
Galliard *v.* Laxton (1862) 2 B & S 363 78
Gambrell *v.* Earl of Falmouth (1835) 4 Ad & El 73
195, 210
Gargrave *v.* Smith (1690) Salk 220; (1691) 1 Salk 221 79, 110
Garland *v.* Carlisle (1873) 4 Cl & Fin 693 182
Garrett *v.* Wilkinson (1848) 2 De G & Sm 244 158
Garstin *v.* Asplin (1815) 1 Madd 150 161
Gas Light & Coke Co *v.* Hardy [1886] 17 QBD 619 157
Gas Light & Coke Co *v.* Herbert Smith & Co (1886) 3 TLR 15 157
Gauntlett *v.* King (1857) 3 CBNS 59 71, 148
Gawan, *ex parte* Barclay, *Re* (1855) 5 De G M & G 403 146
Gawler *v.* Chaplin (1848) 2 Exch 503 66, 205
Gayford *v.* Chouler [1898] 1 QB 316 192
Gee *v.* Liddell (No 1) (1866) 35 Beav 621 41
Gegg *v.* Perin (1845) 9 JP 619 36
General Mutual Life Assurance Society *v.* Feltwell Fen 2nd
District Drainage Board [1945] KB 394 14
General Steel Wares Ltd *v.* Clarke, *Re* (1956) 20 WWR 215 153
George *v.* Chambers (1843) 11 M & W 149 186
Gibbons *v.* Hickson [1885] 55 LJQB 119 125
Gibbs *v.* Cruickshank [1873] LR 8 CP 454 187, 188
Gibbs *v.* Stead (1828) 8 B & C 528 94
Gibson *v.* Chaters (1800) 2 Bos & P 129 69
Gibson *v.* Ireson [1842] 3 QB 39 169
Gilding *v.* Eyre (1861) 10 CBNS 592 69
Giles *v.* Grover (1832) 6 Bligh NS 277; (1832) 1 Cl & Fin 72 80, 127
Giles *v.* Spencer (1857) 3 CBNS 244 21
Gill *v.* Jose (1856) 6 E & B 718 223
Gill *v.* Wilson (1853) 3 ICLR 544 90
Gillan *v.* Arkwright (1850) 16 LTOS 88 36
Gillingham *v.* Gwyer (1867) 16 LT 640 97

Gillott *v.* Aston (1842) 12 LJQB 5 68, 70
Gilman *v.* Elton (1821) 3 B & B 75 168
Gisbourn *v.* Hirst (1710) 1 Salk 249 168
Gislason *v.* Rural Municipality of Foam Lake [1929] 2 DLR 386 211
Gladstone *v.* Padwick [1871] LR 6 Exch 203 43, 128
Glasbrook *v.* David & Vaux [1905] 1 KB 615 220
Glasspoole *v.* Young (1829) 9 B & C 696 141
Glover *v.* Coles (1822) 1 Bing 6 173
Glynn *v.* Thomas (1856) 11 Exch 870 228
Godding, *Re* [1914] 2 KB 70 54, 57-8
Godlonton *v.* Fulham & Hampstead Property Co Ltd [1905] 1 KB 431 190
Godwin, *Re* [1935] Ch 213 53
Goldschmidt *v.* Hamlet (1843) 1 Dow & L 501 55
Goldsmith *v.* Harris (1928) 3 DLR 478 153
Gomersall *v.* Medgate (1610) 80 ER 128 31
Gonsky *v.* Durrell [1918] 2 KB 71 174
Goode *v.* Langley (1827) 7 B & C 26 217
Goodlock *v.* Cousins [1897] 1 QB 558 178, 206
Gordon *v.* Harper (1796) 7 Term Rep 9 160
Gorton *v.* Fuller [1792] 4 TR 565 165, 167
Gough *v.* Wood [1894] 1 QB 713 144
Gould *v.* Bradstock (1812) 4 Taunt 562 101
Governor of the Poor of Bristol *v.* Wait (1834) 1 Ad & El 264 174
Grace *v.* Morgan (1836) 2 Bing NC 534 215
Graham *v.* Spettigne [1885] 12 AR 261 18
Graham *v.* Witherby [1845] 7 QB 491 55
Grainger *v.* Hill (1838) 4 Bing NC 212 182
Grant *v.* Grant (1883) 10 PR 40 152
Gray *v.* Fuller [1943] 1 KB 694 142, 144
Gray *v.* Raper (1866) 1 CP 694 49
Gray *v.* Stait [1883] 11 QBD 668 36
Great Central Railway Co Ltd *v.* Bates [1921] 3 KB 578 107
Great Ship Co, *Re* [1863] 9 LT 432 60
Greater London Council *v.* Connolly [1970] 2 QB 100 86
Green *v.* Austin (1812) 8 Camp 260 91
Green *v.* Ducket [1883] 11 QBD 275 200, 227
Green *v.* Goddard (1704) 2 Salk 641 28
Green *v.* Leney & Another (1933) unreported, December 11 98
Green *v.* Stevens [1857] 2 H & N 146 161
Green *v.* Wroe (1877) WN 130 232
Greenwood *v.* Sutcliffe [1892] 1 Ch 1 197
Gregory *v.* Cotterell (1855) 5 E & B 571 72
Gregory *v.* Hill (1799) 8 TR 299 29
Grey *v.* Sheriff of Middlesex 1 Comp 387 67
Griffin *v.* Scott (1726) 1 Barn KB 3; (1726) 2 Ld Raym 1424, Stra 717 132, 194, 203

Griffith, *ex parte* Official Receiver, *Re* (1897) 4 Mans 217 49
Griffiths *v.* Stephens (1819) 1 Chitt 196 187
Grimwood *v.* Moss (1872) 7 CP 360 21
Groom *v.* Bluck (1841) 2 Man & G 567 193
Grove, *ex parte* (1747) 1 Atk 104 50
Grove *v.* Aldridge (1832) 9 Bing 428 37
Grunnnell *v.* Welch [1906] 2 KB 555 211
Grymes *v.* Boweren (1830) 6 Bing 437 146
Guest *v.* Cowbridge Railway Co (1868) 6 Eq 619 79
Gunn *v.* Bolckow, Vaughan & Co (1875) 10 Ch App 491 198
Guy *v.* Rankin (1883) 23 NBR 49 168
Gwinnet *v.* Philips [1790] 100 ER 780 37
Gwynn, *ex parte* Veness, *Re* [1870] 10 Eq 419 55

H *v.* Sandwell MBC [1993] Legal Action, August 113, 123, 175
Hackney Furnishing Co *v.* Watts [1912] 3 KB 225 170
Haddow *v.* Morton [1894] 1 QB 565 178
Hale *v.* Castleman (1746) 1 Wm Bl 2 69
Hale *v.* Saloon Omnibus Co (1859) 4 Drew 492 39
Hall *v.* Davis (1825) 2 C & P 33 29
Hall *v.* Hatch (1901) 3 OLR 147 140
Halliwell *v.* Heywood (1862) 10 WR 780 223
Hancock *v.* Austin (1863) 14 CBNS 634 100
Hannigan *v.* Burgess [1888] 26 NBR 99 10, 186
Harding *v.* Hall [1866] 14 LT 410 219
Hardistey *v.* Barney (1696) Comb 356 140
Harper *v.* Carr (1797) 7 TR 270 75, 88
Harper *v.* Taswell [1833] 6 C & P 166 203
Harpur's Cycle Fittings, *In Re* [1900] 2 Ch 731 61
Harris, ex *parte* [1885] 16 QBD 130 190
Harris, *In Re* [1931] 1 Ch 138 53
Harris *v.* Lombard New Zealand [1974] 2 NZLR 161 182
Harris *v.* Shipway (1744) Bull NP 182a 19
Harris *v.* Thirkell [1852] 20 LTOS 98 33
Harrison *v.* Barry (1818) 7 Price 690 90
Harrison *v.* Paynter (1840) 6 M & W 387 206
Hartley *v.* Larkin (1950) 155 EG 270 108
Hartley *v.* Moxham [1842] 3 QB 701 117
Harvey *v.* Harvey [1884] 26 Ch D 644 12
Harvey *v.* Mayne (1872) Ir 6 CL 417 29
Harvey *v.* Pocock [1843] 11 M & W 740 110
Harwell *v.* Burwell Sir W Jones 456 152
Haselar *v.* Lemoyne (1858) 5 CBNS 530 232-3
Hassall, *ex parte* Brooke, *In Re* [1874] 9 Ch 301 57
Hatch *v.* Hale [1850] 15 QB 10 197
Hawkins *v.* Walrond (1876) 1 CPD 280 204
Hawtry *v.* Butlin [1873] 8 QB 290 42

Haydon, *ex parte* Halling, *Re* [1877] 7 Ch D 157 55
Hayne's Case (1614) 12 Co Rep 113 158
Haythorn *v.* Bush (1834) 2 Cr & M 689; (1834) 2 Dowl 641 152, 180
Hayward Builders Supplies Ltd *v.* Mackenzie (1956) 2 WWR 591 153
Headland *v.* Coster [1904] 1 KB 219 CA; [1905] 1 KB 219; [1906] AC 286 HL 2, 223
Heathcote *v.* Livesley [1887] 19 QBD 285 55
Heaton *v.* Flood (1897) 20 OR 87 120
Heaton & Dugard Ltd *v.* Cutting [1925] 1 KB 655 164
Heawood *v.* Bone [1884] 13 QBD 179 170, 171
Hefford *v.* Alger (1808) 1 Taunt 218 187, 188
Hellawell *v.* Eastwood [1851] 6 Exch 295 142
Henchett *v.* Kimpson (1762) 2 Wils 140 90, 91
Henderson, *ex parte* Lewis, *Re* (1871) 6 Ch App 626 120
Henley, *ex parte* Fletcher, *Re* [1877] 5 Ch D 809 118
Herries *v.* Jamieson (1794) 5 TR 553 95, 155
Heseltine *v.* Heseltine [1971] 1 All ER 952 160
Heseltine *v.* Simmons [1892] 2 QB 547 43
Hetherington *v.* Groome [1884] 13 QBD 789 42
Hickman *v.* Massey [1900] 1 QB 752 109, 226
Higgins *v.* M'Adam [1829] 3 Y & J 1 55
Hill, *ex parte, In Re:* Roberts [1877] 6 Ch D 63 47
Hill (Frank), *ex parte* Holt & Co, *Re* [1921] 2 KB 831 154
Hill Pottery, *Re* (1866) LR 1 Eq 649 59
Hille India Rubber, *Re* [1897] WN 20 59
Hilliard *v.* Hanson [1882] 21 Ch D 69 68, 71, 112
Hills *v.* Renny (1880) 5 Ex D 313 180
Hills *v.* Street [1828] 5 Bing 37 228
Hinks, *Re* [1878] 7 Ch D 882 57
Hislop *v.* Hislop (1950) WN 124 41
Hitchin *v.* Campbell 2 Bla 829 45
Hobson *v.* Gorringe [1897] 1 Ch 182 144
Hobson *v.* Thelluson [1867] 2 LRQB 642 104
Hockey *v.* Evans [1887] 18 QBD 390 179
Hodder *v.* Williams [1895] 2 QB 663 104
Hodges *v.* Lawrence (1854) 18 JP 347 97
Hoe's Case (1600) 5 Co Rep 896 207
Hogarth *v.* Jennings (1892) 1 QB 907 81, 82, 107-8
Holland, *ex parte* Warren, *In Re* [1885] 15 QBD 48 53
Holland *v.* Hodgson (1872) 7 CP 328 142, 144
Hollinshead *v.* Egan [1913] AC 564 169
Holman *v.* Tuke [1672] Win 80 34
Holmes *v.* Brigg (1818) 8 Taunt 508 158
Holmes *v.* Sparks & Nicholas (1852) 12 CB 242 218
Holmes *v.* Watt (1935) 2 KB 300 50
Holroyd *v.* Marshall [1862] 10 HL Cas 191 43, 139
Holt *v.* Somback Co Car 103 210

Honig *v.* Redfern [1949] 2 All ER 15 171
Hooper *v.* Annis (1838) 2 JP 695 214
Hooper *v.* Lane [1857] 6 HL Cas 443 67, 68
Hopkins *v.* Adcock [1772] 2 Dick 443 210
Hopkins *v.* Gudgeon [1906] 1 KB 690 42
Hopkins *v.* Nightingale (1794) 1 Esp 99 100
Horne *v.* Lewin (1700) 1 Ld Raym 639 197
Horsefall *v.* Davey NPC 147 37
Horsfield *v.* Brown [1932] 1 KB 355 76, 78
Horsford *v.* Webster (1835) 1 CM & R 696 165, 169
Horsley *v.* Cox [1869] 4 Ch App 92 140
Horton *v.* Arnold (1731) Fortes Rep 361 173
Horton *v.* Ruesby (1686) Comb 33 80
Horwich *v.* Symond (1915) 84 LJKB 1083 143
Hoskins *v.* Knight [1813] 1 M & S 245 90
Howard Perry & Co *v.* British Railways Board [1980] 2 All ER 579 181
Howell, *ex parte* Mandleberg, *In Re* [1895] 1 QB 844 49
Howell *v.* Dawson [1884] 13 QBD 67 179
Howell *v.* Listowel Rink & Park Co (1886) 13 OR 476 143
Howes *v.* Young [1876] 1 Ex D 146 57, 217
Hoye *v.* Buck (1840) 1 Man & G 775 76
Hudd *v.* Ravenor (1821) 2 Brod & Bing 662 203, 210
Hudson *v.* Fletcher (1909) 12 WLR 15 104
Hughes *v.* Smallwood [1890] 25 QB 232 90
Hull *v.* Pickersgill (1819) 1 Brod & Bing 282 233
Hulme *v.* Brigham [1943] 1 KB 152 142, 143
Hulse (Sir Edward), *In Re* [1905] 1 Ch 406 144
Humphreys, *ex parte* Kennard, *Re* (1870) 21 LT 684 50
Hunt *v.* Braines 4 MR 402 210
Hunt *v.* Hooper (1844) 12 M & W 664 92
Hunt *v.* Pasman (1815) 4 M & S 329 70
Hunter, *Re* (1912) 8 DLR 102 124
Hunter *v.* Westbrook (1827) 2 C & P 578 158
Hurley, *Re* (1893) 1 WR 653 221
Hurry *v.* Rickman & Sutcliffe [1831] 1 Mood & R 126 71
Husband, *Re* (1875) LR 19 Eq 438 58
Husky Oil & Refining Ltd *v.* Callsen Re: Weber & Sheriff of Battlefield (1964) 45 DLR 396 122
Hutchings *v.* Morris (1827) 6 B & C 464 199
Hutchins *v.* Chambers [1758] 1 Burr 579 10, 210, 214
Hutchins *v.* Scott (1837) 2 M & W 809 67
Hutchison *v.* Birch (1812) 4 Taunt 619 117

Ile de Ceylon, The [1922] P 256 161
Imperial Steamship & Household Coal Co Ltd, *In Re* (1868) 32 LJ Ch 517 61
Imray *v.* Magnay (1843) 11 M & W 267 207

Inkop *v.* Morchurch (1861) 2 F & F 501 36
International Marine Hydropathic, *Re* [1884] 8 Ch D 470 59
International Pulp & Paper Co Ltd, *Re* (1876) 3 Ch D 594 48
Interoven Stoves Co Ltd *v.* F W Hubbard [1936] 1 All ER 263 22
IRC *v.* Pearlberg [1953] 1 All ER 388 23
IRC *v.* Rossmeister [1980] AC 952 77
Iredale *v.* Kendall (1879) 40 LT 362 33
Islington BC *v.* Harridge [1993] *The Times*, June 30, 7 CL 191 16
Izod *v.* Lamb [1830] 1 Cr & J 35 161

Jackson *v.* Hanson (1841) 8 M & W 477 187
Jackson *v.* Irvin (1809) 2 Camp 48 124
Jackson *v.* Litchfield [1882] 8 QBD 474 154
Jacob *v.* King [1814] 5 Taunt 451 187
Jacobs *v.* Humphrey (1834) 2 Cr & M 413 203
James W Elwell, The [1921] P.351 141, 157
Jamieson *v.* Trevelyan (1855) 10 Exch 748 188
Jamieson's Tow & Salvage Co Ltd *v.* Murray [1984] 2 NZLR 144 136
Jarmain *v.* Hooper (1843) 7 Scott NR 663; (1843) C Man & G 827 68, 72
Jays Furnishing Co *v.* Brand & Co [1914] 2 KB 132 172
Jeanes *v.* Wilkins (1749) 1 Ves Sen 194 80, 206, 207
Jelks *v.* Haywood [1905] 2 KB 460 161
Jenings *v.* Florence (1857) 2 CBNS 467 69
Jenkins, *In Re* [1904] 90 LT 65 55
Jenkins *v.* Biddulph (1827) 4 Bing 160 222
Jenkinson *v.* Brandley Mining Co [1887] 19 QBD 568 43
Jenner *v.* Yolland (1818) 6 Price 3 166, 204
Jennings *v.* Mather [1901] 1 QB 108 151
Jennyngs *v.* Playstowe Cro Jac 568 31
Jermyn, *ex parte* Elliott, *Re* (1838) 3 Deac 343 50
John *v.* Jenkins (1832) 1 Cr & M 227 36
Johnson, *Re* [1880] 15 Ch D 604 151, 152
Johnson, *ex parte* Rayner, *Re* [1872] 7 Ch App 325 55
Johnson *v.* Evans (1844) 7 Man & G 240 54
Johnson *v.* Faulkner [1842] 2 QB 925 173
Johnson *v.* Leigh (1815) 6 Taunt 246 98
Johnson *v.* Pickering [1908] 1 KB 1 80, 151
Johnson *v.* Upham (1859) 2 E & E 250 71, 116, 199, 200
Johnstone *v.* Hudlestone (1825) B & C 922 19
Jones *v.* Atherton (1816) 7 Taunt 56 128
Jones *v.* Biernstein [1899] 1 QB 470; (1900) 1 QB 100 33, 129, 138
Jones *v.* Chapman (1845) 14 M & W 124 75
Jones *v.* Gooday (1842) 9 M & W 736 213
Jones *v.* Jones [1889] 22 QBD 425 33
Jones *v.* Lewis (1836) 7 C & P 343 117
Jones *v.* Lock [1865] 1 Ch App 25 40
Jones *v.* Maynard [1951] Ch 572 159

Jones *v.* Parcell & Thomas [1883] 11 QBD 430 54
Jones *v.* Powell (1826) 5 B & C 647 173
Jones *v.* Robinson (1843) 11 M & W 758 223
Jones *v.* Swansea City Council [1989] 3 All ER 162 235
Jones *v.* Vaughan (1804) 5 East 445 75
Jones Bros (Holloway) Ltd *v.* Woodhouse [1923] 2 KB 117 160, 161, 184
Jons *v.* Perchard (1797) 2 Esp 507 227
Jordan *v.* Binckes (1849) 13 QB 757 210
Jory *v.* Orchard (1799) 2 B & P 39 75
Joule *v.* Jackson (1841) 7 M & W 450 168, 169
Joy, *ex parte* Cartwright, *In Re* (1881) 44 LT 883 54
Joynson *v.* Oldfield (1847) 8 LTOS 468 217

Kanhaya Lal *v.* National Bank of India (1913) 29 TLR 314 193
Kay *v.* Grover (1831) 7 Bing 312 76
Keen *v.* Priest (1859) 4 H & N 236 182
Keene *v.* Dilke (1849) 4 Exch 388 186
Keightley *v.* Birch 3 Camp 521 90, 205, 208
Kemp *v.* Christmas (1898) 79 LT 233 33, 127
Kempe *v.* Crews (1697) 1 Ld Raym 167 173
Kendall *v.* Wilkinson [1855] 24 LJMC 89 17
Kent *v.* Fittall [1906] 1 KB 60 171
Kerbey *v.* Denby [1836] 2 Gale 31 12
Kerby *v.* Harding (1851) 6 Exch 234 138, 196
Kern, P E & B E, *Re* [1932] 1 Ch 555 56
Kershaw *v.* Automatic Salesman Ltd (1937) 4 LJCCR 60 180
Key, *ex parte, In Re:* Skinner [1870] 10 Eq 432 57
Khazanchi *v.* Faircharm Investments [1998] 2 All ER 901 107, 116, 127, 135, 200, 201, 205
Kidd & Clements *v.* Docherty (1914) 27 WLR 636 156
Kilpin *v.* Ratley [1892] 1 QB 582 40
King *v.* Birch [1842] 3 QB 425 70
King *v.* England (1864) 4 B & S 782 208
Kingston City *v.* Rogers (1899) 31 OR 119 152
Kirk *v.* Gregory (1876) 1 Exch 55 117, 184
Kirkland *v.* Briancourt (1890) 6 TLR 441 20
Kirkpatrick *v.* Kelly (1781) 3 Doug KB 30 100
Knight, *ex parte* Voisey, *In Re* [1882] 21 Ch D 442 86
Knotts *v.* Curtis (1832) 5 C & P 322 203, 214
Knowle *v.* Blake (1821) 5 Bing 499 35
Koppel *v.* Koppel [1966] 2 All ER 187 159
Kotchie *v.* The Golden Sovereigns Ltd [1898] 2 QB 164 178

Ladd *v.* Thomas (184) 4 Jur 797 107
Lake *v.* Bellers (1698) 1 Ld Raym 733 67
Lamb W T *v.* Rider [1948] 2 KB 331 78
Lamb *v.* Wall (1859) 1 F & F 503 96, 107, 183

Lamont *v.* Southall (1839) 5 M & W 416 65
Lampleigh *v.* Brathwaite 1 Sm LC 151 193
Lancashire Cotton Spinning Co, *In Re* [1887] 35 Ch D 656 60
Lancashire Waggon Co Ltd *v.* Fitzhugh (1861) 6 H & N 502 160, 206
Lane *v.* Sewell (1819) 1 Chit 175 223
Langdon *v.* Traders' Finance Corporation Ltd (1966) 1 OR 655 153
Langford *v.* Selmes (1857) 3 K & J 220 21
Laroche *v.* Wasborough (1788) 2 TR 737 70
Late *v.* McLean (1870) 8 NSR 69 156
Launock *v.* Brown (1819) 2 B & A 592 103
Lavell & Co *v.* O'Leary [1933] 2 KB 200 33, 34, 123, 125, 138, 201
Lavell *v.* Richings [1906] 1 KB 480 167
Lavies, *ex parte* Stephens, *In Re* [1877] 7 Ch D 127 146
Lawrence *v.* Turner (1934) 3 WW 353 168
Lawrence Chemical Co *v.* Rubinstein [1982] 1 WLR 284 190
Lawson *v.* Story (1694) 1 Ld Raym 19 33
Lawton *v.* Lawton (1743) Atk 13 145
Lea *v.* Rossi (1855) 11 Exch 13 176
Lee *v.* Cooke (1858) 3 H & N 203 210
Lee *v.* Dangar, Grant & Co [1892] 1 QB 231;
(1892) 2 QB 337 110, 194, 211, 229
Lee *v.* Gansel [1774] 1 Cowp 1 99, 207
Lee *v.* Gaskell [1876] 1 QBD 700 143
Lee *v.* Lopes (1812) 15 East 230 90
Lee *v.* Smith [1854] 9 Exch 662 19
Leery *v.* Goodson [1792] 4 Term Rep 687 228
Legg *v.* Evans (1840) 6 M & W 36 161
Lehain *v.* Philpott (1876) 35 LT 855 22
Leigh *v.* Taylor [1902] AC 157 143
Leward *v.* Basely 1 Ld Raym 62, I Hawk PC 130 28, 31
Lewis *v.* Baker [1905] 1 Ch 46 21
Lewis *v.* Davies [1914] 2 KB 469 90
Lewis *v.* Gompertz (1837) Will & Woll & Dav 592 70
Lewis *v.* Owen [1894] 1 QB 102 29
Lewis *v.* Read (1845) 13 M & W 834 232
Liford's Case (1614) 11 Co Rep 466 142
Lindsey *v.* Lindsey (1710) Salk 291 99
Linotype-Hell Finance Ltd *v.* Baker [1993] 1 WLR 321 14
Lister *v.* Brown (1823) 1 C & P 121; (1823) 3 Dow & Ry KB 501 36
Lithgow, *ex parte, In Re:*Fenton [1878] 10 Ch D 169 57
Little *v.* Magle (1914) 7 WWR 224 35
Liverpool Loan Co, *ex parte, In Re:* Bullen [1872] 7 Ch App 732 57
Liverpool Marine Credit *v.* Hunter (1868) LR 3 Ch App 479 227
Lloyd (David) *Re* [1877] 6 Ch D 339 58
Lloyd *v.* DPP [1991] *The Independent,* June 21;
[1992] 1 All ER 982 135, 136
Lloyd *v.* Sandilands (1818) 8 Taunt 250 117

Lloyds & Scottish Finance (1966) 127
Loader *v.* Hiscock [1858] 1 F & F 132 NP 55
Lock *v.* Heath (1892) 8 TLR 295 40
Lodge *v.* Rowe (1875) 1 VLR 65 32
Lole *v.* Betteridge [1898] 1 QB 256 53
London Borough of Hackney *v.* White [1995] 28 HLR 219 78
London, Chatham & Dover Railway Co Ltd *v.* Cable [1899] 80 LT 119 179
London Cotton Co Ltd, *Re* (1866) LR 2 Eq 53 59, 60
London County Council *v.* Hackney BC [1928] 2 KB 588 186
London & Devon Biscuit Co, *Re* [1871] LR 12 Eq 190 59
London & Eastern Counties Loan & Discount Co *v.* Creasey [1897] 1 QB 768 143
London & North Western Railway Co *v.* Giles (1869) 33 JP 776 174
London Permanent Building Society *v.* De Baer [1969] 1 Ch 321 14
London Pressed Hinge Co Ltd, *In Re* [1905] Ch 576 163
London & Scottish Finance Ltd *v.* Modern Car & Caravans (Kingston) Ltd [1964] 2 All ER 732 131-2
London & Westminster Loan & Discount Co *v.* London & North Western Railway Co [1893] 2 QB 49 21
London Wharfing and Warehousing Co, *Re* (1885) 54 LJ Ch 1137 70
London & Yorkshire Bank *v.* Belton [1885] 15 QBD 457 166
Long *v.* Clarke [1893] 1 QB 119 99, 100, 101
Longbottom *v.* Berry [1869] 5 QB 123 144
Longendale Cotton Spinning Co, *In Re* [1878] 8 Ch D 150 62
Loring *v.* Warburton (1858) EB & E 507 199, 228
Loton *v.* Devereux (1832) 3 B & Ad 343 70
Love, *ex parte* Official Receiver *v.* Kingston on Thames County Court Registrar, *In Re* [1952] 1 Ch 138 55
Lowe *v.* Dorling [1905] 1 KB 501; [1906] 2 KB 772 190-1, 233
Lowthal *v.* Tomkins (1740) 2 Eq Cas Abr 380 80
Lucas *v.* Nockells (1833) 10 Bing 157 79
Lucas *v.* Tarleton (1858) 3 H & N 116 213
Ludmore, *Re* [1884] 13 QBD 415 56, 218
Lumsden *v.* Burnett (1898) 2 LR QB 177 CA 89, 123, 126, 130-1, 224
Lundy Granite Co, *ex parte* Heavan, *In Re* (1871) LR 6 Ch 462 50
Lusty, *Re* (1889) 60 LT 160 139
Lyford *v.* Tyrrel [1792] 1 Anst 85 12
Lynne *v.* Moody (1729) 2 Stra 851 214
Lyon *v.* Tomkies (1836) 1 M & W 603 206
Lyon *v.* Weldon [1824] 2 Bing 334 203, 206
Lyon & Co *v.* London City & Midland Bank [1903] 2 KB 135 143
Lyons *v.* Elliott [1876] 1 QBD 210 165
Lyons *v.* Golding (1829) 3 C & P 586 75

Macgregor *v.* Clamp & Son [1914] 1 KB 258 10, 148
Mackalley's Case (1611) 77 ER 828 96
Mackay *v.* Merritt (1886) 34 WR 433 54

Mackenzie, Neil, *ex parte* Sheriff of Hertfordshire, *Re* [1899] 2 QB 566 90
Mackie *v.* Warren (1828) 5 Bing 176 68, 70
Mackintosh *v.* Pogose [1895] 1 Ch 505 39
Mafo *v.* Adams [1970] 1 QB 548 183
Magnay *v.* Burt [1843] 5 QB 381 96
Manby *v.* Scott [1663] 1 Mod Rep 124 158
Manchester Brewery *v.* Coombes [1901] 2 Ch 608 18, 21
Manchester City Council *v.* Robinson (1991) 10 Legal Action 84
Manders *v.* Williams (1849) 4 Exch 339 160
Manning *v.* Lunn (1845) 2 C & K 13 197
Margot Bywaters Ltd, *In Re* [1942] 1 Ch 121 61
Marley Tile Co Ltd *v.* Burrows [1978] QB 241 57
Marriage, Neave & Co, *Re* [1896] 1 Ch D 663 9, 164
Marylebone Vestry *v.* Sheriff of London [1900] 2 QB 591 56
Maryport Haematite Iron & Steel Co Ltd, *In Re* [1892] 1 Ch 415 146
Maskell *v.* Horner [1915] 3 KB 106 228
Masters *v.* Farris [1845] 1 CB 715 191
Masters *v.* Frazer (1901) 85 LT 611 167
Masters *v.* Green [1888] 20 QBD 807 166
Matthews *v.* Buchanan [1889] 5 TLR 373 43
Matthias *v.* Mesnard (1826) 2 C & P 353 169
Mavor *v.* Croome (1823) 7 Bing 261 50
May *v.* May (1863) 33 Beav 81 158
M'Carthy, *Re* (1881) 7 LR Ir 437 49-50
McCollas, *ex parte* McLaren, *Re* [1881] 16 Ch D 534 120
McCornish *v.* Melton (1834) 3 Dowl 215 70
McCreagh *v.* Cox & Ford (1923) 87 JP 133;
(1923) 92 LJKB 855 10, 11, 202
McIntyre *v.* Stata & Crysler (1854) 4 CP 248 122
McKay *v.* Douglas [1919] 44 DLR 570 100
McKenzie, *Re* (1899) 2 QB 566 91
McKinnon *v.* McKinley [1856] 1 PEI 113 100
McLeod *v.* Butterwick (1996) 1 WLR 995; [1996] 3 All ER 236;
[1998] 2 All ER 901 CA 127, 134, 200
McLeod *v.* Girvin Telephone Association (1926) 1 DLR 216 148
McMullen & Sons *v.* Cerrone [1994] 1 BCLC 152 47
McPherson *v.* Temiskaming Lumber Co Ltd [1913] AC 145 80
Mead, *ex parte* Cochrane, *Re* [1875] 20 Eq 282 50
Mears *v.* Callender [1901] 2 Ch 388 145
Mechelen *v.* Wallace (1836) 7 Ad & El 54n 21
Mediana, The [1900] AC 113 184
Meehan, *Re* (1879) 6 Nfld LR 172 118
Meggy *v.* Imperial Discount Co Ltd [1878] 3 QBD 711 125
Megson *v.* Mapleton (1884) 49 LT 744 223, 232
Melford *v.* London (1321) 14 Ed II, Sel Soc v86 38
Mellor *v.* Leather (1853) 1 E & B 619 186
Melluish *v.* BMI (No 3) [1994] 2 WLR 795 143

Memco, *Re* (1986) Ch 86 48
Mennie *v.* Blake (1856) 6 E & B 842 186
Messing *v.* Kemble 2 Camp 116 71
Metro Cab Co Ltd *v.* Munro (1965) 48 DLR 701 153
Metropolitan Properties Co Ltd *v.* Purdy [1940] 1 All ER 188 89
Meux *v.* Jacobs [1875] 7 App Cas 481 144
M'Fadden *v.* Jenkyns [1842] 1 Ph 153 41
Milborn's Case (1586) 77 ER 420 96
Mildmay *v.* Smith (1671) 2 Wms Saund 343 209
Miles *v.* Furber [1873] 8 QB 77 21, 168
Miles *v.* Harris (1862) 12 CB 550 217-18, 242
Miller *v.* Curry [1893] 25 NSR 537 101
Miller *v.* Green (1831) 2 C & J 142 173
Miller *v.* Parnell (1815) 5 Taunt 370 211
Miller *v.* Solomon [1906] 2 KB 91 44, 139, 178
Miller *v.* Tebb (1893) 9 TLR 515 100
Millwood Colliery Co, *ex parte* (1876) 24 WR 898 58
Milner *v.* Rawlings (1867) 2 Exch 249 208
Milton *v.* Green 2 B & P 158 76
Milward *v.* Caffin (1779) 2 Wm Bl 1330 75
Moffatt *v.* Lemkin (1993) unreported 150
Moir *v.* Munday (1755) Say 181; (1755) 1 Burr 590 107, 214
Money *v.* Leach (1765) 3 Burr 1742 76
Montague *v.* Davies Benachi & Co [1911] 2 KB 595 61
Moore *v.* Drinkwater (1858) 1 F & F 134 144, 185
Moore *v.* Lambeth County Court Registrar [1970] 1 QB 560; [1970] 1 All ER 980 68, 109, 213
Moore, Nettlefold & Co *v.* Singer Manufacturing Co Ltd [1904] 1 KB 820 208
Morgan, *In Re* [1881] 18 Ch D 93 151
Morgan, *Re* [1904] 1 KB 68 220
Morris *v.* Matthews (1841) 2 QB 293 187, 189
Morris *v.* Salberg [1889] 22 QBD 614 68
Morrish *v.* Murrey (1844) 13 M & W 52 98
Morse *v.* Ouse Drainage Board [1931] 1 KB 109 7
Mortimer *v.* Cragg (1878) 3 CPD 216 CA 117, 217, 219, 242
Morton *v.* Woods [1869] 4 QB 293 20
Moseley *v.* Rendell [1871] 6 QB 338 151
Moser, *In Re* [1884] 13 QBD 738 146
Moss *v.* Gallimore (1779) 1 Doug KB 279 195-6
Mostyn *v.* Stock [1882] 9 QBD 432 57
Mounsey *v.* Dawson (1837) 6 A & E 752 187
Moyse *v.* Cocksedge [1745] Barnes 459; [1748] Willes 636 10, 110
Mudhun Mohun Doss *v.* Gokul Doss (1866) 10 Moo Ind App 563 214
Mullet *v.* Challis [1851] 16 QBD 239 117
Mungean *v.* Wheatley (1851) 6 Exch 88 188

Munroe & Munroe *v.* Woodspring District Council (1979) CLY 2226 99, 103, 108
Munster *v.* Johns (1850) 16 LTOS 245 168
Murgatroyd *v.* Dodworth & Silkstone Coal & Iron Co [1895] 65 LJ Ch 111 21
Murgatroyd *v.* Wright [1907] 2 KB 333 79
Muspratt *v.* Gregory [1838] 1 M & W 633 167
Myers *v.* Washbrook [1901] 1 KB 360 41

Nantes *v.* Corrock 9 Ves 177 141
Nargett *v.* Nias (1859) 1 E & E 439 166, 191
Nash *v.* Dickinson (1867) 2 CP 252 118, 128, 217, 218
Nash *v.* Lucas (1867) LR 2 QB 590 100, 102
National Commercial Bank of Scotland Ltd *v.* Arcam Demolition & Construction Ltd [1966] 2 QB 593 122, 123
National Guardian Assurance Co Ltd, *ex parte, In Re:* Francis [1878] 10 Ch D 408 122, 127
National Westminster Bank *v.* Powney (1990) 2 WLR 1084 78
Dr Needham's Case (1691) 12 MR 5 80
Needham *v.* Rivers Protection & Manure Co [1875] 1 Ch D 253 60
Ness *v.* Stephenson [1882] 9 QBD 245 171
Neumann *v.* Bakeaway [1983] 1 WLR 1016 182, 205, 206
Never Stop (Railway) Ltd *v.* British Empire Exhibition (1924) Inc [1926] Ch 877 145
New City Constitutional Club Co, *ex parte* Russell, *Re* [1887] 34 Ch D 646 163
New South Wales Taxation Commissioners *v.* Palmer [1907] AC 171 92
New York Life Assurance Association & Fullerton, *Re* (1919) 45 OLR 606 141
Newcastle, Duke of, *In Re* (1869) 8 Eq 700 139
Newman *v.* Anderton (1806) 2 Bos & PNR 224 85
Newsum Sons & Co Ltd *v.* James [1909] 2 KB 364 178
Nixon *v.* Freeman (1860) 5 H & N 647 96, 100
North Wales Produce & Supply Co Ltd, *Re* [1922] 2 Ch 340 43
North Yorkshire Iron Co, *Re* [1878] 7 Ch D 661 51, 52, 60
Norton *ex parte* Todhunter, *Re* (1870) 10 Eq 425 54
Norweb plc *v.* Dixon (1995) 1 WLR 636 93
Norwich Union Insurance Society *v.* Preston [1975] 1 WLR 813 12
Noseworthy *v.* Campbell (1929) 1 DLR 964 118
Notley *v.* Buck (1828) 8 B & C 160 58
Nott *v.* Bound (1866) LR 1 QB 405 228
Nowlin *v.* Anderson (1849) 6 NBR 497 91
Nugent *v.* Kirwan (1838) 1 Jeb & Sy 169
Nutting *v.* Jackson (1773) Bull NP 24 75

Oak Pits Colliery, *Re* [1882] 21 Ch D 322 52
O'Brien *v.* Brodie [1866] 1 Exch 302 55

Observer Ltd *v.* Gordon [1983] 1 WLR 1008 207
Opera, *Re* [1891] 3 Ch 260 164
Opperman *v.* Smith (1824) 4 Dow & Ry KB 33 36
Overseers of the Poor of Manchester *v.* Headlam [1888] 21 QBD 96 27
Overseers of Walton on the Hill *v.* Jones [1893] 2 QB 175 26
Owen *v.* Leigh (1820) 3 B & Ald 470 173, 205
Owen & Smith *v.* Reo Motors [1934] 151 LT 274 110, 185
Owens *v.* Wynne [1855] 4 E & B 579 209
Oxenham *v.* Collins (1860) 2 F & F 172 21
Oxley, *In Re* [1914] 1 Ch 602 152

P B Manufacturing *v.* Fahn [1967] 2 QB 1059;
(1967) 1 WLR 1059 127, 180
Padfield *v.* Birne (1822) 3 Brod & Bing 294 140
Page *v.* Vallis (1903) 19 TLR 393 191
Paget *v.* Perchard (1794) 1 Esp 205 124
Pain *v.* Whittaker [1824] 1 Ry & M 99 160
Palmer *v.* Bramley [1895] 2 QB 405 198
Palmer *v.* Crone [1927] 1 KB 804 75
Palmer *v.* Stanage (1661) 1 Lev 43 85, 210
Pape *v.* Westcott [1894] 1 QB 272 22
Papillon *v.* Backne [1658] 2 Hardr 480 107
Parker *v.* Harris 1 Salk 262 86
Parry *v.* Duncan (1831) 7 Bing 243 188
Parry *v.* Jenkins (1832) 1 CR & M 227 36
Parsons *v.* Gingell (1847) 4 CB 545 168
Parsons *v.* Hind (1866) 13 WR 860 143
Parsons *v.* Lloyd (1772) 3 Wils 341 68
Paston *v.* Carter [1883] Cab & El 183 170
Patoclus, The (1857) Swa 173 183
Payne *v.* Drew (1804) 4 East 523 79
Peacock *v.* Purvis (1820) 2 Brod & Bing 362 91, 166
Peake *v.* Carter [1916] 1 KB 652 155, 180
Pearce, *Re* [1885] 14 QB 966 119
Pearson *v.* Graham [1837] 6 AE 899 54
Pearson, *ex parte* West Cannock Colliery Co, *Re* (1886) 3 Morr 157 54
Pease *v.* Chaytor (1863) 1 B & S 658 214
Penoyer *v.* Bruce (1697) 1 Ld Raym 244 95, 154
Penton *v.* Browne (1664) 1 Keb 698 104
Penton *v.* Robert (1801) 2 East 88 145
Peppercorn *v.* Hofman [1842] 9 M & W 618 122
Percival *v.* Stamp (1853) 9 Exch 167 69, 185
Perdana Properties *v.* United Orient Leasing (1981) 1 WLR 1496 169, 170
Perdrian Rubber Co Ltd *v.* Sadek (1928) SRQ 114 168
Perkins *v.* Butterfield (1627) Het 75 202
Perkins *v.* Plympton (1831) 7 Bing 676 69, 186
Perkins Beach Lead Mining Co, *Re* [1878] 7 Ch D 371 59

Perry & Co *v.* Emerson (1906) 1 KB 1 96
Pfeiffer *v.* Sheldheim [1921] 59 DLR 631 18
Philips *v.* Thompson (1684) 3 Lev 191 54
Phillips *v.* Berryman (1783) 3 Doug 286 214
Phillips *v.* Birch (1842) 2 Dowl NS 97 70
Phillips *v.* Viscount Canterbury (1843) 11 M & W 619 224
Phillips *v.* General Omnibus Co (1880) 50 LJQB 112 46, 69
Phillips *v.* Henson (1877) 3 CPD 26 171
Phillips & Another *v.* Rees (1889) 24 QBD 17 216, 219
Phipps *v.* Boardman [1965] Ch 992 232
Pickard *v.* Marriage (1876) 1 Ex D 364 43
Pickard *v.* Sears (1837) 6 A & E 469 157
Piggot *v.* Wilkes (1820) 3 B & Ald 502 100
Piggott *v.* Birtles [1836] 1 M & W 441 166, 214-15
Pilling *v.* Stewart [1895] 4 BCR 94 150
Pilling *v.* Teleconstruction Co Ltd (1961) 111 LJ 424 206-7
Pinches *v.* Harvey [1841] 1 QB 368 68
Pinero *v.* Judson (1829) 6 Bing 206 21
Pit *v.* Hunt (1681) 2 Cas in Ch 73 140
Pitcher *v.* King [1844] 5 QB 758 72, 139
Pitt *v.* Shew [1821] 4 B & Ald 206 203
Pitt *v.* Snowden (1752) 3 Atk 750 81
Place *v.* Flagg (1821) 4 M & R 277 146
Planned Properties *v.* Ramsdens Commercials (1984) *The Times*, March 2 121
Plant *v.* Collins [1913] 1 KB 242 176
Plas-y-Coed Collieries Co Ltd *v.* Partridge Jones & Co [1912] 2 KB 345 208
Plas-yn-Mhowys Coal Co, *Re* (1867) LR 4 Eq 689 59
Pledall *v.* Knapp (1581) 123 ER 356 202
Plevin *v.* Henshall 91833) 10 Bing 24 184
Plummer, *ex parte* (1739) 1 Atk 103 50
Polini *v.* Gray [1879] 12 Ch D 438 14
Pollock, *Re* (1902) 87 LT 238 54
Polkinhorne *v.* Wright [1845] 8 QB 197 29
Pontin *v.* Wood [1962] 1 QB 594 70
Pool *v.* Crawcour (1884) 1 TLR 165 39
Poole's Case (1703) 1 Salk 368 145
Poole *v.* Longueville 2 Wms Saund 284 99
Poole Firebrick & Blue Clay Co, *In Re* (1873) LR 17 Eq 268 61
Porphrey *v.* Legingham 2 Keble 290 191
Potter, *Re* (1874) 18 Eq 381 172
Potter *v.* Bradley & Co [1894] 10 TLR 445 22
Potter *v.* North [1669] 1 Wms Saund 347(c) 233
Potts *v.* Hickman [1940] 4 All ER 491 HL; [1941] AC 212 10, 89, 202
Poynter *v.* Buckley (1833) 5 C & P 512 205
Preece *v.* Corrie (1828) 5 Bing 24 21

Price *v.* Harwood (1811) 3 Camp 108 72
Price *v.* Helyar [1828] 4 Bing 597 54
Price *v.* Messenger (1800) 2 Bos & P 158 76, 77
Prime *v.* Philips (1614) 1 Salk 222 98
Printing & Numerical Registering Co, *Re* [1878] 8 Ch D 535 63
Prior, *ex parte* Osenton, *Re* [1869] 4 Ch App 690 60
Proctor *v.* Nicholson (1835) 7 C & P 67 161
Progress Assurance Co, *ex parte* Liverpool Exchange, *Re* (1870) LR 9 Eq 370 51
Provincial Bill Posting Co *v.* Low Moor Iron Co [1909] 2 KB 344 22, 142, 167
Prude *v.* Beke (1310) Hil 4 Ed II 187
Prudential Mortgage Co *v.* St Marylebone (Mayor) [1910] 8 LGR 901 160
Pugh *v.* Arton (1869) 8 Eq 626 146
Pugh *v.* Griffith (1838) 7 Ad & El 827 117
Pulbrook *v.* Ashby (1887) 56 LJQB 376 19
Pullen *v.* Palmer (1696) 3 Salk 207 19

Quick *v.* Staines (1798) 1 B & P 293 151
Quinlan *v.* Hammersmith & Fulham LBC (1988) 153 JP 180 97

R. *v.* Atkinson [1976] Crim LR 307 CA 77
R. *v.* Backhouse (1771) Lofft 61 102
R. *v.* Baker *ex parte* Guildford Overseers [1909] 73 JP 166 27
R. *v.* Beacontree JJ *ex parte* Mercer (1970) Crim LR 103 114
R. *v.* Beauchamp (1827) 5 LJOSMC 66 32
R. *v.* Benn & Church [1795] 6 Term Rep 198 10
R. *v.* Bird (1679) 2 Show KB 87 199, 219
R. *v.* Birmingham Justices *ex parte* Bennet (1983) 147 JP 82 88
R. *v.* Blenkinsop [1892] 1 QB 43 26
R. *v.* Bradshaw (1835) 7 C & P 233 32
R. *v.* Brenan (1854) 6 Cox CC 381 32
R. *v.* Briggs [1883] 47 JP 615 30
R. *v.* Bristol City Magistrates' Court *ex parte* Willsman (1991) 156 JP 409 26
R. *v.* Burchet [1723] 8 Mod Rep 208, 88 ER 209 186
R. *v.* Burnley JJ *ex parte* Ashworth (1992) 32 RVR 27 38
R. *v.* Butterfield (1893) 17 Cox CC 598 32, 195
R. *v.* Cardiff Justices *ex parte* Salter (1985) 149 JP 721 75
R. *v.* Carrick DC *ex parte* Prankerd (1998) *The Times,* September 1 5
R. *v.* Castro (1880) 5 QBD 490 33
R. *v.* Clacton JJ *ex parte* Commissioners of the Customs & Excise (1987) 152 JP 120 88, 192
R. *v.* Clarke (1835) 4 Nev & M 671 103, 104, 105
R. *v.* Judge Clements *ex parte* Ferridge [1932] 2 KB 535 211
R. *v.* Cotton (1751) Park 112 35, 92

R. *v.* Dudley Justices *ex parte* Blatchford (1992) RVR 63 37, 106
R. *v.* Epping Magistrates *ex parte* Howard & Leach (1996) 7 CLY 521 113, 175
R. *v.* Finlay (1901) 13 Man LR 383 31
R. *v.* Fisher (1865) LR 1 CCR 7 192
R. *v.* Foster (1852) 6 Cox CC 25 192
R. *v.* Frereday (1817) 4 Price 131 223
R. *v.* Gazikom Aba Dore (1870) 7 Bom Cr Ca 83 31
R. *v.* German (1891) 66 LT 264 88
R. *v.* Gillespie [1904] 1 KB 174 27
R. *v.* Gopalasamy (1902) ILR 25 Mad 729 36
R. *v.* Guildford Justices *ex parte* Rich (1996), *The Times*, May 17 88
R. *v.* Hampstead Magistrates' Court *ex parte* St Marylebone Property Co plc (1995) Legal Action, September 1996 67, 113, 174, 175, 236
R. *v.* Harron [1903] 6 OLR 666 28
R. *v.* Hereford Magistrates' Court *ex parte* MacRae (1998) *The Times*, December 31 17, 87, 88
R. *v.* Higgins [1851] 21 ICLR 213 31, 32
R. *v.* Holsworthy Justices *ex parte* Edwards [1952] 1 All ER 411 30
R. *v.* Howson (1966) 55 DLR 582 136
R. *v.* Jetherell [1757] Park 176 218
R. *v.* Justices of Devon (1813) 1 M & S 411 175
R. *v.* Justices of London [1899] 1 QB 532 113
R. *v.* Ledgingham 1 Vent 604 214
R. *v.* Liverpool JJ *ex parte* Greaves (1979) RA 119 113
R. *v.* Locker [1971] 2 QB 321 198
R. *v.* Monkhouse (1743) 2 Stra 1184 187
R. *v.* Monkman [1892] 8 Man LR 509 30
R. *v.* Morgan (1780) Cald 156 37
R. *v.* Mortimer (1906) 70 JP 542 88
R. *v.* Myers (1786) 1 TR 265 103
R. *v.* Nicholson [1901] 65 JP 298 32
R. *v.* Noonan (1876) 10 ICLR 505 34
R. *v.* Norwich JJ *ex parte* Trigger (1987) 151 JP 465 88
R. *v.* Osbourne (1818) 6 Price 94 156
R. *v.* Paget [1881] 8 QBD 151 16
R. *v.* Palmer (1802) 2 East 411 223
R. *v.* The Parking Adjudicator *ex parte* London Borough of Wandsworth [1996] 154
R. *v.* Judge Philbrick & Morey *ex parte* Edwards (1905) 2 KT 108 227
R. *v.* Pigott (1851) 1 ICLR 471 31
R. *v.* Purdy (1974) 3 WLR 367 78
R. *v.* Rabbitts (1825) 6 D & R 341 37
R. *v.* Radnorshire JJ [1840] 9 Dowl 90 37
R. *v.* Raines (1853) 1 E & B 855 187
R. *v.* Rapay (1902) 7 CCC 170 75
R. *v.* Robinson (1835) 1 C M & R 334 218

R. *v.* Royds *ex parte* Sidney (1860) 1 QSCR 8 75
R. *v.* St Dunstan (Inhabitants) (1825) 4 B & C 686 146
R. *v.* Sheriff of Essex (1839) 8 Dowl PC 5 210
R. *v.* Sheriff of Leicestershire (1850) 9 CB 659 209
R. *v.* Sloper & Allen (1818) 6 Price 114 92
R. *v.* Smith (1780) Doug KB 441 29
R. *v.* Smith *ex parte* Porter [1927] 1 KB 478 222, 223
R. *v.* Speed [1940] 4 All ER 491 HL; 12 MR 328 10
R. *v.* Tacey (1821) Russ & Ry 452 192
R. *v.* Walshe (1876) IR 10 CL 511 31
R. *v.* Wells (1807) 16 East 278 80
R. *v.* Williams (1850) 4 Cox CC 87 31
Rai & Rai *v.* Birmingham City Council [1993] unreported 117, 174, 175
Railton *v.* Wood [1890] 15 App Cas 363 50
Ramsay *v.* Margrett [1894] 2 QB 18 159
Rand *v.* Vaughan (1835) 1 Bing NC 767 36
Rapley *v.* Taylor & Smith (1883) Cab & El 150 214
Ratcliffe *v.* Burton (1802) 3 Bos & P 223 98
Ratt *v.* Parkinson [1851] 15 JP 356 74
Rawlence & Squarey *v.* Spicer [1935] 1 KB 412 211
Rawlinson *v.* Mort (1905) 93 LT 555 40
Rawlinson *v.* Oriel (1688) Comb 144 80
Ray *v.* Ray (1813) Coop 264 151
Rayner, *ex parte, In Re:* Johnson [1872] 7 Ch App 732 55
Read *v.* Burley [1597] Cro Eliz 549 167
Read *v.* King [1997] 1 CL 5 30
Reddell *v.* Stowey (1841) 2 Moo & R 358 152
Redman Builders, *Re* [1964] 1 All ER 851 58, 60-1
Reed *v.* Harrison (1778) 2 Wm Bl 1218 194
Reed *v.* Thoyts [1840] 6 M & W 410 44
Regent United Service Stores, *Re* [1878] 8 Ch D 616 51
Regnart *v.* Porter [1831] 7 Bing 451 18
Rendell *v.* Roman [1893] 9 TLR 192 22
Revill *v.* Newberry [1996] 2 WLR 239 29
Reynell *v.* Champernoon [1631] Cro Car 228 9, 137
Reynolds *v.* Coleman [1887] 36 Ch D 453 70
Rhodes *v.* Hull (1857) 26 LJ Ex 265 69, 70, 186
Rhymney Railway Co *v.* Price (1867) 16 LT 395 186, 187
Ricardo *v.* Maidenhead Board of Health (1857) 27 LJMC 73 235
Rich *v.* Woolley (1831) 7 Bing 651 31, 37
Richards, *Re* [1879] 11 Ch D 676 60
Richards, *ex parte* Astbury & Lloyds Banking Co, *Re* [1869] 4 Ch App 630 142, 144
Richards *v.* Overseers of Kidderminster [1896] 2 Ch 212 164
Richards *v.* W Middlesex Waterworks Co (1885) 15 QBD 660 232
Richardson *v.* Jackson (1849) 8 M & W 298 197

Richardson *v.* Tuttle (1860) 8 CBNS 474 209
Richardson *v.* Wright (1875) 10 Ex D 367 177
Ridgway *v.* Lord Stafford (1851) 6 Exch 404 204
Riseley *v.* Ryle (1843) 12 LJ Ex 322 90
River Swale Brick & Tile Works Ltd, *In Re* The (1883) LJ Ch 638 20, 165
Rivers *v.* Cutting [1982] 3 All ER 69 CA 154
Roberts, *ex parte* Brook, *In Re* [1878] 10 Ch D 100 146
Roberts, *ex parte* Hill, *Re* [1877] 6 Ch D 63 10
Roberts *v.* Roberts [1884] 13 QBD 794 42
Robertson *v.* Hooper (1909) 12 WLR 5 77
Robertson *v.* Miller [1904] 3 NB Eq Rep 78 70
Robinson *v.* Briggs (1870) 6 Exch 1 118
Robinson *v.* Burnell's Vienna Bakery Ltd [1904] 2 KB 624 164
Robinson *v.* Hoffman (1828) 4 Bing 562 19
Robinson *v.* Jenkins [1890] 24 QBD 275 176
Robinson *v.* Peace (1838) 7 Dowl 93 140
Robinson *v.* Waddington [1849] 13 QBD 753 200
Robson *v.* Biggar [1907] 1 KB 690 219, 224, 225
Rocke *v.* Hills (1887) 3 TLR 298 212
Roden *v.* Eyton (1848) 6 CB 427 66, 203
Rodgers *v.* Parker (1856) 18 CB 112 173, 212, 213
Rodwell *v.* Phillips (1842) 9 M & W 501 156
Roe *v.* Birkenhead Railway (1851) 7 Exch 36 233
Roe *v.* Hammond (1877) 2 CPD 300 216, 220
Roe *v.* Kingerlee (1986) Crim Law Review 735 192
Rogers, *In Re* [1911] 1 KB 641 56
Rogers, *ex parte* Villars, *Re* (1874) 9 Ch App 432 202, 204
Rogers *v.* Birkmore (1736) 2 Stra 1040 85
Rogers *v.* Kenmay [1846] 9 QB 592 161
Rogers, Eungblutt & Co *v.* Martin [1911] 1 KB 19 169, 190
Rogerstone Brick & Stone Co Ltd, *In Re* [1919] 1 Ch 110 145
Rogier *v.* Campbell [1939] Ch 766 232
Rollason, Rollason *v.* Rollason, *In Re* [1887] 34 Ch D 495 162
Romer & Haslam, *Re* [1893] 2 QB 286 198
Rondeau Le Grand & Co *v.* Marks [1918] 1 KB 75 159
Rook *v.* Wilmot (1590) 78 ER 465 68
Rookes *v.* Barnard [1964] AC 1129 109, 183, 185
Rorke *v.* Dayrell (1791) 4 TR 402 53
Rossiter *v.* Conway (1894) 58 JP 350 28
Rothschild *v.* Fisher [1920] 2 KB 243 210
Roundwood Colliery Co, *In Re* (1897) 1 Ch 373 51, 61, 163
Rowles *v.* Rowles (1750) 1 Ves Sen 348 40
Roy *v.* Fortin [1915] 26 DLR 18 150
Rush *v.* Baker (1734) Cun 130 56
Russell, *Re* (1870) 18 WR 753 167, 169
Russell, *In Re* [1885] 29 Ch D 254 62
Russell *v.* Buckley (1885) 25 NBR 264 100

Russell *v.* Rider (1834) 6 C & P 416 104
Rutherford *v.* Lord Advocate (1931) 16 Tax Cases 145 23, 196
Rutland's, Countess of, Case (1605) 6 Rep 53 67
Ryan *v.* Shilcock (1851) 7 Exch 72 100, 101

S, *Re* (an infant) [1958] 1 All ER 783 16
Sabloniere Hotel Co, *In Re* (1866) LR 3 Eq 74 61
Sabourin *v.* Marshall (1832) 3 B & Ad 440, 110 ER 158 186
Sales Agency *v.* Elite Theatres [1917] 2 KB 164 120
Salford Van Hire (Contracts) *v.* Bocholt Investments [1995] 2 EGLR 50; [1996] RTR 103 4, 170
Salinger, *Re* [1877] 6 Ch D 332 57
Samuel *v.* Duke (1838) 3 M & W 622 80
Samuels, *Re* [1935] Ch 341 56
Sanders, *ex parte* Sergeant, *Re* (1885) 54 LJQB 331 84
Sanders *v.* Davis [1885] 15 QBD 218 144
Sandon *v.* Jarvis (1859) EB & E 935 103
Sanxter *v.* Foster (1841) Cr & Ph 302 112
Sargent's Trusts, *Re* (1879) 7 LR Ir 66 141
Satterthwaite, *Re* (1895) 2 Mans 52 42
Saunders *v.* White [1902] 1 KB 472 42
Saunderson *v.* Baker & Martin (1772) 3 Wils 309 72
Scarfe *v.* Halifax (1840) 7 M & W 288 44, 72
Scarlett *v.* Hanson [1883] 12 QBD 213 139, 176
Schalit *v.* Joseph Nadler Ltd (1933) 2 KB 79 81
Scheibel *v.* Fairbairn (1799) 1 Bos & Pul 388 69
Schlenker *v.* Moxsy (1825) 3 B & C 789 190
Schott *v.* Scholey [1807] 8 East 467 139, 141
Schulter, *ex parte, In Re:* Matanle [1874] 9 Ch App 409 54
Scobie *v.* Collins [1895] 1 QB 375 21
Scorell *v.* Boxall (1827) 1 Y & J 396 156
Scott *v.* Uxbridge & Rickmansworth Railway Co (1866) 1 CP 596 197
Searle *v.* Blaise (1863) 14 CBNS 856 56
Seaton *v.* Lord Deerhurst [1895] 1 QB 853 46
Secretary of State for War *v.* Wynne [1905] 2 KB 845 168
Selby *v.* Greaves (1868) LR 3 CP 594 85
Sells *v.* Hoare [1824] 1 Bing 401 71
Semaynes Case (1604) 5 Co Rep 91a; (1604) Yelv 29; [1604] All ER 62 98, 102, 103
Serjeant *v.* Nash Field & Co (1903) 2 KB 304 21
Seven *v.* Mihill (1756) 1 Keny 371 91
Shaftesbury, Earl of *v.* Russell (1823) 1 B & C 666 141
Sharpe *v.* Fowle [1884] 12 QBD 385 190
Shattock *v.* Craden (1851) 6 Exch 725 207
Shaw *v.* Earl of Jersey (1879) 4 CPD 359 112
Shaw *v.* Kirby [1888] 52 JP 182 209, 211
Sheers *v.* Brooks (1792) 2 H Bl 120 98

Sheffield & South Yorkshire Permanent Benefit Building Society *v.* Harrison [1885] 15 QBD 338 144
Shenstone & Co *v.* Freeman [1910] 2 KB 84 169
Shephard *v.* Cartwright [1955] AC 431 40
Sherman, *Re* (1915) 32 TLR 231 149
Shipwick *v.* Blanchard (1795) 6 Term Rep 298 181-2
Shoppee *v.* Nathan & Co (1891) 1 QB 245 229
Shorland *v.* Govett (1826) 5 B & C 485; (1826) 108 ER 181 110, 226
Shuckborough *v.* Duthoit (1892) 8 TLR 710 57
Shuttleworth & Hancock, *ex parte, In Re:* Deane (1832) 1 Deac & Ch 223 209
Sibeth, *ex parte* Sibeth, *Re* [1885] 14 QBD 417 172
Simpson *v.* Hartropp (1744) Willes 512 166, 168
Simson *v.* Harcourt (1744) Esp NP 167
Simultaneous Colour Printing Syndicate *v.* Foweraker [1901] 1 KB 771 163
Singleton *v.* Williamson (1862) 7 H & N 747 182
Six Carpenters', The, Case (1610) 8 Co Rep 146; (1610) All ER 292; (1610) 77 ER 695 107, 182, 199, 211, 212
Skeate *v.* Beale (1840) 11 Ad & El 983 228
Skidmore *v.* Booth (1854) 6 C & P 777 105
Slater *v.* Hames (1841) 7 M & W 413 223
Slater *v.* Pinder [1871] 6 Exch 228 119
Smalcomb *v.* Buckingham (1697) 12 Mod Rep 146 72
Small *v.* National Provincial Bank of England [1894] 1 Ch 686 145
Smallcomb *v.* Cross & Buckingham (1697) 1 Ld Raym 252 207
Smart *v.* Hutton (1833) 8 A & E 568n 72
Smart Bros *v.* Holt [1929] 2 KB 303 169
Smith, *ex parte* (1890) 7 TLR 42 114
Smith, *Re* [1989] 3 All ER 897 52
Smith, *Re* (1990) 2 AC 215 47
Smith, *ex parte* Spooner, *Re* [1874] 10 Ch App 168 53
Smith *v.* Ashforth [1860] 29 LJ Exch 259 66, 121, 215
Smith *v.* Birmingham Gas Co (1834) 1 Ad & El 526 77
Smith *v.* City Petroleum [1940] 1 All ER 260 145
Smith *v.* Cox [1940] 2 KB 558 197-8
Smith *v.* Critchfield [1885] 14 QBD 873 68, 176, 177, 179
Smith *v.* Egginton (1837) 7 A & E 167 111, 194
Smith *v.* Egginton (1855) 10 Exch 845 197
Smith *v.* Enright (1893) 69 LT 724 183, 188
Smith *v.* Goodwin (1833) 4 B & Ad 413 197, 198
Smith *v.* Keal [1882] 9 QBD 352 72
Smith *v.* Mulcahy [1934] 1 KB 608 184, 186
Smith *v.* Pritchard (1849) 8 CB 565 72, 74
Smith *v.* Russell 3 Taunt 400 91
Smith *v.* Shepherd (1519) 78 ER 945; Cro Eliz 710 98, 115
Smith *v.* Smith [1733] 2 Stra 953 40

Smith *v.* Smith [1971] 115 Sol Jo 444 17
Smith *v.* Torr (1862) 3 F & F 505 201
Smith & Hartogs, *Re* [1895] 73 LT 221 20
Sneary *v.* Abdy [1876] 1 Ex D 299 204, 217, 219
Snedeker *v.* Waring (1854) 12 NY 170 142
Snowballe *v.* Goodricke (1833) 4 B & Ad 541 73
Sodeau *v.* Shorey (1896) 74 LT 240 177
Solers *v.* Wotton (1405) YB 7 Hen 4 fo 27 p.15 187
Solomon, *ex parte* Dressler, *In Re* [1878] 9 Ch 252 52
Sorrell *v.* Paget [1949] 2 All ER 609 18, 200
South Kensington Co-operative Stores, *In Re* [1881] 17 Ch D 161 52
South Rhondda Colliery Co, *In Re* (1898) 60 LT 1260 61
South Wales Electricity plc *v.* DMR Ltd (1997) 4 CL 210 183
Southam *v.* Smout [1963] 3 All ER 104;
[1964] 1 QB 308 29, 100, 101, 104, 106
Sperry Inc *v.* CIBC (1985) 17 DLR 236 188
Spice *v.* Webb & Morris (1838) 2 Jur 943 130
Spyer *v.* Phillipson [1930] 2 Ch 183 146
Squire *v.* Huetson [1841] 1 QB 308 162
Standard Manufacturing Co, *Re* [1891] 1 Ch 639 164
Stanfill *v.* Hickes (1697) 1 Ld Raym 280 20
Stanley *v.* Wharton (1821-22) 9 Price 301 36, 37
Stear *v.* Scott [1984] unreported 135
Steel Linings *v.* Bilby & Co [1993] RA 27 66, 112, 113, 175
Stephens *v.* Elwall (1815) 4 M & S 259 233
Stepney BC *v.* Woolf [1943] KB 202 95
Stevens *v.* Hince (1914) WN 148 41
Stevens *v.* Marston (1890) 60 LJQB 192 19
Stevenson *v.* Wood (1805) 5 Esp 200 50
Stewart *v.* Rhodes [1900] 1 Ch 386 85
Stimson *v.* Farnham (1871) 7 QB 175 209
Stinton N K, *Re* (1900) 109 LT Jo 427 218
Stirch *v.* Clarke (1832) 4 B & A 113 76
Stock *v.* Holland [1874] 9 Exch 147 57
Stockdale *v.* Hansard (1840) 11 A & E 297 209
Stoke-on-Trent BC *v.* W J Wass Ltd [1988] 1 WLR 1406 107
Storey *v.* Robinson 6 Term Rep 139 173
Stratford *v.* Twynan (1822) Jac 418 202
Suffield & Watts, *ex parte* Brown, *In Re* [1888] 20 QBD 693 49
Sunbolf *v.* Alford (1838) 3 M & W 248 150
Swaffer *v.* Mulcahy [1934] 1 KB 608 10, 157
Swales *v.* Fox [1981] 2 WLR 814 106
Swann *v.* Earl of Falmouth & Jennings (1828) 8 B & C 456 125
Swann *v.* Sloan (1895) 29 ILT 109 10, 148
Sweet *v.* Turner [1871] 7 QB 310 193
Swire *v.* Leach (1865) 18 CBNS 479 110
Sykes *v.* Sykes [1870] 5 CP 113 152

Symonds *v.* Kurtz (1889) 61 LT 559 77, 78

T W Hobbs & Co Ltd *v.* Hudson [1890] 25 QBD 232 37
Tadman *v.* Henman [1893] 2 QB 168 21-2
Taggs Island Casino Hotel Ltd *v.* Richmond upon Thames BC [1967] RA 70 164
Talentine *v.* Denton Cro Jac 111 18
Tancred *v.* Allgood (1859) 4 H & N 438 207
Tancred *v.* Leyland (1851) 16 QB 669 195, 214
Tapling & Co *v.* Weston (1833) Cab & El 99 168
Tate *v.* Gleed [1784] 2 Wms Saund 290a 169
Taunton *v.* Sheriff of Warwickshire [1895] 2 Ch 319 163-4
Taylerson *v.* Peters (1837) 7 A & E 110 21
Taylor, *ex parte* Steel & Plant Co, *Re* [1878] 8 Ch D 183 60
Taylor *v.* Baker (1677) 3 Keb 788/2 Lev 203 199
Taylor *v.* Bekon [1878] 2 Lev 203 197
Taylor *v.* Cole [1791] 3 TR 292 109
Taylor *v.* Eckersley [1877] 5 Ch D 740 43, 120
Taylor *v.* Jones 2 Atk 600 141
Taylor *v.* Lanyon (1830) 6 Bing 536 90
Taylor *v.* Richardson (1800) 8 TR 505 72-3
Tellus Super Vacuum Cleaners *v.* Ireland (1938) LJNCCR 54 180
Templeman *v.* Case [1711] 10 MR 24 184, 186
Tennant *v.* Field (1857) 8 E & B 336 126, 133, 199
Thomas, *Re* [1876] Diprose's Friendly Society Cases 64 51
Thomas, *Re* (1881) 44 LT 781 143
Thomas, *Re* (1899) 1 QB 460 217
Thomas *v.* Harries (1840) 1 Man & G 695 125
Thomas *v.* Kelly [1888] 13 App Cas 506 42
Thomas *v.* Lulham [1895] 1 QB 400 37
Thomas *v.* Mirehouse [1887] 19 QBD 563 91
Thomas *v.* Patent Lionite Co [1881] 17 Ch D 250 51
Thomas *v.* Peek [1888] 20 QBD 727 74
Thompson *v.* Mashiter (1823) 1 Bing 283 168
Thompson *v.* Shaw (1836) 5 LJCP 234 19
Thompson *v.* Wood [1842] 4 QB 493 66
Thomson *v.* Clark [1596] 78 ER 754 202
Thornton *v.* Adamson (1816) 5 M & S 38 36
Thornton *v.* Cruther [1769] unreported 2
Thorp *v.* Hurt (1886) WN 96 20
Three Rivers DC *v.* Governor and Company of the Bank of England [1996] 3 All ER 558 236
Throssell *v.* Leeds City Council (1993) 41 Adviser 22 96, 220
Thurso New Gas Co, *In Re* [1889] 42 Ch 486 60
Thwaites *v.* Wilding [1883] 12 QBD 4 129, 190, 211
Tibber (1991) 135 SJ 408 191
Tidey, *Re* (1870) 21 LT 685 54

Till, *ex parte, In Re:* Mayhew [1873] 16 Eq 97 51
Times Furnishing *v.* Hutchings [1938] 1 KB 775 161, 170
Timmins *v.* Rawlinson Bl Rep 533 19
Tinkler *v.* Poole (1770) 5 Burr 2657 181
Tomlinson *v.* Consolidated Credit & Mortgage Corp (1889) 24 QBD 135 36
Toomer *ex parte* Blaiberg, *Re* [1883] 23 Ch D 254 53
Toomey, D P *v.* King (1952) CLY 260 57
Topham *v.* Greenside Glazed Firebrick Co [1887] 37 Ch D 281 42
Toussaint *v.* Hartop (1816) Holt NP 335 124
Tower Finance & Furnishing Co *v.* Brown (1890) 6 TLR 192 39
Townsend, *In Re* (1880) 14 Ch D 132 202
Townsend, *ex parte* Hall, *Re* [1880] 14 Ch D 132 55
Townsend *v.* Charlton [1922] 1 KB 700 88
Townsend *v.* Sheriff of Yorkshire (1890) 24 QBD 612 226
Traders' North Staffordshire Carrying Co, *ex parte* North Staffs Railway Co, *Re* (1874) LR 19 Eq 60 48
Trent *v.* Hunt (1853) 9 Exch 14 195
TSB *ex parte* Botham (1996) EGCS 149 143, 144
Tufton *v.* Harding (1859) 29 LJ Ch 225 180
Tufuyo *v.* Haddon [1984] NZ Recent Law 285 109
Tummons *v.* Ogle (1856) 6 E & B 571 188
Tunbridge's Case [1582] Cro Eliz 8 174
Turner *v.* Barnes (1862) 2 B & S 435 21
Turner *v.* Bridgett [1882] 8 QBD 392 57
Turner *v.* Cameron [1876] 5 QB 306 143, 167
Turner *v.* Hinks [1882] 8 QBD 392 57
Turnor *v.* Turner (1820) 2 Brod & Bing 107 188, 189
Tutthill *v.* Roberts (1673) 89 ER 256 85
Tutton *v.* Darke (1860) 5 H & N 647 96, 100
Twentieth Century Equitable Friendly Society, *Re* (1910) WN 236 59
Twigg *v.* Potts (1834) 3 LJ Ex 336 108

Underhill *v.* Wilson [1830] 6 Bing 697 72
Union Bank of Manchester *v.* Grundy [1924] 1 KB 833 218
United Counties Trust Ltd & Duncombe *v.* Swaffield (1939) 6 LJCCR 79 130
United Scientific *v.* Burnley Council [1978] AC 904 19
Usher *v.* Martin [1889] 24 QBD 272 176
Usher *v.* Walters (1843) 4 QB 553 222

Vasper *v.* Eddows [1702] Holt KB 256 18, 98
Vaspor *v.* Edwards (1702) 12 MR 658 33, 202, 211
Vaudeville Electric Cinema Ltd *v.* Muriset (1923) 2 Ch 72 142, 143
Vaughan *v.* Davis (1793) 1 Esp 257 36
Vaughan *v.* McKenzie (1968) 1 All ER 154 28-9, 102

Veal *v.* Warner (1669) 1 Mod Rep 20 69
Venners Electrical & Cooking Appliances *v.* Thorpe [1915] 2 Ch 404 58, 61
Vertue *v.* Beasley (1831) 1 Mood & R 21 199
Vicarino *v.* Hollingsworth (1869) 20 LTNS 780 127
Villas, *ex parte, In Re:* Rogers [1874] 9 Ch App 432 53
Vining, *ex parte* Hooman, *Re* (1870) LR 10 Eq 63 120
Vinkensterne *v.* Ebden 1 Ld Raym 384 10
Voisey, *ex parte* [1882] 21 Ch D 442 19

W M Long & Co, *ex parte* Cuddeford, *Re* (1888) 20 QBD 316 217, 219
Wade *v.* Marsh (1625) Lat 211 19
Waghorne *v.* Langmead (1796) 1 Bos & P 571 80
Wakeman *v.* Lindsay [1850] 14 QB 625 196
Walkden Metal Sheet Co Ltd, *Re* [1960] 1 Ch 170 57
Walker *v.* Hunter (1845) 2 CB 324 69
Wallace *v.* King (1788) 1 H Bl 13 212, 213
Waller *v.* Weedale (1604) Noy 107 202
Walley *v.* M'Connell [1849] 13 QBD 903 72
Wallis *v.* Savill [1701] 2 Lut 493 209
Wallrock *v.* Equity & Law Life Assurance Society [1942] 2 KB 82 190
Walmsley *v.* Milne (1859) 7 CBNS 115 142
Walsh *v.* Lonsdale [1882] 21 Ch D 9 18, 112
Walter *v.* Rumbal (1695) 1 Ld Raym 53 195
Walton, T D, *Re* [1966] 1 WLR 869 53
Wansborough *v.* Maton (1836) 4 A & E 884 147
Ward *v.* Dalton (1849) 7 CB 643 55
Ward *v.* Henley (1827) 1 Y & J 285 188
Ward *v.* Macauley (1791) 4 D & E 489 160
Ward *v.* Shew [1833] 9 Bing 608 81
Washborn *v.* Black (1774) 11 East 405 121, 122, 126-7, 138
Waterer *v.* Freeman (1617) Hob 205 69
Waterloo Life (No. 2), *Re* (1862) 32 LJ Ch 371 59
Waterman *v.* Yea (1756) 2 Wils 41 188
Watkinson *v.* Hollington [1944] KB 202 95
Watson *v.* Birdell (1845) 14 M & W 57 70
Watson *v.* Main (1800) 3 Esp 15 36
Watson *v.* Murray [1955] 1 All ER 350 121, 185, 215
Watson *v.* Park Royal (Caterers) Ltd [1961] 2 All ER 346 176
Watson *v.* White [1896] 2 QB 9 74
Weaver *v.* Bush (1798) 8 TR 78 29
Webb *v.* Frank Bevis [1940] 1 All ER 247 145
Webber *v.* Hutchins (1841) 8 M & W 319 70
Weeton *v.* Woodcock [1840] 7 M & W 14 146
Welch *v.* Kracovsky (1919) 3 WWR 361 99, 101
Wells, *In Re* [1929] 2 Ch 269 51
Wells *v.* Gurney (1828) 8 B & C 769 96

Wells *v.* Moody [1835] 7 C & P 59 214
Welsh *v.* Bell (1669) 1 Vent 37 66, 135, 173
Welsh *v.* Myers (1816) 4 Camp 368 37
Welsh *v.* Rose (1830) 6 Bing 638 165
Wentworth *v.* Bullen (1829) 9 B & C 840 70
Werth *v.* London & Westminster Loan & Discount Co (1889) 5 TLR 521 96, 126
West *v.* Automatic Salesman Ltd [1937] 2 All ER 706 180
West *v.* Nibbs (1847) 4 CB 172 110, 199
Westbury *v.* Twigg & Co [1891] 1 QB 77 61
Westwood *v.* Cowne [1816] 1 Stark 172 203
Whalley *v.* Williamson (1836) 7 C & P 294 101
Wharfland *v.* South London Co-operative Building Co [1995] *The Times*, April 25 22
Wharton *v.* Naylor (1848) 6 Dow & L 136; [1848] 12 QB 673 91
Wheeler *v.* Stevenson (1860) 6 H & N 155 171
Whimsell *v.* Giffard (1883) 3 OR 1 CAN 119
White *v.* Binstead (1853) 22 LJCP 115 92
White *v.* Greenish (1861) 11 CBNS 209 187
White *v.* Morris (1852) 11 CB 1015 41, 68
White *v.* Wallis (1759) 2 Wils 87 214
White *v.* Wiltshire (1619) 79 ER 476 117
Whitehead *v.* Bennett (1858) 27 LJ Ch 474 145
Whitehead *v.* Taylor (1837) 10 A & E 210 232
Whitmore *v.* Black (1844) 2 Pow & L 445 55
Whitworth *v.* Maden (1847) 2 C & K 517 203, 213
Whitworth *v.* Smith (1832) 5 C & P 250 182, 213
Wigram *v.* Cox [1894] 1 QB 792 155
Wilbraham *v.* Snow (1670) 2 Saund 47 127
Wilder *v.* Speer (1838) 8 Ad & El 547 121, 132
Wildy *v.* Mid-Hampshire Railway Co (1868) 16 WR 409 163
Wilkinson *v.* Downton [1897] 2 QB 57 111
Wilkinson *v.* Peel [1895] 1 QB 963 20
Willey *v.* Hucks [1909] 1 KB 760 57
William Hickley Ltd, *In Re* [1962] 1 WLR 555 58
Williams, *ex parte* [1893] 14 NSWLR 395 3, 106
Williams, *ex parte* Jones, *Re* (1880) 42 LT 157 118, 128
Williams *v.* Holmes (1853) 8 Exch 861 169
Williams *v.* Ladner [1798] 8 TR 72 17
Williams *v.* Lewsey (1831) 8 Bing 28 89
Williams *v.* Mostyn (1838) 4 M & W 145 71
Williams *v.* Roberts (1852) 7 Exch 618 37
Williams *v.* Stern [1879] 5 QB 409 225
Williams *v.* Stevens (1866) 1 PC 352 232
Williams *v.* Stiven [1846] 9 QB 14 20
Williams *v.* Williams & Nathan [1937] 2 All ER 559 67
Willis, Winder & Co *v.* Combe [1884] 1 Cab & El 353 185

Willoughby *v.* Backhouse [1824] 2 B & C 821 71, 214
Willows *v.* Ball (1806) 2 Bos & Pull 376 141
Wilmot *v.* Rose (1854) 3 E & B 563 156
Wilson, *Re* [1985] AC 750 16
Wilson, *ex parte* Lord Hastings, *Re* (1893) 10 Morr 219 52
Wilson *v.* Ducket (1675) 2 Mod Rep 61 140, 167
Wilson *v.* Lombank [1963] 1 All ER 740 117
Wilson *v.* Tummam (1843) 6 M & G 236 71, 72
Wilson *v.* Weller [1819] 3 Moore CP 294 186
Wiltshear *v.* Cottrell (1853) 1 E & B 674 147
Wiltshire *v.* Barrett [1966] 1 QB 312 111
Winchester Cigarette Machinery Ltd *v.* Payne (No.2) [1993] *The Times*, December 15 14
Winn *v.* Ingilby (1822) 5 B & Ald 625 144
Winter *v.* Bartholemew (1856) 11 Exch 704 179
Winter *v.* Lightbound [1720] 1 Stra 301 69
Winter *v.* Miles (1809) 10 East 578 97
Winter *v.* Winter [1861] 4 LT 639 40
Winterbourne *v.* Morgan (1774) 11 East 395 194, 203
Withernsea Brickworks, *Re* [1880] 16 Ch D 337 60
Withers *v.* Berry (1895) 39 Sol Jo 559 44
Witt *v.* Banner [1887] 20 QBD 114 42
Wolfe *v.* Summers (1811) 2 Camp 631 150
Wollaston *v.* Stafford (1854) 15 CB 278 128
Wood *v.* Clarke (1831) 1 C & J 484 169
Wood *v.* Dixie (1845) 7 QB 892 39
Wood *v.* Hewett [1846] 8 QB 913 142
Wood *v.* Nunn (1828) 5 Bing 10 126
Wood *v.* Wood (1843) 4 A & E 397 140
Woodcock *v.* Titterton (1864) 12 WR 865 20
Woodcroft *v.* Thompson 3 Lev 48 214
Wooddye *v.* Coles (1595) Noy 59; 74 ER 1027 69, 205, 206
Woodgate *v.* Knatchbull (1787) 2 TR 148 73, 222
Woodham, *ex parte* Conder, *Re* (1888) 20 QB 40 217
Woodland *v.* Fuller (1840) 11 Ad & El 859 79
Woods, *In Re* [1931] 2 Ch 320 56
Woods *v.* Durrant (1846) 6 M & W 149 121
Woods *v.* Finnis (1852) 7 Ex 363 72
Woolford's Estate *v.* Levy [1892] 1 QB 772 56
Woollen *v.* Wright (1862) 1 H & C 354 72
Wootley *v.* Gregory (1828) Y & J 536 195
Wormer *v.* Biggs [1845] 2 Car & Kir 31 18
Wormsley, *ex parte* Gill, *Re* [1957] 19 ABC 105 38
Wotton *v.* Shirt [1600] Cro Eliz 742 209
Wren *v.* Weild [1869] 4 QB 730 69
Wright *v.* Child [1866] 1 Ex 358 73, 205
Wylie *v.* Birch [1843] 4 QB 566 69

Wystow's Case (1523) YB 14 Hen VIII fo 25 pl 6 143

Yates, *In Re* [1888] 38 Ch D 112 144
Yates *v.* Eastwood (1851) 6 Exch 805 206, 228
Yates *v.* Ratledge (1860) 5 H & N 249 91
Yelloly *v.* Morley (1910) 27 TLR 20 107
Yeoman *v.* Ellison (1867) 2 CP 681 20
York *v.* Flatekval (1971) 3 WWR 289 153
Young, *In Re* (1880) 43 LT 576 43
Young *v.* Broughton Waterworks Co (1861) 31 LJQB 14 187
Young *v.* Dalgety (1987) 1 EGLR 117 142, 145
Young *v.* Dencher [1923] 1 DLR 432 9, 132
Young *v.* Roebuck [1863] 2 H & C 296 55
Young *v.* Short (1883) 3 Man LR 302 150
Youngs *v.* Youngs [1940] 1 KB 760 43

Zoedone, *Re* (1884) 32 WR 312 61
Zouch *v.* Willingdale 1 H Bl 311 21

TABLE OF STATUTES

Administration of Justice Act 1970	93
Agricultural Credits Act 1928	164-5
Agricultural Holdings Act 1986	86, 146-7, 166, 169, 191
Agricultural Tenancies Act 1995	147
Animals Act 1971	9
Air Force Act 1955	95
Apportionment Act 1870	49, 52
Army Act 1955	95
Bankruptcy Act 1883	45, 120
Bills of Sale Acts 1878 and 1882	41, 42, 43, 120
Car Tax Act 1983	5
Child Support Act (CSA) 1991	8, 25, 85, 149, 222, 237
Constables Protection Act 1750	74, 75-6
Consumer Credit Act 1974	6, 11, 44, 162, 169
Consumer Protection Act 1987	139
County Courts Act (CCA) 1984	8, 45
Part VIII	73
s.14	30
s.7	15
s.76	150
s.77	16
s.87	199
s.88	15
s.89	147
s.90	122
s.91	140
s.92	32, 33
s.93	202
s.98	178, 206, 207
s.99	79
s.100	177, 178, 180
s.101	177, 178, 180
s.102	89, 91
s.103	97
s.111	11
s.114	47
s.115	61
s.116	51
s.123	73
s.124	74

s.125 8, 213
s.126 74
s.144 187
Criminal Attempts Act 1981 32
Criminal Damage Act 1971 114, 191
Criminal Law Act 1967 106
Criminal Law Act 1977 114
Crown Proceedings Act 1947 103, 186
Customs and Excise Management Act 1979 5
Deserted Tenements Act 1817 39
Diplomatic Privileges Act 1971 95, 97
Distress (Costs) Act 1817 2, 224
Distress for Rent Act (DRA) 1689 1, 8, 32, 199, 203, 215
s.1 195, 203, 206
s.2 172, 173
s.3 33
s.4 191
Distress for Rent Act (DRA) 1737 1-2, 8
s.1 35
s.2 35
s.3 37
s.4 37
s.7 37
s.8 172-3
s.9 121, 173, 201
s.10 2, 116, 121, 125, 134, 194, 201, 204
s.16 39
s.17 39
s.18 19
s.19 212
s.20 71, 213
Electricity Act 1989 158
Execution Act 1844 89
Finance Act 1989 7, 89
Finance Act 1994 7
Finance Act 1996 7
Gas Act 1986 157
Hosiery Act 1843 155
Housing Act 1988 88
Income Tax Act 1988 23
Improvement of Land Act 1864 5
Insolvency Act 1986 38, 45-54, 56-8, 60-3, 120
Judgments Act 1838 140
Justices of the Peace Act 1979 74, 75
Land Drainage Act 1991 7
Landlord and Tenant Act 1709 89-92
s.1 49, 53, 56, 89, 90, 92

s.6 20, 79, 90, 167
s.7 20, 90, 167
Landlord and Tenant Act 1730 18, 21
Landlord and Tenant Act 1851 166
Law of Distress Amendment Act (LDAA) 1888 2, 148
s.4 167, 189
s.5 203, 204
s.6 203
s.7 81, 82
Law of Distress Amendment Act 1895 2, 82, 83, 189
Law of Distress Amendment Act 1908 2
s.1 170
s.2 190, 233
s.4 161, 164, 171, 172
s.4A 44, 169
s.5 170
s.6 190
Law of Property Act 1925 5, 18, 81
Law Reform (Married Women and Tortfeasors) Act 1935 158
Limitation Act 1980 78, 79
Local Government Finance Act 1988 6, 27
Local Government Finance Act 1992 6, 27
Magistrates' Court Act 1980 7
s.35 213
s.59 87
s.75 17
s.77 16
s.78 77, 117, 199, 213, 229
s.79 198
ss.82-84 88
s.93 87
s.111 192
s.123 77
s.125 82
s.127 79
Malicious Communications Act 1988 94
Married Women's Property Act 1964 159
Metropolitan Police Courts Act 1839 189
Naval Discipline Act 1957 95
Offences Against the Person Act 1861 30, 111
Partnership Act 1890 155, 180
Perjury Act 190
Police and Criminal Evidence Act 105
Post Office Act 1969 168
Railway Companies Act 1867 155-6
Railway Rolling Stock Protection Act 1872 156
Rates Act 10

Rehabilitation of Offenders Act 1974 83
Rent Act 1977 88
Reserve and Auxiliary Forces (Protection of Civil Interests) Act 1951 95
Reserve and Auxiliary Forces (Protection of Civil Interests) Act 1953 183
Road Traffic Act 1991 8, 24, 81, 154
Road Traffic Regulation Act 1984 133
Sale of Farming Stock Act 1816 156-7, 169
Sale of Goods Act 1979 162
Sheriffs' Act 1887 6, 81
s.8 30
s.20 73, 217, 229
s.29 73, 114, 229
Solicitors' Act 49
Statute of Exchequer 191, 214
Statute of Gloucester 1278 39
Statute Law (Reform) Act 1993 155
Statute of Marlborough 1267 1, 66, 97, 98, 115, 201, 214
Statute of Westminster 98, 115, 223
Supreme Court Act (SCA) 1981 6
s.138 79, 80, 150
s.138A 203, 204
s.138B 177, 206, 207
Taxes Management Act (TMA) 1970 7
s.61 82, 89, 103, 202, 203, 206
s.62 89, 92
Theft Act 1968 198, 228
Torts Act 1977 185
Torts (Interference with Goods) Act 1977 181, 184, 186
Value Added Tax Act 1994 7, 23, 33
Vehicle Excise and Registration Act 1994 133
Water Industry Act 1991 158

STATUTORY INSTRUMENTS

Child Support (Collection and Enforcement)
  Regulations 1992 — 8, 25, 77, 199, 222
  sch.1 — 216
  sch.2 — 221, 224
Civil Procedure Rules (CPR) 1999 — 6, 13-14, 181, 226
  Part 23 — 8, 85, 95, 155, 178, 204
Council Tax (Administration and Enforcement)
  (Amendment) Regulations 1998 — 81, 85
Council Tax (Administration and Enforcement)
  Regulations 1992 — 6
  reg.34 — 26
  reg.45 — 77, 97, 158, 195, 197, 199, 213, 222
  reg.46 — 174
  reg.47 — 38
  reg.52 — 211, 219
  sch.5 — 216, 221, 222, 224, 226
Council Tax (Alteration of Lists and Appeals) Regulations 1993 — 27
County Court Fees Order 1982 — 218
County Court Rules 1981 — 45, 73
  O.1 — 150
  O.6 — 188
  O.7 — 96
  O.10 — 158
  O.25 — 15, 154, 155
  O.26 — 11-12, 78, 79, 85, 86, 165, 195, 204, 218
  O.33 — 177, 178, 179
  O.37 — 16, 71
  O.38 — 226
  O.48 — 24, 155
  O.48B — 199
  O.50 — 187
Distress for Customs and Excise Duties
  Regulations 1997 — 7, 96, 148
Distress for Rent Rules 1920 — 223
Distress for Rent Rules 1988 — 8, 81, 83-5, 122, 131, 134, 194, 224
  Appendix 1 — 216
  r.10 — 218, 223
  r.11 — 226
  r.12 — 195, 201, 218

Enforcement of Road Traffic Debts (Certificated Bailiffs) Regulations 1993 8, 81, 82, 216, 218, 221
Enforcement of Road Traffic Debts Order 1993 8, 177
art.4 202, 213
art.7 199
art.9 147
art.11 122
art.13 203
art.14 206
art.15 79
High Court and County Courts Jurisdiction Order 1991 (amended 1999) 6
Insolvency Rules 1986 45, 46, 53, 55, 62
Insolvent Estates of Deceased Persons Order 1986 45
Insolvent Partnerships Order (IPO) 1994 45
Magistrates' Court (Forms) Rules 1981 77, 87
Magistrates' Court Rules 1981 7
r.53 87
r.54 77, 117, 147, 198, 199, 202, 203, 208, 209
r.55 198
Non-Domestic Rating (Collection and Enforcement) (Local Lists) Regulations 1989 6, 27, 38
reg.14 77, 97, 149, 158, 195, 197, 199, 213, 222
reg.15 174
reg.19 219
sch.3 216, 221
Non-Domestic Rating (Collection and Enforcement) (Local Lists) Regulations 1998 81, 85
Rules of the Supreme Court 1965 6, 69, 70
O.2 70
O.17 6, 43, 150, 176-81
O.45 6, 11, 195
O.46 6, 12, 78, 85, 102, 208
O.47 6, 204, 217
O.48B 79, 85
O.65 96
O.80 158
O.81 154
Sheriff's Fees (Amendment) Order 1956 122, 217, 229
Valuation and Community Charge Tribunals (Amendments) Regulations 1993 27
Value Added Tax (General) Regulations 1985 7, 87
Value Added Tax Regulations 1995 7
r.65 202, 203, 206

PART ONE – LEGAL CONTEXT

Chapter One

HISTORY AND DEVELOPMENT

"A landlord's right to distrain for arrears of rent is itself only a survival of one among a multitude of distraints which both in England and other countries belonged to a primitive period when legal procedure still retained some of the forms of a semi-barbarous custom of reprisals . . ."[1]

The origins of the right of self help by distraint are remote and pre-date the earliest collections of monarch's laws, whether we consider Ireland and Wales or Anglo Saxon England (for more discussion see Kruse 1998 2). In early mediaeval times the power was increasingly adopted by weak courts to compel both attendance by defendants and the payment of debts. Later its use by the courts narrowed to the enforcement of judgments.

From about 1300 onwards statute law began to codify and control the common law, by setting limits to the use of distress and providing remedies for wrongful use of the power[2]. From about 1600 we see the outlines of the present enforcement system emerging clearly – distress in the courts is now referred to as execution, common law distress comprises distress for rent and distress damage feasant and forms of statutory distraint begin to be distinguished, such as distress for poor rates introduced by an Act of Elizabeth I (for further discussion see Kruse in CBA, forthcoming 1999). In light of much of the previous discussion, it is interesting to note the issues addressed over the centuries. The problems and deficiencies that Parliament sought to improve included the following:

- *excessive distress and place of seizure:* the Statute of Marlborough 1267 introduced fines for excessive distress and made it illegal to distrain off premises and on roads unless cattle were being deliberately driven off to avoid seizure.
- *offences and remedies:* the Distress for Rent Act 1689 introduced penalties of treble damages for poundbreach and rescous and double damages and full costs for wrongful distress. The Distress for Rent Act 1737 introduced the right of distress after fraudulent removal and a penalty of double damages. It also differentiated illegal and irregular distress. Since this time there has been no major alteration in the structure of bailiffs' offences or remedies.

[1] Bowen LJ in *American Concentrated Must* v. *Hendry* (1893) 57 JP 521.
[2] See generally *F A Enever,* 1931, in Appendix Three.

- *costs:* there has been legislation on permissible fees since the Act of Elizabeth I to prevent oppression and extortion through excess sheriff's fees (29 Eliz c4). The Distress (Costs) Act 1817 extended such control to distress and was intended to "*protect people of small means from the exorbitant charges of those to whom the execution of warrants was entrusted*"[3]. There have been many successive statutes and statutory instruments and costs are still an area of concern to the legislature, and recent years have seen deliberate steps to harmonise the scales applicable to the different forms of the remedy.

- *walking possession*: the origin of alternative forms of impounding may be traced back to s.10 Distress for Rent Act 1737. It allowed a landlord to "*impound or otherwise secure*" goods "*in such place or on such part of the premises . . . as shall be most fit and convenient*" for the purpose of impounding. The Act also created a penalty of treble damages for poundbreach. The courts subsequently held that impounding on the premises had to be by moving and locking up the goods i.e. visibly securing them against the tenant and all others. If the goods could not be secured in this way, they had to be removed (e.g. *Thornton* v. *Cruther* [1769] (unreported)). The strict procedure was then mitigated for the convenience of landlords and tenants by development of the walking possession agreement. The tenant agreed to the goods being distrained but left undisturbed. It is indeed possible that impounding in this manner with the tenant's consent had been happening since before 1737 anyway, but it has grown in prevalence since, to the exclusion of almost every other means of impounding. The problem is that whilst the courts have accepted that this might be impounding effective against the tenant, such an agreement was not a means of impounding that visibly secured it against strangers. In this way it did not comply with the case law developed under s.10 Distress for Rent Act 1737 and has led to the many arguments about abandonment and poundbreach discussed later. As a consequence a widely accepted (and indeed fundamental) practice is of uncertain legality and efficacy (see also Kruse, 1998 1).

- *exempt goods:* the Law of Distress Amendment Act 1888 extended privilege from distress for rent to those classes of goods protected from execution in the county court. This tendency to harmonise the classes of protected goods in line with the civil courts has accelerated in the last decade. The Law of Distress Amendment Act 1908 introduced protection for third parties' goods.

- *certification:* the Law of Distress Amendment Act 1888 introduced the need for rent bailiffs to hold certificates. The Law of Distress Amendment Act 1895 introduced court powers to cancel certificates and penalties for levying without one. Since this Act there has been no substantial change to the regulation of private bailiffs. This is despite a massive increase in the use of distress over the last few decades. The Lord Chancellor's Department raised the possibility of far reaching reform in 1992, but as described below little has actually come of these proposals.

Though there have been efforts to harmonise the law, these have not been coordinated, and have consequently been undermined by the proliferation of forms of

[3] *Headland* v. *Coster* [1904] 1 KB 219 CA.

distress and multiplication of slightly differing regulations on such matters as costs and exempt goods. To emphasise this, it is interesting to note that the major concerns of the latter part of the nineteenth century- protected goods and control of bailiffs, are still areas being given attention by the legislature in the late twentieth century.

However, one major issue to which the courts and academics have repeatedly returned has not been seriously addressed by Parliament. This is whether distress as a remedy should be abolished altogether. The attitude of the courts may be summarised by the following quote: *"Distress is a relict of old times and should not be extended in any way . . ."*[4]. Nonetheless, over the last decade the use of distraint has continued, and even increased (e.g. the introduction of distraint for road traffic penalties). There has been some piecemeal reform, as described, but no attempt to address the general faults of the remedy, despite mounting judicial criticism. Lord Denning in 1982 characterised distress as "*an archaic remedy which has largely fallen into disuse*". In 1986 the Law Commission examined distress for rent[5] and described it as "*difficult and distasteful*" and "*riddled with intricacy and inadequacy*". In light of "*its many uncertainties, anomalies and archaisms*", they concluded that "*Its useful life is now spent and cannot be resuscitated*". The Commission quoted with approval the remark of Sir Jack Jacob that "*its very existence as legal remedy besmirches the fabric of English civil justice*".

In February 1991 the Law Commission published its final report to Parliament on distress for rent[6]. The Commission concluded that, even after considering the responses to the consultation from landlords, bailiffs and others, abolition was still a better solution than piecemeal reform. The report included a draft bill for this purpose. This bill was taken no further, and piecemeal changes to the system of distress have continued.

In July 1992 the Lord Chancellor's Department announced that, in response to public and media concern over the enforcement of community charge, it would conduct a broad review of bailiffs' powers[7]. This initially promised a radical overhaul of the management and control of bailiffs combined with a reform of the law itself. In the event, neither has happened. The major changes proposed in the control of bailiffs have been contracted to some improvements in the certification process, described later. The matter has clearly lost its political priority, as it was not until late 1996 that further steps were taken on the consultation. A group of interested individuals including representatives of creditors, bailiffs and consumers was assembled to consider how the matter could be concluded but after three meetings of the working party limited proposals were put forward which may be implemented in late 1999[8].

In July 1997 Customs and Excise introduced substantial changes to VAT distraint, such as a list of exempt goods copied from Scotland and a new fee scale. Modest changes were made to the use of distraint in enforcing council tax in April 1998. Another piecemeal reform was a revision in the road traffic penalty scale of fees.

[4] Windeyer J in *ex p Williams [1893] 14 NSWLR 395.*

[5] Law Commission Working Paper No. 97, HMSO.

[6] *Landlord & Tenant: Distress for Rent*: Law Commission No. 97, Cmnd 138? HMSO.

[7] *A Review of the Organisation & Management of Civil Enforcement Agents: Consultation Paper*- Lord Chancellor's Department, 1992.

[8] See Lord Chancellors Department 'Modification and Strengthening of the Bailiff Certification and Complaints Procedure', September 1998.

These isolated improvments are welcome but the overall system remains uncoordinated. More hope may lie with a far reaching review of enforcement powers announced by Lord Chancellor's Department in early 1998[9]. This will be a long term project, initially for two years, examining county court enforcement primarily (and the future role of its bailiffs), but also looking at the use of private bailiffs (except in magistrates' courts, which will be the subject of a separate review) and returning also to the 1991 Law Commission report.

It will thus be seen that although, recently, there have been improvements in the regulation of bailiffs and of the process of distress, they have been patchy and uncoordinated. There seems to be a lack of political will or legislative energy to take on the (admittedly) huge problem of reforming the whole system.

Commentary

It therefore appears that if there is to be substantial or immediate change the onus rests with the judiciary, bailiffs, creditors and legal practitioners[10]. The courts have shown a willingness to update the law when presented with an opportunity (e.g. *Salford Van Hire* v. *Bocholt, Re: ELS, Eller* v. *Grovecrest*[11]). Trade bodies are also starting to take steps to improve procedures e.g. the complaints procedures described in chapter 12. The elements already exist to enable the law to be revised without the need for major statutory intervention (see Kruse 1998 1). All the involved parties would benefit from efforts to place the law on a modern, coherent basis without any need to try to apply authorities that are Victorian (and often older) and which reflect a commercial and judicial system no longer applicable to present (or future) needs and experiences.

[9] Lord Chancellor's Department, Enforcement Review, Consultation Paper 1: 'How can the enforcement of civil court judgments be made more effective?' June 1998.

[10] See author's article "Reform or review?" in Legal Action, June 1996.

[11] Respectively [1995] 2 EGLR 50; [1995] Ch 11; [1995] QB 272.

Chapter Two

CURRENT REGIME

2.1 Introduction

Any study of the law of distress is complicated by the range of different forms that the remedy takes. In addition to the ten forms described below, numerous other forms of distress exist or have existed but have fallen into disuse or been abolished. These include the following:

- *car tax* – Customs and Excise can distrain on defaulting car importers[1];
- *excise duties* – Customs and Excise can distrain on defaulting excise traders' stock and assets[2];
- *rent charges created under Improvement of Land Act 1864*: interest due under s.64 of the Act is enforceable by distress in the same manner as a rent charge under s.121 LPA 1925;
- *harbour rates and dues* – harbour authorities or undertakers may levy distress; and,
- *market tolls and stallages* – may be collected by distress by a market owner (a person or council).

The above list contains forms of distress that are rarely seen[3] or are purely historic, as a consequence of which no further reference will be made to them in the text.

As is outlined below, there are currently ten forms of distress in active use, enforced by four different types of bailiff, with the law for each subtly different. Despite these differences between the various forms of the remedy, there are common principles running through every form of seizure which will be discussed in detail in Part Three. The 10 active forms may be divided into three categories as follows.

2.2 Execution

Execution generally refers to the process of enforcement of civil court judgments, whether by charging order, garnishee order etc. More specifically it refers to the seizure of goods to recover judgment debts.

High Court execution: The sheriff's officer may enforce the following judgments by seizure and sale of the defendant's goods:

[1] Car Tax Act 1983.

[2] Section 117 Customs & Excise Management Act 1979.

[3] But see *R* v. *Carrick D.C. ex parte Prankerd* (1998) *The Times*, September 1 in which the use of distress for harbour rates to collect mooring charges was held illegal.

- High Court judgments of any amount;
- all county court judgments for over £5000 where the debt does not arise from an agreement regulated by the Consumer Credit Act 1974; and,
- county court judgments of between £600 and £5000 which do not arise from an agreement regulated by the Consumer Credit Act 1974 and where the creditor requests transfer from the county court to the High Court for this purpose[4].

The sheriff's officer is a private bailiff, but is also an officer of the Supreme Court. They are regulated by the Sheriff's Act 1887 plus the relevant provisions of the Supreme Court Act and RSC. Day by day their instructions come through the county's undersheriff, who can be a useful contact for negotiation.

County court execution: the Court Service employs bailiffs in each county court who are responsible for enforcing all warrants and serving process within that court's area. The bailiff may enforce the following judgments by seizure and sale of the defendant's goods:

- all judgments based on debts arising from agreements regulated by Consumer Credit Act 1974;
- all county court judgments of less than £1000; and,
- any other judgment of an amount up to £5000[5].

Woolf reforms: with the introduction of the Civil Procedure Rules 1999 on April 26 1999, there are major changes to commencing and procedures in the High Court and county court, but few changes to enforcement. Part 50 CPR retains elements of the previous court rules in schedules. Schedule 1 comprises the surviving RSC and includes Orders 17 (interpleader) and 45, 46, and 47 concerning execution. Schedule 2 comprises the surviving CCR, orders 25 and 26 dealing with execution and 0.33 on interpleader. All have minor procedural amendments but are substantially unaltered.

2.3 Statutory distraint

For reasons that will be explained in the commentary section later, the term "distraint" is preferred to "distress" to describe the seizure of goods by bailiffs to enforce liabilities due under statute. A number of debts can be recovered by this means:

Local taxes: both council tax[6] and national non-domestic rate[7] (NNDR) for businesses are enforceable by seizure of goods. Distraint may be levied by either local authority officers or by private bailiffs.The legislation is expanded upon by guidance such as local authority codes of practice (see 12.2) and that contained in chapter 4 of the Council Tax Practice note No 9 "Recovery & Enforcement" issued by Department of the Environment in 1992.

[4] Article 8 High Court and County Courts Jurisdiction Order 1991(as amended on April 26 1999).

[5] As above.

[6] Local Government Finance Act 1992 and Council Tax (Administration and Enforcement) Regulations 1992.

[7] Local Government Finance Act 1988 and Non-Domestic Rating (Local Lists) (Collection and Enforcement) Regulations 1989.

Drainage rates – under Land Drainage Act 1991 s.54(1) a drainage board may recover arrears of drainage rates by a levy of distress in the same manner as a local authority may recover NNDR. Rates are raised by assessment on agricultural land and buildings and special levies on non-agricultural properties in order to finance flood defences and the like. The occupier of a chargeable agricultural property may appeal to the valuation tribunal about the determination of the annual value (s.45). Any other matter can be appealed to the Crown Court (s.51). These matters cannot be raised as a defence in recovery proceedings. A liability order made by the magistrates' court may be enforced by distress only upon the goods and chattels of the liable person (s.54(5)(a)) though the goods need not be in the board's area (*Morse* v. *Ouse Drainage Board* [1931] 1 KB 109) the drainage board need not enforce if it feels that the expenses of collection will not be met (s.54(6)).

Income tax: the Collector of Taxes may levy distraint to collect any unpaid taxes[8]. Distress is used by the Revenue over 30,000 times per annum, but in 75 per cent of these cases it is against companies who have not paid PAYE.

VAT: Customs and Excise may use their own officers or private bailiffs to levy for arrears of VAT. Customs and Excise (C&E) have the power to distrain for VAT under para 5(4) sch. 11. VAT Act 1994 and reg.65 VAT (General) Regulations 1985, as amended by Part XXV, reg 212 VAT Regulations 1995[9].

Insurance premium tax: Customs and Excise may also levy distress to collect tax due from any insurer which they are refusing to pay (Sch. 7 Part III para. 7(7) Finance Act 1994). The tax is charged at 2.5% on any taxable insurance contract made after October 1st 1994. These contracts include most policies except those for motor vehicles for the disabled, credit facilities and various ships and aircraft. Like VAT tax may be assessed in the absence of a return, there is a right of appeal to tribunal, and various penalties for non-payment and non-compliance. Like VAT these include a penalty for breach of a walking possession agreement (para. 19, sch 7). The tax is enforced by distraint in the same manner as VAT.

Landfill tax: is also collected by C&E under Part III, Finance Act 1996. It is a tax on the disposal of waste in landfill sites throughout the UK. Site operators are liable for the tax at a rate of £7 per tonne on any disposal made after October 1st 1996. Tax can be assessed where C&E feel that too little is being paid. There is again a right of appeal to tribunal, interest and penalties for non payment and a penalty of 50% of the tax due for breach of walking possession (Part V, para. 24, sch 5). The tax is enforced by a levy of distress in the same manner as VAT.

Magistrates' court orders: private bailiffs may be used by magistrates courts to collect unpaid orders[10]. The police are also empowered to enforce such warrants, but rarely if ever do so nowadays. Where a defendant defaults on payment of any sum adjudged to be paid following summary conviction or an order, the magistrates court can enforce by distraint. The sums recoverable by this means are civil debts (i.e. tax and national insurance contributions), damages, compensation orders and fines,

[8] Sections 61–62 Taxes Management Act 1970 as amended by ss.152–3 Finance Act 1989.

[9] See too Distress for Customs and Excise Duties Regulations 1997.

[10] Sections 75–78 Magistrates Court Act 1980 and r.54 Magistrates Court Rules 1981.

including those from the Crown Court, Court of Appeal and House of Lords. Many courts restrict distress for fines to fixed penalty offences (e.g. fines for motoring offences) or for sums under a level of £100–150.

Child support maintenance: the Secretary of State for Social Security is empowered to levy distraint to collect arrears of maintenance due to the Child Support Agency (CSA)[11]. They may also collect other amounts of maintenance due to a parent with care at the same time and may enforce "interim maintenance orders" (provisional assessments imposed as a penalty on the absent parent for not supplying the information required) by distress. Private bailiffs are employed. Additional powers are also contained in the Child Support (Collection and Enforcement) Regulations 1992 and in the CSA's detailed code of practice for its bailiffs. This code is very lengthy and detailed and deals with many aspects of the distraint process. Its general spirit is that distraint should be levied in an "humane, firm but fair manner" and considerable attention is paid to how the bailiff approaches the matter.

Road traffic penalties: local authorities may use private bailiffs to levy for unpaid orders for road traffic penalties[12]. Any sum payable for a parking offence in England and Wales is recoverable by a new form of warrant of execution as if payable under a county court order. These penalties were introduced progressively in Greater London but are now applicable throughout the whole of England & Wales if local councils wish to adopt the powers. (All London boroughs have, but outside the capital only a few authorities have so far, including Oxford, Winchester and High Wycombe.) Road traffic distraint is a complex amalgam of county court execution, distress for rent and special provisions all of its own. It is a confusing area to deal with, as there are seven different statutes regulating the process.

Where an individual contravenes parking regulations a parking attendant employed by the borough can impose a penalty charge and may either fix notice of this on the car or give it to the driver. If the owner does not pay in 28 days' notice is served on him giving a further 28 days in which to pay. If the person does not pay then a "charge certificate" is issued and the penalty increases by 50%. After a further 14 days the local authority applies to for a county court order enabling it to recover the penalty. Local authorities may also use distraint to recover sums ordered be paid following an adjudication by a parking adjudicator under s.73 RTA 1991. See 3.2.6 for more detail.

2.4 Common law distress

Distress for rent – arrears of unpaid rent may be collected by means of distress, either by the landlord or by using a private certificated bailiff. A range of provisions govern the remedy, some very old[13]. The remedy not only applies to rent but also to rent charges (*Dodds* v. *Thompson* [1866] 1 CP 133).

[11] Child Support Act 1991, s.35.

[12] Section 78, Part II, Road Traffic Act 1991; Enforcement of Road Traffic Debts Order 1993 (which extends the relevant sections of the County Courts Act i.e. ss.85–104 and 125, to these debts, but with important amendments); Enforcement of Road Traffic Debts (Certificated Bailiffs) Regulations 1993 (which apply the Distress for Rent Rules 1988).

[13] For example, Distress for Rent Rules 1988 and Distress for Rent Acts 1689 and 1737.

Distress damage feasant: distress to remedy damage to crops caused by stray cattle has now been replaced by a statutory remedy[14]. The remedy of distress damage feasant remains for trespassing chattels (e.g. *Reynell* v. *Champernoon* [1631] Cro Car 228; *Ambergate, Nottingham & Boston & Eastern Junction Co* v. *Midland Railway Co* [1853] 2 El & Bl 792), but was generally regarded as obsolete until recently when it was revived to provide a legal basis for the practice of clamping wrongfully parked cars by private firms (see 8.4.8 later). Any land trespass or private nuisance may be levied for if the person could sue for damages for the same wrong, but there is no right of distress damage feasant for other wrongs. It is immaterial if the chattel's original entry on the land was lawful.

Commentary

The above threefold division is not one that is always clearly appreciated by either lawyers or bailiffs. There has been a tendency, understandable perhaps but nevertheless erroneous, to group together all forms of distress, both common law and statutory, as if they were the same remedy. This false classification has been the source of much confusion and many mistakes. There is a real difference between distress at common law and distress under an Act of Parliament. It is an important distinction as it has serious implications for the duties and powers of the bailiff, debtor and third parties.

Common law distress has developed primarily through case law over the centuries. Statutory distraint is a power to seize goods granted under a particular statute. The absence of extensive case law and the deliberate delimitation of each party's rights by the relevant statute usually means that there are much greater powers for the bailiff in statutory distraint. Where detail is absent on the procedure for a particular form of distress under an Act of Parliament it has been common to infer rights from other forms of distress, normally distress for rent. This has for instance until recently particularly been the practice of the Inland Revenue and Customs and Excise, though specific regulations have now begun to displace this. There is abundant case law on common law distress which is capable of filling all the gaps in statutory provision. Despite the occasional confident remarks by judges – for example "*It is agreed that the power of distress for rates is not like the power of the landlord to distrain: we all know the difference*"[15], the tendency to extend the provisions of distress for rent is a longstanding and "*unfortunate confusion*"[16] which still continues. The consequences can include wrongful actions by bailiffs, bad advice by legal practitioners and other advisers and mistaken acts by debtors and other involved parties.

As the following case law illustrates, an analogy based on similarity of names is not a safe one: the truer analogy for statutory distraint is with execution in the civil courts.

- *Distraint for local taxes:* most of the case law concentrates on differentiating distraint for rates from distress for rent.

[14] Animals Act 1971.
[15] Lindley LJ in *Re: Marriage, Neave & Co* [1896] 2 Ch D 663.
[16] Beck J in *Young* v. *Dencher* [1923] 1 DLR 432.

– *Hutchins* v. *Chambers* [1758] 1 Burr 579: This was the first case which fully explored this issue. The main question was whether plough beasts were protected in distraint for rates. A clear judgment summarising the law was delivered by Lord Mansfield who held that seizure under the Rates Acts and similar statutes is much more analogous to execution than rent distress. The purpose of rent distress is to compel payment. Statutory distress is more like execution as goods can be sold immediately to clear the debt. It was stated specifically that a "*common law exemption* [from distress for rent] . . . *doth not extend to cases where the distress is given in the nature of an execution, by any particular statute*".

– *Potts* v. *Hickman* [1940] 4 All ER 491 HL: this case concerned the rights of a landlord in distress for rates when rent was also due. The law was extensively reviewed by the law lords who quoted *R.* v. *Speed* [1940] 4 All ER 491 HL: 12 MR 328 in which Holt J said "*when a statute says money 'shall be levied by distress', that is an execution*". From *R.* v. *Benn & Church* [1795] 6 Term Rep 198 is quoted "*a warrant of distress for rates [is] in the nature of an execution*". The judgment was that there was no doubt that a distress for rates is "*analogous to, and in some respects is, an execution*".

See also *Moyse* v. *Cocksedge* [1748] Willes 636; *Re: Roberts ex parte Hill* [1877] 6 Ch D 63; *Swann* v. *Sloan* (1895) 29 1LT 109 and *McCreagh* v. *Cox & Ford* (1923) 87 JP 133.

- *fines distraint*: in *Hannigan* v. *Burgess* [1888] 26 NBR 99 the courts considered an attempt to replevy goods seized in distress for a fine. Fraser J described the distraint as "*an execution issued by a Justice, and the proceedings under such a distress are entirely different from those under a distress for rent. . . . Goods sold under a distress issued upon a conviction are sold in like manner as goods taken under a fieri facias.*" See also *R.* v. *Speed* [1940] 12 MR 328.
- *taxes distraint:* in *McGregor* v. *Clamp* [1914] 1 KB 288 Bray J held "*The right of distress by the Crown was really by way of execution*". Lush J added that whilst tools of the trade might be protected in distress for rent there is "*no such limit in case of distress by the Crown for taxes. Although the mode of recovery is by distress, yet the process is really analogous to execution on a judgment*".
- *miscellaneous forms of distraint:* see also *Vinkensterne* v. *Ebden* (distress for harbour dues)[17] and *Swaffer* v. *Mulcahy* (distress for tithe rent charge)[18].

Thus it may be seen that execution is the closer analogy to distress under statute. Like distress for rent it provides plentiful case law to guide practitioners and its procedures are, on examination, always far more like statutory distraint than are those of rent distress. Two examples of this will suffice:

– *Place of levy*: statutory distraint and execution may be levied anywhere in the bailiff's "jurisdiction". The landlord may only levy at the rented property.

– *Time of levy*: statutory distraint and execution may be levied at any time. The landlord may only levy between sunrise and sunset.

[17] [1698] 1 Ld Raym 384

[18] *Halsburys Laws*, para. 204 vol 13.

Numerous other decisions could be cited but in conclusion readers are simply referred to Halsbury's *Laws*[19] which states that the "*rules governing . . . distress for rent are not applicable to distress for rates or for taxes or under the summary jurisdiction* [in magistrates court]".

Practitioners must nevertheless be exercise caution when making any analogies. In *McCreagh* (1923) 87 JP 133, McCarlie J states at 134 "*The poor law code is complete in itself. It contains many and detailed provisions . . . It contains many matters of procedure peculiar to its own purpose*". Reference to outside sources, even if that is most properly to execution, should still be made with care, bearing in mind the unique nature of each process. Regulations specific to execution cannot be imported into the statutory remedies, but the common law principles of execution should be applicable. Nonetheless, as a reminder of the fundamental difference between the procedures, throughout the rest of this book seizure of goods under statute will be termed distraint, whilst levies under common law powers will be called distress.

2.5 Other forms of bailiff action

Although not the concern in any detail of this book, below are outlined the other forms of civil process that are enforced by bailiffs, by way of contrast with the seizure of goods.

2.5.1 Warrants of delivery

Warrants of delivery may be issued in the High Court (RSC O.45 r.4) or county court (CCR O.26 r.16) as a means of enforcing delivery orders made in fixed date actions, for instance for the recovery of goods subject to a hire purchase agreement. Though it is not necessary (at least for cases in respect of Consumer Credit Act regulated agreements) for the creditor to use the court bailiffs to enforce the warrant, as a private bailiff may be used, the powers of the bailiffs in either case will be the same. They will only be able to seize such goods as are specified in the order, or goods to their value it that was given as an alternative by the court. The bailiffs have no power of forced entry in order to enforce the warrant. If the warrant is issued by the court, application may be made on notice to suspend it.

2.5.2 Warrants of possession

Possession warrants (writs in the High Court) are issued in actions for the recovery of possession or for forfeiture in order to enforce the order made by the court (RSC O.45 r.3; CCR O.26 r.17). The court bailiff must be used to enforce such warrants. As they are concerned with the recovery of real property, by their nature they permit entry to be forced if necessary in order to execute the warrant. Under s.111(1) CCA the county court bailiff is not empowered by such a warrant to do more than remove the occupiers of the property (which may include any third parties present, i.e. not just the tenant or mortgagor party to the proceedings). A possession warrant may be combined with a warrant of execution allowing seizure of goods in order to recover any arrears or costs due under the order (CCR O.26 r.17(3)). This also applies in the High Court (RSC O.45 r.3(4)), but the rule for the sheriff's officer is that in enforcing

[19] [1934] 1 KB 608.

a writ of possesion s/he should deliver vacant possession to the plaintiff. Thus, both persons and goods should be removed at the time of eviction (*Norwich Union Insurance Society* v. *Preston* [1975] 1 WLR 813). The general rules on duration of warrants and leave to issue applicable to execution apply to warrants/writs of possession (RSC O.46; CCR O.26 r. 17(6) and see 6.1.3.).

2.5.3 Warrants of arrest

Much of the law on the enforcement of arrest warrants is the same as that for distress, and the authorities are interchangeable. Thus an arrest warrant issued in a civil matter, such as under a judgment summons, cannot be levied on a Sunday (*Lyford* v. *Tyrrel* [1792] 1 Anst 85) and an outer door may not be forced in order to enter to execute it (*Kerbey* v. *Denby* [1836] 2 Gale 31).

There is however an exception where the bailiff enforcing is a warrant of committal for contempt of court by arrest. In such cases the officer may, after notice, break open the outer door of the house of the party to be arrested (*Brigg's Case* 1 Roll Rep 336; *Burdett* v. *Abbot* [1811] 14 East 1; *Harvey* v. *Harvey* [1884] 26 Ch D 644). It also appears that such process may be enforced on a Sunday – see Chitty J in *Harvey* v. *Harvey* at 651, referring to a case in *Willes* Reports on p. 459.

PART TWO – PRE-LEVY TACTICS

Chapter Three

PREVENTING SEIZURE

This chapter examines the strategies open to the client to avoid or prevent a levy by the bailiff actually taking place. Enforcement may have been threatened, a warrant may even have been issued, but it will be assumed in most cases that the bailiff will not have made great progress with the levy itself.

3.1 Staying enforcement of warrants

It may be possible to persuade a creditor to voluntarily withdraw a warrant, but this will normally only be in a situation where terms of payment have been agreed. Only in three situations is it possible to apply to court to have a warrant stayed by order.

3.1.1 High Court

The High Court has been most profoundly effected by the changes introduced by the new Civil Procedure Rules. Previously the typical practice was for judgment to be entered for full payment of the full sum forthwith. Instalments were *only* possible if the defendant applied for a stay of execution.

With effect from April 26, 1999, High Court procedure is brought into line with that in the county court. When admitting the claim on form N9A the debtor is invited to provide financial details and to request time to pay by instalments, which are likely to become the norm, determined usually by court staff (if not accepted by the claimant) for sums up to £50,000, and by judges in other cases (CPR Part 14). On default execution may issue and a stay would then be necessary.

If judgment is entered in default, or perhaps on summary judgment (under CPR Parts 12 and 24 respectively), it is more likely to be on terms of payment in full forthwith. If payment is not made, execution may again issue and stay will be required.

Application can be made at any time after the judgment is entered, which will normally be after the sheriff has visited the premises and levied (O.47 r.1). Application may be made even though the debtor neither acknowledged service of the writ of summons nor stated in the response that a stay of execution would be sought.

In the first and third cases the application must be made by application on N244 under CPR Part 23 stating the grounds of the application and supported by an affidavit substantiating those grounds and disclosing details of the debtor's income, expenditure, assets and liabilities where inability to pay is the reason for seeking the stay (O.47 r.1(3)). Even though such an affidavit is not formally required to support a request made at the time that judgment is entered, it may be advisable to have one prepared in advance as a precaution, and the court may well require it – especially if consideration of the request is adjourned to a later date. The application and affidavit must be served on the judgment creditor at least four days before the date set for the hearing of the application. It is obviously also important to notify the sheriff of the request and it can be possible to arrange extra time to make the application by speaking to the sheriff's officer.

The Court can stay execution if it is satisfied that the conditions set out in O.47 r.1 are met and either there are "*special circumstances which render it inexpedient to enforce the judgment or order*" or "*the applicant is unable from any cause to pay money*". The court may well require the defendant to attend to be examined on the evidence given in the affidavit and to produce supporting documentation such as details of current bills, salary and debts. The Court has broad discretion to stay the execution either absolutely or for such period and subject to such conditions as it thinks fit. All these considerations must however be conducted in light of the fact that the plaintiff should only be deprived of an immediate opportunity to enforce the judgment if there is good reason (*Winchester Cigarette Machinery Ltd* v. *Payne (No. 2)* [1993] *The Times*, December 15). Stays may be granted for limited periods on money judgments (*General Mutual Life Assurance Society* v. *Feltwell Fen 2nd District Drainage Board* [1945] KB 394).

Orders staying execution that the court may make include the following:

- a stay on terms of payment, whether by instalments or by a lump sum or sums;
- an indefinite stay with liberty to apply or for a set period with a review at the end thereof;
- a stay subject to a moratorium for a set period; or,
- a stay subject to a charging order (if the debtor consents).

Readers should also note that under O.45 r.11 the Court has a general power to stay execution of a judgment or order, and to give other relief, on the ground of matters that have arisen since the date of judgment being entered. This may be done on whatever terms the Court thinks just. It has been held in *London Permanent Building Society* v. *De Baer* [1969] 1 Ch 321 that the effect of this provision is to enable the Court to consider matters which would have prevented the original order being made, or would have led to a stay if they had already occurred at the date of the order. The predecessor of O.45 r.11 (O.42 r.27) spoke of "facts which have arisen too late to be pleaded" – which makes clear the real intention of this rule. Application should again be made by summons and affidavit.

Execution may also be stayed where a judgment is being appealed. This by application under O.59 r.13 and special circumstances will have to be shown to persuade the Court of the need to deprive plaintiffs of their rights. These may include the possibility of enforcement ruining or precipitating the bankruptcy of the defendant (*Linotype-Hell Finance Ltd* v. *Baker* [1993] 1 WLR 321), the likelihood that if the debt or damages were to be paid to the plaintiff, they would not be recoverable if the appeal were successful (*The Annot Lyle* [1886] 11 P 114) and situations (*Polini* v. *Gray* [1879] 12 Ch D 438) where refusing a stay would render the appeal nugatory. Such stays may be on terms such as a requirement that the plaintiff be paid without undue delay if the appeal fails or that the appellant's assets are preserved in the meantime, other than for satisfying essential liabilities.

3.1.2 County court execution

Under s.88 CCA the county court has a general power to stay any execution issued in proceedings, whether for the whole sum due or an instalment thereon, where the paying party is unable for any reason to satisfy the order. This stay may be on such terms and for such periods as the court thinks fit, and may be renewed periodically until the cause of the inability to pay has ceased.

In respect of execution warrants, the power to suspend the warrant is exercised under O.25 r.8 CCR. The debtor applies on prescribed form N245, providing details of his/her income, expenditure and other liabilities, both those subject to court orders and those which as yet are not, and making an offer of payment. This form is copied to the judgment creditor, who is given fourteen days in which to object to the application. If no objection is received the court office will suspend the warrant on the terms proposed. If the judgment creditor objects to the payment terms offered on the N245, a court officer will determine the rate of payment and suspend the warrant accordingly. Either party may challenge such a decision within fourteen days by application for "reconsideration" on N244. The matter will be transferred to the court local to the debtor if necessary and will be heard before the district judge, who may confirm, set aside or vary the order as he thinks fit.

Where the judgment creditor's objection is to suspension of the warrant as such, rather than to terms of payment, a hearing will be arranged before district judge, with at least two days' notice being given to each party. Under O.25 r.8(10) where the district judge suspends a warrant the debtor may at the same time be ordered to pay the costs of the warrant and any fees or expenses incurred before its suspension, and sale of sufficient of the goods may be ordered to cover such fees, expenses and costs. Probably because most warrants are suspended very soon after issue without any hearing taking place, other than the fee being added onto the judgment debt – which is automatic upon issue of the warrant – the author has never encountered such orders being made to recover costs.

If any of the terms of the suspension are not complied with, the judgment creditor may apply for the warrant to be reissued. This actually rarely seems to happen, and generally once a warrant is suspended, one may regard it as effectively set aside or cancelled.

The court also has powers under s.71(2) CCA to suspend or stay any judgment or order where the person cannot pay the whole sum or any instalment. This can be done for such time and on such terms as the court thinks fit, and can be renewed periodically. This provision is slightly broader in its application than s.88 and O.25 and can be of particular help where the defendant cannot pay at all. This is because of the way that the court's guidance to its staff on processing N245 applications is written. The instructions from Court Service are that an application making an offer of no payment must be treated as no offer at all, and cannot be considered. Instead whatever terms are requested by the judgment creditor should form the order. An application under s.71(2), being an application on notice to district judge on N244, will not be treated in the same way and will not encounter the same administrative problem.

As in the High Court, execution may be stayed on application where a judgment is being appealed either to Circuit Judge (O.37 r.8) or to the Court of Appeal (s.77).

Commentary

Problems are sometimes experienced in making application on N245 where the bailiff has yet to either visit or enter the debtor's property. Some courts will refuse to accept the form until the bailiff has had an opportunity to enter the premises and conduct a levy (see Counter levies at 8.4.7). The justification given for this is that unless the bailiff has thus secured the judgment creditor's position, if the debtor defaults on the terms of the suspension, it may be more difficult for the bailiff to enforce the re-issued warrant. There is no statutory justification for this kind of approach and Lord Chancellor's Department has given clear guidance to courts that N245 applications must not be refused, regardless of when in proceedings they are submitted (see *Court Business*, December 1993, item B2673). Despite this statement, refusals still do occur. If such problems are encountered and the warrant is subsequently executed, the court still has jurisdiction to suspend on the basis that the application may be regarded as having been made at the time that the defendant tried to submit it to court – see *Islington Borough Council* v. *Harridge* [1993] *The Times,* June 30, 7 CL 191, in which an application to stop an eviction was refused on the basis that there was no judge in the court available to hear it when the tenant's solicitor attended. If practitioners encounter this problem from either the bailiffs or counter staff at the court, the first stage is obviously a complaint within the court and then within Court Service. A threat of judicial review of the Chief Clerk's refusal may also be effective. Comparison may be made with stays of execution in the High Court, which may be sought both on receipt of the writ and on pronouncement of judgment, as well as after seizure. This indicates that there is no necessity for there to be an actual levy before the county court has the power to suspend. The court is suspending a warrant, executed or not, rather than a levy.

3.1.3 Magistrates' court distraint

A magistrates' court may, if it thinks it "expedient", postpone the issue of a warrant until such time and on such conditions as it thinks just (s.77(1) MCA). Applications for postponement may be made as often as necessary (*Re: Wilson* [1985] AC 750). This means that, at the hearing at which the decision is taken to issue a warrant to bailiffs, the court can further delay the enforcement provided certain terms – usually for instalment payment – are met.

There is however no specific power to suspend warrants *after* they have been issued, unlike in the civil courts. However magistrates' courts do have discretionary powers to grant "stays of execution" in very exceptional cases. Victorian authorities indicate that these exist. For example it has been held that the court may suspend, on terms, the enforcement of "a sum of money claimed to be due and recoverable on complaint to a Court of Summary Jurisdiction" (*R.* v. *Paget* [1881] 8 QBD 151); whilst more recent cases have confirmed the power to grant a stay (*Re S (an infant)* [1958] 1 All ER 783 and *B(BPM)* v. *B(MM)* [1969] 2 WLR 862).

However, these cases also show that magistrates have only a discretionary power, not a duty, to grant a stay and that this power is only likely to be exercised where there are exceptional circumstances. This may be, for example, where an appeal is pending or where the welfare of a minor might be effected (*Smith* v. *Smith* [1971] 115 Sol Jo 444). Equally it has been held that an appeal against a maintenance order is not grounds to stay its enforcement (*Kendall* v. *Wilkinson* [1855] 24 LJMC 89) and that once the court has confirmed liability, it cannot suspend a warrant (*Barons* v. *Luscombe* [1835] 3 Ad & El 589). Most recently a Divisional Court decision on this has been reported – *Crossland* v. *Crossland* [1993] 1 FLR 175. In this matrimonial case a distraint warrant was issued to collect unpaid arrears of maintenance and a levy occurred. The husband applied by complaint for the magistrates to suspend the warrant and, on their refusal, appealed by way of case stated. Sir Stephen Brown, P held that there was no inherent jurisdiction to suspend and "*that once having issued (the warrant) . . . the matter was out of the court's hands*" and the justices were *functus officio* – they had discharged their duty. This position was re-emphasised in *R.* v. *Hereford Magistrates' Court, ex parte MacRae* (1998) *The Times,* December 31 in which the court noted that the legislation was conspicuous by its silence as to any power to suspend or revoke a warrant. There are good reasons for this: as costs would be named by the bailiff when the warrant was issued to them.

Thus, although some courts will allow defendants to apply to vary the terms of payment of an order under s.75(2) MCA and at the same time suspend a warrant, many more will refuse to entertain any application whilst the warrant is in the bailiff's hands. There is no way round such a problem and the client's only option then will be to deal with and perhaps try to negotiate with the bailiff, for which see later.

3.1.4 Other cases

In all other forms of distress the decision to issue the warrant lies solely with the creditor, so any stay on enforcement will be solely a matter of negotiation with that creditor. As in the courts, the agreeing of terms of payment will be essential to any concession given to the debtor.

3.2 Liability for the sums claimed

This section will examine the nature of the liabilities for which distress may be levied, and the various means available to dispute a claim. In many cases these arguments will be commenced after the distress has been taken, and it will be necessary to try to agree a stay of enforcement as described at 3.1 in order to allow negotiations to take place.

3.2.1 Distress damage feasant

Although distress damage feasant is a remedy for trespass to property, it is not invalid because there has been no actual damage, provided that the distrainor could have sued for nominal damages. Professor Glanville Williams (1939) "Liability for Animals" – suggests that "it would be the better policy to provide proof of actual damage", but it is not possible to say with certainty whether one can distrain for mere encumbering of property as opposed to physical injury: some authorities indicate that this may be possible (see for example *Bromhall* v. *Norton* (1690) 2 Jo 193; *Williams* v. *Ladner* [1798] 8 TR 72; *Baker* v. *Leathes* [1810] Wight 113).

Distress may be levied by the owner of the property or others with an interest in it that may be damaged by the trespass. The damages claimable include damage to land, to chattels thereon, and possibly to the owner or family or employees (*Boden* v. *Roscoe* [1894] 1 QB 608). Distress may be levied even if the value of the chattel taken is disproportionate to the damage done (i.e. there is no concept of "excessive distress" – for which see 10.8.3 later). However distress damage feasant cannot be levied on chattels that have left the property (*Vasper* v. *Eddows* [1702] Holt KB 256) or on chattels that remain but are doing no damage (*Wormer* v. *Biggs* [1845] 2 Car & Kir 31). Distress cannot be taken for past damage, only for damage by chattels still on the land and doing damage (*Buist* v. *McCombe* [1883] 8 AR 598 or *Graham* v. *Spettigue* [1885] 12 AR 261). The latter case also shows that only the trespassing chattel can be seized, not another in its name. Distress cannot be levied for damage anticipated in the future (*Pfeiffer* v. *Sheldheim* [1921] 59 DLR 631), though the threat of imminent damage seems to be a permissible basis for a distress (*Sorrell* v. *Paget* [1949] 2 All ER 609). Distress cannot be levied if the owner has contributed to or permitted the trespass, for instance by failing to properly secure their premises.

A claim can be made for losses incurred whilst taking chattels to the pound or whilst in a pound. Charges cannot be made for the use of the pound, as impounding is mandatory if the remedy is employed.

Use of the remedy bars a later action for trespass. If a dispute as to liability arises, the best course of action is probably either to replevy the goods or to pay the compensation claimed and then sue to recover it (see chapter 10). If the dispute is as to the damages claimed, the debtor may sue (see chapter 10).

3.2.2 Distress for rent

When may the landlord distrain? The right of a landlord to distrain exists automatically when land or premises are let (*Manchester Brewery* v. *Coombs* [1901] 2 Ch 608). It need not be expressly reserved and there is no need for a written tenancy agreement (*Walsh* v. *Lonsdale* [1882] 21 Ch D 9) although it may be excluded by the terms of the tenancy agreement or lease. The following specific conditions must also be satisfied:

- the rent payable must relate to occupation of land upon which distress may be levied and formerly only applied to "rent service" payable as an incident of tenure for possession of premises. Rent cannot be levied in respect of rent for incorporeal hereditaments (*Talentine* v. *Denton* (1605) *Cro Jac* 111; *Capel* v. *Buszard* [1829] 6 Bing 150), but by statute it may be levied for a rent charge (s.121(2) Law of Property Act 1925) and for a "rent seck" (s.5 Landlord and Tenant Act 1730).

- the rent must be in arrears on a current tenancy *and* must be certain (*Regnart* v. *Porter* [1831] 7 Bing 451; and see 6.4.1). There are no "arrears" for which distress can be levied until the day after payment falls due (*Dibble* v. *Bowater* (1853) 2 E&B 564), the tenant being able to pay the rent at any time during the day on which it falls due (*Duppa* v. *Mayo* (1669) 1 Saund 287). If the rent is due on the last day of the term of tenancy, and is not paid, distress will *not* be possible the next day as the term will be over (Co Litt 47 and see later). Longer may have to be allowed if time to pay is given by the landlord (*Clun's Case* (1613) 10 Co Rep 127a). It does not alter this situation that the rent is payable in advance, if it is not paid on the day it is due (*Lee* v. *Smith* [1854] 9 Exch 662). Payment of course terminates the right to distrain, though it has been held that giving a cheque in payment does not suspend the landlord's remedy until it is cashed (see *Harris* v. *Shipway* (1744) Bull NP 182a and 10.3 later). The rent due must be certain (see 6.4.1 later) – even if the rent varies if it can be calculated or a minimum figure is set, distress may be levied.

- the distrainor must hold the reversion no matter how short, even if s/he is a tenant who has sublet for their term less just one day (*Wade* v. *Marsh* (1625) Lat 211). The reversion must be vested in the landlord at the time the rent fell due, even though it is not necessary to hold the reversion for the whole period over which it accrued (*Thompson* v. *Shaw* (1836) 5 LJCP 234). A joint landlord may distrain for the full sum due, with or without the consent of the other joint landlords (*Pullen* v. *Palmer* (1696) 3 Salk 207; *Robinson* v. *Hoffman* (1828) 4 Bing 562).
- though distress cannot be used after the end of a tenancy (see below), if any tenant gives notice to quit and then does not leave, under DRA 1737, s.18 the landlord can levy (or sue) for double the former rent for the period during which the former tenant remains (*Timmins* v. *Rawlinson* (1764) 1 W.Bl Rep 533; *Johnstone* v. *Hudlestone* (1825) B&C 922). The landlord thus can levy for mesne profits which otherwise would not be the subject of distress. This right ceases as soon as the tenant leaves (*Booth* v. *Macfarlane* (1831) 1 B & Ad 904). The notice received from the tenant must be valid, in the sense that it complies with the common law requirements as to period and expiry date (*Farrance* v. *Elkington* (1811) 2 Camp 591).
- rent must be lawfully due. This is to be determined by the true construction of the agreement (*C H Bailey* v. *Memorial Enterprises* [1974] 1 All ER 1003) and it may be that the sum due can only be ascertained after the due date for payment. Thus where the rent may be subject to a review clause, any higher sum ascertained by this procedure will become payable retrospectively once it has been determined (*United Scientific* v. *Burnley Council* [1978] AC 904). In this connection it is worth noting that a distinction is sometimes made between the "distrainable rent" (the certain sum due) and other amounts that may be due under the lease (e.g. extra sums due on review) – see for example *ex parte Voisey* [1882] 21 Ch D 442. The Court in *United Scientific* questioned whether this distinction was any longer applicable, but did not rule upon it in order to reach their decision. Reference was made to Foa's "General Law of Landlord and Tenant" which suggests that the common law right to distrain only applies to rent in the strict mediaeval sense and not to other contractual sums due under the agreement. *NB*, if separate agreements exist between landlord and tenant, related to but distinct from the letting of the land, these may not be the subject of distress. See *Pulbrook* v. *Ashby* (1887) 56 LJQB 376 or *Stevens* v. *Marston* (1890) 60 LJQB 192 in which brewers who were landlords of pub premises sought to distrain in respect of sums due under agreements to supply drink to the licensed premises. Such agreements should be registered as bills of sale and as they were not, the levies were illegal.

If rent has been tendered, albeit late, then unless time was made of the essence in the lease, it is no longer unpaid and is not lawfully due (*Bird* v. *Hildage* [1948]

1 KB 91). In this case the tendered rent was refused and was paid into court. The landlord was held liable for the costs of the proceedings. *Bird* v. *Hildage* also held that permitting unpunctual payment of the rent in the past without protest does not justify the tenant assuming it will be permitted in the future, nor waive a right to levy for arrears. Even if the landlord has accepted a reduced sum of rent for a period, on default the whole sum may be levied (*Re: Smith & Hartogs* [1895] 73 LT 221). If the rent is due, the landlord may then distrain on the day immediately after the rent has fallen due for all or part of the arrears. If the rent is due on a Sunday, the landlord can distrain on a Monday (*Child* v. *Edwards* [1909] 2 KB 753).

- the nature of the tenancy is immaterial. It may agreed orally or in writing; it may be a tenancy at will (*Morton* v. *Woods* [1869] 4 QB 293) or a normal weekly tenancy (*Yeoman* v. *Ellison* (1867) 2 CP 681). Clauses in the tenancy extending the right to distrain do not destroy the common law entitlement to the remedy (*In Re: The River Swale Brick & Tile Works Ltd* (1883) LJ Ch 638). Thus clauses permitting distress on privileged goods are legal (*Re: River Swale*), as are clauses permitting distress for sums that are not rent (*Doe d Elney* v. *Benham* [1845] 7 QB 976) or permitting distress off the rented premises – provided that those premises are associated with the demised property (*Daniel* v. *Stepney* [1874] 9 Exch 185). If several tenants occupy the land subject to one rent, the landlord can levy distress on any one for the rent due from all (*Woodcock* v. *Titterton* (1864) 12 WR 865).

- if the tenant is allowed to hold over at the end of the term, the landlord can distrain (*Beavan* v. *Delahey* [1788] 1 Hy Bl 5). Under ss.6, 7 Landlord and Tenant Act 1709 distress can be used within six months of the end of the lease or tenancy provided that the landlord does not change and that the tenant personally remains in occupation. If the tenant remains in occupation at the end of the term of a tenancy in such a manner as to indicate that the tenancy has been renewed, distress may be levied in the normal manner, and the Act will not apply (*Dougal* v. *McCarthy* [1893] 1 QB 736). The Act also does not apply if the tenant remains in occupation of only part of the premises under a new tenancy agreement (*Wilkinson* v. *Peel* [1895] 1 QB 963). Indeed, if a new tenancy is granted, any arrears under the old tenancy cannot be the subject of distress (*Stanfill* v. *Hickes* (1697) 1 Ld Raym 280). The Acts do not apply where the tenancy has been terminated by forfeiture (*Kirkland* v. *Briancourt* (1890) 6 TLR 441) but do seem to apply where the tenant remains under a notice to quit (*Williams* v. *Stiven* [1846] 9 QB 14) or as a statutory tenant. Note that in levies under these provisions the tenant loses the protection of basic household goods and tools granted by statute (see 9.22.2).

- the landlord need not demand the rent or give notice before distraining unless this is stipulated for in the tenancy agreement (*Cranley* v. *Kingswell* (1617) Hob 207). The distress itself is a demand and the common law rules on demanding rent need not be complied with (that is, a demand made on the premises for the sum due on the day it falls due – *Thorp* v. *Hurt* (1886) WN 96). Thus if the lease allows the rent to be demanded in advance at any time during a rental period, this may be done and distress may be levied immediately without the need for "reasonable notice" to the tenant (*London & Westminster Loan & Discount Co* v. *London & North Western Railway Co* [1893] 2 QB 49).

When may the landlord not distrain? Distress cannot be employed if any of the following conditions apply:

- if the tenancy has expired; if a tenancy has been terminated by forfeiture (*Grimwood* v. *Moss* (1872) 7 CP 360; *Serjeant* v. *Nash Field & Co* (1903) 2 KB 304); or by a notice to quit (*Murgatroyd* v. *Dodworth & Silkstone Coal & Iron Co*.[1895] 65 LJ Ch 111). Acceptance of rent, or levying distress, after the issue of a notice to quit does not act as a waiver of any breach of the tenancy unless the clear intention is to create a new tenancy (*Clarke* v. *Grant* [1950] 1 KB 104 but see *Zouch* v. *Willingdale* (1790) 1 H Bl 311). If the old tenancy has ended, and a new tenant has entered the premises, distress may not be levied even though a few goods of the old tenant may remain behind (*Taylerson* v. *Peters* (1837) 7 A&E 110).

- if there is no demise. A contract for a lease is not sufficient to entitle a person to levy distress (*Dunk* v. *Hunter* (1822) 5 B & Ald 322), nor is entry by a tenant in anticipation of a grant of a lease or an agreement for a lease, unless the conditions for a tenancy at a fixed rent can be implied (*Pinero* v. *Judson* (1829) 6 Bing 206) or unless there is subsequent execution of the lease or a clause in an agreement permitting distress (*Carrington* v. *Saldin* (1925) 133 LT 432; *Manchester Brewery* v. *Coombs* [1901] 2 Ch 608). A landlord also cannot distrain if conditions precedent to a tenancy remain to be satisfied – for example if a house is to be furnished by the landlord prior to the letting, he may not distrain until this is done (*Mechelen* v. *Wallace* (1836) 7 Ad & El 54n).

- if new premises are involved; if a new lease has been granted or if an action has been commenced against the ex-tenant as a trespasser (*Bridges* v. *Smyth* (1829) 5 Bing 410).

- if the tenant has been led to believe that the remedy will not be used by the landlord (*Miles* v. *Furber* [1873] 8 QB 77) or if agreement is made to postpone distress (*Giles* v. *Spencer* (1857) 3 CBNS 244; *Oxenham* v. *Collins* (1860) 2 F&F 172).

- if the tenancy has been terminated by death: in *Scobie* v. *Collins* [1895] 1 QB 375 a tenancy at will ceased on the death of the tenant therefore a distress was trespass. However if a tenant dies and their personal representative enters and holds over, distress may be levied. This cannot be done if the spouse alone remains in occupation (*Turner* v. *Barnes* (1862) 2 B&S 435).

- where the distrainor does not hold the reversion. If there has been an assignment of the lease, the distrainor must have reserved the express power to distrain if assigning his/her whole interest (*Preece* v. *Corrie* (1828) 5 Bing 24). A demise of the whole term or longer equals an assignment (see s.5 L&TA 1730 and *Langford* v. *Selmes* (1857) 3 K&J 220). Thus in *Lewis* v. *Baker* [1905] 1 Ch 46, the defendant sublet the property for a term exceeding the original lease. When he levied distress for the rent, the court held it to be illegal. See too *Tadman* v. *Henman*

[1893] 2 QB 168 in which a reversion by estoppel was held to justify distress, but not against third party goods.

- against the assignee of a lease if the landlord consented to the assignment, knowing the assignor owed rent (*Pape* v. *Westacott* [1894] 1 QB 272; *Wharfland* v. *South London Co-operative Building Co* [1995] *The Times,* April 25). However the assignee is bound by the power of distress in the pre-existing lease and cannot object to its use against them (*Daniel* v. *Stepney* [1874] 9 Exch 185).
- if court action has been commenced (*Chancellor* v. *Webster* [1893] TLR 568; *Potter* v. *Bradley & Co* [1894] 10 TLR 445). Conversely the landlord cannot sue so long as distress is held even if it is insufficient because as long as the distress is held in the manner of a pledge, the debt is suspended (*Edwards* v. *Kelly* (1817) 6 M&S 204; *Lehain* v. *Philpott* (1876) 35 LT 855).
- if a person with a licence to occupy is involved (*Rendell* v. *Roman* [1893] 9 TLR 192; *Provincial Bill Posting Co* v. *Low Moor Iron Co* [1909] 2 KB 344; *Interoven Stoves Co Ltd* v. *F W Hubbard* [1936] 1 All ER 263).

If a tenant wishes to dispute the right of the landlord to levy distress, for any of the reasons outlined, this may be done by an action for illegal distress or by replevin. See respectively chapters 7 and 9. The entire development of the remedy of replevin was driven by the need to define the limits and nature of the landlord and tenant relationship, and almost all the early year book reports dealing with replevies of illegal distresses are concerned not with the manner of the distress itself but the exact terms of the lease upon which it was based.

For what may the landlord distrain? The landlord may distrain for the full sum due, or only a portion, and may include with that all sums treated as rent in the reddendum (see 6.4.1 later). It used to be held that there is no right of set off even for repairs (*Absolon* v. *Knight & Barker* (1743) 94 ER 998). However the Court of Appeal in *Eller* v. *Grovecrest Investments Ltd* [1995] 2 WLR 278 held that there was no difference between a claim for rent arrears by court action and a claim by distress. In both the respective rights of landlord and tenant should be considered. A cross claim for damages by the tenant could be used by way of set off as a defence against a claim for rent by distress. An injunction was granted in the *Eller* case to restrain a levy where the damages claim exceeded the rent due. Set off can be excluded by the agreement, but it will have to be an explicit term and a covenant to pay "without deductions" is not sufficient (*Electricity Supply Nominees* v. *IAF Group* (1993) 2 EGLR 95).

3.2.3 High Court and county court judgments

If a claim is disputed the action will *have* to be contested. This will involve the filing of a defence and/or a counter claim. The problem for the judgment debtor faced with execution is that judgment will already have been entered against them. This may be for one of two reasons:

- they have already disputed the claim and lost, either at arbitration or trial. If this is the case challenging the judgment may be difficult unless there is scope for an appeal (and they are not out of time) or they can seek to have the judgment set aside because they failed to attend the hearing; or,

- alternatively the judgment may have been entered in default of a defence. In this case application may again be made to set the judgment aside. It will be necessary to show convincing reasons why the person did not respond the first time around – for instance, the originating process went astray and they were not previously aware of the action; and secondly that they have arguable defence with some prospect of success.

In the High Court application to set aside is on summons and affidavit, in the county court on notice on application form N244.

3.2.4 Income tax

By the time enforcement proceedings for tax are commenced, whether by distress or by court action, the time for challenging liability has, in theory at least, been lost (*Rutherford* v. *Lord Advocate* (1931) 16 Tax Cases 145).

Under the old system of assessment prior to 1994, if no tax return was made by the client liability was estimated by the Inspector. Nonetheless it is normally possible for the taxpayer to persuade the collector to stay tax enforcement whilst an application to submit a late appeal is made to the Commissioners. Issues as to the merits of an assessment cannot be raised during recovery proceedings and tax is properly recoverable where the right of appeal has been lost or not taken up (*IRC* v. *Pearlberg* [1953] 1 All ER 388). If the tax is improperly assessed the taxpayer cannot replevy after distraint (*Allen* v. *Sharp* (1848) 2 Exch 352). If however there has been no valid assessment on the debtor, the distraint may be unlawful (*Berry* v. *Farrow* [1914] 1 KB 632).

For businesses beginning after April 6, 1994, from the tax year 1994-1995, and in all other cases from 1996-1997, self assessment applies (s.60 ICTA 1988). Tax returns should be made with self assessments included (unless made before September 30th each year, in which case the Revenue will do the calculations). In the absence of a return a "determination" is made by the Inspector (s.28C(1A)). This is treated as a self assessment until superseded by one (s.28C(3)). A determination must be made within five years of the filing date (s.28C(5)) and this can be amended by filing a self assessment within twelve months. There is no right of appeal on these matters. If the self assessment displacing a determination does not include a tax calculation, enforcement will continue until the Inspector has done the computation. Again the Collector should be asked to wait whilst the new liability is calculated.

3.2.5 VAT

As with income tax, if no quarterly return is made VAT liability is assessed under s.73 VATA. By the time enforcement has begun, the right of appeal to the VAT Tribunal is formally passed (s.83/4). That said, if the trader can supply evidence that the assessed sum is excessive it would be unusual for distress not to be stayed to allow a late appeal to be filed. The Customs and Excise normally accept these, however "frail the excuse" to quote "Croners". Bailiffs may also be ordered to abandon the levy if the firm deregisters for VAT during the levy process, which should be borne in mind as a tactic. Deregistration is possible if the trader can satisfy Customs and Excise that turnover has fallen below, and will remain below, £48,000 for the following year.

3.2.6 Road traffic penalties

If an individual has contravened parking regulations a parking attendant may impose a penalty charge by either fixing notice of this on the car or giving it to the driver. If the owner does not pay in 28 days notice is served on them by the local authority under s.66 RTA stating that there are a further 28 days in which to pay and that the charge will increase thereafter. If the person does not pay then a "charge certificate" is issued and the penalty is increased by 50% (para. 6, sch. 6 RTA). After a further fourteen days the local authority may apply to Northampton county court for an order that it may recover the penalty as if it were payable under a county court judgment (para. 7 sch. 6). The court's procedure is laid down by O.48B CCR.

The debtor has two opportunities to challenge the penalty. Under para. 4 sch. 6 RTA s/he may challenge the notice to owner by making representations to the local authority, on the ground that:

- s/he did not own the vehicle at the time of the offence;
- the vehicle was parked without the owner's consent, e.g. after being stolen;
- the owner is a hire firm and the vehicle was on hire at the time of the offence; or,
- the parking offence did not occur.

Representations should be made within 28 days of service of the notice to owner and local authorities may (and do) disregard later submissions. The local authority must consider and respond to any valid representations and may cancel the notice to owner or reject the representations. If the owner's representations are rejected, he may appeal to the parking adjudicator within 28 days, or pay the penalty (paras. 4 & 5, Sch. 6). If an appeal to the adjudicator is unsuccessful, the owner has 28 days in which to pay, otherwise the local authority may issue a charge certificate.

If the penalty is subject to a court order and is at the stage of distress, the owner may still challenge liability by means of a statutory declaration to Northampton county court parking enforcement centre, on forms obtainable from the court. This declaration should be made within 21 days of service of the order on the grounds that:

- s/he did not receive the notice to owner;
- representations against it were ignored, or
- there has been no response to an appeal to the parking adjudicator (para. 8(1) sch. 6).

Late appeals can be accepted (para. 8). If the county court accepts it, the effect of the declaration is to revoke the court order and cancel any charge certificate. The matter is then passed back to the council who may issue a new notice to owner or refer it to the adjudicator (para. 8(7) sch. 6). If the adjudicator accepts the representations, the original notice to owner is cancelled. If the penalty is upheld the owner has another opportunity to pay – presumably a further 28 days.

One issue that is unclear is the status of any charges that the bailiffs have incurred in levying the warrant. The court rules state that "any execution issued on the [cancelled] warrant shall cease to have effect". It is unclear if this is intended to have retrospective effect, so that monies paid to the bailiffs by the owner should be refunded. One presumes that this should happen, and one may note that in execution the sheriff cannot proceed to recover any fees after execution is withdrawn, stayed or otherwise cancelled (see chapter 11).

3.2.7 Child support maintenance

As with local taxes, considered below, the first problem with challenges to liability is that the distress warrant rests upon a liability order made by the magistrates' court. The scope for opposing liability orders is even more restricted in respect of the CSA than it is in respect of local taxes.

The first stage in the enforcement process is the issue of an arrears notice, about eight days after a payment has been missed. It states the sum due plus any interest that is recoverable. Interest is not chargeable on any arrears due since April 17, 1995 and could not be collected on certain debts – such as those due to CSA error or which were paid within 28 days of being demanded. Arrears due before April 17, 1995 continue to attract interest at one per cent over base rate. The figures should always be checked. It is still possible at this stage to negotiate a payment arrangement. Cases are passed to litigation where arrears exceed £25, an agreement for the payment of arrears has been broken or not reached and a deduction from earnings order cannot be implemented or is ineffective (s.33 CSA). Arrears will not be enforced where the absent parent is under 18 years' old or where the debt is more than six years' old (reg. 28(3) CS(C&E) Regulations).

The absent parent must be given seven days' notice of the application for the liability order (reg. 27(1)). The notice must state the arrears due plus interest (reg. 27(2)). If part payment is made the application can proceed for the balance without needing a new notice to be served (reg. 27(3)). Application must be to the court with jurisdiction for the place where the absent parent lives. The magistrates' court must make a liability order if satisfied that payments are due but unpaid. The court cannot question the maintenance assessment itself (s.33(4)) but some courts may adjourn the matter if a review or appeal are pending. There is no provision, in magistrates' court civil proceedings, for setting aside orders as in the civil courts.

It will therefore be necessary to approach the CSA to negotiate a stay on enforcement whilst the assessed sum is challenged. It is common knowledge that the formula for child support maintenance is complex and that there are frequent problems with its calculation by the CSA. The calculation of maintenance should always be checked – computer programs exist to do this. Absent parents facing distress will probably fall into three categories: the self employed; those on benefits other than Income Support and income based Job Seekers Allowance; and those whose income derives from capital. In none of these cases is the preferred means of enforcement, the deduction from earnings order, possible, thus the liability order and distress will be issued. The inherent complications of the CSA formula will be compounded in these cases – for example, by assessment of the income of a self employed person. Problems may arise where the period used for the assessment of income is unrepresentative of a client's average income: the CSA can be asked to consider recalculating on a different periods accounts. If the client has particularly high special expenses, such as travel to work costs or the costs of contact with the children, the CSA may be asked to consider a "departure" from their standard formula.

3.2.8 Local taxes

The major difficulty in preventing distraint for local taxes is that it follows a liability order. The case is conducted by the magistrates' court as a complaint: the case is made on the balance of probabilities.

Council tax At the hearing of a summons for an order for council tax the local authority will have to satisfy the justices that the bill has been properly demanded, is due and remains unpaid. The local authority must present evidence on the following:

- that the council tax has been fixed by resolution by the local authority;
- sums have been demanded in accordance with the regulations (that is, demand, reminder and final notices have been sent at the correct intervals);
- full payment of the amounts due has not been made by the due dates;
- reminders and final notices have been issued as required;
- the sum has not been paid within seven days of the reminder or final notice being issued and that the full amount has become payable;
- the summons was served for the full sum due at least seven days after the sum became payable; and,
- the full sum claimed has not been paid.

The council's evidence may be produced by certificate, such as a certified copy signed by the appropriate officer showing the council's resolution setting the charge and a certificate confirming that computer records have been properly compiled. The taxpayer may defend on the following grounds at the magistrates' court:

- the amount has not been demanded in accordance with the regulations;
- the debt is statute barred (see reg. 34 CT (A&E) Regulations and 6.1.3);
- the amount has been paid; or,
- that s/he is not the person named on the summons.

Even if sums have been incorrectly billed in the past, if the authority's error is realised and any balance due is then pursued, this is lawful even if it is several years later (*R.* v. *Blenkinsop* [1892] 1 QB 43). It appears that, where the full sum has been correctly demanded, default on any later agreement to allow payment by instalments will not necessitate a further demand (*Overseers of Walton on the Hill* v. *Jones* [1893] 2 QB 175).

If satisfied that a case has been made by the billing authority, the justices must make a liability order. This will identify the sum recoverable. If the sum claimed has been reduced, e.g. by benefit, the order will be a sum greater than that due. It remains valid but the excess amount is treated as being paid. If the debtor owes more than is on the order, the local authority may enforce up to the sum due on the order, but will need a new order for the balance. A liability order cannot be refused because a benefit claim is pending (*R.* v. *Bristol City Magistrates Court ex parte Willsman* (1991) 156 JP 409). It appears that the court may refuse a liability order for the full amount if the debtor has tendered part payment which has been refused, so as to avoid incurring excessive costs and fees for the debtor (*R.* v. *Gillespie* [1904] 1 KB 174). If only the court costs are unpaid there is discretion whether or not to allow enforcement (*R.* v. *Baker ex parte Guildford Overseers* [1909] 73 JP 166) but enforcement should probably *not* proceed (*Cotton* v. *Kaldwell* (1833) 2 Nev & M 391.

Liability cannot be challenged before the justices on the basis of any other matters. These are the subject of appeal to the Valuation Tribunal (see Council Tax (Alteration of Lists and Appeals) Regulations 1993) and include such issues as:

- whether the debtor is liable;
- whether the property is a chargeable dwelling;
- entitlement to a disability reduction;
- entitlement to a discount.

The court cannot refuse a liability order on such grounds (*Overseers of the Poor of Manchester* v. *Headlam* [1888] 21 QBD 96; *Dixon* v. *Blackpool and Fleetwood Tranroad Co* [1909] 1 KB 860). The fact that an appeal has been made to the Tribunal does not terminate liability for the sum due, which should still be paid. Some councils will suspend recovery action to allow an appeal to be heard. If an appeal succeeds, overpaid tax can be refunded or credited against future liabilities.

Appeals on valuation matters are to the Tribunal on a standard form that they can supply. If the ground for the appeal is liability, this is initially to the local authority (see s.16, LGFA 1992 and Valuation and Community Charge Tribunals (Amendments) Regulations 1993, regs. 35–37).

National non-domestic rates The procedure for the recovery of business rates (NNDR) is very similar to that described above for council tax. The court must be satisfied that the debt has been correctly demanded on successive notices in accordance with regs. 11(1) and 12(1) NNDR (C&E)(LL) Regulations and that it is still due and unpaid, in which case an order shall be made (reg. 12(4)). Even if payment is made between issue and hearing, an order could still be made for reasonable costs (reg. 12(7)). A liability order can deal with more than one person or more than one sum (reg. 13(1)). The defences available to the trader are that the debt is paid, that it has not been correctly demanded or that it is statute barred (reg. 12(3)). Liability may also be challenged on the basis of the valuation; entitlement to exemption under sch. 3 of the LGFA 1988 because of the nature of the property; discretionary relief under s.47, for instance because the liable body is a charity; non-occupation under s.45 or reduction or remission under s.49. All these issues must be dealt with outside the court.

3.2.9 Magistrates' court

If faced with distress for a criminal penalty the client will have two options – either to appeal the original decision to convict and fine, or to seek more time to pay the sum due. Appealing the conviction is a matter for criminal specialists. If time to pay is sought, application will have to be made to the court.

When a penalty is imposed, the court is required to assess the defendant's means and relate the fine to ability to pay. A date may be set by which, if any part of the fine remains unpaid, the defendant will have to appear for a further means enquiry. Magistrates rarely invite requests for extended time to pay. The rule is that enforcment of a penalty should begin immediately, so an immediate payment may be requested and a distress warrant may be issued straight away, but suspended on terms of payment. If the defendant then fails to pay within the allotted time, the court may issue a summons or warrant to bring them back for a further enquiry as to means.

3.3 Resisting distress

Whilst the debtor may be entitled to take certain steps to prevent the levy taking place, it is also possible for him/her to commit offences, either intentionally or not. The most likely offences to arise are interference with seized goods or violent resistance to a levy. In cases of alleged illegal resistance, it is up to the prosecution to show that all the elements of the offence have been committed (*R.* v. *Harron* [1903] 6 OLR 666).

3.3.1 Refusing entry

As will be fully described in chapter 7, entry cannot be made against the debtor's will. If this is ignored or if a forced entry is discovered it is permissible for the debtor to resist entry within limits[1]. However, ejecting a bailiff who has entered legally can lead to forced re-entry and to the commission of an offence. The courts have sanctioned the use of reasonable force by the debtor in three different contexts:

- *bailiff's status not disclosed*: In *Broughton* v. *Wilkerson* (1880) 44 JP 781 Broughton, a county court bailiff, attended at Wilkerson's house to levy. The defendant held the door open whilst they discussed the matter. An argument developed and when the bailiff forced entry, a fight ensued. The bailiff neither produced the warrant nor made his purpose clear. As the bailiff had no right to force entry he was not thereafter in execution of his duties. As a result there was not an assault on a court officer.
- *entry is forced:* wherever bailiffs exceeds their powers the debtor may resist. In *Rossiter* v. *Conway* (1894) 58 JP 350 the defendant bailiff was seeking to levy distress for rates. He took Mrs. Rossiter by surprise when she opened the door, jamming his arm in as she tried to close it. When Conway entered the house she punched him. Mrs Rossiter was charged with assault but it was held she had authority to admit or exclude any person from the house and was therefore entitled to resist a forced entry. Similarly in *Vaughan* v. *McKenzie* [1968] 1 All ER 1154 two county court bailiffs used force to enter. One was then struck on the head but it was ruled that an assault on a court officer had not occurred because of the prior illegal entry.
- *permission to enter refused or withdrawn:* In *Davis* v. *Lisle* [1936] 2 KB 434 two police officers entered premises to make enquiries relating to an offence. They had no permission and no warrant to enter. Davis told them to leave and then punched and abused PC Lisle. It was held that this was not assault upon an officer in the execution of his duty because, as soon as they were told to leave ("not without emphasis"), they had no right to remain and were trespassers. This case highlights

[1] *Green* v. *Goddard* (1704) 2 Salk 641 – "it is lawful to oppose by force" and see *Leward* v. *Basely* (1695) 1 Ld Raym 62.

an important point which will receive more consideration later, namely that the bailiff's right to enter appears to be, in some respects, a revocable licence (see 7.4)

The problem in these situations is determining the measure of reasonable force that may be employed by the debtor or occupier. The example of *Vaughan* above is not entirely helpful as there could well have been a criminal assault – the issue decided was that it was not an assault upon a court officer. It is probably safe to assume that something less than the amount of force used in that case will be reasonable and lawful, whether from the debtor or from others. In *Collins* v. *Renison* [1754] Say 138/96 ER 830 the defendant was found liable for trespass in upsetting a ladder upon which the plaintiff was standing. Even though this was done "gently . . . thereby doing as little damage as possible to the plaintiff" it was still thought that such a degree of force was not justified in the defence of land. More recently this area has been examined in *Revill* v. *Newberry* [1996] 2 WLR 239, which held that trespassers are still owed a duty of care. There should be a warning or alternative attempt to repel an intruder before any action likely to cause significant injury to the trespasser, if he is not posing a threat to the occupier or likely to do irreparable damage to the property. This elaborates on the existing authorities which held that force may be used to remove a peaceable trespasser *after* a request to leave has been ignored (*Hall* v. *Davis* (1825) 2 C&P 33), though if force is used to enter, no request to leave is necessary (*Weaver* v. *Bush* (1798) 8 TR 78) – this is also the case if force is employed after a peaceable entry (*Polkinhorne* v. *Wright* [1845] 8 QB 197 at 206). If the occupier meets with resistance, more force may be employed, the limits on this escalation being the value of the property concerned, the amount of harm threatened to it and the above mentioned duty of care.

We may also consider here the position of dogs on the premises. The law is that it is an offence to set on or urge a dog to attack, worry or put any person in fear and that the keeper will be liable for any damage or injury caused. Even if the dog is kept to guard a property, the owner may be liable if the animal prevents access by or injures innocent visitors on lawful business. The person may sue if their entry is under a legal right.

Offences by the debtor. The use of violence and threats of violence to eject a bailiff from premises which have been legally entered can lead to forced re-entry (see 7.4.4) and possibly prosecution for assault or an action for trespass to person brought by the trespassing bailiff (see *Gregory* v. *Hill* (1799) 8 TR 299 and 7.6 later). Note also that an action for false imprisonment/trespass would lie for unlawfully imprisoning a person in order to compel restitution of property (*Harvey* v. *Mayne* (1872) IR 6 CL 417) – the bailiff could also use force to escape (see 8.1.1). It is an offence at common law to obstruct the execution of powers granted by statute (*R.* v. *Smith* (1780) Doug KB 441). The person can be fined or imprisoned up to two years at the court's discretion. A good example is *Southam* v. *Smout* [1963] 3 All ER 104 in which the county court bailiff entered legally by a closed but unlocked door in order to arrest the debtor. The son-in-law of the debtor objected to this entry of his house without his permission and assaulted the bailiff when he refused to leave. This was held to be an offence. However if the debtor (or her goods) had not been in the house, the bailiffs would have been trespassing on third party premises (see 7.3.3).

A debtor may be guilty of criminal contempt if s/he obstructs a sheriff's officer or county court bailiff in the execution of their duty – for instance, by assaulting the officer (*Lewis* v. *Owen* [1894] 1 QB 102). The court may commit or fine the offender.

This will be so even if there are minor errors in the writ. In *R.* v. *Monkman* [1892] 8 Man LR 509 it was held unlawful to resist a sheriff's officer executing three writs of fi fa which were incorrect as to the date of judgment on each. The sheriff is under a duty to enforce a writ that is on the face of it regular, and such errors were mere irregularities that could be amended.

If a sheriff's officer is resisted, he may arrest and imprison the guilty parties (s.8(2) Sheriff's Act 1887 and see 2 Coke Inst. p. 193 citing 8 Ed. II Execution 252: "And it is holden for a maxim of law, that it is not lawful for any man to disturb the ministers of the King in the due execution of the Kings writ, or process of law"). The county court may, under s.14 CCA, commit and/or fine any person who assaults an officer whilst in execution of his duty. The bailiff may arrest the offender without a warrant and take him/her before the judge. A recent example is the two consecutive custodial sentences of three months given to a defendant who attempted to run down two bailiffs with his car (*Read* v. *King* [1997] 1 CL 5). If a person is committed, they can appeal and apply for release pending their appeal, no notice of which need be served on the bailiff (*Brown* v. *Crowley* [1963] 3 All ER 655). The alternative remedy for an officer who is the victim of an assault would be to lay an information before a magistrates court under the Offences Against the Person Act 1861. Although it has been held that the justices have no jurisdiction over assaults arising during execution (*R.* v. *Briggs* [1883] 47 JP 615) the correct procedure for the court would be to treat it as only triable on indictment and accordingly take depositions and commit it for trial at the Crown Court if there is a prima facie case to be made out (*R.* v. *Holsworthy Justices ex parte Edwards* [1952] 1 All ER 411).

Defence by debtor. It would be a defence for the debtor to say that he honestly, but mistakenly, believed the victim was not a court officer or not acting in execution of his duty (*Blackburn* v. *Bowering* [1994] OC 3 All ER 380 CA). The prosecution must show not that the defendant knew that the complainant was an officer acting in execution of his duty but that there was an assault i.e. an intentional or reckless show or application of unlawful force. As the use of reasonable force is lawful in self defence, if such force is applied to an officer as would be reasonable had he not been an officer, in the belief that he was not an officer, then the defendant has a good plea of self defence, even if his belief was unreasonable. Thus if the defendant believed he was being attacked by persons who were not court officers, and only reasonable force necessary to repel the attack is used, the use of force was not assault and the prosecution must prove he did not act reasonably or honestly in self defence.

Equally if the county court order is void or ultra vires resistance by the owner of the goods is not unlawful obstruction (*R.* v. *Finlay* (1901) 13 Man LR 383). It is not illegal obstruction if the sheriff is entering third party premises when neither the person nor the goods of the debtor are present (*R.* v. *Gazikom Aba Dore* (1870) 7 Bom Cr Ca 83; see also 7.3.3 later).

In conclusion therefore, there seems nothing wrongful in the debtor peaceably denying entry to a bailiff, whether by actively refusing entry or simply not opening the door to the bailiff. Provided that they have the will and persistence to do this, the strategy should be successful and there would be no recourse against them within the law of distress.

3.3.2 Protecting goods from seizure

The debtor may resist seizure that is unlawful by taking back the goods that are being seized. However if used at the wrong time or in the wrong circumstances, such an action risks being an offence – either rescue or poundbreach.

Recaption: it is legal for a person to simply seize back their own illegally distrained goods before they are impounded, where:

- the distress is illegal in respect of place, goods being seized or because there is no debt due (*Cotsworth* v. *Betison* (1696) 1 Ld Raym 104; *R.* v. *Pigott* (1851) 1 ICLR 471; *R.* v. *Walshe* (1876) IR 10 CL 511 and generally see Co. Litt. 160b);
- where seized chattels are being abused or neglected by the distrainor who has taken them out of the place where they were originally impounded for an illegal use (*Gomersall* v. *Medgate* (1610) 80 ER 128);
- where a valid tender is refused (*Bevill's Case* (1585) 4 Rep 11b and see 10.3);
- in distress damage feasant if the taking of chattels is not in "fresh pursuit", that is, immediately consequent upon the trespass, then retaking by the owner is lawful;
- the levy is on an order of which there is no record at court (*R.* v. *Carroll* (1828) 2 Ir L Rec 53); or,
- where the warrant is invalid because it does not comply with the prescribed form (*R.* v. *Williams* (1850) 4 Cox CC 87) and provided that the relevant statute does not contain an exception in such circumstances (see 6.1.1).

The levy being resisted must be illegal in its execution, and rescue cannot be used to challenge some other aspect of the process – for example, an objection to being held liable to rates is a matter of appeal, and does not justify rescue (*R.* v. *Higgins* [1851] 2 ICLR 213). Both forcible recapture and forcible resistance to wrongful seizure are also lawful and are defences in actions for assault (*Leward* v. *Basely* I Hawk PC 130), though the level of force permissible may be difficult to determine (*Blades* v. *Higgs* (1861) 10 CBNS 713). The more recent case of *Devoe* v. *Long & Long* (1951) 1 DLR 203 confirms that the right of recaption may be exercised to recover goods wrongfully taken using whatever force is reasonably necessary and entering onto another's property to do so if necessary, provided that that can be peaceable and without any breach of the peace (*Rich* v. *Woolley* (1831) 7 Bing 651). Rescue must be by the owner of the goods, or by his agent, but not by a stranger (FNB 1026). Thus, if the goods of two persons are wrongfully taken, each must rescue his own (*Jennyngs* v. *Playstowe Cro* (1620) *Jac* 568).

It is stated in "Buller's Nisi Prius" (7th edition, p.61 following FNB 102F) that it is not rescue to disturb a bailiff who is in the process of making a distress but who has not yet secured possession the distrainors remedy would be an action on the case. This is cited also in "Woodfall on Landlord & Tenant" at 9.168, though there are no modern authorities. By contrast Coke (2 Inst p161) and Viner's Abridgment, citing Litt f237, state that resisting distress is as much an offence as actual rescue (this appears to be unique to distress for rent, see 3.3.5).

Two separate wrongful acts that can be committed by the debtor-rescue and poundbreach. The latter is most likely to occur, though the offences are often referred to simply as rescue (e.g. s.92 CCA). Both are offences at common law and torts for which the bailiff may sue in trespass.

Rescue (or rescous) is interference with seized goods in possession of the person distraining (Co Litt 160) not yet impounded. In earlier times there was a distinct time lag between seizure and impounding during which the debtor could seek to recover items (*Cotsworth* v. *Betison* (1696) 1 Salk 247). To constitute rescue there must be something equal to a breach of the peace, or likely to prove a breach of the peace, plus taking in the presence of the keeper (*Lodge* v. *Rowe* (1875) 1 VLR 65).

Rescous is both a criminal offence under the Distress for Rent Act 1689 and a civil tort leading to a penalty of treble damages, based on the debt due. The bailiff can also use the right of recaption, i.e. pursue and re-take the goods, and an attempt to rescue justifies an assault (*Anon* (1705) 11 Mod Rep 64).

The common law remedy for rescue which would be applicable, for instance, to statutory distraint is a special action for trespass by the creditor on the goods seized, in which a claim for any assault on the bailiff may also be made (FNB 101D). The person sued may defend on the grounds outlined earlier.

Poundbreach is interference with impounded goods and is the offence most likely to be committed in these days of walking possession agreements. It is an offence to breach a pound even if the distress was unlawful, as the impounded goods are now in the custody of the law and the poundbreach is thus a trespass to the Crown and a breach of the peace (*Anon* (1535) 1 And 31; *R.* v. *Nicholson* [1901] 65 J P 298). To constitute poundbreach there must be a criminal intention (*Lodge* v. *Rowe* (1875) 1 VLR 65 and see *Abingdon RDC* v. *O'Gorman* later).

Poundbreach is an offence, whether or not there is a breach of the peace and whether or not the seized items have been improperly stored, simply because it is a violation of legal custody (*R.* v. *Beauchamp* (1827) 5 LJOSMC 66). The offence of poundbreach can apply to statutory distraint as well as distress for rent (*R.* v. *Higgins* [1851] 2 ICLR 213). The bailiff's warrant is *prima facie* evidence of his authority and there is no need to prove that the sum was properly due in order to prosecute poundbreach (*R.* v. *Brenan* (1854) 6 Cox CC 381). It is not a defence to say that the distress was illegal – the breach of the pound is the gist of the proceedings, and it is not necessary to examine the cause of the distress in detail (see for example *Company of Proprietors of Parrett Navigation* v. *Stower, Trott & Munckton* (1840) 6 M&W 564 or FNB 101). The offender can be prosecuted for an indictable offence at common law (*R.* v. *Butterfield* (1893) 17 Cox CC 598; *R.* v. *Bradshaw* (1835) 7 C&P 233). It can also be an offence for a person to attempt to commit poundbreach (s.1 Criminal Attempts Act 1981). For a person to be convicted, it has been held that there should be clear evidence of them knowingly engaging in or assisting in the commission of the offence (per Lord Hanworth MR at 218 in *Lavell & Co* v. *O'Leary* [1933] 2 KB 200). The committal can be for an unlimited period (*R.* v. *Castro* (1880) 5 QBD 490) or a fine can be for an unlimited amount, though based on the person's means and the gravity of the offence (*Beeche's Case* (1608) 77 ER 559).

In addition to the criminal remedy, there are two civil general remedies for poundbreach. One is a common law right of action for damages which would be applicable to most forms of statutory distraint. There is also right of recaption, which would bar the civil action (*Vaspor* v. *Edwards* (1702) 12 MR 662). There are also three special remedies as described below. In all cases of poundbreach, the cause of action lies with the impounder, not the person upon whose property goods are impounded (FNB 100E, 33 Hen VIII pl. 56).

There is a specific remedy for landlords under s.3 Distress for Rent Act 1689. The landlord may sue in the local county court by a special action for the wrong sustained. Such an action is a penal action and the plaintiff is not therefore entitled to an affidavit of documents or the other preparations normal prior to trial (*Jones* v. *Jones* [1889] 22 QBD 425). Action may be taken against either the owner or actual offender, but if the landlord recovers against the offender, action may not later be taken against the owner (Sir Bartholemew Shower's Observations, fol 162/3).

The penalty is treble damages for both rescue and poundbreach. Treble costs can also be awarded (*Lawson* v. *Story* (1694) 1 Ld Raym 19). The basis upon which the damages are calculated is the value of the goods seized (*Cyril Morgan (Holdings)* v. *Dyer* (1995) 11 CLY 193). No special damages need to be proved by the landlord (*Kemp* v. *Christmas* (1898) 79 LT 233). The same case also indicated that although the plaintiff may have already recovered damages in respect of the offence (in this instance, an action for negligence against the bailiff) this does not provide the offender with a defence, although it may be used in mitigation of the damages awarded. Note that in *Firth* v. *Purvis* (1793) 5 TR 432 the pound was breached *after* tender was refused by the plaintiff landlord, who insisted on the goods seized. In the circumstances treble damages were held excessive and were reduced to single damages. For the remedy to arise it is not important where the goods were impounded but if they are fraudulently removed to third party premises and then rescued by a third party the DRA probably doesn't apply (*Harris* v. *Thirkell* [1852] 20 LTOS 98). Normally it is held that the landlord may not protect seized goods by suing for trespass or conversion (but see commentary later), though an action for the common law tort of rescue may be possible (*Iredale* v. *Kendall* (1879) 40 LT 362).

Under s.68 VATA there is a civil penalty for breach of any walking possession agreement of 50 per cent of the VAT due. The debtor will not be liable if s/he can convince the Commissioners or, on appeal, a VAT Tribunal, that there is a reasonable excuse for the breach. Lack of funds is **not** a reasonable excuse.

In respect of county court execution s. 92 CCA states that any person rescuing seized goods is liable to prison of one month and/or a fine up to level 4 (£2500). He may be arrested and brought before a judge by the bailiff. Arrest will either be on the spot if they are caught by the bailiff, or alternatively following a summons from the court. In High Court execution retaking seized goods can be treated as a criminal contempt – see 3.3.1 earlier.

Naturally in instances where an offence is alleged, arguments can arise as to whether poundbreach or rescue have indeed occurred and these will involve questions as to whether impounded goods have been abandoned (*Dod* v. *Monger* (1704) 6 Mod 215) or were properly impounded in the first place. There will be no abandonment, and therefore an offence will have been committed, where possession is adequately retained or the bailiffs *intends to retain* it. See for example *Jones* v. *Biernstein* (1900) 1 QB 100 in which a rent bailiff took an inventory and then remained in close possession until he left the house over the weekend. The tenant re-took the goods in his absence but was held guilty of poundbreach as abandonment had not occurred. The bailiff had abandoned actual possession of the goods for no necessary reason, but as he intended to return (as shown by the inventory), the distress was not abandoned completely and the bailiff remained in "constructive possession". Abandonment *has* occurred and/or no offence is committed where:

- *the authorised bailiff is not in possession*: even where possession had been abandoned due to threats and violence by the defendant, it was held not to have been rescue because the goods had been left in the care of bailiffs' assistants and not the officer named on the warrant (*R.* v. *Noonan* (1876) 10 ICLR 505).
- *there is no adequate impounding*: in *Alwayes* v. *Broom* (1695) 2 Lutw 1262 it was held that it is not poundbreach to remove goods from a pound left unsecured (see to Co. Litt 47b citing 3 Ed. III trespass II). Equally it is not an offence for the debtor to change the lock on the pound (for example, the room selected by the landlord on the tenant's premises) provided that no goods are removed. The distrainor may, though, have a special action on the case against the tenant (*Anon* [undated] cited under *Holman* v. *Tuke* [1672] Win 80).
- *poundbreach occurs before removal*: in *Lavell & Co* v. *O'Leary* [1933] 2 KB 200 a tenant, Mr. Wong Gee, signed a walking possession agreement with bailiffs who distrained for rent arrears on goods in his business premises, the "Canton Cafe". Wong then got a removals firm to take the goods away. The firm was found not guilty of poundbreach because they took the goods from the landing outside the property. Wong Gee was guilty as he had moved the goods there after they had been impounded within his premises. The court asserted that a walking possession agreement is valid against all the world (but contrast this with the next case).
- *removal is by an innocent third party*: in *Abingdon RDC* v. *O'Gorman* [1968] 3 All ER 79 CA a landlord distrained for rent upon a hired television set, amongst other things. Notice was given to the tenant who signed a walking possession agreement. However he later asked Mr O'Gorman from the television hire firm to remove the rented set. They were not informed of the levy when doing this. The bailiff began an action for treble damages. The Court of Appeal held that the hire firm was not guilty of poundbreach because the walking possession agreement did not validly impound the goods against strangers. A person cannot be guilty of poundbreach unless s/he has a guilty mind, i.e. knows of the impounding. O'Gorman was not guilty as he was not covered by the agreement. If he had been, he should have been notified of the seizure so that he could serve notice on the landlord of his claim to the goods (see 9.22.2).

As will be returned to at 8.2.1 the courts have frequently manifested dissatisfaction with the common lack of notice of walking possession on third parties and the risk of poundbreach. In *Dixon* v. *McKay* (case heard (1903), case reported [1912] 21 Man LR 762) it was held that seizure by means of walking possession was "reasonably sufficient" as far as the debtor was concerned but might not be for third party buyers – and in *Dodd* v. *Vail* (1913) 9 DLR 534 walking possession was held to be valid seizure against those with notice of the seizure but third parties would not necessarily be aware of it. Ideally bailiffs should secure effectual and continuous (i.e. close) possession (*Little* v. *Magle* (1914) 7 WWR 224, citing *Dixon* above) if they wish to ensure that the seized goods are protected from interference by all parties with a possible interest in them.

- *distress damage feasant*: in *Knowle* v. *Blake* (1821) 5 Bing 499 cattle seized in distress damage feasant were left by the distrainor on the owner's property. Later they were taken by the plaintiff to his own premises, but were freed by the defendant owner. It was held that there was no rescue as leaving the items on the owner's property constituted abandonment.

Commentary

The penalties for poundbreach and rescue seem, to modern eyes, excessive and irrational (see Law Commission 1986). The damages bear little relationship to the actual loss incurred by the plaintiff. The main consolation in this must be that these offences are rarely prosecuted. Probably many of the instances of interference with seized goods occur when debtors sell them to raise funds to clear the sums due, and bailiffs will of course be pragmatic and take the amount tendered, rather than pursue any alleged wrongdoing. It is worth noting in passing that in execution the bailiff has, by seizure, got a special property in the goods upon which it is possible to found an action for conversion (9.26). It is often said that it is not possible in distress for rent for the landlord to sue in the same way as the impounding gives no such interest (*R.* v. *Cotton* (1751) Park 112). The author has argued (Kruse 1998, 1) that this is based on outdated authorities and that they should now be disregarded. Damages for conversion would be a fairer measure of the plaintiff's loss than some of the penalties described above.

3.3.3 Concealing or removing goods

It is not illegal for the debtor to hide items of value on the property prior to the levy. Most bailiffs tend to make only a fairly cursory search, despite a common law duty to use "reasonable diligence" in a search, so this strategy may succeed. Removing items from the property prior to a levy is also legal, except that in distress for rent the debtor risks the offence of fraudulent removal (see below) and in execution by the sheriff entry may be forced to third party premises (see 7.4.4). Other bailiffs can peaceably enter third party premises to search for goods (see 7.3.3). The debtor is not obliged to say where any goods are, so it is usually extremely unlikely that a bailiff will be able to discover their new location. The only factor operating in the bailiff's favour is that after a while the debtor is likely to tire of not having the use of goods, so that they will be retrieved. At this point if the levy has not been terminated it is possible for the bailiff to return and try again.

Fraudulent removal occurs when a tenant removes goods in order to defeat a levy of distress for rent, leaving insufficient goods for distress behind. The landlord can pursue and sell goods fraudulently or clandestinely removed within 30 days of their removal (s.1 DRA 1737), provided that they have not been sold in good faith and for valuable consideration to a person not privy to the fraud (s.2 DRA), and if s/he can show the following:

- *there is a right to distrain* – there must of course be rent arrears, although the landlord does not need to show that distress was actually contemplated (*Stanley* v. *Wharton* (1822) 9 Price 301). Any distress that *is* levied must be lawful (*R.* v. *Gopalasamy* (1902) ILR 25 Mad 729). There is no presumption by the court that the distress was lawful, and the prosecution must prove this. In the absence of such prove, the defendant cannot be convicted as the court will regard them as exercising their right of private defence of their property against unlawful interference. If the tenancy has been terminated and the tenant is no longer in possession the landlord cannot follow goods and seize them. In *Gray* v. *Stait* [1883] 11 QBD 668 the landlord terminated the tenancy and the same day the tenant moved out, leaving a quarter's rent unpaid. The landlord seized goods at the tenant's new home. This was wrongful. If the tenant holds over under 8 Anne c.14 s.6 the power to distrain continues (see 3.2.2).
- *the removal was fraudulent* – i.e. it was done wilfully, knowingly and deceitfully to deprive the landlord. The burden of proof is on the landlord (*Parry* v. *Jenkins* (1832) 1 CR & M 227; *Inkop* v. *Morchurch* (1861) 2 F & F 501). Removal need not be clandestine to be fraudulent (*Opperman* v. *Smith* (1824) 4 Dow & Ry KB 33) but a secretive removal at night is very likely to be fraudulent (*Watson* v. *Main* (1799) 3 Esp 15; *Furneaux* v. *Fotherby* (1815) 4 Camp 136; *Vaughan* v. *Davis* (1793) 1 Esp 257). It has been suggested that if the tenant removes goods, thinking that s/he has a right to do so, this removal is probably not fraudulent (*John* v. *Jenkins* (1832) 1 Cr & M 227);
- *the removal was to defeat a levy of distress*. The court must decide if it was fraudulent even if the tenant admits it was to avoid distress (*John* v. *Jenkins* (1832) 1 Cr & M 227). The tenant need not personally remove goods so long as s/he allows it to be done (*Lister* v. *Brown* (1823) 1 C & P 121);
- *no sufficient goods* remained (*Gegg* v. *Perin* (1845) 9 JP 619; *Gillan* v. *Arkwright* (1850) 16 LTOS 88): readers need to note the complex rules on goods seizable in distress for rent, for which see 9.22;
- *the removal occurred after the arrears accrued* (*Watson* v. *Main* (1799) 3 Esp 15; *Rand* v. *Vaughan* (1835) 1 Bing NC 767). The tenant has all day to pay the rent due, and distress cannot be made until the next day therefore it appears that goods removed on the day rent falls due are not fraudulently removed (*Dibble* v. *Bowater* (1853) 2 E&B 564; *Re: Aspinall* [1961] Ch 526);
- *removal was by the tenant* or by a third party acting at his/her instigation. The tenant will still be liable for the acts of a third party if privy to the fraud (*Lister* v. *Brown* (1823) 3 Dow & Ry KB 501). A third party is only liable if s/he knew of the fraudulent purpose of the removal (*Brooke* v. *Noakes* [1828] 8 B&C 537): see also the next paragraph;
- *the goods removed belonged to the tenant* and were distrainable (*Thornton* v. *Adamson* (1816) 5 M & S 38). Goods not the property of the tenant (e.g. on a bill of sale in arrears) are outside these provisions (*Tomlinson* v. *Consolidated Credit & Mortgage Corp* (1889) 24 QBD 135) therefore when the goods were seized on default by the mortgagor, there was no fraudulent removal. The fact that this may be in breach of the terms of the Bills of Sale Acts is not an issue for the landlord as these statutes exist to protect the mortgagor, not third parties. This exemption from the offence applies regardless of whether the creditor is aware of an imminent distress (*Bach* v. *Meaks* [1816] 5 M&S 200).

If the landlord has grounds to suspect that goods are inside entry may be forced during day time to any locked or secured premises, that is any house, barn, stable, outhouse, yard or close (DRA 1737 s.7). If entry is to be forced a constable must be present (*Rich* v. *Woolley* (1831) 7 Bing 651; *Cartwright* v. *Smith & Batty* (1833) 1 Mood & R 284) but the landlord need not request the goods first (*Williams* v. *Roberts* (1852) 7 Exch 618). If entry is to be forced to a house, an oath should be made before a justice of the peace first, to the effect that there is a reasonable ground to suspect that goods are present.

There is a civil penalty for fraudulent removal by the tenant, and any person wilfully and knowingly assisting (which can include the trustee of a bankrupt tenant – *Welsh* v. *Myers* (1816) 4 Camp 368). This is payment of double damages to the landlord (s.3 DRA 1737) and is recoverable by action. The damages are to be measured by the value of the goods removed (*Gwinnet* v. *Philips* [1790] 100 ER 780; *Brooke* v. *Noakes* [1828] 8 B & C 537). In such a penal action, the normal directions and rights as to discovery etc. do not apply, therefore the plaintiff landlord cannot for instance administer interrogatories to the defendant (*T W Hobbs & Co Ltd* v. *Hudson* [1890] 25 QBD 232).

Alternatively a criminal sanction is available. Under s.4 DRA 1737, when the goods do not exceed £50 in value, the landlord may lay an information in the magistrates' court, either that in the area where goods were removed or where they were taken (*R.* v. *Morgan* (1780) Cald 156). The landlord's right to sue still applies even if the debt is under this ceiling (*Horsefall* v. *Davey* (1816) NPC 147; *Stanley* v. *Wharton* (1822) 9 Price 301). The court can order a penalty of double the value of the goods removed which is payable as a fine within a time set by the court. If prosecuted before the magistrates it must be shown that the offence was committed "wilfully and knowingly" (*R.* v. *Radnorshire JJ* [1840] 9 Dowl 90). The justices do not need to specify the goods removed, so long as they find that the value is below the prescribed level (*R.* v. *Rabbitts* (1825) 6 D&R 341). The magistrates' decision can be appealed to the Crown Court under s.5 DRA 1737 (*R.* v. *Cheshire JJ* (1833) 5 B & Ad 439) and if the party appealing enters into a recognizance with sufficient sureties for double the sum ordered to be paid and on condition that s/he appears at the Crown Court, enforcement of the justices' order shall be stayed in the meantime (s.6).

3.3.4 Consequences of a failed levy

If the bailiff fails to gain entry or find any adequate goods, a return of "no goods" or "no sufficient distress" is made to the creditor and other enforcement may then be attempted by them. Case law makes it clear that the bailiff must have made reasonable efforts to actually enter or search for goods to be able lawfully to make such a return (*Thomas* v. *Lulham* [1895] 2 QB 400). Nil returns can be made if the goods are hidden (*Doe d Haverson* v. *Franks* (1847) 2 Car & Kir 678), if entry is obstructed (*Doe d Cox* v. *Roe* (1847) 5 Dow & L 272) or refused (*R.* v. *Dudley Justices ex parte Blatchford* (1992) RVR 63) or if goods are already subject to seizure, or become so under a claim for priority by the Crown – for which see 6.6.2 (*Grove* v. *Aldridge* (1832) 9 Bing 428).

The link between a failed levy and further enforcement is important because the various regulations specify the conditions that must be satisfied by the bailiff to enable other steps to be taken. In local tax recovery the billing authority may seek to have the debtor committed to prison where the bailiff reports that "he was unable (for whatever reason) to find any or sufficient goods of the debtor on which to levy the amount" (reg. 47(1) CT(A&E) Regulations; reg. 16(1) NNDR(C&E) Regulations). If the bailiff fails to make any proper levy at all, then a nil return is not correct and an application for committal cannot be based upon it (*R.* v. *Burnley JJ, ex parte Ashworth* (1992) 32 RVR 27). Similar rules apply where, following a failed execution by a sheriff's officer or county court bailiff, the judgment creditor wishes to enforce by petitioning for bankruptcy on the basis that execution has been returned unsatisfied in whole or in part (s.268(1)(a) Insolvency Act 1986). This was examined in *Re: A Debtor (No. 340 of 1992)*[1994] 3 All ER 269 CA and the court held that the failure of the sheriff to gain access on unstated occassions at unstated hours did not justify a return of the writ as "unsatisfied". The court made a distinction between an unexecuted and an unsatisfied writ (see also *Re: Worsley ex parte Gill* [1957] 19 ABC 105) and stated in this case that the return that the writ was unsatisfied was merely the bailiff's opinion on the effect of what he has done (or failed to do) – the court is not bound by this opinion. The writ orders goods to be seized: where this has not been done at all the return in question was at least irregular as it could not be justified by what the bailiff had actually done.

3.3.5 Resistance to distress for rent: Advisers should beware that, at common law, resistance to levies of distress for rent can give rise to a number of offences. Their origin is essentially feudal, as refusal of rent by various means was interpreted as denial of landlord's '*seisin*' *i.e.* an undermining of his/her rights of possession. Though in practice obsolete in everyday applications of property law, seisin remains a technical aspect of freehold ownership. Furthermore given that distress for rent is still an essentially proprietary remedy available to landlords, it is likely that these offences remain valid (at least between freeholder and tenant): some are confirmed by statute.

Mere denial of the rent to the landlord is not wrongful (a 'disseisin') without more deliberate resistance (Co Litt 160b citing 3 Ed III 75 & 8 Hen VI 11). If more active steps are taken to deny the landlord, the tenant may be liable for one of the following:

- *Forestalling* – which is where a tenant waylays or threatens the landlord or bailiff with force and in such a manner that he does not distrain or demand the rent (*Noy's Maxims* c. 23 p. 55; Co Litt 161b);
- *Enclosing* – which is where the tenant bars the landlord's entry (Co Litt 160b). For example see the case of *Melford* v. *London* (1321) 14 Ed II, Sel Soc v86. Before the Eyre of London an assize of novel disseisin was passed for the landlord on the basis that the tenant had wrongfully deprived his lord of his rent, and the ability to levy it, by leaving the rented premises empty and refusing to give the landlord the key so he could attempt to levy for the rent due. Judgment was given against the tenant for the rent due;
- *Resistance* which is physical prevention of a levy by the tenant (Co Litt 160b).

In all these instances the remedy would appear to be an action for trespass on the case, in which the landlord can recover the arrears, damages and costs (*Noy's Maxims* p.55; Co Litt 257b citing Hen VI 20).

The final denial of the landlord has a remedy in statute:

- *Land is left 'fresh':* If the tenant leaves no distrainable goods on the property it is said to be 'fresh'. Premises should be open and sufficient to the landlord's distress (Co Litt 153b). Coke includes enclosing (see above) in this category as if property is so "immured or inclosed about" that the landlord cannot enter and distrain, the effect is the same (2 Co Inst 295). There is a special remedy applicable to cases where distress for rent fails because the tenant has deserted the premises, leaving land uncultivated without any sufficient distress. The landlord, finding no-one in possession, may request that two justices view the premises and put the landlord in possession if at least six months' rent remains unpaid and they are satisfied the property is abandoned. For more details see DRA 1737 ss. 16, 17 and Deserted Tenements Act 1817: readers referring to older authorities may encounter this as a writ of '*cessavit per biennium*' under Statute of Gloucester 1278 (6 Ed 1 c.4).

3.4 Transfers to third parties

Transferring goods to relatives, children or friends puts them beyond the reach of bailiffs in many cases and in genuine cases, if a third party then removed his/her goods before distress, they could not be sued (*Pool* v. *Crawcour* (1884) 1 TLR 165). The fact that the debtor has disposed of goods to a third party just prior to a levy in order to defeat the seizure does not necessarily void the disposition merely because of the circumstances in which it occurred. If the bargain was for good consideration with a genuine intention to pass property it will be valid (*Wood* v. *Dixie* (1845) 7 QB 892). It is not necessary for both parties to act in good faith, so long as there is good faith on the part of the purchaser (*Mackintosh* v. *Pogose* [1895] 1 Ch 505). The same might apply to bills of sale and purchase and lease back (*Tower Finance & Furnishing Co* v. *Brown* (1890) 6 TLR 192). The deal will not be invalidated by the purchaser's knowledge of the intended execution provided that proof of payment and change of possession can be shown (*Hale* v. *Saloon Omnibus Co* (1859) 4 Drew 492).

If items genuinely transferred to third parties are taken, the person generally has a remedy – interpleader in the courts, a declaration of ownership versus the landlord or an injunction and action for wrongful interference (see chapter 9). A third party may prove ownership by making a statutory declaration. If a third party's goods are in the hands of the debtor through fraud or theft they may be recovered by the true owner (*Earl of Bristol* v. *Wilsmore* (1823) 2 Dow & Ry 755).

Various means of transfer have been tried. The most common are outlined below.

3.4.1 Gifts

A gift, properly undertaken, will put property beyond the reach of bailiffs. Gifts may be effected by several means – by deed, by declaration of trust or by delivery. It is likely that the last is the method most commonly tried by individuals, though trusts are discussed at 3.4.2.

To make (and prove) an effective gift, the debtor will have to demonstrate the following:

- that the transfer of property was made with no intention of its return; and,
- that there was clear and distinct act of gift.

All property, real and personal, corporeal and incorporeal, may be given. We are interested in personal property and the main means of giving personal chattels is by transfer and retention of possession. Without actual delivery a gift of chattels won't be effective, thus if the donor wishes to retain possession, a gift will have to be by bill of sale instead, for which see 3.4.3. Actual manual delivery is not essential, though an oral gift without some act of delivery will be ineffective (*Smith* v. *Smith* [1733] 2 Stra 953). Examples of successful and failed gifts follow.

- *donee is put in possession by donor* – In *Kilpin* v. *Ratley* [1892] 1 QB 582 a father verbally gave furniture to his daughter. They were in a room in her home where some of the furniture was stored. There was no manual delivery and after the gift the furniture remained where it was. The court held that he had done all he could to complete the gift and there was no need to go through "the mere formality of handling furniture in order to complete the gift".
- *donee is put in constructive possession by the donor* – for example by handing over the key to a warehouse where goods are stored (*Rowles* v. *Rowles* (1750) 1 Ves Sen 348); by touching and words (*Rawlinson* v. *Mort* (1905) 93 LT 555); or by delivery of part as representative of the whole (*Lock* v. *Heath* (1892) 8 TLR 295 – the gift of a chair).
- *the nature of the donee's possession is changed* – for example in *Winter* v. *Winter* [1861] 4 LT 639 a barge was given to the donor's employee who had previously been in possession of it as employee, but who subsequently used it as his own. In *Cain* v. *Moon* [1896] 2 QB 283 it was held that prior delivery, such as for safe keeping, can be converted into delivery as a gift by changing the capacity in which the item is held.
- *intention alone is not enough* – in *Jones* v. *Lock* [1865] 1 Ch App 25 a father put a cheque into his baby son's hand and declared it to be the son's. The father died soon after and the cheque was found still to be in his possession. His declaration in favour of his son was never followed through by investment or the like and thus was not an effective gift.

Gifts between family members can be problematic. There is no reason why a gift cannot be made to a child provided that it is effected properly (*Shephard* v. *Cartwright* [1955] AC 431). Between husband and wife the situation is more complex. They may give each other gifts of chattels and so on, but the need for a clear and distinct gift and evidence of intention is even more important. A gift must be unequivocal. If the facts are consistent with both a gift and an intention to share use with a spouse, no gift has occurred. See for example, *Re: Cole ex parte Trustee of Bankrupt's Property* [1964] 1 Ch 175 – the bankrupt husband had told the wife that goods in a house were all hers, but they continued to live together and share the chattels. No delivery or change of possession could be shown, and as a result title remained vested in his trustee. In *Bashall* v. *Bashall* (1894) 11 TLR 152 a husband allegedly gave a pony and trap to his wife. Again both continued to use it and the wife's claim was held unproved. Delivery is needed to effect a gift to a spouse who does not have existing possession (*Hislop* v. *Hislop* (1950) WN 124). An act showing an intention to change ownership may be sufficient, even if chattels are still shared, but mere letters written and signed by one spouse giving furniture to the other are not enough (*In Re: Bretton's Estate* [1881] 17 Ch D 416).

3.4.2 Trusts

It is not unheard of for debtors, particularly small firms, to try to protect property by putting it in trust. As noted above this may be done by declaration of trust.

A valid trust of personal property may be created in writing (*Gee* v. *Liddell (No. 1)* (1866) 35 Beav 621) or by oral declaration of the trust (*M'Fadden* v. *Jenkyns* [1842] 1 Ph 153). If the trust is created in writing no particular form must be followed so long as all the material terms of the trust are contained – the parties, the property concerned and the objects of the trust. The written instrument will have the advantage of being proof that can be shown to any bailiff calling to seize. However the problem is that written assignments of chattels will tend to fall under the Bills of Sale Acts (see 3.4.3) unless they are covered by one of the statutory exemptions – amongst others, they are for the benefit of creditors of the grantor, they are marriage settlements or they are in the ordinary course of business. As none of these exemptions are likely to apply, the trust may have to comply with the technicalities of the Acts. One way to escape this problem and still have some written proof of the trust is where the assignment is complete without writing, such as by delivery, and the document simply refers to or confirms this transaction. Such evidence of the declaration of trust can be prepared at a later date to the creation of the trust itself. At common law although only an absolute interest in chattels could be created by a trust it is now possible to create limited interests in all chattels except those exhausted by personal use. This does not include a business' stock or farming stock (*Myers* v. *Washbrook* [1901] 1 KB 360; *Breton* v. *Mockett* [1878] 9 Ch D 95).

A trust is effective as most bailiffs cannot seize equitable interests in property (see 9.1.2). As against strangers, the trustee and beneficiary are one person in equity, so possession of the trust property by the beneficiary is regarded as possession by the trustee (see *White* v. *Morris* (1852) 11 CB 1015). Thus the trustee may sue in conversion even if the trust property is retained and enjoyed by the beneficiary (*Barker* v. *Furlong* [1891] 2 Ch 172). Note however that it has been held that where the whole beneficial interest is vested in the debtor(s), the trust will **not** be allowed to defeat the creditor (*Stevens* v. *Hince* (1914) WN 148). Clearly, this strategy is only going to succeed where the property can be held on trust for more than one person, perhaps the debtor and spouse/cohabitee jointly (provided that they are not joint debtors).

Finally we may note that trusts that are created for an illegal purpose or against the public interest are void. We may speculate whether a trustee in the circumstances described, who is forced to sue or interplead to protect the alleged trust property, may meet with some scepticism on the part of the courts as to the validity of the trust they seek to defend.

3.4.3 Bills of Sale

Assignment of goods under bill of sale is a means of transferring the property in goods whilst retaining the possession of them. It can afford effective protection for them against bailiffs, whether the purpose is the benefit of another creditor by the provision of security for the credit extended or the debtors's own protection, where the bill of sale is made with a friend or relative. For instance, it has been sucessfully used between husband and wife in respect of household goods that both continue to use (*French* v. *Gething* [1922] 1 KB 236; *Re: Satterthwaite* (1895) 2 Mans 52). This strategy is not uncommon but can face considerable problems. Bills of sale are regulated by the Bills of Sale Acts 1878 and 1882 and numerous formalities and procedures must be followed for them to be effective against bailiffs. The following outlines the key elements to which attention should be paid.

The bills of sale legislation is concerned with documents rather than transactions. Thus any transfer of property, if put into writing, can be liable to be treated as a bill of sale and will have to comply with the following requirements (*Hopkins* v. *Gudgeon* [1906] 1 KB 690). Gifts by deed or by declaration of trust can be included if the property remains with the donor and no effective transfer to another can be shown. Mortgages and charges of goods by companies are in the main outside the Acts, but instead see 9.21 on debentures. The statutory requirements which must be complied with are described below.

A bill of sale document must exist in the correct form. The 1882 Act contains a standard form in its schedule which must be closely, though not exactly, followed (*Roberts* v. *Roberts* [1884] 13 QBD 794). The statutory form identifies the parties, the loan and the terms of its repayment and allows the goods to remain in the possession of the owner unless s/he is in breach of the bill under s.7 of the 1882 Act, for instance by default, bankruptcy or by allowing the goods to be taken in execution. If two or more individuals grant a bill of sale over their goods, their shares should be identified if they are unequal, otherwise the bill will be void (*Saunders* v. *White* [1902] 1 KB 472). Repayments of the loan do not have to be in equal amounts (*Re: Cleaver ex parte Rawlings* [1887] 18 QBD 489) nor do the instalments have to comprise equal amounts of interest (*Edwards* v. *Marston* [1891] 1 QB 225). Bills will be void where the times of payment are unspecified (*Hetherington* v. *Groome* [1884] 13 QBD 789) or the interest rate is not stated (*Blankenstein* v. *Robertson* [1890] 24 QBD 543). A bill failing to comply with the statutory requirements is wholly void (s.9 1882 Act and see *Davies* v. *Rees* [1886] 17 QBD 408).

An inventory of mortgaged goods must be attached. The bill of sale document itself does not describe the goods and chattels mortgaged, therefore an inventory will be attached (s.4 1882 Act). This must specifically describe the goods concerned (*Thomas* v. *Kelly* [1888] 13 App Cas 506) and too vague an inventory will render the bill ineffective in respect of any personal chattels not properly described (*Witt* v. *Banner* [1887] 20 QBD 114). If there could be no problem identifying the items concerned, more general words may be permissible (*Davidson* v. *Carlton Bank* [1893] 1 QB 82).

A bill of sale may be made in respect of most goods and chattels, including furniture, growing crops and fixtures. Trade machinery are for the purposes of the Acts treated as personal chattels rather than fixtures (s.5 1878 Act), so all machines, plant and equipment in factories and workshops may be assigned, but the bill must be registered – see below (*Hawtry* v. *Butlin* [1873] 8 QB 290). Trade machinery does not, however include machines supplying power or gas, water or steam: any assignment of such items does not require registration (*Topham* v. *Greenside Glazed Firebrick Co* [1887] 37 Ch D 281). Even if a bill is void in respect of personal chattels, it will not prejudice the status of other items included in it, such as fixtures (*Re: North Wales Produce & Supply Co Ltd* [1922] 2 Ch 340) or excluded trade machinery (*Re: Burdett* [1888] 20 QBD 310). If the bill includes an assignment of real chattels as well as personal chattels, it is void (*Cochrane* v. *Entwistle* [1890] 25 QBD 116). The grantor of the bill must be owner of the personal chattels comprised in the bill otherwise it will be void (s.5 1882 Act) – this includes after acquired property, but not fixtures, plant and trade machinery acquired to replace items mentioned in the schedule to the bill (s.6 1882 Act).

Consideration must have been given and must be stated in the document. A minimum advance of £30 is prescribed; anything less than this renders the bill void (s.12 1882 Act). The loan should have been made at the same time as the bill, unless it is to be made by instalments, in which case this should be disclosed in the bill (*In Re: Young* (1880) 43 LT 576). If the consideration is not truly stated, the bill is not wholly void, but is void only in respect of any personal chattels comprised in it (*Heseltine* v. *Simmons* [1892] 2 QB 547).

Witnesses should attest the making of the bill (s.10 1882 Act). Failure to do this renders the bill void. An affidavit should accompany the bill detailing its proper execution and attestation, the true date of execution and the residence and actual occupation of the grantor (the debtor) and every witness. Again failure to comply with these provisions avoids the bill (*Matthews* v. *Buchanan* [1889] 5 TLR 373).

Registration of the bill must take place to make it valid (s.10 1878 Act and see *Pickard* v. *Marriage* (1876) 1 Ex D 364; *Youngs* v. *Youngs* [1940] 1 KB 760). The bill and inventory, a copy of these and the affidavit must be presented within seven days to Queens Bench Division of the High Court (s.8 1882 Act), otherwise it will be void in respect of any personal chattels assigned. Registration must be renewed every five years (s.11 1878 Act) and failure to do this makes the bill wholly void (*Fenton* v. *Blythe* [1890] 25 QBD 417), as a result of which it will be ineffective against a bona fide execution creditor (*Jenkinson* v. *Brandley Mining Co* [1887] 19 QBD 568).

Enforcement of the bill of sale is by the mortgagee (the secured lender) taking of possession of the goods given as security. This seizure would put the goods beyond the reach of the bailiff just like seizure by another bailiff (*Taylor* v. *Eckersley* [1877] 5 Ch D 740; *Donaghue* v. *Campbell* [1901] 2 OLR 124). If goods subject to a bill are seized in distress before the debt secured by the bill has been called in by the creditor, that creditor would have no right to possession of the goods and could not sue the bailiff for conversion. A bill dated after the date of a levy will not be effective (*Gladstone* v. *Padwick* [1871] LR 6 Exch 203). However this statement needs to be qualified as the effectiveness of a bill differs according to the debt being enforced by distress:

- *execution* cannot be levied on mortgaged goods (*Holroyd* v. *Marshall* [1862] 10 HL Cas 191; *In Re: Cuthbertson ex parte Edey* [1875] 19 Eq 264) and the execution creditor may be liable to the grantee of a bill for a levy on assigned goods (*Condy* v. *Blaiberg* [1891] 55 JP 580). Interpleader can protect the goods if this happens (see 9.2.5). If interpleader is begun by the mortgagee it is normally the practice to order sale and divide the proceeds (O.17 r.6 RSC).
- *magistrates' court* distraint is prevented on mortgaged goods.
- *local tax* distraint on mortgaged goods is prevented.
- *income tax* distraint can take place under s.14 of 1882 Act

- *rent distress* is not prevented, unless a Consumer Credit Act default notice has been served by the mortgagee (s.4A LDAA 1908). However the mortgagee could remove the goods without it being fraudulent (see 3.3.3). If the landlord does distrain, it seems he is not liable to account to the grantee for any surplus (*Evans* v. *Wright* (1857) 2 H&N 527). The grantee may pay off the distress and then sue the grantor (*Edmunds* v. *Wallingford* [1885] 14 QBD 811).

In all cases the validity of a bill may be open to challenge by a bailiff through the courts. In *Miller* v. *Solomon* [1906] 2 KB 91 it was observed that bills of sale could be used to try to defeat seizure but that "*It could not be right that a bill of sale holder, whose security is for a small sum on goods of large value, should be allowed to put an execution creditor in this dilemma and permit goods to escape execution . . .*". Thus the court might not allow "the furtherance of a dishonest purpose". See also *Reed* v. *Thoyts* [1840] 6 M&W 410: if a person purports to dispose of goods under a fraudulent bill of sale, although it may be valid as against the other party to the agreement, from the point of view of creditors seeking to levy distress or execution, the bill is void and the property in it remains in the debtor.

3.4.3 Furniture Leases

Another quite common approach, especially amongst small firms, is for the debtor to transfer his/her assets to a friend or relative and then lease the items back again. Distress for rent would not be prevented by this technique if the transfer were to a spouse or business partner: in most other cases it might be effective protection against seizure. For example see *Withers* v. *Berry* (1895) 39 Sol Jo 559 – a husband gave property to his wife by a deed of gift. After they separated the furniture was leased back to him – but it was held not to be in his possession and thus not seizable in execution. However the courts may regard these arrangements as simply stratagems to avoid legal enforcement and refuse to uphold them in any action brought by the debtor for wrongful interference following seizure (*Scarfe* v. *Halifax* (1840) 7 M&W 288).

Chapter Four

INSOLVENCY

The insolvency of the debtor individual or company can have a major impact on the ability of bailiffs to proceed. The procedures involved in entering insolvency are not dealt with here but there are numerous books available describing these aspects of the system. Insolvency procedure is laid down by four separate bodies of statute.

- For individuals and companies the Insolvency Act 1986 and Insolvency Rules 1986 apply. These provide a code for the insolvency of firms and individuals and lay down procedures to be followed in administering their affairs. The legislation splits into two parts. The first part deals with the insolvency of firms, the second with that of individuals. Parliament created parallel forms of insolvency for both companies and individuals.
- The insolvency of partnerships is dealt with separately by the Insolvent Partnerships Order 1994 (IPO) which modifies the relevant provisions of the Insolvency Act as necessary. A partnership may be wound up as an unregistered company (see below) under articles 7 & 9 IPO. Winding up can occur concurrent with the bankruptcy of the partners (articles 8 & 10) or partners can be bankrupted alone on their own petitions or a creditor's (article 11). A Company Administration Order may be made under article 6. Article 4 applies the Company Voluntary Arrangement procedure to partnerships with the relevant amendments though the partners may need personal Individual Volentary Arrangements too. Everything said about the separate procedures applies to the partnership forms.
- For deceased bankrupts the Insolvent Estates of Deceased Persons Order 1986 applies. This applies the Insolvency Act 1986 to the administration of deceased insolvents' estates with the adaptions contained in Sch. 1 to the Order. Part I of the Schedule applies certain provisions, including s.285 dealing with restrictions on enforcement and ss.346 and 347 dealing with limitations on distress and execution. Part III applies the IVA procedure.
- A more informal insolvency can be achieved by a person by seeking an Administration Order in the county court. The legislation relating to this is found in the County Courts Act 1984 and County Court Rules 1981. Although as a result this may seem to be a purely civil court procedure, its origin is in the Bankruptcy Act 1883 and it should be viewed as a form of bankruptcy.

Bailiffs must treat claims to be insolvent seriously and take reasonable time to investigate them (*Ayshford* v. *Murray* (1870) 23 LT 470). If a bailiff proceeds to sell after the insolvency has been confirmed, he may be in contempt of court (*Re: Bryant* (1876) 4 Ch D 98) though the trustee may simply sue for conversion (*Hitchin* v. *Campbell* (1772) 2 W.Bl 829; *Bailey* v. *Bunning* (1665) 1 Lev 174).

This chapter will examine the effects of the different forms of insolvency, rather than the forms themselves, as it will be assumed that readers will have some familiarity with the general structure of the insolvency legislation. Some bailiffs' actions, such as distress for rent and execution, must be singled out for special treatment as they are treated separately in law. All references will be to the Insolvency Act and Insolvency Rules unless otherwise stated.

4.1 Stays on proceedings and other legal process

The *general* effect of insolvency is to stay all enforcement proceedings against the debtor and the estate, in order to ensure fair treatment of all creditors. This section examines the relevant provisions in the different forms of insolvency and their detailed implications.

4.1.1 Relevant provisions

Individual voluntary arrangements The initial stage of the IVA procedure is for the debtor to formulate repayment proposals with an Insolvency Practitioner acting as "nominee" and draw up a detailed repayment scheme for presentation to the creditors. To buy time for this work to be done, the debtor can apply to the court for an interim order (s.253). The interim order lasts for 14 days initially (s.255(6)) and allows the nominee time to prepare a report for the court on the IVA proposal. Section 252(2) provides that: *"An interim order has the effect that, during the period for which it is in force: . . . b) no other proceedings, and no execution or other legal process, may be commenced or continued against the debtor or his property except with the leave of the court."* Under s.254 the court may similarly stay any action, execution or other legal process against the debtor whilst an interim order application is pending.

The effect of interim orders has been explored in a number of cases most recently *In Re: A Debtor (Nos. 13A & 14A-IO-1995)* (1995) 1 WLR 1127. The judgment is a useful summary of the argument that has taken place on the interpretation of the phrases "*no other proceedings . . . or other legal process*" (see 4.1.2). It will be seen that the protection offered by interim orders is quite severely circumscribed and a range of remedies are not affected by the making of such an order. However once a voluntary arrangement is made all creditors are bound by it (s.260(2)). Enforcement could not then continue and, for instance, to proceed with an execution would be malicious and wrongful (see 5.2 and *Phillips* v. *General Omnibus Co* (1880) 50 LJQB 112; *Seaton* v. *Lord Deerhurst* [1895] 1 QB 853).

Bankruptcy Whilst a petition is pending the bankruptcy court may, on application from the debtor (or presumably, any other interested party), stay any "action, execution or other legal process" against the property or person of the debtor (s.285(1)). Property includes goods, chattels and money (s.436). Equally a court where a case is taking place against the debtor, for instance a magistrates' court dealing with a liability order application, may stay proceedings or allow them to continue on terms (s.285(2)). In short, court action may be prevented whether in a civil court or criminal court, but the court cannot inhibit distraint, though it is likely to be effected by the "three month rule" (see 4.6).

Enforcement after a bankruptcy order is made is dealt with primarily by s.285(3).

Subject to ss.346/347 (see later for details of these special rules on execution and distress for rent) no creditor whose debt is provable in the bankruptcy may have any remedy or take any steps against the person or property of the bankrupt. The effect of this is to completely bar enforcement of an existing debt. As for other and future debts, see 4.4.4.

Administration orders When any county court is notified of an administration order application by another court, proceedings against the person in that court are stayed. Once an administration order is by a county court made, no creditor included on the order can take any action against the person or property of the debtor except with leave of the court and on such terms as may be imposed (s.114 CCA). This also applies to any creditor initially listed on the debtor's application, even though their debt is not subsequently included in the order because the court decided that it should be excluded. These creditors too will need leave of court before being able to enforce even though they are not being paid through the Administration Order. This will particularly effect local taxes and fines which are often excluded after objections by the local authority or magistrates' court. There are a couple of exceptions to this as detailed later.

4.1.2 What are proceedings?

Individual Voluntary Arrangements During interim orders execution by civil court bailiffs is specifically stayed. Magistrates' courts would seem to need leave to issue distraint warrants. In respect of local taxes and child support maintenance it would seem that obtaining the initial liability order needed for enforcement of these debts would certainly need leave of court (see *Re: Smith* (1990) 2 AC 215). This being the case distraint is probably prevented as a result. There is no modern authority on this, but cases based on a right of distraint under a warrant issued by the magistrates suggest that such levies will be regarded as "legal process" and will accordingly require leave. See *ex parte Hill, In Re: Roberts* [1877] 6 Ch D 63 in which a gas company levying distress under a justice's warrant was held to be enforcing a form of execution by way of legal process. The modern liability order permits enforcement of the sum due by the means permitted by the regulations, but seems sufficiently analogous to mean that the older case law still applies.

Bankruptcy As described at 4.1.1, a bankruptcy order has various detailed effects which are examined in detail there.

*4.1.3 What are **not** proceedings?*

As no court action is required for distraint for rent, income tax and VAT it has been held that they are not legal process or proceedings and thus they may continue uninhibited despite an interim order or bankruptcy petition. For instance in *Mc Mullen & Sons* v. *Cerrone* [1994] 1 BCLC 152 the court considered s.252(2)(b) and held that distress for rent was not covered as it is a self help, non-judicial remedy. It is however understood that Crown departments generally choose not to distrain in such circumstances.

4.2 Special exceptions to stays

In some forms of company insolvency the coverage of stays of execution is more extensive, or can be subject to specific exemptions in certain circumstances.

4.2.1 Company Administration Orders

Under s.10 when a petition for an administration order is presented, and until the order is made or dismissed, no proceedings, execution or other legal process may be commenced or continued, and no distraint may be levied. Under s.11(3)(d) when a company administration order is made, no execution or distress can occur except with the leave of the court and subject to its terms or with the administrator's consent. All bailiffs' actions are therefore prevented.

4.2.2 Windings up

An important general point to note is that the wording relating to enforcement against insolvent companies differs from that dealing with other debtors (contrast what follows with the case for bankruptcy at 4.1.1). Reference is made to any "proceeding" against the company. It has been held that this word includes distraint. A number of decisions, culminating in *Re: Memco* (1986) Ch 86, have expressed discomfort that distraint should be regarded as an "*action or proceeding*" under ss.126 and 130, but have felt bound by the long line of authority. To explain the difference between this and the effect of IVAs and bankruptcy orders we may note that the word used is "proceeding" not "proceedings". Discussing this phrase in *Re: International Pulp & Paper Co Ltd* (1876) 3 Ch D 594, Sir George Jessell, MR, stated that it should be construed as generally as possible. This approach was followed in *Eastern Holdings Establishment of Valduz* v. *Singer & Friedlander Ltd* [1967] 2 All ER 1192 and it has been held that winding up bars a range of procedures, including interpleader (*Eastern Holdings*) and rates recovery in the magistrates' court (*Re: The Flint, Coal & Cannel Co Ltd* (1887) 56 LJ Ch 232) as well as distraint.

Under s.126(1), between the presentation of a winding up petition and a winding up order being made, any action or proceeding pending against the company in either the High Court or Court of Appeal can be stayed. Also any other pending action or proceeding may be restrained by the bankruptcy court. Clearly this will affect both execution and distraint.

During winding up by the court the assets of the company are protected from enforcement (ss.128 and 130). Under s.128 any distress or execution is void if initiated after the winding up commenced, i.e. after the petition was presented. Two points must be made. First **all** enforcement is effected. There is no differentiation between that for pre-insolvency provable debts and post-insolvency non-provable debts unlike bankruptcy (see 4.1.4). Secondly, void means void to all intents so that the creditor retains no interest under an execution, even against third parties (*In Re: Artistic Colour Printing ex parte Fourdrinie* [1882] 21 Ch D 510). The restriction includes distress for both rent and rates (*Re: Traders' North Staffordshire Carrying Co ex parte North Staffs Railway Co* (1874) LR 19 Eq 60) and, one may presume, all other forms of statutory distraint. However this apparent bar on enforcement is subject to the powers contained in s.130(2) (see 4.4.1).

Partnership insolvencies A partnership may be wound up as an unregistered company. Part V of the Act deals with their liquidation. The effect of such winding up on enforcement against the partnership is that, at any time between the presentation of the petition and the making of the winding up order, the court may stay any action or proceeding against the firm (s.221(1) applying s.126 etc.). Under s.227 the same also applies to proceedings against any of its contributories if the application for a stay is made by a creditor. Also, under s.228 the making of the winding up order will restrict a creditor's rights to begin or continue enforcement against any contributory of the firm except with leave given on application to the bankruptcy court and on such terms as it might impose (*Gray* v. *Raper* (1866) 1 CP 694).

4.3 General exceptions to restriction

Some forms of enforcement by bailiffs receive special treatment in all forms of insolvency.

4.3.1 Distress for rent

A landlord retains the right to distrain in certain circumstances. A limited right is set in statute for personal insolvency. The power to levy against a limited company will depend upon when the distress was commenced. In both forms of insolvency, there can be an ongoing right to distrain.

Personal insolvency During bankruptcy the landlord is granted a limited right of distress (s.347). Generally rent arrears are irrecoverable by distress and will have to be proved for like every other debt of the tenant. However under s.347(1) the landlord may distrain for rent due, but only for the six months immediately prior to the beginning of the bankruptcy, i.e. the date when the order was made.

Where distress follows the order, even by minutes, anything other than the six months' element must be proved for and cannot be the subject of distress (*Re: Bumpus ex parte White* [1908] 2 KB 330). If the tenant goes bankrupt during a rental period, the Apportionment Act 1870 will apply to apportion sums due before and after the commencement of the insolvency, and distress may be levied at the end of the period for any sum accrued due before the bankruptcy (*Bishop of Rochester* v. *Le Fanu* [1906] 2 Ch 513; *In Re: Howell ex parte Mandleberg* [1895] 1 QB 844). If the landlord neglects to distrain and allows goods to be sold by the trustee, the only remedy will be to prove for the rent debt in the bankruptcy (*Anon ex parte Descharmes* 1 Atk 102). For the same reason a landlord who fails to actually distrain cannot claim any priority over any creditor who has obtained some sort of security, such as a solicitor with a charge under the Solicitors' Act (*In Re: Suffield & Watts ex parte Brown* [1888] 20 QBD 693).

If the landlord distrains between the petition and order, any surplus over and above the six months' rent plus costs, or any sums in respect of rent due after the distress, shall be held by the landlord on trust as part of the bankrupt's estate (subs. 2). The trustee may seek a court order to recover such sums (*Re: Crook ex parte Collins* (1891) 66 LT 29). An agreement between landlord and bankrupt tenant not to levy distress on terms of taking the dead stock of the rented farm at a valuation, though this may be beneficial to the estate, cannot enable the landlord to recover more rent than the six months recoverable under the Act (*Re: Griffith ex parte Official Receiver* (1897) 4 Mans 217).

Where a landlord is entitled to claim rent due from the sheriff executing upon goods under s.1 L&TA 1709 etc (see 6.6.1), the claim is restricted to six months' rent (subs. 6), but the sheriff is under no liability to account to the trustee for any money paid to the landlord before any notice of the bankruptcy order was received (subs. 7; *Re: M'Carthy*

(1881) 7 LR Ir 437). If the claim is received before the bankruptcy, but not actually paid before the commencement, the trustee will be liable to satisfy the landlord's claim as the goods are already impounded on his behalf (*Re: Driver* (1899) 43 Sol Jo 705) or will have to recompense an execution creditor who has paid the rent but not been repaid by the sheriff (*In Re: Craig & Sons ex parte Hinchcliffe* [1916] 2 KB 497). See also *Re: Jermyn ex parte Elliott* (1838) 3 Deac 343 in which an injunction was granted to restrain an action by the trustee against the execution creditor for the proceeds of goods sold to recover sums paid to release items claimed by a landlord. These sums do not form part of the bankrupt's estate and the trustee is not entitled to retain them. However if a landlord neglects either to levy or to make any claim until after sale by the sheriff and the supervention of bankruptcy, the preferential rights granted by the statute are lost (*Re: Davis ex parte Pollen's Trustees* (1885) 55 LJQB 217). For similar reasons, if a rent claim is met by the supervisor of a voluntary arrangement for a debtor who later becomes bankrupt, the estate can reimburse the supervisor for the sums paid (*Re: Ayshford ex parte Lovering* [1887] 4 Morr 164); see also *Re: Humphreys ex parte Kennard* (1870) 21 LT 684 where the Official Receiver made a similar payment prior to the appointment of the trustee. The trustee later sought to impugn this arrangement but it was upheld by the court. If the bankrupt wishes to assign the lease but has rent arrears, the arrears may be cleared from the purchase monies and cannot then be reclaimed from the landlord by the trustee. This is because the estate has benefited by the payment and the landlord has waived the right to distrain (*Mavor* v. *Croome* (1823) 7 Bing 261). Equally money paid by a trader after the commencement of bankruptcy to avert imminent distress by a landlord cannot be recovered by the trustee as again the estate has benefited by retaining the goods that may have been seized and the landlord cannot be deprived of his/her legal rights (*Stevenson* v. *Wood* (1805) 5 Esp 200).

After discharge, the landlord cannot distrain upon any of the goods that were comprised in the bankrupt's estate (s.347(5)). Note that these provisions are intended generally to restrict the landlord's rights against property comprised in the estate. The right to seize property not in the estate, but still liable to distress for rent, such as the goods of third parties (see 9.22) is unaffected. Thus in *Railton* v. *Wood* [1890] 15 App Cas 363 the landlord was held able to seize goods subject to a bill of sale and maintain poundbreach when these were wrongfully seized by the mortgagee. As the landlord can seize any goods on the premises, it does not matter whether they have vested in the trustee or not (*In Re: Lundy Granite Co ex parte Heavan* (1871) LR 6 Ch 462). If distress is issued before an insolvency commences it may be completed against the goods found on the bankrupt's premises if s/he is not the tenant (*In Re: Exhall Mining Co Ltd* (1864) 33 LJ Ch NS 595). If a joint tenant has gone bankrupt the landlord may distrain against the non-bankrupt joint tenant for the same arrears, provided no dividends have been paid in the insolvency (*Holmes* v. *Watt* (1935) 2 KB 300). The landlord may distrain on goods, even though they have been sold or assigned by the trustee, if they are not removed promptly from the premises (*ex parte Plummer* (1739) 1 Atk 103) but it seems that if they are sold to a person residing on the premises they are held to have been removed (*ex parte Grove* (1747) 1 Atk 104). This latter case presumably will not apply if the purchaser is the bankrupt tenant's spouse (see 9.22.3 later).

It is lawful for a landlord to levy distress even though the property is vested in the trustee (subs. 9; *Re: Mead ex parte Cochrane* [1875] 20 Eq 282): such property is not in legal custody so as to be exempt from distress (*Re: Collins* (1888) 21 LR Ir 508). It is not possible for the trustee to obtain an order for repayment of sums raised (*Re: Cliffe ex parte Eatough & Co Ltd* (1880) 42 LT 95). Injunctions to prevent such distresses may be made, but only on terms that the landlord is paid the rent allowable, or that the sum is secured for him/her (per Bacon CJ in *ex parte Till In Re: Mayhew* [1873] 16 Eq 97). The trustee may agree to make payment to the landlord to avert an imminent distress: this will generally give the landlord preference over the trustee's costs, as s/he would have had if a levy had actually been made (*Re: Chapman ex parte Goodyear* (1894) 10 TLR 449). If there are no seizable goods, the **only** remedy for the landlord will be to prove for the rent as other remedies against the tenant are barred by the bankruptcy (*Thomas* v. *Patent Lionite Co* [1881] 17 Ch D 250). Leave will generally be given to permit distress begun before the petition to be concluded. If the landlord is in possession under a distress when the insolvency begins, and that possession later becomes tortious because of vesting in the trustee, the trustee may recover damages in conversion but in deciding the measure of damages the landlord must be allowed what the trustee would have had to pay to obtain possession at the start of the bankruptcy – i.e. the arrears claimed (*Cox* v. *Liddell* (1895) 2 Mans 212).

If the landlord levied before bankruptcy, but the tenant had initiated replevin (see 9.28) and had recovered his/her goods, but then gone bankrupt before trial of the replevin claim, the landlord may not make any claim against the goods now in the possession of the trustee. The landlord's only remedy will be against the replevin bond (*Bradyll* v. *Ball* (1785) 1 Bro CC 427).

Under s.116 CCA a landlord may still distrain for rent arrears due after an administration order has been made. The rent **recoverable** is however restricted to an amount of six months' rent due immediately before the date that the order was made and any other sums due may not be levied – instead the landlord will have to enter a claim in the administration order.

Winding up. Rent distress also attracts special provisions in windings up. If rent distress has been initiated before the winding up it may continue unless the liquidator pays any rent due (*Re: Roundwood Colliery Co* (1897) 1 Ch 373). If goods of a company in liquidation are on the premises of a tenant in arrears, for instance as undertenants, they may be seized by a landlord (*Re: Regent United Service Stores* [1878] 8 Ch D 616; *Re: Carriage Co-operative Supply Association ex parte Clemence* [1883] 23 Ch D 154). If distress for rent is put in at premises rented by a company now in liquidation it is illegal under s.128 (see 4.2.2) if the premises are not retained for the purposes of the winding up (*Re: Progress Assurance Co ex parte Liverpool Exchange* (1870) LR 9 Eq 370). The lessor's only remedy would be to prove for the debt (*Re: Coal Consumers Association* (1876) 4 Ch D 625). The landlord can however levy if the property is retained for the purposes of better winding up the firm (*Re: North Yorkshire Iron Co* [1878] 7 Ch D 661).

Continued possession. If the bankrupt tenant continues to occupy the rented premises, he will still be liable to pay rent. As a result there seem to be no restrictions upon the landlord using distress to collect rent arrears accruing after the order (*Re: Binns* [1875] 1 Ch D 285; *Re: Thomas* [1876] Diprose's Friendly Soc Cases 64; *In Re: Wells* [1929] 2 Ch 269). The landlord's rights against third party goods on the premises will not have been altered by the bankruptcy or vesting (*Brocklehurst* v. *Lawe* (1857) 7 E&B

176). The court will not be able to intervene under s.285(1) or (2) because, as described earlier, distress for rent cannot be described as a legal proceeding. Even if the lease has been disclaimed, if the bankrupt is still in occupation the landlord can distrain up until the date of termination (*Briggs* v. *Sowry* [1841] 8 M&W 729). If the tenancy is terminated by notice to quit by the landlord, the landlord may only distrain for rent due up until the notice becomes effective (*Re: Wilson ex parte Lord Hastings* (1893) 10 Morr 219).

If the tenancy vests in the trustee in bankruptcy and s/he does not disclaim, he may become personally liable for the rent (*Burrell* v. *Jones* (1819) 3 B&A 47). Vesting occurs where the tenancy is not exempt from the effects of the Insolvency Act. Exempt tenancies include those which are assured, secure and protected. Thus it will be business, unprotected and agricultural tenancies and restricted contracts that are most likely to vest. Landlords may therefore prove (or distrain within the limits described) for the rent due before the insolvency, but their rights in respect of rent accruing after the date of commencement are unaffected and the trustee may be liable to distress under privity of estate (*In Re: Solomon ex parte Dressler* [1878] 9 Ch 252).

In company insolvencies a landlord may levy if the demised premises are retained for the purposes of better winding up the firm (*Re: North Yorkshire Iron Co* [1878] 7 Ch D 661). Rent payments in such circumstances are regarded as a debt contracted for the purpose of the winding up and should be paid in full like any expense properly incurred by the liquidator (*Re: Oak Pits Colliery* [1882] 21 Ch D 322). See also *In Re: South Kensington Co-operative Stores* [1881] 17 Ch D 161, a voluntary winding up case, in which it was held that rent due must be apportioned under the Apportionment Act 1870 – the landlord being entitled to prove for rent due up until the commencement of the winding up, and being entitled to levy distress for the full rent after that date, for which the firm remained liable as it remained in possession of the premises for the purpose of carrying on the business under the liquidator during the winding up. Enforcement may proceed as normal in the event of non-payment. See also *In Re: Brown Bayley & Dixon ex parte Roberts & Wright* [1881] 18 Ch D 649, in which it was held that distress could be levied for sums due after winding up began where the liquidator remained in possession, as the terms of the lease will continue to apply.

4.3.2 Bankruptcy orders and statutory distraint

It is stated explicitly in s. 347(8) that none of the restrictions affecting landlords during bankruptcy apply to other forms of distraint. It has been suggested that the leading decision on committal for non-payment of rates (*Re: Smith* [1989] 3 All ER 897) bars all forms of enforcement, including distraint, after the bankruptcy order. However the remarks on this in the case are ambiguous and *obiter* and are at variance with both the statute and other decisions. The actual situation is that most forms of distraint are uninhibited by bankruptcy, being exempt from s.285(3). Bailiffs may therefore legally levy against a bankrupt for local taxes, VAT and the like as normal, regardless of the debtor's bankrupt status. Subsection 347(9) emphasises this by stating that property that is included in the estate may be distrained, even though it is vested in the trustee. It is understood that Customs and Excise and the Inland Revenue will not exercise their rights to levy unless, respectively, the debtor continues to trade and incurs further debts or if other creditors also continue to exercise their rights to levy, to the Revenue's possible detriment.

4.3.3 Execution

Special provisions are made in both bankruptcy and all forms of winding up for the sheriff's officer and county court bailiff levying execution for any debt, whether provable or not. The provisions for winding up (ss.183/4) and bankruptcy (s.346) closely mirror each other and will be dealt with together. The rights of the landlord in execution under s.1 L&TA 1709 (see 6.6.1) will still be exercisable (see 4.3.1).

Statute intervenes in certain executions to deprive the creditor of the proceeds. There must be an execution in progress for the relevant sections to apply – it must not have been withdrawn, completed or otherwise abandoned, for instance due to there being no available goods (*Re: Godwin* [1935] Ch 213). Conversely, there being an execution in progress cannot prevent a bankruptcy order being made (*Rorke* v. *Dayrell* (1791) 4 TR 402). There is also a question as to whether the following provisions apply to partnership goods seized from an insolvent partner. It was held in *Dibb* v. *Brooke & Son* [1894] 2 QB 338 that the execution creditors were entitled to the proceeds of sale of such assets as there is nothing in the sections to show that such joint assets vest in the trustee after seizure by the sheriff. If a bankruptcy is annulled the trustee loses his/her right to the proceeds, which revert to the execution creditors (*Diggles* v. *Austin* [1868] 18 LT 890). Equally if one petition is dismissed, and the bailiff pays the creditor, if another petition is presented the proceeds cannot be reclaimed by the trustee (*Re: Condon ex parte James* [1874] 9 Ch App 609). It should also be noted that the fact that an execution may be inhibited by the insolvency does not mean that later levies by other bailiffs will be inhibited in the same way; a bailiff in possession under a subsequent levy, for instance for statutory distraint, may now be able to remove and sell (*Re: Toomer ex parte Blaiberg* [1883] 23 Ch D 254).

Notice The following rights and duties are triggered by the sheriff receiving notice of the insolvency (*ex parte Villas In Re: Rogers* [1874] 9 Ch App. 432). It will often be important for the debtor, in order to protect him/herself, to ensure that proper notice is given. The notice must be served on the sheriff or his recognised agent, not on the bailiff in possession (*In Re: Holland ex parte Warren* [1885] 15 QBD 48; *Bellyse* v. *M'Ginn* [1891] 2 QB 227). Notice can be verbal (*Curtis* v. *Wainbrook Iron Co* [1884] Cab & E 351) and its service is not covered by the rules for service in the Insolvency Rules (*Lole* v. *Betteridge* [1898] 1 QB 256). The notice should be specific enough for the bailiff to be able to identify the bankrupt as the person against whom a levy has been made: in *Re: Smith ex parte Spooner* [1874] 10 Ch App 168 the sheriff had levied against a debtor who was not apparently a sole trader, but went into insolvency as such (see also *Evans* v. *Hallam* [1871] 6 QB 713).

In the county court notice may be implied if the district judge is responsible both for issuing execution and for making a subsequent bankruptcy order, even though direct notice from the Official Receiver is not received until after the statutory period (*In Re: Harris* [1931] 1 Ch 138). In voluntary windings up notice to the sheriff of the meeting at which a resolution to go into voluntary winding up may be made is adequate notice under the Act (*Engineering Industry Training Board* v. *Samuel Talbot (Engineers) Ltd* [1969] 2 QB 270). Contrast to this *Re: T. D. Walton* [1966] 1 WLR 869 in which notice to the sheriff of a meeting of creditors to consider the possibility of voluntary winding up was held insufficient notice, as the meeting would not consider an actual resolution to wind up. The onus of proof lies on the execution creditor, not the trustee, to show that no notice was received (*In Re: Joy ex parte Cartwright* (1881) 44 LT 883; *Pearson* v. *Graham* [1837] 6 AE 899). If there is insufficient evidence to prove notice was not received any sale is invalid and the proceeds must be returned to the trustee (*ex parte Schulte In Re: Matanlé* [1874] 9 Ch App 409; see also *ex parte Dawes In Re: Husband* [1875] 19 Eq 438).

If a bailiff seizes the goods of a bankrupt in execution, even though no notice has been given, he or she will be liable in conversion to the trustee (*Price* v. *Helyar* [1828] 4 Bing 597; *Balme* v. *Hutton* (1833) 9 Bing 471). Any damages that the trustee may recover may be reduced by the bailiff's legitimate expenses.

Incomplete executions Where the execution was issued before the bankruptcy order was made but the process has not yet been completed by sale of goods (or by receipt of the proceeds – *Figg* v. *Moore* [1894] 2 QB 690), the creditor must abandon the seizure and is not entitled to retain the "benefit of that execution" i.e. any title to goods seized or the proceeds of their sale or to any sums paid to avoid the execution (s. 183(1)/s346(1); see for example *Re: Norton ex parte Todhunter* (1870) 10 Eq 425). If the judgment creditor seeks to continue with execution it is wrongful and malicious (see 5.2). After the presentation of a petition, the court can intervene by way of injunction to restrain sale under an execution (*Re: Tidey* (1870) 21 LT 685). The same applies if an execution creditor seeks to enforce a provable debt after discharge (*Davis* v. *Shapley* [1830] 1 B & Ad 54).

If the execution is complete, the plaintiff may retain the money regardless of the bankruptcy. The onus is on the creditor to prove that the execution had been completed. An execution is **not** complete where:

- the bailiff has withdrawn upon agreeing instalment payments (*Re: Ford* [1900] 1 QB 264) or has re-entered when such an arrangement has broken down (*Re: Brelsford* [1932] 1 Ch 24);
- the sheriff has withdrawn permanently with the creditor's consent on payment of a lump sum (*Re: Evans* (1916) 2 HBR 111) or at the order of the court on the appointment of a receiver (*Mackay* v. *Merritt* (1886) 34 WR 433);
- the debtor pays all or part of the debt to the sheriff (*Re: Pearson ex parte West Cannock Colliery Co* (1886) 3 Morr 157) or direct to the creditor (*Re: Godding* [1914] 2 KB 70; *Re: Pollock* (1902) 87 LT 238);
- successive sales occur under the same execution, and although the first is complete and the proceeds have passed to the creditor, other goods remain to be sold to satisfy the full debt. The sheriff's duty is to go on settling the debt until it is cleared. The proceeds of sale in this context mean the whole proceeds of all sales, not just proceeds of a partial sale (*Jones* v. *Parcell & Thomas* [1883] 11 QBD 430);
- there has only been delivery of the writ/warrant to the bailiff (*Philips* v. *Thompson* (1684) 3 Lev 191; *Arminer* v. *Spotwood* (1773) Loft 114; *Re: Davies ex parte Williams* [1872] 7 Ch App 314). There must be an actual levy. Thus where a second writ or warrant is satisfied from the proceeds of a sale made under a prior execution, the proceeds cannot be retained against the trustee unless there has been an actual seizure (*Johnson* v. *Evans* (1844) 7 Man & G 240). Where, however, a prior

writ is set aside, for example on interpleader by the trustee, a subsequent executed writ may still be valid and entitle to the creditor to the proceeds (*Goldschmidt* v. *Hamlet* (1843) 1 Dow & L 501; *Graham* v. *Witherby* [1845] 7 QB 491);

- the bailiff has simply seized and is in possession (*Cole* v. *Davies* (1698) 1 Ld Raym; *ex parte Rayner In Re: Johnson* [1872] 7 Ch App 732; *In Re: Dickenson ex parte Charrington & Co* [1888] 22 QBD 187);
- a sale occurs that is not a sale under the execution (see *Heathcote v Livesley* [1887] 19 QBD 285), and may be fraudulent (*Re: Townsend ex parte Hall* [1880] 14 Ch D 132 – "sale" to a third party with sheriff's consent) or is not a full sale of the goods. In *Ward* v. *Dalton* (1849) 7 CB 643 the sheriff sold some of the goods seized by auction of lotted parts. Deposits were taken on each lot but lots were only separated from the mass of goods and delivered to the buyers after the bankruptcy order had been made. It was held that this was an "inchoate sale" that enabled the trustee to recover the whole of the proceeds;
- the creditor has only begun to prepare for the sale (*In Re: Chinn* [1881] 17 Ch D 839); or,
- proceeds are still held by the bailiff/sheriff (*Bluston & Bramley Ltd* v. *Leigh* [1950] 2 KB 554).

It does not matter that the execution has not been completed because sale has been delayed by an injunction under the Insolvency Rules (*Re: Gwynn ex parte Veness* [1870] 10 Eq 419) or by an interpleader claim (*O'Brien* v. *Brodie* [1866] 1 Exch 302; *Re: Haydon ex parte Halling* [1877] 7 Ch D 157). The trustee will be able to claim any proceeds of sale or possession of the goods from the sheriff (*Re: Johnson ex parte Rayner* [1872] 7 Ch App 325). If the trustee recovers the proceeds an action against the execution creditor for conversion by seizing goods after the commencement of the bankruptcy will probably fail as the proceeds are a fairer measure of damages than the value of the goods at the time of seizure (*Whitmore* v. *Black* (1844) 2 Pow & L 445).

An execution **is** complete if there has been:

- a sale before the presentation of any petition (*In Re: Love ex parte Official Receiver* v. *Kingston on Thames County Court Registrar* [1952] 1 Ch 138; *Higgins* v. *M'Adam* [1829] 3 Y&J 1; *Young* v. *Roebuck* [1863] 2 H&C 296);
- the execution has been settled by a payment of cash and sale of goods to the creditor well before the bankruptcy (*In Re: Jenkins* [1904] 90 LT 65);
- a return of no goods (*Re: Fairley* [1922] 2 Ch 791);
- an interpleader sale (*Re: Chiandetti* (1921) 91 LJKB 70), as well as normal sale or full payment;
- the sheriff has sold goods by bill of sale (*Christie* v. *Winnington* (1853) 8 Exch 287) and has received full payment (*Loader* v. *Hiscock* [1858] 1 F&F 132 NP).

If before the execution is completed, notice of the debtor's bankruptcy is received any goods or money seized or recovered in part satisfaction of the judgment debt must be surrendered, on request, to the trustee as the right to enforce the security given by seizure is lost and the money is a by product of that security (*Re: P.E. & B.E. Kern* [1932] 1 Ch 555. The provisions refer to the sheriff receiving notice after goods have been "taken in execution" (s.346(2)) – this has been held to mean that the sheriff is in possession of them, not that they have had to have been removed as under s1 Landlord & Tenant Act 1709 (*Marylebone Vestry* v. *Sheriff of London* [1900] 2 QB 591). As s.346(1) refers to sums paid to avoid execution, we must conclude that "money recovered" by the bailiff includes these sums.

The costs of the bailiff, up until notice of the bankruptcy was received, constitute a first charge upon the goods, to satisfy which they may be sold by the trustee (s.346(2)). These costs do not include poundage (*Re: Ludmore* [1884] 13 QBD 415), or the costs of preparing for a sale that could not proceed because of the insolvency (*Searle* v. *Blaise* (1863) 14 CBNS 856; *Rush* v. *Baker* (1734) Cun 130) nor do the allowable costs include the costs of an interpleader as this procedure is initiated by the sheriff without the trustee being a party (*In Re: Rogers* [1911] 1 KB 641). The execution creditor or interpleader claimant may instead be liable. Costs also do not include the execution creditor's costs of issuing and serving the writ of fi fa; the sheriff cannot deduct and retain a third party's expenses (*In Re: Woods* [1931] 2 Ch 320).

The wording of the provisions is slightly different for companies and their treatment is consequently also different to bankruptcy. Under s.184(1) after an order, resolution for voluntary winding up or appointment of a provisional liquidator the sheriff has duties imposed upon him. If an execution has not been completed by sale or by receipt or recovery of the full amount due including costs the bailiff will have to deliver to the liquidator the goods or money seized (or received) in part satisfaction though the costs of the execution are a first charge upon this and the liquidator can sell items to pay the sheriff (s.184(2)). Readers should note that this requirement to pass on goods or money must be read in light of the general voiding of incomplete executions under s.183(1). That subsection states that the benefit of an execution may not be retained. It has been established by the courts the benefit is **not** monies paid to the bailiff to avoid sale. Cases such as *In Re: Caribbean Products (Yam Importers)* [1966] Ch 331, and *In Re: Andrew* [1937] 1 Ch 122 have explored the meaning of the phrase "benefit of execution" and explained that it refers not to the money received (which is the "fruits of the execution") but to the security of the charge on the debtor's goods obtained by the issue of execution. The charge enables the creditor to proceed to complete the execution and clear the balance of the judgment debt then due by removal and/or sale and it is this benefit that is lost. This charge subsists as long as the goods are unsold or the debt is not fully satisfied. The creditor issuing a warrant is protected by a priority right preventing other dealing with the goods as long as the execution is in force. To have this priority it does not matter that the security has not been enforced by sale. As a consequence we must take the reference to monies in s.184(2) to refer to money seized by, not paid to, the bailiff. The situation is different in bankruptcy. Payments already made cannot, subject to the next section, be claimed back from the creditor (*Re: Samuels* [1935] Ch 341).

Note that the goods only need to be delivered when asked for by the bailiff. In the absence of such a request, the bailiff's duty is to proceed to sale as usual (*Woolford's Estate* v. *Levy* [1892] 1 QB 772).

Executions over £500. There are further restrictions on an officer levying execution in respect of any completed execution for a judgment of over £500, including bailiff's charges (*ex parte Lithgow In Re: Fenton* [1878] 10 Ch D 169) that leads to the realisation of money by sale or payment to avoid sale. The execution is affected even though the judgment debt is below £500, if the costs take it over the limit (*ex parte Liverpool Loan Co In Re: Bullen* [1872] 7 Ch App 732). The bailiff's costs include levy fees and poundage, but possession fees may be a different matter (*Howes* v. *Young* [1876] 1 Ex D 146). Expenses not actually incurred cannot be included in the £500 figure (*Willey* v. *Hucks* [1909] 1 KB 760). A judgment is not affected if it has been reduced below the limit by the time bankruptcy occurs (*Mostyn* v. *Stock* [1882] 9 QBD 432). Also creditors may avoid this provision and retain the proceeds of sale against the trustee in a number of ways: by abandoning part of their claim (*Re: Salinger* [1877] 6 Ch D 332; *Turner* v. *Bridgett* [1882] 8 QBD 392); by issuing execution for less than the specified sum of £500 *(Re: Hinks* [1878] 7 Ch D 882); or by ordering sale for less than £500, even though execution was issued for more (*Turner* v. *Hinks* [1882] 8 QBD 392).

If the sheriff or bailiff is notified of a pending bankruptcy petition and an order is later made upon that petition, or if notice is served that a winding up petition has been presented against a firm or that a meeting has been called at which a resolution to enter voluntary winding up will be presented, and a compulsory or voluntary winding up results from this, the sums collected will vest in the bankrupt's estate and therefore must be held by the bailiff for 14 days after the notice, or whilst the petition is pending, in case they should be paid over to the trustee (s.346(3)&(4)/s.184 (3) & (4) and see *ex parte Key In Re: Skinner* [1870] 10 Eq 432). The sheriff can deduct the costs of the execution, but this will not include possession fees after the date of the insolvency (*In Re: English & Ayling ex parte Murray & Co* [1903] 1 KB 680).

Sums paid to prevent sale include any payments made under a possession agreement to the sheriff or payment made to the sheriff when he called in order to levy (*Re: Walkden Metal Sheet Co. Ltd* [1960] 1 Ch 170). However, payments made by a third party to the bailiff to avoid seizure are not effected (*Bower & Co* v. *Hett* [1895] 2 QB 337). Also excepted are sums paid into court by an interpleader claimant subject to trial of the claim in order to prevent sale of their goods – they were unsuccessfully claimed by the trustee as representative of the proceeds of sale (*Shuckborough* v. *Duthoit* (1892) 8 TLR 710). The trustee also has no claim to payments made by the debtor to the sheriff without there being any seizure: such payments made under pressure to buy the forbearance of the sheriff are not paid "under an execution" (*In Re: Hassall ex parte Brooke* [1874] 9 Ch 301 – see also *Stock* v. *Holland* [1874] 9 Exch 147 – this seems to include payments made to avoid a sale that the execution creditor has agreed to accept). The 14 day "waiting period" begins with the day of payment or the day that sale takes place (*Re: Cripps, Ross & Co* [1888] 21 QBD 472) and if notice is received after this period has expired, as payment to the sheriff in such circumstances is vested in the creditor and held by the sheriff on the creditor's behalf, the creditor is entitled to receive it (*Marley Tile Co Ltd* v. *Burrows* [1978] QB 241). In county court execution, if the warrant is transferred to a "foreign court" for enforcement, the 14 day period is reckoned from the date that proceeds are received by the foreign court rather than the court of issue (*D P Toomey* v. *King* (1952) CLY 260). If bankruptcy does occur following notice of a petition, money will have to be repaid whether paid to the sheriff, the solicitor or the execution creditor (*Re: Ford* [1900] 1 QB 264; *Re: Godding* [1914] 2 KB 70). If money is paid over to the creditor despite notice of the bankruptcy, the sheriff may be sued by the trustee (*Notley* v. *Buck* (1828) 8 B&C 160) but the sheriff may in turn sue the execution creditor (*Re: Husband* (1875) LR 19 Eq 438). *NB* the fact that the sheriff is holding a debt for 14 days does not render it a debt, even a contingent debt, upon which a petition could also be issued by the execution creditor (*In Re: William Hockley Ltd* [1962] 1 WLR 555).

Under s.346(6) and ss.183(2)(c) & 184(5) the court has the power to set aside the trustee's or liquidator's rights to such extent and on such terms as it thinks fit. These rights may again be set aside by the court as it thinks fit but a very strong case will have to be made, the guiding principle being fair treatment of all creditors. However where the creditor failed to complete execution because the debtor firm was stalling it (and all other creditors) there was no reason for the court to exercise its discretion in favour of that creditor and allow the execution to continue (*Re: Redman Builders* [1964] 1 All ER 851). Those who have purchased property in good faith from the sheriff are protected (s.346(7); s.183(2)(b)). Under s.346(8) it seems to be permissible to issue execution for a non-provable debt, provided that only property acquired since the bankruptcy order, and not claimed by the trustee, is seized. If after acquired property is seized for a debt provable in the bankruptcy, the execution will be set aside by the court on application by the debtor or trustee (*Barrow* v. *Poile* (1830) 1 B & Ad 629).

4.4 Leave to proceed

In windings up, bankruptcy and administration orders, despite the general bar on enforcement after the order, special exceptions can be made in some cases.

4.4.1 Windings up

Despite what was said at 4.2.2 regarding the effect of liquidation on enforcement it has been held (*Re: Bellaglade* [1977] 1 All ER 319; *Venners Electrical & Cooking Appliances* v. *Thorpe* [1915] 2 Ch 404) that distraint issued before a winding up petition was filed may continue unless there are special circumstances such as fraud or unfair dealing which mean that it should be stayed. The apparent bar on enforcement during a winding up under ss.128, 130 is subject to the powers contained in s.130(2).

Under s.130(2) no action or proceeding can be begun or continued *after* an order has been made, *except* with leave of court and on such terms as the court may impose. This supplements the impact of s.128 on distraint. Levies may not be begun, nor may they be continued with, as the term "proceeding" has been held to refer to *any* stage in the levy process – from seizure to sale. However, as stated, leave of court may be given on terms under s.130(2) to allow enforcement such as distraint to continue.

Where the enforcement began before the commencement of the winding up and unless special reasons exist which render it inequitable, such as fraud or unfair dealing (*Re: David Lloyd* [1877] 6 Ch D 339; *Re: Herbert Berry* [1977] 1 WLR 617) distress may continue (*Re: Bellaglade* [1977] 1 All ER 319; *In Re: Exhall Mining Co Ltd* (1864) 33 LJ Ch NS 595). The simple fact of the petition being presented is no ground in itself to restrain an execution (*ex parte Millwood Colliery Co* (1876) 24 WR 898). Appointment of a provisional liquidator prior to a winding up order is not a necessary bar to distress (*In Re: Dry Docks Corporation of London* [1888] 39 Ch

306). The crucial point is when seizure occurs, rather than the issue of the warrant, so if this follows the presentation of the petition, even by minutes, the levy must be stayed (*Re: London & Devon Biscuit Co* [1871] LR 12 Eq 190). Even where execution is issued before or at the same time as the petition, if the liquidator takes possession before the bailiff, the bailiff should be restrained (*Re: Waterloo Life (No. 2)* (1862) 32 LJ Ch 371).

Leave to continue prior distress may be given:

- if the court feels that the creditor has acted properly and simply been prevented from levying before the petition by the resistance of the debtor (*Re: London Cotton Co Ltd* (1866) LR 2 Eq 53);
- if there are sufficient assets to satisfy all creditors so that the issue is simply whether a creditor should be paid now or later, having otherwise acted correctly at all times (*Re: Bastow* (1867) LR 4 Eq 689);
- if subsequent writs have been lodged with the sheriff, even though they have not been levied, provided that he is already in possession under a prior writ (*Re: Hille India Rubber* [1897] WN 20). The court may in such cases restrain sale until the winding up order is made and then order delivery of the property to the liquidator for sale, reserving to the creditors the same priority against the proceeds as if it was a sale by the sheriff (*Re: Plas-yn-Mhowys Coal Co* (1867) LR 4 Eq 689; *Re: Hill Pottery* (1866) LR 1 Eq 649); or,
- if the levy is for an ongoing liability such as rates, which should still be payable and enforceable where the liquidator retains beneficial occupation on the behalf of the company, particularly where the business is carried on, in which case leave to distrain may be given (*Re: International Marine Hydropathic* [1884] 8 Ch D 470). Distraint for rates begun before the winding up commenced may proceed unless the liquidator pays the rates (*In Re: Dry Docks Corporation of London* [1888] 39 Ch 306).

Leave to continue with a levy may not be given, where for instance:

- the court doubts that the warrant was properly issued before the order was made (*Re: Perkins Beach Lead Mining Co* [1878] 7 Ch D 371);
- forced sale under an execution or distress would be injurious to the company and its other creditors (*Re: Twentieth Century Equitable Friendly Society* (1910) WN 236); or,
- to ensure fair treatment of all creditors (*D Wilson (Birmingham) Ltd* v. *Metropolitan Property Developments Ltd* [1975] 2 All ER 814) as it is the courts duty to ensure that there is an "equality of equities" (*In Re: Dimsons Estate Fire Clay Co* [1874] 19 Eq 202).

Terms may be imposed when granting leave, such as in *Re: Bastow* (1867) LR 4 Eq 689 in which the court made an order restricting the levy to moveable property i.e. stock rather than plant. Where the value of goods seized before the petition greatly exceeds the debt due the court may order the liquidator to pay the enforcing creditor off *(Re: Withernsea Brickworks* [1880] 16 Ch D 337). It is also possible that a sale may be allowed to go ahead as sale is not putting an execution or distress in force as contemplated by s.128 (*Re: Great Ship Co* [1863] 9 LT 432).

Where the enforcement is to begin after *the winding up*, it will only be allowed where special circumstances apply (*In Re: Lancashire Cotton Spinning Co* [1887] 35 Ch D 656; see also *The Constellation* (1966) 1 WLR 272). In the absence of special circumstances the court has to stay or restrain the execution to ensure an equal distribution to all creditors of the same class (*Bowkett* v. *Fullers United Electrical Works* [1923] 1 KB 160). Special circumstances that might justify giving leave to continue with enforcement might be where:

- the creditor delayed the enforcement due to representations for indulgence on the part of the company (*Re: Taylor ex parte Steel & Plant Co* [1878] 8 Ch D 183 or *Re: Richards* [1879] 11 Ch D 676);
- where the actions of the company inhibited the bailiff (*Re: London Cotton* (1866) LR 2 Eq 53);
- where the execution creditor has delayed enforcement proceedings due to other proceedings disputing the validity of the insolvency itself (*Re: Prior ex parte Osenton* [1869] 4 Ch App 690); or,
- where the creditor is secured and is proceeding to recover their own property (*Re: Aro Co Ltd* [1980] 1 All ER 1067).

Exceptional circumstances do not include the fact that the creditor may have no other way of recovering their money (*Anglo-Baltic & Mediterranean Bank* v. *Barber* [1924] 2 KB 410). Where part of the claim relates to before the winding up and part to after its commencement, then the latter debt may be enforced with leave whilst the former will have to be proved for (*Re: North Yorkshire Iron Co* [1878] 7 Ch D 661).

4.4.2 Voluntary windings up

As the court need not be involved at all in voluntary windings up, there is as a result no automatic stay on enforcement under ss.128 & 130 as in compulsory liquidations as described at 4.2.2. However the liquidator may apply to the court under s.112 for such protection and the court may use the powers it would have in respect of a court winding up. The earliest stage at which the court can intervene is after a petition has been presented. If the company plans a meeting of members and creditors to consider plans to deal with creditors, this does not justify the court intervening (*Booth* v. *Walkden Spinning & Manufacturing Co Ltd* [1909] 2 KB 368). The impact of court orders can be as follows:

- all enforcement action against the company will usually be stayed, unless the circumstances are exceptional, in order to ensure fair treatment for all creditors (*Needham* v. *Rivers Protection & Manure Co* [1875] 1 Ch D 253; *In Re: Thurso New Gas Co* [1889] 42 Ch 486). Where the company has been stalling all its creditors it is not just and reasonable to give one stalled creditor, who has not been able to complete a levy before the winding up began, preference over other stalled creditors, whether they had completed levies or not (*Re: Redman Builders* [1964]

1 All ER 851). The court will stay threatened as well as actual enforcement (*Re: Zoedone* (1884) 32 WR 312).

- this general bar includes distress for rent (*In Re: South Rhondda Colliery Co* (1898) 60 LT 1260), statutory distraint (*In Re: Margot Bywaters Ltd* [1942] 1 Ch 121) and execution (*Westbury* v. *Twigg & Co* [1891] 1 QB 77). However, note that in the *Bywaters* case the distraint was only begun after the resolution. In such cases the costs of the execution will have to be met by the creditor and not the liquidator (*Montague* v. *Davies Benachi & Co* [1911] 2 KB 595).
- distraint begun before the commencement of the insolvency may be treated differently – see *In Re: Roundwood Colliery* [1897] 1 Ch 373. In such cases only if special reasons such as fraud or unfair dealing make it inequitable for enforcement to continue will it be restrained (*Venners Electrical Cooking & Heating Appliances* v. *Thorpe* [1915] 2 Ch 404).
- although leave to enforce may be given under s.130(2), terms may be imposed by the court, such as that part of the debt only may be enforced (eg: *In Re: G Winterbottom Ltd* [1937] 2 All ER 232 where only part of several years' rent arrears were recoverable by distress).
- the manner of exceptional circumstance that may lead the court to allow enforcement to continue include deception of the bailiff (*Armoduct Manufacturing Co Ltd* v. *General Incandescent Co Ltd* [1911] 2 KB 143); use of winding up as a deliberate way of avoiding payment (*In Re: Imperial Steamship & Household Coal Co Ltd* (1868) 32 LJCh 517) or distress where all assets are subject to floating charges that exceed their value (*In Re: Harpur's Cycle Fittings* [1900] 2 Ch 731).
- the court may, when staying enforcement commenced *after* the commencement of the winding up, impose terms, such as that the creditor be permitted to prove for the debt plus court costs (*In Re: Poole Firebrick & Blue Clay Co* (1873) LR 17 Eq 268; *In Re: Sabloniere Hotel Co* (1866) LR 3 Eq 74).

4.4.3 Administration orders

The power also exists under s115 CCA for the court, at the request of a creditor, to issue execution against the debtor where it is believed his/her property is worth more than £50. This process will be a normal county court execution.

4.4.4 Future debts and bankruptcy

If new debts arise after a bankruptcy order the situation is more complex. If there are no existing debts proved for in the bankruptcy then the creditor can proceed as normal to commence any action or other legal proceedings save that enforcement could be stayed on application under s.285(1) or (2) – see 4.1.1. In most cases there may be little reason to bar enforcement as bankruptcy does not absolve the debtor of responsibility for ongoing or subsequent liabilities. However if the creditor has already proved for a debt in the bankruptcy, leave of court is required to pursue any debt arising later- see s.285(3(b)). If debts accrue after the bankruptcy order has been made, they are largely unaffected by it and can be collected in the normal fashion. The only possible restrictions are in s.285, subs.(1) or (2).

4.5 Security

Certain creditors are given preferential treatment in insolvency. Those with security (e.g. a mortgage on property) are in the most favourable position, getting paid first from the assets before any other claim is dealt with and, as will be seen, being largely unaffected in enforcing their security (s.285(4)). This is of relevance in distress and execution because of the decision of the High Court in *Re: A Debtor (No. 10 of 1992)* (1995) *The Times*, February 1st which held a bailiff's walking possession agreement to be security within the meaning of s.383 of the Act. Section 383 reads "*a debt is secured . . . to the extent that the person to whom the debt is owed holds any security for the debt (whether mortgage, charge, lien or other security) over any property of the person by whom the debt is owed*". This decision did not create any new legal principle but simply revived an established principle. It could have a profound effect on debtors if the creditor suspects that the person may be contemplating or facing insolvency, as a prompt levy before any order is made would put the creditor in a preferential, secured position. A right of distress in itself is not a form of security (*In Re: Russell* [1885] 29 Ch D 254). It also seems undisputed that a creditor who has both levied distress and removed the seized goods will be regarded as secured (*ex parte Birmingham Gaslight & Coke Co, In Re: Adams* (1870) 11 Eq 204). It would appear that this right of security will be effected where a petition is presented by the execution creditor in question and it will have to be surrendered in whole or in part (see s.269 Insolvency Act 1986 and *In Re: Chidley and In Re: Leonard* [1875] 1 Ch D 177).

Creditors levying distraint against bankrupts have broad powers, which are supplemented by these provisions. Restrictions on enforcement do not apply to secured creditors (s.285(4) and see for example *In Re: Longendale Cotton Spinning Co* [1878] 8 Ch D 150). Under s.285(5) where any goods of a bankrupt are held by any person by way of any pledge, pawn or other security, the Official Receiver when acting as interim receiver or during the course of investigations into the bankrupt's affairs may, after written notice, inspect them with a view to redeeming the security. The security cannot then be realised without leave of court and unless the trustee has had a reasonable opportunity to inspect the goods and redeem. Equally under s.311(5) after the trustee has been appointed, where any goods are similarly subject to some form of security, the trustee may serve notice again with a view to exercising the bankrupt's right of redemption. The notice has the same effect as under s.285(5). By rules 6.117 to 6.119, the trustee may give notice to redeem at the creditor's proved value. The creditor then has 21 days in which to revalue the security and call on the trustee to settle for that sum. If either valuation is disputed, the trustee can require sale. It seems that the effect of these latter provisions is that a creditor with walking possession may be paid even sooner than their already preferential position might suggest. They may be compared with similar powers to dispose of goods subject to security and to clear the secured debt that apply to companies (e.g. s.15 for administrators and s.43 for administrative receivers).

Personal insolvency None of these rights would appear to be exercisable if goods have not been seized before a Bankruptcy Order, after which date the estate vests in the trustee and probably seizure should be before the date of the petition's presentation, otherwise the impounding being challenged as a void disposition. In respect of IVAs, interim orders do not prevent most forms of distraint, so it will be worthwhile creditors seeking to exercise their right of distraint as they will then be in a preferential position for payments and a creditors' meeting could not affect their rights without their consent, as was ruled in the case in question.

Company insolvencies In CAOs no security may be enforced by the taking of any steps (s.11(3)(c)). As taking steps to enforce security covers more than court proceedings (*Bristol Airport* v. *Powdrill* [1990] Ch 744) it would appear to include removal under a walking possession agreement. If seizure precedes a winding up, the distraining creditor will be treated as secured as in bankruptcy (*Re: Printing & Numerical Registering Co* [1878] 8 Ch D 535; *Re: Blue Bird Mines* [1942] 44 WALR 85) and thus will have priority to any preferential creditors (*Re: D S Paterson & Co Ltd* (1931) OR 777). This is subject to any specific limitations such as the "three month rule".

4.6 Three month rule

In both bankruptcy and all forms of winding up special provisions apply to bailiffs levying any form of distress immediately prior to the court making an order against the insolvent firm or individual. The section relating to firms is s.176, that relating to bankrupt persons is s.347. What may be termed the "three month rule" applies where the any person, whether landlord or other bailiff, distrains on a debtor and that person or firm is declared bankrupt or is wound up within three months of the levy (ss.176(1), 347(3)).

In the case of companies if the assets of the company are insufficient to cover preferential debts, the seized goods, or the proceeds of their sale, are charged with those preferential debts to the extent that they cannot be satisfied from the assets (s.176(2)). Any person who must surrender goods or money as a result of this will also rank as a preferential creditor for payment after the other creditors with priority. Their position relative to other creditors is determined by the proceeds of sale of the goods by the liquidator but they will not be entitled to payment from those proceeds (s.176(3)). The provisions do not effect s.128 which voids any post petition levy (s.176(1)).

In the case of levies against bankrupts, any goods seized or proceeds of sale realised, other than any amount held by the landlord on trust for the bankrupt's estate under s.347(2) (i.e. rent arrears accrued more than six months before the bankruptcy or any later rent due), shall be charged with the amount of any preferential debts that cannot otherwise be met from the bankrupt's estate. If the bailiff hands over goods or cash to the trustee as a result of this provision, he or she ranks as a preferential creditor to the extent of the sum paid over or the proceeds of sale of the goods but not so as to receive any money from the sums realised from the distraint.

Chapter Five

WRONGFUL DISTRESS: FORMS AND REMEDIES

It is possible for a bailiff to make a variety of errors in his procedure or conduct. These are classed generally as wrongful distress (or execution). It is important to be clear about how and when these may arise and their consequences, in order to ensure that actions to which clients are subject are legal. It should be noted that special rules and remedies apply to the High Court sheriff and are dealt with separately.

5.1 Forms of wrongful distress

Wrongful distress can take three forms – illegal, irregular or excessive:

- *Illegal Distress* In law an illegality is any act that is forbidden by law: that is a departure from or neglect of the proper formalities. For bailiffs illegality will occur where there is no right to distrain (e.g. the debt has been paid, or its amount tendered) or where an unlawful or unauthorised act is committed during the levy, such as distress at the wrong time, on exempt or third party goods, with forcible entry or when goods not previously seized are removed and sold). The distress will be void from the beginning (*Attack* v. *Bramwell* (1863) 3 B & S 520 and see 7.5.2 on trespass *ab initio*). Even if a valid warrant is levied at the same time as an invalid one, this will not be a defence against an action for illegal distress on the invalid warrant (*Lamont* v. *Southall* (1839) 5 M&W 416).

  Illegal distress is a trespass, so an action for illegal distress is simply an action for damages for trespass to land or goods or for conversion. The measure of damages will be the same as in the ordinary tort action, and the plaintiff may simply sue for damages for trespass or wrongful interference instead of for illegal distress as such. As in all torts nominal damages at least are recoverable for infringement of the plaintiff's rights, but particularly if special damages are sought some causal connection between tort and loss will have to be shown. It is also probable that only such damages as are reasonably foreseeable and not too remote are recoverable. The plaintiff has the burden of proof, but this is discharged if s/he shows that, on the balance of probabilities, the tortious distress caused or contributed to the damage.

- *Irregular Distress* Irregular distress is a creation of statute, and does not apply to all forms of distress (see 10.8 later). An irregularity is anything done in the wrong manner or without the proper formalities. It may be waived or consented to by the other party or rectified by the court by the award of damages for the costs caused by it. The validity of the act done is not affected. Thus in bailiffs' law this offence occurs when the levy is correct but subsequent events are not, e.g. selling goods at an undervalue, sale after the debt and costs have been paid or failing to give proper notices. It is more of a technical offence than illegal distress and as the remedy is only the actual damage suffered by the plaintiff, which may be negligible or difficult to prove depending on the nature of the irregularity, it is likely that this will be encountered very infrequently.

- *Excessive Distress* There is a common law duty to avoid an excessive levy, but for rent it was also codified in the Statute of Marlborough 1267. The offence occurs when more goods are taken than are reasonably required to satisfy the debt and costs (for example an excessive levy occurred when £100 of goods were taken for a debt of less than £1 – *Baker* v. *Wicks* [1904] 1 KB 743). Judging the value of the goods etc must take into account the nature of the forced sale which will have to take place: the bailiff must therefore exercise a reasonable and honest discretion (*Roden* v. *Eyton* (1848) 6 CB 427). Sale at an undervalue does not necessarily mean the levy was excessive (*Thompson* v. *Wood* [1842] 4 QB 493). The debtor may sue for excessive distress even though the sale, less expenses, does not clear the debt due (*Smith* v. *Ashforth* [1860] 29 LJ Exch 259). It is no defence for the bailiff to say that allowance was being made for possible claims by the landlord, for which see 6.6.1 and *Gawler* v. *Chaplin* (1848) 2 Exch 503, nor is it acceptable to say that excess was seized in case unforeseen circumstances might have rendered a levy for less insufficient (*Aldred* v. *Constable* [1844] 6 QB 370). There will be no basis for a claim if there was only one thing to take, even if its value greatly exceeded the sum due (*Welsh* v. *Bell* (1669) 1 Vent 37; *Field* v. *Mitchell* [1806] 6 Esp 71; *Avenell* v. *Coker* [1828] Mood & M 172). There is no basis for a claim based on an intention to seize alone, such as goods being entered on an inventory, as no actual wrong will have been done (*Beck* v. *Denbigh* (1860) 29 LJCP 273). In distress damage feasant, seizure of a chattel whose value greatly exceeds any damage done is legal if its trespass is causing that damage.

  Because they often fail to appreciate the nature of sale at auction and the prices likely to be raised by the process, plus the natural tendency to overvalue one's own goods, debtors often feel that there has been an excessive levy when there has not. Simon Brown LJ in *Steel Linings* v. *Bibby & Co* [1993] RA 27 observed that "*where the allegation advanced was one of excessive distress, debtors should expect a generally sceptical reaction to their own estimation of the goods' worth. In short, the civil courts would not allow themselves to become a ready means of escaping the proper processes and consequences of . . . distress*". Consequently it is fair to assume that successful actions for excessive distress will be rare.

An attempt to levy distress may be as wrongful as an actual levy, and the same remedies will be applicable. See for example:

- *Hutchins* v. *Scott* (1837) 2 M & W 809 in which a tenant in rent arrears was visited by the landlord's bailiff and pressed for payment of the due rent plus the expenses of the levy. Nothing was touched and no inventory made but the tenant paid under protest. Hutchins later sued for excessive distress. It was held that the tenant could not say that no actual distress has occurred just because nothing was taken, no one remained on the premises and no inventory was made. The bailiff, Scott, had said "unless you pay . . . I shall take your goods". The payment made was thus "an agreement not to go through a mere ceremony".
- *Bissicks* v. *Bath Colliery* (1877) 2 Ex D 459: in which it was held that going to the debtor's house, showing him the warrant and demanding payment, otherwise a man would remain in possession, was sufficient seizure to entitle the sheriff to fees. "*It is enough if the sheriff's officer goes down to the premises with the warrant and gets payment. He can only receive payment by virtue of the warrant, which is his authority, and the debtor can . . . in order to avoid the inconvenience of a levy and sale..pay.*" Cockburn CJ went on to say that the warrant was "virtually executed" if both sides agree to avoid the trouble of seizure and sale by agreeing payment.
- *R* v. *Hampstead Magistrates Court ex parte St Marylebone Property Co plc* (1995) Legal Action Sept 1996, p. 21: recently this case confirmed that *Hutchins* v. *Scott* is still good law and applicable to distraint for local taxes. On judicial review a liability order was quashed, thus rendering the distraint issued under it wrongful. The damages arising from this were the amount paid by the company in excess of the rates that were due. This sum was the court costs and bailiffs' fees plus interest.

5.2 Wrongful execution

The general principles of offences described above apply to both the county court bailiff and the sheriff's officer, but because of their special office and status, the detailed position of the latter is notably different.

Sheriff's officers As with other bailiffs, the sheriff is liable for any action done in excess of the authority given by the writ, and thus for any fraud, omission or wrongful act. The legal position of sheriffs and county court bailiffs is the same except that an order of a superior court is in all cases a protection to the officer executing it unless he exceeds his mandate and he is not bound to take notice of any defect or irregularity in the writ, even though obvious and apparent (*Countess of Rutland's Case* (1605) 6 Rep 53; *Brown* v. *Watson* (1871) 23 LT 745; *Williams* v. *Williams & Nathan* [1937] 2 All ER 559; *Barclays Bank* v. *Roberts* [1954] 1 WLR 1212). As a public officer with duties to judgment debtors, if he knows, or might by reasonable care have discovered that a writ was void, the sheriff will be guilty of culpable negligence if he seizes under it (*Hooper* v. *Lane* (1857) 6 HL Cas 443). The sheriff must prove the validity of a judgment debt where the debtor has assigned chattels in fraud of creditors (*Lake* v. *Bellers* (1698) 1 Ld Raym 733). If the sheriff wishes to seize such goods under a writ of fi fa he must prove the judgment, not just rely on the writ (*Grey* v. *Smith* (1808) 1 Camp 387), as the assignment is good except as against the judgment creditor, and the sheriff will trespass by seizing third party goods unless there is a valid judgment

(*White* v. *Morris* (1852) 11 CB 1015). Liability arises here from taking the goods of an innocent party, not because the judgment is bad.

Improper execution is categorised differently to wrongful distress due to the nature of the writ upon which the levy is based. Execution is at royal command, with the consequence that wrongdoing in its performance is viewed more seriously. Improper execution may be either wrongful or irregular, though the distinction is not absolute and 17 Halsbury's Laws, para. 457, n.1 suggests that all improper levies are wrongful, the only differentiating factor being the actual damages that the plaintiff could prove.

A *wrongful execution* occurs in three ways:

- *where it is authorised by neither the judgment nor the writ:* there are many examples of such execution. The levy may be excessive (provided that the plaintiff can show it to be "obviously" so – *Moore* v. *Lambeth County Court Registrar* [1970] 1 QB 560). The execution may be at the wrong address (*Morris* v. *Salberg* [1889] 22 QBD 614; *Jarmain* v. *Hooper* (1843) 7 Scott NR 663) or against the wrong person's goods (*Hilliard* v. *Hanson* [1882] 21 Ch D 69; *Smith* v. *Critchfield* [1885] 14 QBD 873). It may even be because the judgment has been satisfied or valid tender has been made (*Cubitt* v. *Gamble* [1919] 3 TLR 223; *Rook* v. *Wilmot* (1590) 78 ER 465 ; *Clissold* v. *Cratchley* [1910] 2 KB 244) or because there is no writ to justify it (*Cameron* v. *Lightfoot* (1778) 2 Wm Bl 1190; *Parsons* v. *Lloyd* (1772) 3 Wils 341), for example where a writ is executed after it has been set aside by the court (*Belshaw* v. *Chapman Marshall* (1832) 4 B&A 336).

  The remedy against wrongful executions in such circumstances is for the aggrieved party to take an action for trespass (*Hooper* v. *Lane* (1857) see p. 6 HL Cas 443), the measure of damages being the same as if the wrongdoer had no official character. There is no need to prove that malice was involved in such an action (*Clissold* v. *Cratchley* [1910] 2 KB 244). Although wrongful execution is trespass, it is not trespass *ab initio* and the levy remains good (*De Gondouin* v. *Lewis* [1839] 10 Ad & E 117). Such actions will be against the sheriff and may be against the execution creditor if they instructed the sheriff to act in the wrongful manner (*Morris* v. *Salberg* [1889] 22 QBD 614; *Jarmain* v. *Hooper* (1843) 7 Scott NR 663). The sheriff may seek protection from the action by way of interpleader (see 9.25 later).

  However an execution *is* void and *is* trespass *ab initio* if the debt was paid (*Clissold* v. *Cratchley* above) and the court may set the execution aside. If execution is set aside restitution of goods, or their value if they have been sold, may also be ordered (see "irregular execution" below). A plaintiff can of course issue another writ even if the first is void (*Mackie* v. *Warren* (1828) 5 Bing 176).

- *where it is issued without reasonable cause or maliciously*: a levy is illegal if malice is involved in its issue or conduct (*Cash* v. *Wells* (1830) 1 B & Ad 375; *Pinches* v. *Harvey* [1841] 1 QB 368; *Gillott* v. *Aston* (1842) 12 LJQB 5). Malice means an act done intentionally without just cause, or any act motivated by a dishonest, irrelevant or improper motive. For example an action lies where a person maliciously and without probable cause procures execution to be levied for a sum higher than the judgment debt (*Churchill* v. *Siggers* (1854) 3 E&B 929), where a judgment creditor issues a second writ whilst the first remains unreturned (*Waterer* v. *Freeman* (1617) Hob 205; *Wren* v. *Weild* [1869] 4 QB 730) or where the judgment creditor maliciously issues execution for the whole debt when part has been paid or refuses tender and proceeds to execution (*Gilding* v. *Eyre* (1861) 10 CBNS 592). Execution may also be malicious where it is levied excessively (*Wooddye* v. *Coles* (1595) Noy 59; *Jenings* v. *Florence* (1857) 2 CBNS 467) or where the judgment creditor continued to enforce after the judgment debtor became insolvent (*Phillips* v. *General Omnibus Co* (1880) 50 LJQB112).

The defendant's remedy is to claim damages in an action on the case (*Scheibel* v. *Fairbairn* (1799) 1 Bos & Pul 388), the damages awarded being assessed on the degree of malice proved (*Gibson* v. *Chaters* (1800) 2 Bos & P 129), with an exemplary award possible. In the absence of proof of malice on their part, action cannot be taken against a judgment creditor (*Phillips* v. *General Omnibus Co* (1880) 50 LJQB 112 – an action for detention of goods failed as the "ingredient of malice" was absent). See also *Crozer* v. *Pilling* (1825) 4 B&C 26 and *De Medina* v. *Grove* [1847] 10 QB 172.

- *where the levy is otherwise in breach of court rules or common law powers*: an illegal execution also occurs wherever the procedure of the sheriff does not follow that laid down by the Rules of the Supreme Court or fails to comply with the duties imposed by case law. Thus execution is wrongful if goods are seized after a stay of execution has been ordered (*Childrens* v. *Saxby* (1683) 1 Vern 207; *Winter* v. *Lightbound* [1720] 1 Stra 301) or has been agreed between judgment creditor and debtor (*Veal* v. *Warner* (1669) 1 Mod Rep 20; *Bikker* v. *Beeston* (1860) 29 LJ Exch 121). A levy is illegal if there was forced entry (*Curlewis* v. *Lawrie* [1848] 12 QB 640) or if execution occurred on a Sunday without leave of court having been obtained by the sheriff. Execution is also wrongful if the sheriff ignores the instructions of the judgment creditor (*Walker* v. *Hunter* (1845) 2 CB 324) or if the sheriff alters the writ or warrant (*Hale* v. *Castleman* (1746) 1 Wm Bl 2). In such cases the debtor can sue for damages for trespass with no need to prove malice (*Percival* v. *Stamp* (1853) 9 Exch 167; *Duke of Brunswick* v. *Sloman* (1849) 3 CB 317). Restitution will be ordered if necessary.

  Although illegal execution is trespass it is not void, even if there has been forced entry (Littleton J at YB 18 Ed IV fo 4 pl 19). The court may void the execution but if the sheriff simply exceeded his authority the execution is not automatically void. If the cause of action is breach of duty by the officer, the measure of damages is the actual loss incurred, though the plaintiff should at least get a nominal sum (*Wylie* v. *Birch* [1843] 4 QB 566).

- *Irregular execution* occurs if the rules of court are not followed. Essentially it is distinguished from wrongful execution by the fact that it is concerned with the form of the writ or warrant, not the manner of its execution. Typically some mistake will have been made in issue which the court is able to rectify. As irregularity involves genuine error or a technical flaw, no wrong will normally be committed and damages will rarely be awarded unless malice or actual damages are shown (*Rhodes* v. *Hull* (1857) 26 LJ Ex 265). Damages may be allowed if for instance goods have been sold under the irregular execution (*Perkins* v. *Plympton* (1831) 7 Bing 676). If a writ is set aside for irregularity, rather than amended, an action for damages for trespass may be taken against the execution creditor (*Loton* v. *Devereux* (1832) 3 B & Ad 343).

Examples of irregularity include a levy by an unauthorised officer (*Rhodes* v. *Hull* (1857) 26 LJ Ex 265); an execution which does not exactly follow the terms of the judgment (*Fisher* v. *Magnay* (1843) 6 Scott NR 588; *Phillips* v. *Birch* (1842) 2 Dowl NS 97; *Re: Cobbett* (1861) 10 WR 40); a levy for the wrong sums (*Wentworth* v. *Bullen* (1829) 9 B & C 840; *Davis* v. *Shapley* (1830) 1 B & Ad 54; *King* v. *Birch* [1842] 3 QB 425; *Cobbold* v. *Chilver* (1842) 4 Man & G 62).

The remedy in cases of irregular execution is for the debtor to apply for the execution to be set aside and for restitution to be ordered if necessary (*Rhodes* v. *Hull* (1857) 26 LJ Ex 265). The judgment debtor has the option of waiving any irregularity (*Lewis* v. *Gompertz* (1837) Will & Woll & Dav 592). The judgment creditor may seek to have the proceedings amended.

Proceedings are not automatically nullified by an irregularity but can be if it is serious enough (see RSC O.2 r.1). An order is a nullity if it fails to comply with an essential provision and can be set aside by the court "*ex debito justitiae*" under its inherent jurisdiction (*Craig* v. *Kannsen* [1943] KB 256 CA). Normally the court will correct an irregularity by giving leave for the creditor to amend the process (e.g. *Laroche* v. *Wasbrough* (1788) 2 TR 737; *Evans* v. *Manero* (1841) 7 M&W 463; *Re: London Wharfing & Warehousing Co* (1885) 54 LJ Ch 1137). Execution will only usually be set aside where the debtor has suffered prejudice as a result or has become insolvent (*Hunt* v. *Pasman* (1815) 4 M&S 329; *Webber* v. *Hutchins* (1841) 8 M&W 319). When setting aside, terms cannot be imposed on the sheriff, who will be protected from action by the writ provided that it was not obviously void or beyond the court's jurisdiction (*Gillot* v. *Aston* (1842) 12 LJQB 5 and see above). The application for setting aside must be made by summons or motion by the debtor without delay in a reasonable time (*Austin* v. *Davey* (1844) 4 LTOS 160). It has been held one year is unreasonable delay (*Reynolds v. Coleman* [1887] 36 Ch D 453), as was four months (*Pontin* v. *Wood* [1962] 1 QB 594). The setting aside does not prevent the creditor issuing another writ (*McCornish* v. *Melton* (1834) 3 Dowl 215; *Mackie* v. *Warren* (1828) 5 Bing 176).

Restitution may be ordered if execution is set aside and should be included as a term on the same order. If restitution is not ordered a separate application may be made by summons (see Chitty's "Archbolds" QB Practice 14th edn p. 830) or a writ of restitution may be issued on ex parte application on affidavit against the execution creditor. If the goods have been sold, the sum to be ordered to be paid as restitution to the owner should be the sale value, not the real value of the goods (*Robertson* v. *Miller* [1904] 3 NB Eq Rep 78). As to the effect of irregularity on sale see 10.5.6.

County court bailiffs An order of an inferior court is not of itself, at common law, conclusive protection to the officer operating under it. The officer must scan the terms of the order and if, on the face of it it appears to be an order the court could not legally make, he is justified in not enforcing it since he is supposed to know the law and know that the document is a nullity (*Andrews* v. *Morris* [1841] 1 QB 3; *Carratt* v. *Morley* [1841] 1 QB 18; *Watson* v. *Birdell* (1845) 14 M&W 57). If the order is good on the face of it the bailiff is fully protected in its execution – even though aware that in the circumstances it was illegally issued. Wrongful execution by the county court bailiffs is broadly the same as described above for sheriffs. In addition to the general rights to sue, if execution is irregular the court can set it aside in whole or in part under O.37 r.5 CCR.

5.3 Remedies

As already suggested, a range of remedies exist, some under statute, some at common law. The debtor may choose to:

- sue for a tort actionable per se (trespass to land, goods or person, and breach of duty by public officers). Proof of the wrong done will suffice (*Williams* v. *Mostyn* (1838) 4 M&W 145);
- take an "action on the case" where the damages (general and consequential) claimed must be proved. This would include negligence and actions for excessive distress (*Messing* v. *Kemble* (1800) 2 Camp 116);
- sue on a statutory provision, which provide remedies for various offences that may be committed typically under distress for rent. Examples include actions for distress off the demised property or upon the highway – for which see later. It is also possible to sue on the "equity" of a statutory provision – in other words, where an Act imposes a duty but creates no specific penalty for breach, it may still be possible to base an action for wrongful distress upon failure to comply (*Johnson* v. *Upham* (1859) 2 E&E 250);
- replevy;
- pay under protest and then sue to recover the sums paid.

The debtor may only employ one remedy at a time. In *Hilliard* v. *Hanson* [1882] 21 Ch D 69 a man applied for interpleader and an injunction successively: the latter was refused until the first proceedings were decided. Reaching an agreement with the bailiff regarding payment or sale does not debar the debtor from later taking action against the bailiff (*Sells* v. *Hoare* [1824] 1 Bing 401; *Willoughby* v. *Backhouse* [1824] 2 B&C 821). If the bailiff tenders amends before an action is begun, the plaintiff should not get judgment (s.20, Distress for Rent Act 1737).

5.4 Who can be sued?

Normally any action taken will be against the bailiff who levied and any creditor authorising the illegal act (*Hurry* v. *Rickman & Sutcliffe* [1831] 1 Mood & R 126). In illegal distress the action will always be against the bailiff, the creditor may only be sued if they authorised or ratified any unlawful act by their agent (*Gauntlett* v. *King* (1857) 3 CBNS 59 – see 12.1.2 later). If such authorisation or ratification has been given then, to cite Tindal CJ in *Wilson* v. *Tumman* (1843) 6 M&G 236: "all who procure a trespass to be done are trespassers themselves". The situation is different in execution because of the special liability of the sheriff. Special rules also exist for magistrates' distress.

5.4.1 Sheriffs' liability

The sheriff is an agent of the plaintiff and must execute a writ if it is regular, dealing with writs in the order in which they were received (*Dennis* v. *Whetham* (1874) LR 9 QB 345). The sheriff is liable for damages to the creditor if he does not follow this procedure (*Smalcomb* v. *Buckingham* (1697) 12 Mod Rep 146) or if he executes with unreasonable delay or negligence (*Re: Essex Sheriff, Terrell* v. *Fisher* (1862) 10 WR 796) or fails to levy at all (*Pitcher* v. *King* [1844] 5 QB 758). However the sheriff also has duties to the debtor, the debtor's trustee in bankruptcy and to the debtor's landlord, and is generally liable for any act not covered by the authority of the writ or warrant which would by itself be trespass or conversion (*Re: A Debtor (No. 2 of 1977)* (1979) 1 WLR 956). Thus the sheriff is not merely liable for putting the execution process in train, he is absolutely liable for every aspect of his subordinates' conduct (*Ackworth* v. *Kempe* [1778] 99 ER 30; *Underhill* v. *Wilson* [1830] 6 Bing 697). If the sheriff seizes the wrong goods under a valid warrant he acts on behalf of the court not the execution creditor (*Wilson* v. *Tumman* (1843) 6 M&G 236; *Woollen* v. *Wright* (1862) 1 H&C 354). The sheriff will be liable to an action even if the execution creditor's solicitor directs him to seize particular goods. It is not within the solicitor's authority to instruct the sheriff how to perform his duty and an innocent execution creditor is not liable for torts arising from verbal instructions given to the bailiff (as opposed to directions on the writ itself) (*Smith* v. *Keal* [1882] 9 QBD 352; and contrast *Jarman* v. *Hooper* (1843) C Man & G 827)

Anything done illegally is imputable to the sheriff as if it was done as part of the execution or was purported to be part of the execution – for example, the sheriff was liable for false imprisonment where the bailiff arrested a debtor in the absence of sufficient goods for seizure under a fi fa (*Smart* v. *Hutton* (1833) 8 A&E 568n). The sheriff will be liable for any act done in purported exercise of the officer's duty, even if it is contrary to instructions (*Scarfe* v. *Halifax* (1840) 7 M&W 288 at 290). Any deputy appointed by the sheriff's officer is also the sheriff's responsibility (*Gregory* v. *Cotterell* (1855) 5 E&B 571 – sheriff liable when goods were seized after payment). The sheriff is liable despite the fact that there is no proof that the act or omission has been ratified (*Saunderson* v. *Baker & Martin* (1772) 3 Wils 309 – third party goods were seized under the writ). The sheriff can be sued for wrongfully retaining possession of goods after the true facts of ownership become apparent (*Dunstan* v. *Patterson* (1857) 2 CBNS 495) though if the original seizure arises from misrepresentation by the owner, s/he may be estopped from suing (see also *Price* v. *Harwood* (1811) 3 Camp 108). If a person is silent upon a mistake in process, they may be assumed to have acquiesced to it (*Fisher* v. *Magnay* (1843) 12 LJCP 276) and may be estopped from any remedy. However if the third party protests against the mistaken execution, the sheriff will be liable for any consequent damages (*Walley* v. *M'Connell* [1849] 13 QBD 903) even where the protest is accompanied by a payment to prevent execution (*Baron De Mesnil* v. *Dakin* [1867] 3 QB 18). That money is paid under duress and can be recovered by an action for money had and received – see later.

The sheriff is not liable if the action of bailiff is not under the colour of the writ or done in pretended execution of it and is quite outside his duty and is not done for the purpose of executing the warrant (*Woods* v. *Finnis* (1852) 7 Ex 363; *Smith* v. *Pritchard* (1849) 8 CB 565). The sheriff is not liable if the bailiff acts after the warrant has been withdrawn (*Brown* v. *Copley* (1844) 8 Scott NR 350). If a person persuades a bailiff to act contrary to his duty, he cannot later complain about that particular breach of duty but the sheriff has a general responsibility in the matter (*Taylor* v. *Richardson* (1800) 8

TR 505) and thus may be sued for any other misconduct by which the plaintiff suffered damage (*Cook* v. *Palmer* (1827) 6 B&C 739; *Botten* v. *Tomlinson* (1847) 16 LJCP 138; *Crowder* v. *Long* (1828) 8 B&C 598). Thus, where the debtor persuaded the bailiff not to advertise and to delay the sale this interference did not bar an action for damages arising from the negligent conduct of the sale leading to disposal at an undervalue (*Wright* v. *Child* [1866] 1 Ex 358). The sheriff is not liable for criminal acts committed without his authority (*Woodgate* v. *Knatchbull* (1787) 2 TR 148).

Sheriffs' officers are also liable for damages for their wrongful acts. It will be necessary to prove that the sheriff authorised the conduct complained of, so merely showing that the bailiff is bound to the sheriff is not enough (*Drake* v. *Sikes* (1797) 7 TR 113); the original warrant will have to be produced or proved (*Snowballe* v. *Goodricke* (1833) 4 B&Ad 541). Notice of certain facts to the sheriff, such as setting aside of a writ, is notice to the sheriff's officers too, so that they will also be liable for any wrongful act that occurs (*Belshaw* v. *Chapman Marshall* (1832) 4 B&A 336).

Under s.29(2) Sheriffs Act 1887 it is an offence for either a sheriff, under-sheriff, sheriff's officer or bailiff to breach any of the provisions of the Act, or be guilty of any wrongful act or neglect or default in the execution of their office. This will clearly include any wrongful levy of execution as well as making improper charges in violation of s.20 of the Act (for which see 11.3.4). Any such offence may be punished as a misdemeanour (s.29(1)) or as contempt of the Supreme Court (s.29(5)).

The debtor or other aggrieved person also has a personal remedy in that they may sue under s.29(2) in the High Court. The Court may order the officer to forfeit a penalty of £200 and pay all damages suffered by the person aggrieved (presumably to be assessed as in trespass) plus the costs occasioned by the complaint. Proceedings should be commenced no later than two years after the alleged offence (s.29(7)). The court may stay any proceedings and order the offence be dealt with by other means (s.29(8)). See for example *Bagge* v. *Whitehead* [1892] 2 QB 355 CA in which the debtor sued the sheriff for failing to exempt from seizure the basic wearing apparel, bedding and tools of the trade protected by statute. It was held in this case that the sheriff was not liable for the £200 penalty as only the officer guilty of an illegal act can be subject to the forfeit. However general damages were awarded at common law. Lopes J held "*Acts done criminaliter are alone dealt with by s.29, not acts done civiliter, in respect of which the remedy against the sheriff remains the same as before the Act.*"

5.4.2 *County court liability*

nature of the liability of county court district judges and bailiffs is set out in Part CCA and is modelled largely on sheriffs' liability and partly on constables' ity.

ıder s.123 every district judge is responsible for the acts of bailiffs appointed to assist him just as a sheriff is responsible for acts of officers, e.g. the district judge is responsible if execution is against the wrong person. These provisions have been explored in several cases. In *Burton* v. *Le Gros* [1864] 34 LJQB 91 it was held that the high bailiff (now district judge) in a county court is liable to the same extent as the sheriff for the wrongful acts of any bailiff or persons employed by them, so that the high bailiff could be sued if the bailiff executing the warrant failed to follow the procedure laid down in the County Court Rules. See 5.4.1 on sheriff's liability. Whilst the position of the high bailiff/district judge has been said to be that of standing in the place of the sheriff in terms of all relevant legislation (*Bennett* v. *Powell* (1855) 3 Drew 326) caution must be exercised as the county court office is a creation of statute and "it is fallacious to liken a high bailiff in all respects to a sheriff " (per Smith J in *Thomas* v. *Peek* [1888] 20 QBD 727 at 728). Although this responsibility is created by statute, the district judge will also be liable under common law, like the sheriff, and can be sued by anyone injured by the bailiff's failure to carry out his statutory duties. Thus in *Watson* v. *White* [1896] 2 QB 9 it was held that an action will lie against the district judge at the party aggrieved by neglect in the performance of his duties, notwithstanding the powers of the judge, under s.124 CCA, to order the bailiff to pay damages. As s.124 is only concerned with providing a summary remedy to judgment creditors aggrieved by the bailiff's actions (see for instance *Domine* v. *Grimsdall* [1937] 2 All ER 119), the continued existence of the common law remedy is beneficial to other parties.

There are limits on a district judge's liability. The district judge of a court where a warrant is issued cannot be liable for the wrongful acts of a bailiff in a "foreign" court in executing the warrant (*Smith* v. *Pritchard* (1849) 8 CB 565) – even though a bailiff from the issuing court may assist in the wrongful execution. *Smith* v. *Pritchard* shows also that the district judge is responsible only for acts done under the supposed authority of the warrant, such as forced entry, but not unassociated acts such as assault.

Further under s.126 a person cannot take action against the bailiff for anything done in obedience to the warrant unless demand in writing for inspection of warrant is made at the bailiff's office and the bailiff refuses or neglects to comply within six days. The bailiff shall not have judgment made against him if the warrant is produced at the trial, despite any defect or irregularity in it. Compare the Constables Protection Act 1750 s.6 at 5.4.4. This protection was examined in *Aspey* v. *Jones* (1884) 54 LJQB 98 which confirmed that both the district judge and the bailiff are protected,even though there may have been no jurisdiction for the judge to have made the order upon which the warrant is based. If the action is for the mere fact of seizure (not its mode) and if this was done in conformity to the warrant and if this is produced and is regular, the officers are protected. See also *Dews* v. *Riley* (1851) 11 CB 434: the bailiff or clerk of the court is a mere ministerial officer and if they act in performance of a duty placed upon them by statute, such as enforcing a warrant, they are not liable for trespass even if the order being enforced is bad; see also *Andrews* v. *Morris* [1841] 1 QB 3.

5.4.3 Justices' liability

In the case of magistrates' court distress the scope for action against justices is limited because of the effect of ss.44, 45 Justices of the Peace Act 1979. Under s.44 justices may not be sued for any act or ommission in the execution of their duty in respect of any matter within their jurisdiction. This is despite negligence on their part (*Everett* v. *Griffiths* [1921] AC 631), informality (*Ratt* v. *Parkinson* [1851] 15 JP 356) or irregularity (*Bott* v. *Ackroyd* [1859] 23 JP 661). Even when the justices act beyond their jurisdiction, any act or ommission in purported execution of their duty may only be the subject of an action if done in bad faith (s.45). Acting in excess of jurisdiction thus may not be actionable if it is the result of an error or misdirection – for instance, for lack of sufficient evidence (*Palmer* v. *Crone* [1927] 1 KB 804; *R.* v. *Cardiff Justices ex parte Salter* (1985) 149 JP 721). Under s.50 of the Act the High Court or county court may set aside with costs any action wrongly brought against a justice of the peace.

5.4.4 Constables' and other officers' liability

Constables or other officers enforcing a warrant issued by justices have a duty to act strictly according to the terms of the warrant. If they do not they can be sued. However if the officer acts in obedience to the warrant, s/he has a good defence to any action in tort as s/he is protected by s.6 Constables Protection Act 1750. Provided that he or she complies within six days with any written demand for sight of or an opportunity to copy the warrant, the officer will not face judgment as a result of any defect in the justices' jurisdiction. If the officer complies with the demand for the warrant the justices must be sued as co-defendants and judgment cannot be given against the officer for any defect in the justices' jurisdiction. The officer merely needs to produce the warrant at the trial to be entitled to judgment in his/her favour. As already described, it may be very difficult to enter any judgment for trespass or conversion against justices nowadays, though if a judgment is entered against them, even though the case is dismissed against the constable or officer, costs can be awarded against the justices. If no demand for a copy of the warrant is made, the constable may be protected from damages for seizing goods under an illegal distress warrant (*Palmer* v. *Crone* [1927] 1 KB 804). A constable is under a duty to enforce a justices' warrant, even though it is known to be defective, so resisting the execution can be an offence (*R.* v. *Royds ex parte Sidney* (1860) 1 QSCR 8; *R.* v. *Rapay* (1902) 7 CCC 170) and the proper procedure will be to challenge the magistrates' jurisdiction following the procedure under the 1750 Act.

Section 6 has been held to apply to any person acting by order of a constable (*Jones* v. *Chapman* (1845) 14 M&W 124) and to any "officer", not just a constable, enforcing a magistrates' warrant. Thus "all inferior officers" enforcing a warrant issued for rates are entitled to protection in any action, for instance for conversion (*Lyons* v. *Golding* (1829) 3 C&P 586) – but not replevin (*Milward* v. *Caffin* (1779) 2 Wm Bl 1330; *Fletcher* v. *Williams* (1805) 6 East 283), where the validity of the warrant is disputed (*Harper* v. *Carr* (1797) 7 TR 270; see also *Nutting* v. *Jackson* (1773) Bull NP 24). Today it will probably not be possible to count distraint issued under liability orders for local taxes and child support maintenance as equivalent to distress warrants issued for rates by justices under previous legislation. As a result the 1750 Act will no longer relevant to such bailiffs and will only apply to those enforcing magistrates' orders for fines, maintenance and civil debts by distress.

For details of the nature of the demand, see *Clark* v. *Woods* [1848] 2 Ex 395; *Jory* v. *Orchard* (1799) 2 B&P 39. A demand is not invalid because it requires compliance in less than six days (*Collins* v. *Rose* (1839) 5 M&W 194). The person charged with execution of the warrant must receive it, not a subordinate (*Clarke* v. *Davey* (1820) 4 Moo 465). If the officer refuses or neglects to comply with the demand, action may be begun immediately, but if it is delayed, the constable may still comply before the writ or summons is issued (*Jones* v. *Vaughan* (1804) 5 East 445). A substantial rather than literal compliance with the section may be sufficient to protect the officer (*Atkins* v. *Kilby* (1840) 11 Ad & El 777).

A distinction needs to be made between cases where an action may lie against the justices for exceeding their jurisdiction and actions against the officer for exceeding the authority of the warrant (*Milton* v. *Green* (1804) 5 East 233). Thus in an action against the bailiffs for a wrongful and malicious excessive distress, there is no need to demand the warrant under s.6 prior to commencing action as the bailiffs had clearly not been acting in obedience to their authority (*Hoye* v. *Buck* (1840) 1 Man & G 775). Thus an action for unauthorised distraint will not require prior compliance with s.6 (*Kay* v. *Grover* (1831) 7 Bing 312; *Cotton* v. *Kaldwell* (1833) 2 Nev & M KB 399), nor will an action for excessive distraint (*Stirch* v. *Clarke* (1832) 4 B&A 113). If it is doubtful whether the officer was acting in obedience to the warrant, it should be demanded (*Price* v. *Messenger* (1800) 2 Bos & P 158). A constable is protected if s/he obeys an unlawful warrant, but not if s/he executes a lawful warrant in an unlawful way (*Horsfield* v. *Brown* [1932] 1 KB 355), in which case the officer may be sued, but not the justices (*Money* v. *Leach* (1765) 3 Burr 1742). A constable may be sued even though s/he believes that s/he is acting under the warrant for example by taking the wrong person's goods (*Price* v. *Messenger* as above), by levying excessively or by levying without having the warrant available (see 6.1.2).

The Act protects against defects in jurisdiction, not against defects in the form of the warrant. If there are faults with the form, the bailiffs' protection may be derived from elsewhere (see 6.1.1).

Chapter Six

COMMENCING LEVIES: ISSUE

6.1 Warrants

6.1.1 Form

The beginning of the process of recovery of debt by distress is the instruction of the bailiff. This is typically done by the issue of a "warrant", a written authority from the creditor or court to the distrainor. From the warrant the bailiff derives his powers and rights (*Smith* v. *Birmingham Gas Co* (1834) 1 Ad & El 526). Without a warrant the distress would be illegal. In *Symonds* v. *Kurtz* (1889) 61 LT 559 a person other than that named on the warrant carried out the distress. This was held to be trespass. If the bailiff holds more than one warrant against the same person, there is nothing irregular in seizing under more than one at once (*Robertson* v. *Hooper* (1909) 12 WLR 5).

The form of the warrant will vary from one type of distress to another but typically specifies the debt due and commands the bailiff to seize and sell goods and immediately pay over the proceeds to the creditor. In the case of distraint for fines the warrant must be in writing (r. 54(1) MCR & Magistrates' Courts (Forms) Rules 1981: form 48 – fines; form 109 – civil debts) whilst for VAT prescribed form 823 is used. In other forms of distraint there is no requirement that they should be in writing.

In several regimes it is provided that any defect in the warrant or original order will not invalidate the levy. For instance under reg. 45(7) CT(A&E) Regulations and reg. 14(7) NDR (C&E)(LL) Regulations or under reg. 30(3) CS (C&E) Regulations distraint is not unlawful because of any defect in the liability order and a bailiff will not be a trespasser as a result. Thus a trivial error that does not detract from the general sense of a warrant does not invalidate it (though see *IRC* v. *Rossmeister* [1980] AC 952), but it will be invalid if some important detail, such as the address, is wrong (*R.* v. *Atkinson* [1976] Crim LR 307 CA). Damages cannot be claimed for a wrongly calculated sum (*Bavin* v. *Hutchinson* (1862) 6 LT 504).

It is worth noting that many magistrates' courts neglect to correctly issue warrants because they only enter the name of a firm of bailiffs rather than named employees. However, s.78(1) MCA provides that a warrant is not void because of any defect so long as it states that the sum has been adjudged to be paid. It would therefore not be possible for the bailiff to be sued for trespass (*Price* v. *Messenger* (1800) 2 Bos & Pull 158) however the defendant can claim any special damages caused by the defect in the warrant (s.78(3)). A similar provision relates to defects in other court process (s.123) and the guidance in "Stone's Justices Manual" is that a minor error that does no injustice should be disregarded.

6.1.2 Production of warrant

There is no right for the debtor to see a distress warrant, unlike a police search warrant, and no duty for the bailiff to show it (*Buller's Case* (1587) 1 Leon 50) but in

Symonds v. *Kurtz* (1889) 61 LT 559 the court held that it is a general principle of law that every person whose home is entered is entitled to know the authority under which this is done and be able to see whether that authority is followed.

It has been held that at common law a constable enforcing a magistrates' arrest warrant can be sued for an illegal act not in execution of his duty by failing to have the warrant with him when levying, as he should be able to produce his authority if required (*Galliard* v. *Laxton* (1862) 2 B&S 363; *Codd* v. *Cabe* (1876) 1 Ex D 352). The warrant does not have to be in the officer's physical possession provided that it is under his control and can be easily and quickly produced – for instance in a vehicle parked close by (*R.* v. *Purdy* (1974) 3 WLR 367). It is not acceptable that a warrant is available at an office nearby (*Horsfield* v. *Brown* [1932] 1 KB 355; *De Costa Small* v. *Kirkpatrick* [1979] 68 Cr App R 186). This common law rule is explained by Roskill LJ in *R.* v. *Purdy* at 365 – "*Where a person is being arrested on a warrant otherwise than for a criminal offence, it is essential that he should be able to know for what he is being arrested . . .; he can . . . "buy" his freedom from arrest by instant payment of the sum stated on the warrant*". From this it would appear that the same principle is capable of being extended to distress warrants where again the debtor may prevent immediate taking of their goods, rather than their person, by immediate payment.

6.1.3 Validity and Limitations

The debtor may be able to challenge the validity of a warrant of the basis that enforcement of the debt is time barred, or that the warrant itself has expired. The Limitation Act 1980 is, in fact, of limited assistance in this matter. The Act is applicable to all classes of action, which includes any proceeding in a court of law (s.38(1)). This is defined as including any form of initiating process, such as the summons for a liability order for local taxes (*China* v. *Harrow* UDC [1954] 1 QB 178). It does **not** refer to the issue of execution on a judgment, to which special rules apply, nor does it apply to the recovery of taxes and duties by the Crown (s.37(2)). We may accordingly summarise the limitations that apply as follow.

- Execution – in the civil courts it is necessary for the judgment creditor to obtain permission of court before issuing execution where six years or more have elapsed since the date of the judgment (RSC O.46 r.2(1)(a); CCR O.26 r.5(1)(a)). Application is made on notice under CPR Part 23, without the need to serve it on the defendant, supported by affidavit, though the court may direct that notice be served on the debtor, so that the judgment debtor would have an opportunity to make representations.

  Failure to apply for permission is an abuse of process (*London Borough of Hackney* v. *White* [1995] 28 HLR 219) and the execution may be set aside by the court on application by the debtor. The Limitation Act 1980 does not apply to applications for leave to issue execution (*National Westminster Bank* v. *Powney* (1990) 2 WLR 1084) as there is a distinction between the right to take an action and the procedural right or remedy to issue execution (*Berliner Industriebank Aktiengesellschaft* v. *Jost* [1971] 1 QB 278; *W T Lamb* v. *Rider* [1948] 2 KB 331).

  High Court and county court warrants are then valid for twelve months from the date of issue (RSC O.46 r.2(3) & CCR O.26 r.6) but they can be extended, or the permission renewed.

- Crown distraint – there seems to be no limit on the validity of warrants (*Elliot* v. *Yates* [1900] 2 QB 370).
- In the case of magistrates' court orders, there is no limitation placed upon criminal proceedings by the Limitation Act (see *AG* v. *Bradlaugh* [1885] 14 QBD 667). There are limitations on the commencement of civil and criminal proceedings within the Magistrates' Court Act 1980 (s.127(1)) but there seems to be no time limit on the validity of a warrant issued to enforce an order.
- Road traffic distraint is modelled on county court execution. Thus a warrant is valid for twelve months but cannot be renewed (O.48B r.5(6)) and under O.26 r.5 (as applied by O.48B r.5(1)) a warrant cannot be issued without permission of court if more than six years have elapsed since the original order.
- There are no limits on the duration of rent distress warrants but there are limits on when distress for rent can be used. Distress should be levied within six months of the end of the lease as long as the landlord still has an interest in the property and the former tenant is still in possession i.e. the person is holding over under s.6 Landlord and Tenant Act 1709. The maximum time allowed for enforcement of rent arrears is six years after they have accrued (s.19 Limitation Act 1980). Up to six years' arrears are enforceable, even if more than that are due (*Doe d Davy* v. *Oxenham* (1840) 7 M&W 131).

A distress made upon an invalid warrant or unenforceable debt would be illegal. See 5.1 for details of how to challenge this. In other forms of distraint there is no limit on the validity of the warrant.

6.1.4 Binding effect of execution warrants and writs

When a writ of *fieri facias* or warrant of execution is issued, a warning notice is usually sent to the debtor. The purpose of this is to notify the debtor that ownership rights over all goods are "bound in the debtor's hands" from the date the sheriff/bailiff received the writ/warrant (s.138(1) SCA; CCA s.99; for road traffic penalties article 15(1) ERTDO applying CCA s.99). The receipt of the writ is the important date (*Gargrave* v. *Smith* (1690) Salk 220), so a writ received by the sheriff before a writ issued on an earlier judgment will have priority (*Guest* v. *Cowbridge Railway Co* (1868) 6 Eq 619). If a warrant is issued in one county court but transferred to another for enforcement, the time of binding is when the warrant is issued by the second court (*Birstall Candle Co* v. *Daniels* [1908] 2 KB 254). If the creditor loses the right to seize goods because there is delay by the court between the application for the warrant and its issue by the court office, the binding will be held to be effective from the time of issue, thus giving the execution creditor priority (*Murgatroyd* v. *Wright* [1907] 2 KB 333).

"Bound" means that the sheriff has acquired the legal right to seize the goods though, notwithstanding this binding effect, ownership continues with the judgment debtor until sale and does not vest in the sheriff (*Payne* v. *Drew* (1804) 4 East 523). As the property in the goods is not altered the debtor can legally deal with the goods until seizure (*Lucas* v. *Nockells* (1833) 10 Bing 157). However a charge upon the goods has been created for the creditors (*Woodland* v. *Fuller* (1840) 11 Ad & El 859). Note that this charge is not such as will give priority in bankruptcy if there has only been binding, but not actual seizure (*In Re: Davies* (1872) LR 7 Ch 314). The sheriff has acquired a special property in the goods which enables him to sell as officer of the court. Any transfer or assignment of the goods from the date of binding will be subject to the sheriff's right to follow and seize the goods (*Ehlers, Seel & Co* v. *Kauffman & Gates* (1883) 49 LT 806). The binding effect of the writ effects any transaction occurring on the same day – such as a deed of gift, which will be rendered ineffective (*Boucher* v. *Wiseman* (1595) Cro Eliz 440).

The binding effect of the writ is only defeated if the goods have been purchased in good faith without notice of the fact that a writ has been issued and remains unexecuted by seizure (*Samuel* v. *Duke* (1838) 3 M & W 622; *McPherson* v. *Temiskaming Lumber Co Ltd* [1913] AC 145). Alternatively the sheriff can recover the value of the goods from the purported purchaser, rather than pursuing and seizing the items themselves (*Cockburn* v. *Jeanette* (1942) 3 DLR 216). Disposal of the goods other than by sale in market overt will be void (*Giles* v. *Grover* (1832) 6 Bligh NS 277). Binding only effects the debtor's general property, not any special property (s.138(4)(a)) thus hired or mortgaged goods and the like are not bound until actual seizure and may be removed without any fear of pursuit by the owner (*Allan* v. *Place* (1908) 15 DLR 476). Note also that binding only applies to goods and not to other property e.g. money, which are not affected until actual seizure (*Johnson* v. *Pickering* [1908] 1 KB 1).

At common law the binding power operated differently, being effective from the date of the "teste" of the writ, that is, the date it was issued by the execution creditor. It has been held that the common law rule still applies to the Crown (*Jeanes* v. *Wilkins* (1749) 1 Ves Sen 194). This will give later Crown writs priority over those delivered earlier (*R.* v. *Wells* (1807) 16 East 278; and see 6.6.2), though again a *bona fide* sale in market overt will defeat the binding power (*Lowthal* v. *Tomkins* (1740) 2 Eq Cas Abr 380). It has also been held that the statutory binding provisions are only for the protection of genuine purchasers of the judgment debtor's goods, and do not apply to executors of the debtor's goods, in whose hands the property is bound from the date of issue, not delivery (*Horton* v. *Ruesby* (1686) Comb 33; *Rawlinson* v. *Oriel* (1688) Comb 144; *Anon* (1690) 2 Vent 218; *Dr Needham's Case* (1691) 12 MR 5; *Waghorne* v. *Langmead* (1796) 1 Bos & P 571). The same naturally also applies to administrators (*Farrer* v. *Brooks* (1673) 1 MR 188).

6.2 Distrainor

The qualifications needed by the distrainor will vary from regime to regime, as will the remedies for failing to comply with these requirements. In most cases complaint can be made to the employer, in some cases to a trade body (see chapter 12). The county court also has a role in this as it grants certificates to private bailiffs (see 6.2.10). In many cases there is no statutory stipulation as to who may levy, though creditors may restrict themselves, for instance by insisting that only certificated bailiffs levy.

6.2.1 Distress for rent

In distress for rent either the landlord or a certificated bailiff may distrain (*Re: Caidan* (1942) Ch 90). The landlord may include executors and administrators acting on behalf of a deceased landlord, receivers under Law of Property Act 1925 s.109(3) and receivers appointed by the court (*Pitt* v. *Snowden* (1752) 3 Atk 750). If the land is held on trust, only the trustee, not the beneficiary, may distrain (*Schalit* v. *Joseph Nadler Ltd* (1933) 2 KB 79). However if the landlord has simply authorised payment to be made to another person, they cannot distrain (*Ward* v. *Shew* [1833] 9 Bing 608). Unless the landlord is a corporate body, s/he may distrain in person. In the latter case, and most often otherwise, a private bailiff, who must be certificated, will be used, being instructed by the issue of a warrant. If the landlord distrains in person, the sale may be passed to an agent, who need not hold a certificate. If the landlord is a company, the director most hold a certificate to be able to distrain (*Hogarth* v. *Jennings* (1892) 1 QB 907). Distress without a certificate is trespass (s.7 LDAA 1888). The bailiff must produce a certificate and any letter of appointment from the landlord for the tenant or any other person present who appears to be in control of the premises (r.12(1)).

6.2.2 Road traffic distraint

The Enforcement of Road Traffic Debts (Certificated Bailiffs) Regulations 1993 apply the Distress for Rent Rules 1988 to road traffic distraint. Under reg. 2 any bailiffs holding a general certificate for rent can act under s.78 RTA and any bailiff wishing to act under s.78 needs a general certificate. On levying the certificate should be produced to the debtor or any other person who appears to be in control of their premises (r.12(1) of the Rules).

6.2.3 Local taxes distraint

Generally private bailiffs will be used by the billing authority, though some authorities employ their own staff to levy. Bailiffs enforcing local taxes must be certificated (CT(A&E) (Amendment) Regulations 1998 SI 295; NNDR (C&C) (LL) (Amendment) Regulations 1998, SI 3089). The DoE recommends at para. 4.4 in practice note 9 on council tax collection that references should be taken up by local authorities and that they should be given guidelines on their operations. Bailiffs must carry a written authority from the billing authority. This authority should be shown to the debtor if requested (reg. 45(5) CT (A&E) Regulations; reg. 14(5) NDR (C&E) (LL) Regulations.

6.2.4 Sheriff's officers

High Sheriffs hold their office for one year only and undertake mainly ceremonial duties. An Under-Sheriff will be appointed as deputy to the High Sheriff and often the same solicitor's firm holds the position from year to year. He or she indemnifies the High Sheriff against any liability for wrongful acts and then appoints the sheriff's officer, generally the same firm of bailiffs from year to year. They again execute a bond to indemnify the High Sheriff and have various duties imposed upon them under the Sheriffs Act 1887 and common law (see 5.4.1).

6.2.5 County court bailiffs

County court bailiffs are the only bailiffs who are employed as such by a government department or agency. They are civil servants employed by Court Service and are responsible to the senior district judge within each county court.

6.2.6 Magistrates' courts

Execution of a distraint warrant may be by constables, by persons under a constable's direction or any person to whom it is directed by the constable. A warrant may also be enforced by a person employed by an authority of a prescribed class, authorised in the prescribed manner to execute warrants and acting within that area for which the employing authority is authorised to act (s.125(2) MCA). Generally courts employ a private bailiff's firm who will normally be certificated.

6.2.7 Customs and Excise

The distrainor may be any C&E collector or officer empowered by a warrant signed by a Customs and Excise Officer of rank not below Higher Executive Officer. Alternatively a warrant may be issued by the HEO direct to an "authorised person" to levy distraint. In about 75 per cent of cases C&E now employ private, usually certificated, bailiffs. The levy must be executed by or under the direction of the authorised person.

6.2.8 Inland Revenue

The collector of taxes has sole responsibility for carrying out a distraint (s.61(3) TMA) but is normally accompanied by a bailiff. The collector carries a "Collectors' Warrant" which provides proof of identity if required and confirms that the holder has been appointed by the Commissioners of Inland Revenue to carry out all duties in relation to the taxes for which they are responsible. The accompanying bailiff is required by the Revenue to hold a general certificate or a sheriff's officer's identity card. He may advise on the value of goods, arrange for disposal of goods and act as an independent witness in the event of an alleged irregularity or complaint.

6.2.9 Child Support Agency

Any levy of distraint will be by private bailiffs who should carry written authorisation of the Secretary of State, which should be shown to the debtor on request (reg. CS (C&G) Regulations 30(2)). One firm of private bailiffs has the contract with the CSA for the whole of England & Wales.

6.2.10 Certification

Most private bailiffs, or at least senior partners, directors or officers in a firm will hold a county court certificate. A bailiff must be certificated in order to levy distress for rent (s.7 LDAA 1888, road traffic penalties (reg. 2 Enforcement of Road Traffic Debts (Certificated Bailiffs) Regulations 1993) and from 1998, local taxes (see 6.2.3 above).

However the fact that the court has authorised an individual is used by most bailiffs as a way of demonstrating their suitability and probity when tendering for work. A bailiff may be fined up to level 1 for levying without a certificate (s.2 LDAA 1895). Such distress is also trespass under s.7 LDAA 1888 (*Hogarth* v. *Jennings* [1892] 1 QB 907). It is probably wrongful to use a certificate as a means of identification when levying any other form of distress.

There are two sorts of certificate – the *general* which authorises the holder to levy anywhere in England and Wales and which lasts two years, and the *special* which is valid in respect of a specific distress for rent at named premises for one month, though readers will probably only encounter the former.

The procedure for the granting and challenging of certificates is found in the Distress for Rent Rules 1988.

Application Application for a new certificate or to renew an expired or expiring general certificate is by sworn application to the county court local to where the bailiff lives or works. Information should be provided on their employment, their criminal record (though the Rehabilitation of Offenders Act 1974 applies) and whether they have a history of personal indebtedness – a copy of the county court register of judgments should be provided and they must also reveal whether they or any firm with which they have been involved has ever been insolvent. They must demonstrate a knowledge of the law, for instance by their educational or employment record or by having passed a professional examination. The court will not verify any of this information.

Under r.6 the applicant must also provide a bond or deposit (or satisfy the court that there is sufficient subsisting security) of £10,000 for a general certificate and £750 for a special. This security covers the "due performance of the bailiff's duties" and any reasonable costs and fees incurred in investigating any complaint lodged against the bailiff, or in the cancellation of the certificate.

The application is then heard on oath by a Circuit Judge, who must be satisfied that the applicant is a fit and proper person with sufficient knowledge of the law and does not buy bad debts for a business. Most county court circuit judges are not very familiar with the laws of distress and the hearing is seldom a thorough examination of the applicant's suitability or knowledge.

Complaints The court has a general power to cancel certificates or declare them void at any time (s.1 LDAA 1895). However the matter will normally come before the court by means of a debtor's complaint under the 1988 Rules, though a District Judge taxing a bailiff's bill may also refer the matter for consideration of the certificate if a significant overcharge is felt to have occurred.

Any complaint as to the conduct or fitness of a bailiff should be made to the issuing court (r8(1)). There is no set form for this complaint, and it could be oral, but a written complaint specifying the statute under which it is made and laying out the detailed allegations is naturally preferable. The court sends written details to the bailiff who must respond in writing within fourteen days, or a longer period if the court allows (r.8(2)).

A hearing will be arranged before a Circuit Judge to show cause why the certificate should not be cancelled if the bailiff either does not reply or the reply does not satisfy the Judge that the person remains fit to hold their certificate (r.8(3)). The bailiff is summonsed on notice and the complainant and any other interested party receive a copy (r.8(4)). At the hearing the bailiff may attend and make representations, as may the complainant (r.8(5)). The procedure is determined by the Judge, including what evidence shall be allowed, and the hearing may proceed even in the bailiff's absence (r.8(6)).

After hearing the parties, if the complaint is upheld the Judge may cancel the certificate and/or order that the security be forfeited either wholly or partly to compensate the complainant, to cover any costs and expenses s/he may have incurred and also to cover the court's own costs, expenses and fees. If the certificate is retained but the security forfeit, the bailiff must provide a new indemnity (r.9(2)). The court publicises the cancellation both locally and nationally if the bailiff operates outside the district of that county court and the costs of this are taken from the security (r.9(6)).

It should be noted that even if a certificate is cancelled, it continues to have effect for any possession agreement entered into before the date of cancellation unless the Judge directs otherwise (r.9(4)). It will be necessary for the complainant to make a specific request for such a direction to prevent any levy continuing, presumably most conveniently at the hearing of the complaint.

Conclusions The attractions of this procedure to the complainant are its simplicity, and its cheapness, as no filing fees are incurred. However there are a number of possible difficulties. So far as the hearing is concerned, it is unlikely that Legal Aid will be granted unless the potential damages are considerable. Proper representation before Circuit Judge may therefore be problematic for the debtor. Secondly there are very few reported cases on certification complaints to give guidance to either party on the circumstances in which bailiffs should have their certificates challenged or cancelled. This compounds the obscurity and neglect of the remedy. The only known cases are:

- *Re Sanders ex parte Sergeant* (1885) 54 LJQB 331 – a case in which distress was levied by a certificated bailiff but not within district in which the certificating county court was situated. It was held that no offence had been committed.
- *Manchester City Council* v. *Robinson* (1991) 10 Legal Action 1991. The council applied for revocation of the defendant's certificate on the grounds that he had distrained after a suspended possession order had been made in the county court, that he had used invalid forms (thus showing an insufficient knowledge of the law), that he had used his own pass key to enter the premises and that he was director of the landlord company, despite undertaking in his certificate application not to distrain where he was regularly employed in rent collection. The court held that whilst the bailiff may have acted illegally in some respects, his misconduct was not serious enough to warrant cancellation of his certificate. This was justified particularly by the fact that the defendant gave the court an assurance that he would not use out-dated forms again. Whilst it was suggested that the use of the key was illegal entry, only £100 costs were awarded against the defendant.

These two cases suggest that the attitudes of courts is likely to be that the wrong complained of will have to be very serious, and certainly more than a "technicality", to warrant revocation or a heavy financial penalty.

Thirdly the problem of the obscurity of the remedy is compounded by uncertainty as to the extent of the remedy. The LCD has given their opinion on this, though it may well not be shared by local judges. The LCD suggests that certification complaints may be made in the following situations:

- a levy of rent, road traffic or local tax distress (obviously);
- a levy of any other form of distraint by a certificated bailiff, on the basis that the basic rules of procedure are common to all forms; and,

- a levy by an uncertificated employee of a certificated employer, the argument being that a failure to adequately train or monitor staff suggests a lack of fitness to hold a certificate.

The final issue is that the Rules are so expressed to suggest that the security deposit may only be forfeit to compensate the person in cases of wrongful distress for rent, and not other forms.

6.3 Death of parties

In the civil courts permission is necessary in order to issue execution where either the judgment creditor or debtor has died, or any assets of the deceased have come into the hands of his/her executors or administrators since the date of the judgment (RSC O.46 r.2(1)(b)&(c); CCR O.26 r.5(1)(b)&(c)). Application for leave is *ex parte* on notice under CPR Part 23 with an affidavit. Permission to issue execution against an executor is not equivalent to entering judgment against that executor (*Stewart* v. *Rhodes* [1900] 1 Ch 386).

In distraint there are no such restrictions, except for road traffic distraint, which follows the county court procedure. Under O.26 r.5 (as applied by O.48B r.5(1)) a warrant cannot be issued without permission of court if the defendant has deceased and the estate is in the hands of executors or administrators.

In distress for rent, it has been held that if the tenant dies, but his/her executor or administrator continues in possession of the property, the landlord may distrain on the goods of the deceased in the hands of the executor/administrator (*Braithwaite* v. *Cooksey & Another* (1790) 1 H Bl 465; *Bolton* v. *Canham* (1670) Pollexfen 20).

6.4 Sums leviable

Typically the sums for which the warrant may issue will be the debt plus any court costs incurred (see for instance s.35 CSA or for local taxes reg. 45(2) CT; reg. 14(2)(b) NNDR). Two cases require special mention.

6.4.1 Rent arrears

The landlord may distrain for part of the rent only *(Tutthill* v. *Roberts* (1673) 89 ER 256) so rent for individual periods may be distrained for separately, and in any order (*Palmer* v. *Stanage* (1661) 1 Lev 43). However one sum due on one date must be levied in one levy (*Bagge* v. *Mawby* (1853) 8 Exch 641). If there are several tenancies in one tenant's name, each should be distrained for separately (*Rogers* v. *Birkmire* (1736) 2 Stra 1040).

Service charges, water, fuel and insurance may be recovered by distress if they are treated as rent by the lease i.e they are reserved or recoverable as rent (*Concorde Graphics* v. *Andromeda Investments* (1983) 265 EG 386; *Escalus Properties* v. *Robinson* (1995) 31 EG 71). If the agreement includes such items as part of the use of the land, the landlord can distrain for the whole balance due (*Selby* v. *Greaves* (1868) LR 3 CP 594). Though distress may not be levied for the use of chattels, if furniture is included in a lease, rental for its use may be levied by distress (*Newman* v. *Anderton* (1806) 2 Bos & P NR 224).

The rent payable must be certain in the sense that its quantity, extent and time of payment should be known or be capable of being ascertained (Co Litt 96a; *Parker* v. *Harris* (1692) 1 Salk 262; *GLC* v. *Connolly* [1970] 2 QB 100). Thus if a service charge treated as rent is variable, the sum due must have been agreed by the tenant or otherwise confirmed (e.g. by tribunal). A rent that fluctuates is not uncertain and distress upon it is valid provided that it may be calculated, though based on factors that may vary (*In Re: Knight ex parte Voisey* [1882] 21 Ch D 442). The essential factor is that the sum payable can be worked out (*Daniel* v. *Gracie* [1844] 6 QB 145). If there is no agreed rent, distraint cannot be levied and the landlord must begin a court action (*Dunk* v. *Hunter* [1822] 5 B & Ald 322).

In the case of farms and agricultural holdings, only up to one year's rent may be recovered (s.16 Agricultural Holdings Act 1986) unless the terms of the tenancy defer payment of rent to the next quarter or half year after the date when it is due (s.16(2)) and see *ex parte Bull In Re: Bew* [1887] 18 QBD 642. The tenant may offset any compensation due from the landlord (s.17).

6.4.2 County court

Where a judgment is payable by instalments a warrant cannot be issued until the debtor has defaulted on at least one instalment and so long as no previous execution is outstanding. The warrant can be for a part of the debt or the whole outstanding balance. Part warrants are for £50 or one monthly or four weekly instalments, whichever is the greater (O.26 r.2). Execution ceases if the debt and issue costs are paid. If the bailiff is executing a part warrant and is offered more than the sum being claimed, he may accept any amount up to the full judgment debt and costs.

6.5 Preconditions

For many debts, in addition to simple default in payment, other conditions will have to be satisfied before the debt can be enforced by seizure of goods.

6.5.1 Local taxes

Having obtained a liability order for local taxes in the magistrates' court, the "billing authority" should notify the debtor of the order but is free to use whichever recovery method is most appropriate, although normally a warrant is issued immediately to the bailiff. Certainly distraint must be tried before the billing authority proceeds to committal. It is **not** permissible for the first stage to be omitted just because it appears that there would be no goods worth levying upon (*Re: Brown* [1878] 3 QBD 545). The DoE in its guidance on practice suggests that distraint may be particularly useful against self-employed people or those with savings which exclude them from Income Support.

6.5.2 VAT

The process normally begins with the issue of an internal notice that distraint may be necessary. This "distress advice" is issued in three circumstances:

- where a VAT return is received without full payment;

- where the due date for any payment has passed and the debt is over the current prescribed level (currently £200); or,
- where an assessment indicates that a debt of over the prescribed figure may be due. If a registered person fails to make a complete return, or supply information required by the regulations, tax due may be assessed. When notified to a person it is treated as tax due and recoverable, but may be replaced at any time by a properly declared return.

At this stage C&E will normally try to negotiate by direct personal contact with the debtor. If this fails an "Demand notice for immediate payment" is issued on form 891 under reg. 65(1), and is served by post or hand. If the person then neglects or refuses to pay and at least £200 is still due, a distraint warrant will follow. No time to respond to the demand notice is laid down in law, and it is at the local office's discretion. A distraint warrant may be issued at any time after the refusal or neglect but Customs and Excise must wait thirty days after notification of an assessment before executing a warrant, unless the assessment has been notified in the absence of a return, when distress can take place immediately after a written demand for payment (reg. 65(1) VAT (General) Regulations 1985).

6.5.3 Magistrates' orders

If instalments are in default, enforcement will be for all instalments still unpaid. A distraint warrant will be issued in the following circumstances.

- *Fines* – if the court allowed time to pay or set instalments, or if the defendant was absent at the hearing, distraint cannot be issued until the court has served notice in writing stating the total balance due, the instalments ordered and the date for payments to begin (Form 49 MC (Forms) Rules). Otherwise a warrant will be issued on default. Normally a final demand will be served by the court warning that a warrant may be issued. This will normally invite the debtor to seek further time to pay if this is required.
- *Maintenance* – a warrant will be issued by the magistrates after a hearing to consider whether there is good cause for the failure to pay (s.59 MCA). The hearing will follow a complaint made by the spouse or collecting officer. A request for a complaint can only be made at least 15 days after the date of the original maintenance order itself (s.93 MCA) during which time it is normal to serve a copy of the order on the defendant..
- *Civil debts* – distraint may only be issued if the defendant has received a copy of the order or if the order was made in his/her presence and the warrant was also issued on that occasion (r.53 MCR).

In respect of fines, the Queens Bench Divisional Court has recently clarified the procedure that may be followed by a magistrates court in enforcing a fine by distress (*R.* v. *Hereford Magistrates' Court ex parte MacRae* (1998) *The Times*, December 31). If no payment or response is made following a final demand, it is appropriate to issue a warrant without further proceedings. The court has no duty, and indeed no power, to hold a means inquiry hearing when considering whether to issue distress. Such a hearing is only necessary under ss. 82–84 MCA when the issue of a warrant of committal is being considered. Thus *R.* v. *Birmingham Justices ex parte Bennet* (1983) 147 JP 82, which held that if the evidence reveals a 'reasonable likelihood' that there are distrainable assets, a warrant should be issued, must be understood to apply when the court is "considering committal as an alternative". This also applies to *R.* v. *Clacton JJ ex parte Commissioners of the Customs & Excise* (1987) 152 JP 120. In *R.* v. *Norwich JJ ex parte Trigger* (1987) 151 JP 465 it was held that the use of distraint as an option, and the availability of seizable goods, should be considered before committal is threatened: though not cited in *MacRae* the decision must now be read in light of that case. Nonetheless none of these decisions were an authority for the proposition that there *had* to be a means inquiry in every case, even if only a distress warrant was being considered. The decision in *R.* v. *German* (1891) 66 LT 264, which states that generally, before issue, the court may require evidence of the existence of distrainable goods, held no more than that the justices have a discretion in such circumstances.

The decisions in *R.* v. *Guildford Justices ex parte Rich* (1996) *The Times*, May 17, that in every case the defendant should have an opportunity to make representations at a hearing before the warrant is issued and thus there is a chance for distraint to be further postponed (see 3.1.3) on varied terms of payment (and see too *Harper* v. *Carr* (1797) 7 TR 270), must be distinguished. In that case the defaulter had no notice of the possible issue of distress. In the *MacRae* case the final demand sent specific notice of distress. The decision in *Forrest* v. *Brighton JJ* [1981] 2 All ER 711 that the only exception to the debtor's right to attend is where the person is in prison, though there should still be a hearing, must also now be understood in light of *MacRae*.

MacRae also held that, as no hearing is necessary, it is acceptable for the justices to delegate the task of issuing warrants to a court officer. Whoever makes this decision must still consider the circumstances of the debtor. If the court is satisfied that there are no seizable goods, for instance the debtor's only asset is income, there is no need to attempt to levy, and alternative enforcement such as committal may be used instead (*R.* v. *Mortimer* (1906) 70 JP 542).

6.5.4 Rent

A private landlord must obtain leave of county court to use distress against a protected or statutory tenant under s.147 Rent Act 1977 or an assured or assured shorthold tenant under s.19 Housing Act 1988. Leave is not required for commercial tenancies, secure tenancies or tenants with restricted contract. Application for leave of court is by originating application. At the hearing the court has the same powers as it has in possession proceedings to adjourn, stay or postpone proceedings. The court's discretion to grant or refuse the application is not limited, but should only be exercised after due enquiry into any question that might arise and the tenant should be permitted to show a reasonable and bona fide defence if one exists, for example, whether the rent is due and payable.

Leave may be refused if there is a dispute over the amount payable, though there is no need for a decision to be reached by the court on this question at the hearing of the application for leave (*Townsend* v. *Charlton* [1922] 1 KB 700). If leave is granted, it may be on whatever terms the court thinks fit, and as the court's discretion is absolute an order will only be set aside where it is wrong in principle. Thus in *Metropolitan Properties Co Ltd* v. *Purdy* [1940] 1 All ER 188 the Court of Appeal would not overturn an order suspending leave on condition that a lump sum be paid at once followed by monthly payments thereafter to clear the arrears in under eighteen months. The power certainly exists to suspend leave on conditions that weekly payments are made, provided that the whole weekly rent/mesne profits are covered, plus a sum towards the arrears (*Blanket* v. *Palmer* [1940] 1 All ER 524).

6.5.5 Income tax

Under ss.61–62 Taxes Management Act 1970 as amended by ss.152–3 Finance Act 1989 distraint may be used where tax has been demanded and there has been a neglect or refusal to pay(s.61(1)). A taxpayer will be sent demand notes asking for payment (s.60). Non-payment after demand is evidence of refusal to pay (*Lumsden* v. *Burnett* (1898) 2 LR QB 177). If the demands cannot be proved to have been received by the debtor, the distraint may be unlawful (*Berry* v. *Farrow* [1914] 1 KB 632).

6.6 Competing claims

6.6.1 Landlords' claims

Landlords are given priority rights to claim payment of any rent arrears in both execution and distraint for road traffic penalties under s.1 Landlord & Tenant Act 1709 in the High Court and s.102 CCA for the county court and road traffic bailiffs. Where the goods have been seized under a statutory distraint the landlord cannot demand payment of the rent arrears as distraint is not an execution of a judgment within the meaning of s.1 L&TA – see *Potts* v. *Hickman* [1940] 4 All ER 491 where a bailiff levied for rates arrears on a tenant already in rent arrears. The landlord failed in his claim against the bailiff.

The relevance of the statutory right to tenants is that its invocation, by notice to the bailiff, may at least delay execution – perhaps enabling the debtor to raise funds to clear the sums claimed, or might even persuade the bailiff that it is not worthwhile proceeding, if the available goods are insufficient to cover both rent and judgment.

Restrictions on claim The extent of the rent that may be claimed is limited:

- the landlord may be entitled to receive no more than four times any term's rent where the term is less than one year (s.1 Execution Act 1844) with a maximum of one year's rent. The landlord can claim the maximum rent to which they are entitled, even if they were in the habit of remitting some of the sum due to the tenant (*Williams* v. *Lewsey* (1831) 8 Bing 28). If the tenancy is for a fixed term and has just been renewed, no claim can be made for rent due under the previous lease, even though it falls within the one year limit in claims (*Cook* v. *Cook* (1738) Andrews 217);
- there must be an existing landlord and tenant relationship (*Re: Eastcheap Alimentary Products Ltd* [1936] 3 All ER 276). *Re: Eastcheap* was decided on the basis that there was no tenancy between the company and the landlord. Older authority was cited (*Bennet's Case* (1727) 2 Stra 787 and *Carr* v. *Goslington* (1727) 11 MR 414) which also suggest that if the relationship is of head landlord and subtenant, the Act will not apply. There does appear to be an exception to this

in that the landlord and tenant relationship does not have to be between the judgment debtor and landlord as the legislation applies to any landlord of a property "in which goods are seized", so the tenancy may be with the spouse of the debtor for example (*Hughes* v. *Smallwood* [1890] 25 QB 232). If the lease or tenancy has expired but the tenant is still in possession, under ss.6 & 7 of the 1709 Act the landlord may distrain for up to six months' rent (see 3.2.2): however this does not apply to the landlord's claim against the bailiff under s.1 as this only applies to subsisting tenancies (*Lewis* v. *Davies* [1914] 2 KB 469);

- the landlord can only claim rent due at the time of seizure (*Hoskins* v. *Knight* [1813] 1 M&S 245). A claim for any sums accruing after the date of seizure is barred, though if rent is payable in advance and has fallen due, it may be recovered (*Harrison* v. *Barry* (1818) 7 Price 690);
- the landlord is entitled to payment of up to a full year's rent even if a petition for the debtor's bankruptcy is presented subsequent to the seizure and sale (*Gill* v. *Wilson* (1853) 3 ICLR 544) and despite the fact that the landlord's right to rent would be less under the bankruptcy *(Re: British Salicylates Ltd* [1919] 2 Ch 155). This is so because the 1709 Act has impounded the goods for the benefit of the landlord so they are no longer the debtor's goods. This is contrary to the normal effect of bankruptcy on an execution (see 4.3.3 and *Re: Neil Mackenzie ex parte Sheriff of Herts* [1899] 2 QB 566). However if bankruptcy takes place before the sale, the sheriff will only be able to justify payment to the landlord if it was made in ignorance of the bankruptcy order (*Lee* v. *Lopes* (1812) 15 East 230).

There are also limits as to the seizures against which the landlord may claim:

- the execution cannot be one on a judgment for the landlord (*Taylor* v. *Lanyon* (1830) 6 Bing 536);
- the claim can only be made against one execution even if two are levied (*Dod* v. *Saxby* (1735) 2 Stra 1024);
- the section is not confined to seizure of goods that would be subject to distress for rent (*Riseley* v. *Ryle* (1843) 12 LJ Ex 322).

Generally, however, it has been held that these provisions should be construed liberally in the landlord's favour (*Henchett* v. *Kimpson* (1762) 2 Wils 140).

Bailiff's duties. The bailiff is under no liability to enquire as to the existence of rent arrears or keep the goods in case such a claim emerges. If notice of a claim is received it may be investigated, and a bailiff would be wise to require production of a current tenancy agreement or lease to confirm the landlord's entitlement to claim (*Augustien* v. *Challis* (1847) 1 Exch 279). This said, it would however appear that even slight evidence of the existence of a lease will then be sufficient (per Lord Ellenborough CJ in *Keightley* v. *Birch* (1814) 3 Camp 521). The form of the notice is not important, so verbal notice from a tenant would be sufficient. Certainly, knowledge of the existence of rent arrears is sufficient notice to the bailiff (*Andrews* v. *Dixon* (1820) 3 B & Ald 645); though again matters may be delayed to enable the bailiff to investigate where the tenant disputes the level or existence of arrears (*Nowlin* v. *Anderson* (1849) 6 NBR 497).

The sheriff can seize enough to cover the rent plus the debt on receiving notice from the landlord within five days of the levy (even after sale). If a separate levy must be made for enough to cover the rent, this is a separate proceeding for which separate possession fees may be charged (*Re: Broster* [1897] 2 QB 429).

If the county court bailiff seizes the goods of a third party in error they may not be retained to satisfy a claim by the landlord but must be returned to the owners, even though the landlord could have seized them in distress (*Beard* v. *Knight* (1858) 8 E&B 865; *Foulger* v. *Taylor* (1860) WN 220). However if the sheriff's officer seizes goods belonging to a person who is not the tenant, a claim may be made by the landlord as the L&TA 1709 applies to any "goods and chattels whatsoever" on the premises (*Forster* v. *Cookson* [1841] 1 QB 419; *Duck* v. *Braddyll* (1824) M'Clel 217).

Landlord's duties. The landlord cannot distrain as the seized goods are in the custody of the law (*Peacock* v. *Purvis* (1820) 2 Brod & Bing 362) – whether they are in the sheriff's hands or the hands of a buyer from the sheriff (*Wharton* v. *Naylor* (1848) 6 Dow & L 136), but the goods are "in effect impounded . . . for the landlord's benefit" (*Re: McKenzie* (1899) 2 QB 566). The landlord cannot insist on sale of the goods (*Green* v. *Austin* (1812) 8 Camp 260; *Yates* v. *Ratledge* (1860) 5 H&N 249) but he or she can sue the sheriff if payment is not made out of the proceeds of sale (*Henchett* v. *Kimpson* (1762) 2 Wils 140). It does not effect the landlord's claim that goods were left after the execution upon which distress could have been levied (*Colyer* v. *Speed* (1820) 2 Brod & Bing 67).

If the landlord attempts to recover rent due by distraint it is trespass (*Wharton* v. *Naylor* [1848] 12 QB 673). If the execution is later abandoned, the landlord can proceed with distress as normal (*Seven* v. *Mihill* (1756) 1 Keny 371). Equally if the sheriff fails to seize or impound distress may be levied (*Blades* v. *Arundale* (1813) 1 M&S 711). If the sale is fraudulent, the landlord may distrain (*Smith* v. *Russell* (1811) 3 Taunt 400).

Procedure. Under s102(2) CCA the landlord may within five days of seizure, or before removal of the goods, deliver a written claim stating the rent due and the period to which it applies. The bailiff should then levy for the rent and costs as well and should not sell any of the goods within a further five days unless they are perishable or the tenant has requested their sale (subs 3; *Thomas* v. *Mirehouse* [1887] 19 QBD 563). Under subs. 4 upon sale the bailiff will satisfy first the costs of the sale, then the landlord's claim not exceeding:

- four weeks' rent where the rent is due weekly; or,
- two terms of payment where the letting is on any term of less than a year; or,
- otherwise, one year's rent; and,
- the sum for which the warrant was issued.

Any surplus or left over goods are returned to the debtor (subs. 6). If replevin is commenced, the bailiff can nevertheless sell such portion of the goods as will satisfy the costs of the sale and debt for which execution was commenced (subs. 5). The cost of distress will be calculated on the same basis as any execution and no extra fees may be added (subs. 7).

A similar procedure is followed by the sheriff except that there must be removal of goods off the premises for s.1 to apply – simply seizing the goods will not suffice (*White* v. *Binstead* (1853) 22 LJCP 115). Thus if only a portion of good seized have been removed, this does not enable the section to apply (*Colyer* v. *Speer* (1820) 2 Brod & Bing 67) and this cannot be rectified later. If there is no removal within a reasonable time, the landlord will be able to distrain as normal (*Re: Davis* (1885) 55 LJQB 217). In the High Court the claim is for up to one year's rent in total and once the maximum is paid the levy may proceed as normal. When the claim is received by the sheriff the execution creditor is notified and required to pay the rent due to the sheriff. The subsequent levy by the sheriff will be for both the debt due to the plaintiff and the rent arrears that they have been obliged to discharge.

6.6.2 Crown Priority

It is a long established principle of common law that the Crown is entitled to priority in all recovery proceedings (*New South Wales Taxation Commissioners* v. *Palmer* [1907] AC 171), whether it is enforcing by execution (*R.* v. *Cotton* (1751) Park 112) or by distress (*Attorney-General* v. *Leonard* [1888] 38 Ch D 622). Thus if the Crown seeks to levy and finds a landlord or other creditor already in possession, it may proceed as its debt takes precedence providing the goods have not been sold (*R.* v. *Sloper & Allen* (1818) 6 Price 114). This cannot occur if the earlier levy has proceeded to sale, for then the goods are no longer the debtor's.

This right originates in common law. Now for income tax it is contained in s.62 TMA. Where the debtor has not paid PAYE due for the last year or has not passed on sums deducted from sub-contractors, that tax should be paid by the creditor seeking to levy any execution or distraint on demand to the Collector before sale or removal can proceed. If the enforcing creditor will not pay up the bailiff will be obliged to withdraw. If these sums are not paid within ten days of the demand the Collector can then distrain and sell the goods to recover the tax. A landlord is exempt from this. These provisions do not apply to money seized by the bailiff, nor to money paid to him by the debtor.

The other likely Crown creditor to be encountered in this context is Customs and Excise collecting VAT. If the Department have exercised their right to issue summary proceedings in the High Court and enforce that judgment by execution, the writ will have priority. The more normal course of action for VAT arrears is distraint and, as described above, even a later levy will attain priority

6.6.3 Previous Distress

The basic principle is that goods already seized and in the custody of the law cannot be seized again by a bailiff. Properly each bailiff must wait for the one with a prior levy to complete that levy before proceeding (note that an agreement with the creditor whereby the bailiff will not enforce on terms of payment is equivalent to withdrawing a warrant, so that later levies will gain priority – *Hunt* v. *Hooper* (1844) 12 M&W 664). A more pragmatic approach tends to be followed: if the debtor does not pay, the earlier bailiff will remove and sell and will pass on any surplus proceeds of sale to the second bailiff. If the debtor pays by instalments, the second bailiff request the first to either complete the levy by sale or to withdraw. This will often lead either to sale or an instalment arrangement between the debtor and second bailiff.

Regard must be had to the special rules applicable to civil court bailiffs. In execution and distraint for road traffic penalties the date of issue of the writ or warrant determines priority between them (see 6.1.4). Secondly Court Service has given special guidance to county court bailiffs on how to handle prior levies by private bailiffs levying distraint.

The court will contact the private bailiffs and ask them to either remove or withdraw from possession. If goods are removed the county court bailiff can then levy on what remains. If the private bailiff consents to withdrawal the court bailiff will proceed as normal. If the private bailiffs refuse to either remove or withdraw, court action may be threatened. Removal will not be insisted upon where it is possible for both bailiffs to receive instalments, where instalment payments to the private bailiffs will soon cease or where it is considered that the debtor has no additional goods to seize or funds to make extra payments as insisting on removal would deprive the execution creditor of any hope of recovery.

6.7 Final warnings

Most bailiffs will send notice to the debtor of the fact of that a warrant has been issued, as this may provoke payment without the need to take any further steps. Some regulations include a specific charge in the fee scales for such a letter (for example CSA and road traffic penalties). Some bailiffs are required by statute or internal practice to send notice – see below. Whatever the situation, it is important to check the contents of such communications to be satisfied that no untoward or illegal threats are made. It is an offence under s.40 Administration of Justice Act 1970 to harass a person whilst endeavouring to collect any debt due under contract (this will apply to rent arrears and, presumably, contractual debts being enforced by execution upon a judgment). A person will be guilty of the offence if s/he:

"1a) harasses the other with demands for payment which, in respect of their frequency or the manner or occasion of making any such demand, or of any threat or publicity by which any demand is accompanied, are calculated to subject him or members of his family or household to alarm, distress or humiliation;
b) falsely represents . . . that criminal proceedings lie for failure to pay . . .;
c) falsely represents himself to be authorised in some official capacity to claim or enforce payment".

This section could cover a range of actions. Examples would include threats of imprisonment for failing to allow entry, claims of status as court officers when that is not the case or any threats of violence or racial or sexual abuse.

Any harassment must be deliberate. It would be necessary to show that the bailiff was aware (or could not ignore) the fact that his actions were illegal the fact that acts are *likely* to harass debtors will be sufficient (*Norweb plc* v. *Dixon* (1995) 1 WLR 636). Neglect to make proper enquiries as to the legality of certain actions does not constitute knowledge that an offence is being committed. Both the person making such threats plus anyone who supported or assisted them (eg: an office manager) may be prosecuted in the magistrates' court. On summary conviction the defendant may be fined up to £5000. Any one enforcing a debt by legal process is not effected by this provision so long as their actions are "*reasonable (and otherwise permissible in law)*".

Attention should also be paid to the Malicious Communications Act 1988. Under s1 it is an offence to send any letter or article which conveys a threat or "information which is false and known or believed to be false by the sender" and which it was known would be likely to cause distress or anxiety to the recipient. It is suggested that this may include the not uncommon threat made in letters by bailiffs' firms to break in and remove goods whether or not the debtor is at home. Malicious communications are a criminal offence leading to a fine on summary conviction of up to £2500. The defendant may show that s/he used the threat to reinforce a demand he or she believed there were reasonable grounds for making it and that it was believed that the use of the threat was a proper means of reinforcing the demand.

6.7.1 Income tax

If the tax remains unpaid, a final demand or warning letter giving seven days' notice before distraining on a taxpayer's goods is issued. The time lapse between the original demand and distraint is variable because in the absence of an actual refusal to pay, reasonable time must be allowed before refusal can be inferred. Distraint is unlawful therefore where the collector distrains immediately after demand and in the absence of the occupier (*Gibbs* v. *Stead* (1828) 8 B & C 528). There is no time limit on when distraint may be issued, i.e. the Revenue can distrain after the end of the relevant tax year (*Elliot* v. *Yates* [1900] 2 QB 370).

6.7.2 Execution

When a writ of fieri facias or warrant of execution is issued a warning notice (county court form N326) is usually sent to the debtor. The main purpose of this is to notify the debtor of the binding effect of the writ or warrant (see 6.1.4). This warning also gives the person another opportunity to pay, but will not be sent if it is felt that the debtor may dispose of the goods. In such cases the bailiff visits as soon as possible to attempt to levy the full sum due.

Chapter Seven

COMMENCING LEVIES: INITIAL VISITS

PART ONE – BAILIFFS' RIGHTS

7.1 Liable persons

A bailiff is entitled to levy execution or distress against the goods of the liable person, the debtor, whether that person is an individual or a company. Special rules apply to partnership property (see 9.11), but a debt due from a partnership maybe pursued against any partner, even if s/he is the only surviving member of a firm (*Eddowes* v. *Argentine Loan & Mercantile Agency Co Ltd* (1890) 62 LT 602). If the debt in question is a joint debt it may be enforced against the debtors' sole or joint property. The property of any one of the liable individuals may be seized and the others need not be chased (*Herries* v. *Jamieson* (1794) 5 TR 553). The warrant must follow the judgment or order, so a joint judgment must be enforced by a warrant issued against all defendants (*Abbot* v. *Smith* (1774) 2 Wm Bl 947; *Clarke* v. *Clement & English* (1796) 6 TR 525). This point was confirmed also in *Penoyer* v. *Brace* (1697) 1 Ld Raym 244, which further held that if one of joint debtors has died, enforcement may continue unabated against the other (see also 6.3). Special rules also apply to property jointly owned by the debtor (see 9.3).

Some individuals are specially privileged from enforcement:

- *diplomatic staff* may not have execution levied on them, their family members or their employees (respectively Articles 31(3), 37(1) & 37(2) sch. 1, Diplomatic Privileges Act 1971). Under Article 22(3) of the 1971 Act the privilege extends to the furnishings of diplomatic missions, other property thereon and to vehicles owned by the mission for the transport of the diplomatic staff.
- *armed forces:* neither execution nor distress may be levied upon those volunteering or called up for service in the armed forces without permission of court (s.(2) & (3) Reserve & Auxiliary Forces (Protection of Civil Interests) Act 1951 respectively). Leave is sought by application on notice under CPR Part 23. This does not apply to judgments for damages in tort, to orders for costs, to judgments for debts incurred after the military service began or to orders in criminal proceedings. It also does not effect the power of distress damage feasant (*Watkinson* v. *Hollington* [1944] KB 202), but does refer to other forms of distress than rent, for instance for local taxes (s.6(2) & *Stepney BC* v. *Woolf* [1943] KB 202). Furthermore any military equipment, instruments or clothing supplied to a person in the armed forces may not be seized in execution (s.185 Army Act 1955; s.185 Air Force Act 1955 and s.102 Naval Discipline Act 1957).

If execution is levied against a privileged person, or in a privileged place (see 7.2.1), the process can be set aside, but no action lies against those acting in disobedience of a lawful writ or order, even if malice is alleged (*Magnay* v. *Burt* [1843] 5 QB 381).

7.2 Time

7.2.1 Time of Day

Execution may be levied at any time (*Brown* v. *Glenn* (1851) 16 QB 254 per Lord Campbell at 257). By analogy with execution (see commentary, chapter 2) it seems to be the case in statutory distraint that bailiffs may distrain at any time (see *Throssell* v. *Leeds City Council* (1993) 41 Adviser 22). This is reinforced by the fact that the CSA code of practice for its bailiffs implicitly acknowledges that distraint may be levied at any time by restricting levies to between 7am and 9pm unless the circumstances are exceptional.

The common law rule applicable to distress for rent is that a levy should not occur between sunset and sunrise (*Aldenburgh* v. *Peaple* (1834) 6 C&P 212, *Brice* v. *Hare* (1824) 2 LJOSKB 194, *Tutton* v. *Darke* (1860) 5 H&N 647, *Nixon* v. *Freeman* (1860) 5 H&N 647). A landlord may enter premises at night to prevent removal by third parties so that goods may be levied the next day, though this may still be trespass (*England* v. *Cowley* (1873) 28 LT 67). If the bailiff levies distress for rent at the wrong hour the distress is irregular (*Perry & Co* v. *Emerson* (1906) 1 KB 1) unless the error is waived by the debtor (*Werth* v. *London & Westminster Loan & Discount Co* (1889) 5 TLR 521). In the only reported case on the matter (*Lamb* v. *Wall* (1859) 1 F&F 503) only the "real actual damage" suffered was allowed to the plaintiff – which in this case of distress after sunset and occupation of the plaintiff's premises by the landlord for several hours, preventing her leaving, was held to be only one farthing. However as distress at the wrong time is illegal and is a trespass, the proper measure should be general damages because the tort has been committed (for which see 7.5 later) without any set off for any debt due.

For VAT under reg. 7 DCED Regulations 1997 a levy may only commence between 8am and 8pm on any day of the week, though it may be continued outside that period until it is completed. Where the business facing distraint trades partly within and partly (or wholly) outside these times, the levy may be commenced at any time and on any day that the firm is trading.

In distress damage feasant the common law rule does not apply, and distress may be levied at any time of day or night (*Anon* (1495) YB 11 Hen 7 fo 5 pl 18) as trespass may occur at any time (*Milborn's Case* (1586) 77 ER 420; *Mackalley's Case* (1611) 77 ER 828).

7.2.2 Day of the Week

Distress for rent should not be levied on Sundays (*Werth* v. *London & Westminster Loan and Discount Co* (1889) 5 TLR 520) or on public holidays like Christmas and Easter. Execution may be levied on a Sunday but only with leave of court in an emergency (O.65 r.10 RSC or O.7 r.3 CCR) and otherwise on any day. These restrictions only apply to the original levy, not later visits to the premises (*Atkinson* v. *Jamieson* (1792) 5 TR 25; *Wells* v. *Gurney* (1828) 8 B&C 769). By implication one may assume that similar limitations will apply in statutory distraint. Failing to comply with these restrictions will, as above, render the distress irregular.

Commentary

Neither of the above rules on time of day – either the unlimited rights in execution or the more rustic restrictions of distress for rent – can be regarded as fully acceptable in a modern context. As to day of the week, viewed from a modern perspective, these rules cause few problems as a six day working week is neither unusual or unreasonable.

7.3 Place

The basic rule is that the debtor's goods may be seized wherever they are, normally from premises belonging to the debtor. This includes goods of the debtor found on the highway *(Quinlan* v. *Hammersmith & Fulham London Borough Council* (1988) 153 JP 180: in which bailiffs levied for rates by seizing the car Q. was driving in the street. The case confirmed that statutory forms of distress are not subject to the provisions of the Statute of Marlborough 1267 – see "rent" below).

Although bailiffs executing statutory distress may go anywhere in England and Wales (for example CSA distraint can be levied anywhere in England and Wales – reg. 30(1); as may local taxes – reg. 45(6) CT; reg. 14(6) NNDR), certain limits are placed on other bailiffs' movements.

7.3.1 Execution

The officer levying execution is limited in several respects as to where he may levy:

- the sheriff is restricted to his "bailiwick" and the county court bailiff may only operate within that particular court's area. The county court provisions regarding execution out of the court's area do not apply to warrants for road traffic penalties, though these are modelled on county court procedure (s.103) County Court Act 1984;
- execution may not be levied at royal residences (*Winter* v. *Miles* (1809) 10 East 578; *AG* v. *Dakin* [1820] 4 HL 338) though this does not include the Palace of Westminster (*Combe* v. *De La Bere* [1882] 22 Ch D 316); or,
- at diplomatic premises or the private residences of ambassadors (Articles 22 & 30 sch. 1 Diplomatic Privileges Act 1971).

7.3.2 Distress for rent

The bailiff or landlord can only attend at the "demised", i.e. rented premises (*Capel* v. *Buszard* (1829) 6 Bing 150) unless goods are on common land, have been fraudulently removed elsewhere (see 3.3.3) or the tenant consents to a levy elsewhere.

The landlord may **not** levy off the premises in the street (c.15, Statute of Marlborough 1267). An exception exists where goods are located in the street immediately outside the premises. Two cases, *Hodges* v. *Lawrence* (1854) 18 JP 347 and *Gillingham* v. *Gwyer* (1867) 16 LT 640 suggest that a property includes half the road outside, so in theory a car parked not only in a drive but immediately outside a house can be seized, whereas one directly opposite in the street or outside a neighbour's house cannot. By way of contrast, however, see the remarks of Sir W M Jones in *Beckett* v. *Corporation of Leeds* [1871] 7 Ch App 421.

A second exception exists where the landlord seizes goods off the demised premises and on the highway in 'fresh pursuit'. If the landlord arrives to distrain and sees the tenant in the process of removal, she or he may chase and seize the goods. Coke states that this is because a view of the goods on the premises "is a kinde of possession of them" (2 Inst 131). Such a seizure in hot pursuit is **not** illegal therefore the tenant could not legally rescue his/her goods (see Co Litt 161a). However in distress damage feasant seizure in fresh pursuit is **not** permissible, therefore rescue by the owner would be legal (Co Litt 161a & 3.3.3).

7.3.3 Third party premises

Rather like the landlord's right of pursuit of fraudulently removed goods mentioned above, the bailiff levying execution may attend third party premises if it is believed that the debtor's goods have been removed there in order to avoid execution (*Ratcliffe* v. *Burton* (1802) 3 Bos & P 223). Force may be used as a house is "only a privilege for himself" and the protection from forced entry only applies to the goods of an occupier and his/her family and does not protect goods brought in there to prevent lawful execution (*Semaynes Case* (1604) 5 Co Rep 91a, proposition 5). This conclusion was reached by analogy with c17 Statute of Westminster I: the sheriff may force entry in order to replevy goods wrongfully removed to premises in order to evade replevin. Demand for entry should be made first before force is employed (*Semaynes Case*, proposition 6).

The bailiff of course may enter a third party's premises peaceably in order to search for a debtor's goods (*Biscop* v. *White* (1600) 78 ER 991 – the doors of the stranger's house were found open). However the bailiff will be a trespasser if either no goods are found (*Cooke* v. *Birt* (1814) 5 Taunt 765; *Green* v. *Leney & Another* (1933) unreported case (1933) December 11, even though the debtor may have resided on the premises immediately before the levy and the bailiff therefore had reasonable cause to suspect and believe that the defendant's property was still there (*Morrish* v. *Murrey* (1844) 13 M&W 52). If inner doors are forced in the process, the bailiff also trespasses (*Johnson* v. *Leigh* (1815) 6 Taunt 246).

What may be defined as a stranger's house? It does not include a property where the debtor's goods are ordinarily deposited, or where the debtor is ordinarily resident, though s/he may not be classed as the occupier (see for example *Cooke* v. *Birt* (1814) 5 Taunt 765 or *Sheers* v. *Brooks* (1792) 2 H Bl 120).

7.3.4 Distress damage feasant

Goods may be seized wherever a trespass has occurred, as long as the goods are actually in the process of trespassing and doing damage (*Vasper* v. *Eddows* (1702) Holt KB 256). If the trespassing chattels are removed from the premises, they cannot be seized in fresh pursuit, unless (it seems) the distrainor was already present at the site of the trespass before they are removed (*Clement* v. *Milner* (1800) 3 Esp 95). Chattels on the highway aren't privileged from seizure unless they are using the highway as a highway. The above mentioned provisions of c.15 Statute of Marlborough have been held to apply solely to distress for rent (*Smith* v. *Shepherd* (1591) 78 ER 945; *Prime* v. *Philips* (1614) 1 Salk 222).

7.4 Entry rights

7.4.1 Basic rights

In *Long* v. *Clarke* [1893] 1 QB 119 at 121, Lord Esher, M.R. observes that a bailiff may "*do that which, if any other person did it, would be a trespass*". The basic rule applicable to all forms of distress and execution is that the bailiff has a right of entry which must be exercised without the use of force. If entry is obtained through force, it is an illegal act which is unauthorised by the warrant and the distress is trespass (*Lindsey* v. *Lindsey* (1710) Salk 291; BNP 104a) (*Curlewis* v. *Laurie* [1848] 12 QB 640). A criminal offence may also be committed (see 7.7.1).

7.4.2 Premises

Consideration must be given to which premises these basic rights of peaceable entry apply:

- *debtor's home*: since at least the early seventeenth century the debtor's home has been considered his/her "castle". It is protected from any forced or unwanted entry. This protection against forced entry extends to all buildings within the boundary of the premises (*American Concentrated Must Corporation* v. *Hendry* (1893) 68 LT 742). See also *Munroe & Munroe* v. *Woodspring District Council* (1979) CLY 2226 where bailiffs forced entry into a garage in the plaintiff's garden. The court awarded general damages for trespass, for the value and loss of use of the car and special damages for damage to the garage door;
- *separate, non-domestic premises*: private bailiffs levying distress may enter such premises but must never break in (*Brown* v. *Glenn* [1851] 16 QB 254; *Poole* v. *Longueville* (1680) 2 Wms Saund 288). There is an exception for execution – see 7.4.4 later;
- *flats, maisonettes and bedsits*: A common problem confronted during entry into a block of flats or house in multiple occupation is determining which is the outer door – the common entrance or the door to the premises solely and exclusively occupied by the debtor. The often quoted English case is *Lee* v. *Gansel* [1774] 1 Cowp 1. General Gansel was arrested by a bailiff who entered the property where he lodged by means of an open outer door but then broke into the General's bedroom. Gansel rented rooms in the house of a Mr. Mayo – two rooms on the first floor, with doors opening onto the landing, two rooms on the second floor, with separate doors. He shared the kitchen with Mayo who also lived there and both used the outer door. It was held not to be logical for Gansel to have four outer doors to his premises, therefore the bedroom was legally broken open, for as was held in *Astley* v. *Pinder* (1760) cited by Lord Mansfield CJ @ 6 in *Lee* v. *Gansel* (above) "*an inner door has no protection at all*". This case seems to favour the case for occupiers of flats and houses in multiple occupation. A more definitive answer is given in *Welch* v. *Kracovsky* (1919) 3 WWR 361. In this it was held that a door connecting a suite of rooms occupied exclusively by a tenant in an apartment block with a hallway used by all tenants and leading to the main entrance is an outer door and therefore cannot be forced;
- *hotels and lodgings*: if the debtor is resident in a hotel or lodgings house, it may be

that the debtor would have no protection from forcible entry to the premises in order to seize their goods, and the levy would be valid, though the actual owner of the premises may have a cause of action against the bailiff (see the discussion in *Kirkpatrick* v. *Kelly* (1781) 3 Doug KB 30; *Piggot* v. *Wilkes* (1820) 3 B & Ald 502).

7.4.3 Mode of entry

The strict legal rights of entry apply as by the authorities are reviewed here – but see the later commentary section.

- *doors*: the bailiff may enter an open door (*Budd* v. *Pyle* (1846) 10 JP 203). It would also appear that a bailiff may open and enter an unlocked door having the legal authority under the warrant to open the door in the ordinary way in which other persons may (*Ryan* v. *Shilcock* (1851) 7 Exch 72). Breaking open a door or gate in a wall is trespass (*Long* v. *Clarke* [1893] 1 QB 119). The use of a locksmith to open a door is illegal and otherwise removing or damaging locks and chains is likewise wrongful (per Hardwick CJ [1735] cited in "Viner's Abridgment"). If an obstruction has been placed against the door by a person and s/he permits the bailiff to remove this to enter the door, the entry is legal provided that no force is used (*McKay* v. *Douglas* [1919] 44 DLR 570). If a door is nailed shut, it is illegal to force it open (*Russell* v. *Buckley* (1885) 25 NBR 264). Reasonable force may be used to see if a door is fastened (*McKinnon* v. *McKinley* [1856] 1 PEI 113).

  The front doors of all buildings within the boundary of the property are protected from forced entry (*American Concentrated Must Co* v. *Hendry* [1893] 57 JP 521). Even if a door is within the boundaries of a property and can only be reached by passing through other gates or doors, if it constitutes the entrance to a dwelling, it is protected (*Hopkins* v. *Nightingale* (1794) 1 Esp 99). A door leading into a garden or yard within a property is not an outer door.

- *windows*: a bailiff may climb through an open window (*Nixon* v. *Freeman* (1860) 5 H&N 647; *Tutton* v. *Darke* (1860) 5 H&N 647) or skylight (*Miller* v. *Tebb* (1893) 9 TLR 515) and open one more if necessary (*Crabtree* v. *Robinson* [1885] 15 QBD 812) – though "Clerk & Lindsell on Torts" at 16–33 questions whether these principles can now apply in the light of the decision in *Southam* v. *Smout* [1964] 1 QB 308 at 329.Though a bailiff may open a closed but unfastened door he cannot open a closed but unfastened window as the former gives an "*implicit licence to anyone with lawful business to enter*" whilst the latter gives no such licence as it is not a normal means of entry (*Nash* v. *Lucas* (1867) LR 2 QB 590). David Feldman also questions whether, in light of the discussion of the concept of licence to enter in *Nash* v. *Lucas*, it is now safe to assume that an open window is a licence to enter if a door is locked.

  The bailiff cannot open a closed, latched window (*Hancock* v. *Austin* (1863) 14 CBNS 634) and the fastening securing a window may not be removed (*Bell* v. *Oakley* (1814) 2 M&S 259). A window pane cannot be broken (*Attack* v. *Bramwell* (1863) 3 B&S 520).

- *walls*: a bailiff may climb over a wall or fence or walk across a garden or yard provided these are not damaged (*Long* v. *Clarke* heard (1893), reported (1894) 1 QB 119). A wall cannot be broken down to gain entry, but a hole in an unfinished wall may be passed through (*Whalley* v. *Williamson* (1836) 7 C&P 294).

- *keys*: Use of a landlord's pass key is illegal as entering by such means is not "*the ordinary way in which visitors gain access*" (*Miller* v. *Curry* [1893] 25 NSR 537). It does not matter whether the bailiff found the key or it was provided by a landlord – see *Welch* v. *Krakovsky* (1919) 3 WWR 361. If the key is left in the lock it seems it may be permissible to turn it like a door handle to open the door if it has been left in the lock so as to make the premises accessible to all with a legitimate reason to enter (*Ryan* v. *Shilcock* (1851) 7 Exch 72), though whether such a general authority from the householder to enter in such situations can now be assumed seems to be questioned in the judgment in *Southam* v. *Smout* [1963] 3 All ER 104.

- *other means*: In one case it was even held acceptable for a landlord to take up the floor of his room so as to effect entry into the tenant's room below (*Gould* v. *Bradstock* (1812) 4 Taunt 562). This odd result arises from the fact that the floor was only comprised of boards, and there was no plaster ceiling in the tenant's premises through which the landlord had to break. Thus the boards were not the plaintiff's sole property, nor was any force used. The tenant might have had a remedy for disturbance of his use of the ceiling, but the court felt there was no trepass, Lord Mansfield CJ adding at p. 564 "*What is decided in this case will not do much harm or good as a precedent, for probably the circumstances never happened before, or will ever happen again.*" This is probably true, though readers may note that it has been held that entry via a loft from an adjoining house is illegal (*Anglehart* v. *Rathier* (1876) 27 CP 97). If the door, window or wall are already broken open, it would seem that the bailiff may enter (*Long* v. *Clarke* above). In *Whalley* v. *Williamson* (1836) 7 C&P 294 a levy was conducted at premises that were only part built. The bailiff entered through a hole in the wall and then forced a boarded over window. It was held that this was trespass because the hole was not intended to have a door or window fitted later, therefore it had to be considered that the "outer fence" of the house was the boarded window, which was illegally entered by force.

- *by "invitation":* all the above have implied that the debtor will be absent at the time of the bailiff's attendance, and that s/he will be finding a way in to an empty property as best he or she can. In most cases of course someone will be present to open the door. If the door is opened and the bailiff permitted to enter, this is of course a legal entry. A number of issues arise around this.

  - *strangers* – did the person opening the door have the authority to do so? It is arguable that if they did not, this is not a legal means of entry.
  - *minors* – if a child opens the door either in the absence of the parent or whilst the parent is elsewhere in the house, is the entry legal? Very probably this is not a legal mode of entry.
  - *refusal of entry* – it seems clear from the authorities that if the debtor simply verbally refuses entry before the bailiff is over the threshold the bailiff may not

proceed (*Semaynes Case* (1604) Yelv 29; *Vaughan* v. *McKenzie* [1968] 1 All ER 154).

Many creditors have developed policies to deal with such issues of access. For instance, a VAT warrant permits the bailiff enter any house or premises during the daytime in order to levy distress. If entry cannot be gained a notice is left. If entry is gained but a "person in authority" (i.e. a director, owner or partner) cannot be found VAT form 879A is left. Inland Revenue guidance to collectors of taxes is that they should normally only enter at the invitation of the debtor (or his/her representative).

- *under false pretences*: In general it appears that entry gained under false pretences will not render a levy illegal. The authorities on this are not explicit, but the conclusion may be inferred, particularly from *R.* v. *Backhouse* (1771) Lofft 61. In the course of executing an arrest warrant an officer gained access by pretending he had a note for the attention of the defendant, Backhouse. When the officer was let in and revealed his true purpose, he was assaulted by Backhouse. At the trial the actual circumstances of the assault were disputed, but Backhouse was held culpable and was fined. The means by which the officer entered initially were neither examined nor criticised, from which it may be implied that they were neither thought wrongful nor a mitigating factor in Backhouse's defence.

  Deliberate deception thus seems not to make an entry and seizure wrongful, so we may regard any mistaken deception as similarly not wrongful. In *Cresswell* v. *Jeffreys* (1912) 28 TLR 413 a bailiff instructed to distrain for rent arrears told the tenant that he could not legally seize his livestock. The tenant had intended to remove them from the property but then did not. The bailiff later seized some of the cattle and was then sued for wrongful distress. It was held that the bailiff's remarks were either a misstatement of law or a declaration of an intention to abandon a legal right, but in neither case could they create an estoppel preventing seizure. A misstatement of law cannot create an estoppel and a representation can only do so if it is regarding existing facts, not an intention. The right to distrain was not waived either, as there was no consideration for the waiver.

  It seems that entry under false pretences is only wrongful if a court is misled by the bailiff as part of the procedure. See *Anon* (1758) 2 Keny 372/96 ER 1214 in which a sheriff procured a search warrant by pretending stolen goods were on premises so that he could enter and arrest the occupant. No search was made for any goods. The court regarded the means used to gain entry as "undue" or improper. From this we may deduce that a county court bailiff misleading a district judge in seeking permission to force re-entry, a landlord misleading the justices when applying for a warrant to break open premises after an alleged fraudulent removal or a sheriff's officer dishonestly representing facts in an application for a writ of assistance under RSC O.46 r.3 would all render the levy illegal.

- *assistance*: in *Nash* v. *Lucas* [1867] 2 QB 590 the court dealt with a question yet to be satisfactorily answered – may a bailiff be let in by a third party already on the premises? In *Nash* the bailiff encouraged a workman employed by the landlord to let himself into the house by opening a shut window so that he could then open the locked front door to admit the bailiff. As he acted at the behest of the bailiff the whole entry was held to be illegal. However reference was made to *Sandon* v. *Jarvis* (1859) EB & E 935 where a bailiff arrested a man by touching him through an already broken window. This action was held to be legal and the principle could be extended to "assisted entry".

7.4.4 Initial entry by force

There are a several exceptions to the basic rules outlined above which permit entry to be forced. Nevertheless it is probably safe to say that the courts would expect prior demand for entry to be made first before force is used so as to allow the occupant the opportunity of permitting entry and in order to avoid, if possible, violent resistance (see *Launock* v. *Brown* (1819) 2 B&A 592; *Burdett* v. *Abbot* (1811) 14 East 1).

- *income taxes* – the Inland Revenue collector of taxes may force entry to premises, though some demand for entry should be made first (*Semaynes Case* [1604] All ER 62). A collector may seek a break-open warrant for the purpose of gaining access to premises. This is done by laying an information on oath before a justice of the peace. The warrant will be granted if the JP is satisfied there is a reasonable ground for believing the person is "neglecting or refusing" to pay. The collector may only force entry during the "daytime" (s.61(2)TMA). The collector may call for police assistance when forcing entry and every constable shall "aid and assist in the execution of the warrant and in levying the distress". This presumably only extends to preventing a breach of the peace (see 7.4.6 and *R.* v. *Clarke* (1835) 4 Nev & M 671). It has been held that the collector cannot break in without a constable being present (*Foss* v. *Racine* (1838) 8 C& P 699). Use of the power of forced entry is very rare.

  Despite the judgment in *Semaynes* case it does not seem that this right of forced entry any longer extends to sheriff's officers and county court bailiffs enforcing judgments for tax (s.26(1) Crown Proceedings Act 1947) and certainly in other suits by the Crown, except to those in which the monarch is personally plaintiff, there is no right of forced entry. It does not seem possible to extend the principle in *Semayne* to private bailiffs or local authority officers enforcing local taxes (*Munroe & Munroe* v. *Woodspring DC* (1979) CLY 2226). Similarly bailiffs enforcing a fine by distraint are held to be enforcing a civil process, so that entry may not be forced in such a levy either (*R.* v. *Myers* (1786) 1 TR 265).

- *re-entry* – re-entry may be forced immediately following a legal first entry in two circumstances:

  - *after forcible ejection:* if the bailiff is obliged to leave premises because of threats or the use of force immediately after a lawful first entry or later during the process of seizure and impounding, he may use force to regain entry. Examples include, after peaceable entry – *Eagleton* v. *Gutteridge* (1843) 11 M&W 465 and during seizure (*Francome* v. *Pinche* [1766] Esp NP (3rd edn) 382). Force may be employed in such cases even after a considerable delay – in the case of *Eldridge* v. *Stacy* (1863) 15 CBNS 458 the bailiff returned three weeks after forcible expulsion. However the bailiff must have made a full entry initially, not just a foot in the door (*Boyd* v. *Profaze* (1867) 16 LT 431).

– *after forcible exclusion:* If the bailiff leaves temporarily, and returns to find his way barred, he may again use force to get back in (*Bannister* v. *Hyde* (1860) 2 E&E 627). It was argued in this case that force is justified as being kept out by force is equivalent to being turned out by force (see Wightman J at 631). This right to re-enter will only apply if the bailiff voluntarily leaves for a short time (and on return only goods previously seized may be taken). The bailiff cannot re-enter after a long delay (*Russell* v. *Rider* (1834) 6 C&P 416) because the goods will have been abandoned (see 8.4.1). In *Russell* the landlord's bailiff left in a state of "high excitement, bordering on insanity". The landlord broke in six days later to remove the goods and was found to have trespassed.

No demand need be made before forcing re-entry (*Aga Kurboolie Mahomed* v. *R* (1843) 4 Moo PCC 239). This is because, in the circumstances under discussion, the debtor is taken to know the purpose for which the bailiffs entered and have returned and to be unlawfully obstructing them by preventing entry.

Note that David Feldman (1986) also proposes that, in light of the judgment in *Southam* v. *Smout* (above), it may also be held lawful for a bailiff to use force to open a door in order to summon help (see too *R.* v. *Clarke* (1835) 4 Nev & M 671).

- *separate or non-domestic premises* – may be entered forcibly only in execution, e.g. a workshop (*Hodder* v. *Williams* [1895] 2 QB 663) or a barn (*Penton* v. *Browne* (1664) 1 Keb 698). It is however interesting to note that Bowen J in *American Concentrated Must* v. *Hendry* (1893) WN 67 felt that the decision in Penton was a departure from the older law and that it was "*a misconception to suppose that an outhouse within the curtilage enjoys less immunity than a disconnected outhouse*" i.e. the sheriff had no more right to break in than a landlord or other bailiff. This right does not apply if the non-domestic premises are connected to a dwelling, even though they may have separate entrances and no communicating doors – for instance a flat over a shop (*Hudson* v. *Fletcher* (1909) 12 WLR 15).

  The bailiff should make enquiry as to the presence of goods first (*Hobson* v. *Thelluson* [1867] 2 LRQB 642). These rules refer to premises which are not "connected with or within the curtilage of the dwelling house". Garden sheds and garages are thus protected as they are "parcel of the dwelling house". County court bailiffs will always get the permission of a district judge before such a forced entry. It is understood that sheriff's officers regularly exercise the right to force entry to business premises.

- *stranger's premises* may be entered forcibly by a landlord with a police officer if an oath has been sworn before magistrates to the effect that there are grounds for believing goods have been fraudulently removed there (see 3.3.3). The sheriff may also break into a third party's house if goods have been taken there to avoid execution (see 7.3.3).

- *distress damage feasant:* a distrainor may use reasonable force to enter premises to levy distress damage feasant. This will not invalidate a levy (*Anon* [1412/13] YB 14 Hen 4 13a pl2). This is presumably because it will be their own premises in most cases, so that even if access has been barred by the owner of the trespassing chattels, the occupier of the property may use force upon their own land.

There is no statutory requirement for a property to be left secure after forced entry. Parallels could be drawn with the duties imposed upon the police under the Police & Criminal Evidence Acts or the fuel companies in respect of disconnections, and failure to leave a property secure could form the basis of claims for compensation for damage caused by the forced entry, for property lost if the premises were not secure and for losses arising from the occupier's inability to get back into the property.

7.4.5 Identification

In most cases of distress bailiffs do not have to identify themselves when entering premises. In distress for rent, road traffic penalties, local taxes and child support maintenance only is some document is required by statute. The certificate for rent and traffic penalties should only be shown when levying for such debts. Sheriff's officers will show their "warrant card" (their official identification bearing their photograph and name) on entry. See also 6.1.2 on the production of warrants.

7.4.6 Police attendance

A police officer may be called by a bailiff to attend a levy or forced entry if a threat of violence can be shown (*Skidmore* v. *Booth* (1854) 6 C&P 777). The officer's presence would be to prevent a breach of the peace and not to assist in the seizure. A breach of the peace may be defined as a situation when and where:

- harm is actually done or is likely to be done to a person whether by the conduct of the person against whom the breach is alleged or by someone provoking that breach;
- harm is actually done or is likely to be done to a person's property in his presence, provided that the natural consequences of such harm is likely to be a violent retaliation; or,
- a person is genuinely in fear of harm to him/herself or property in their presence as a result of an assault.

The police can arrest the person who commits, or who they reasonably believe will commit, a breach of the peace.

Guidance given to the Metropolitan Police is that officers asked to attend levies should first check that the warrant is valid; that their entry to the premises should only be by invitation of the occupier or in order to prevent a breach of the peace; that officers should remain impartial and only become involved if an offence is occurring or possible; that they should not assist the bailiff in any way, such as advising the occupier to open the door, and that they should withdraw if the bailiff persists in acting in an illegal manner and report the matter to the creditor instructing them.

A request for police attendance can only be justified by a bailiff if it can be shown that it was necessary because of threats of resistance or violence or similar circumstances met on a previous visit (*R.* v. *Clarke* (1835) 4 Nev & M 671;*Skidmore* v. *Booth* (1854) 6 C&P 777). It is clear from this judgment that the common threat in correspondence to attend with police is at least misleading and should **not** be made as a matter of course.

To conclude therefore, both parties are entitled to have the police present if there is a genuine threat of violence. Other attendance or threats of police attendance are inappropriate and should be taken up with the local constabulary as well as with the bailiffs' firm, even if no action is taken for illegal distress.

7.4.7 Failed entry

If the bailiff fails to gain entry or find any adequate goods on a first visit the bailiff will try once or twice again, very likely at different times, and may make discrete local enquiries in the neighbourhood as to whether the debtor still trades or lives at the address. If they still do not meet with success a return of "no goods" or "no sufficient distress" is made to the creditor. Case law makes it clear that the bailiff must have made reasonable efforts to actually enter or search for goods to be able to make such a return legitimately. Nil returns can be made if the goods are hidden (*Doe d Haverson* v. *Franks* (1847) 2 Car & Kir 678) or entry is obstructed (*Doe d Cox* v. *Roe* (1847) 5 Dow & L 272) or refused (*R.* v. *Dudley Justices ex parte Blatchford* (1992) RVR 63).

Commentary

It will be apparent from the above review of case law on modes of entry that there is no coherent pattern to what is considered lawful or acceptable. One may particularly feel that judicial opinion is moving against means of entry that are not "ordinary means" (see *Southam* v. *Smout* [1964] 1 QB at 329. Thus in *ex p Williams* (1893) 14 NSWLR 395 Windeyer J observes "*persons entering premises must take care not to do so in a way that is calculated to provoke a breach of the peace. Climbing over fences is very likely to annoy people and . . . very serious consequences might ensue if someone thought a burglary was about to be committed*". More recently a more restrictive view still was enunciated in *Swales* v. *Fox* [1981] 2 WLR 814 by Lord Donaldson. Though he took trouble to stress that he was only concerned in the case with the statutory powers of the police under s.3 Criminal Law Act 1967 to use "such force as is reasonable" in aid of a power of arrest, and not the common law position, his views are probably indicative of the general attitude of the courts to modern property rights. In defining forced entry he stated" *In the context of outside premises of course there is no problem unless there is a gate or something of that sort. The constable simply enters and is authorised to do so. . . . But if he meets an obstacle, then he uses force if he applies any energy to the obstacle with a view to removing it. It would follow that, if my view is correct, where there is a door that is ajar but is insufficiently ajar for someone to go through the opening without moving the door and energy is applied to that door to make it open further, force is being used. A fortiori force is used when the door is latched and you turn the handle from the outside and then ease the door open. Similarly if anyone opens a window or increases the opening in any window, or indeed dislodges the window by the application of any energy, he is using force to enter . . .*"

Bearing in mind the views of the Court of Appeal in *Southam* v. *Smout*, and that these views are aimed at limiting the use of permitted reasonable force, the modern attitude to peaceable entry by bailiffs could be even more restrictive. Witness the Chief Justice's judgment in *ex parte Williams* [1893] 14 NSWLR 395 it is remarked "*a number of cases have been cited . . . and in some very fine distinctions are drawn*

. . . it is difficult to draw from the cases any satisfactory principle to apply . . . I think that the safest course to pursue in the interests of the public, and for the preservation of the public peace, will be to hold that entry" should be by normal means. The academic authorities referred to clearly feel that there be a more restrictive approach taken and in *Khazanchi* v. *Faircharm Investments* [1998] 2 All ER 901 Morritt LJ commences his judgment by stating that entry may only be made "with the consent of the occupant or person in possession of the premises". It appears safest to assume that this must be an active consent rather than seeking to rely on any dubious implied licence to enter, especially as such licence is clearly capable of revocation by the debtor. The scope for further litigation to modernise and tighten up the rules on entry seems considerable, and the words of Atkin LJ in *Great Central Railway Co Ltd* v. *Bates* [1921] 3 KB 578 at 582 should be borne in mind "it should be established that nobody has a right to enter premises except strictly in accordance with authority"

PART TWO – REMEDIES FOR WRONGFUL ENTRY

7.5 Trespass to land

Whilst a licence to enter property against an owner's consent may be given by law, for instance, in order to distrain, any unlawful or unjustifiable entry into or upon property is a trespass for which court action may be taken, even though there is no actual damage. Every unjustifiable intrusion is covered, however minor. Every continuance of a trespass, for example from day to day, is a fresh trespass and a fresh cause of action. It is no defence to say that the trespass arose from a mistake as to law or fact, provided that the physical act of entry was voluntary (but see *Papillon* v. *Backne* [1658] 2 Hardr 480, which suggests that the bailiff trespasses only after notice of his error). If the entry is voluntary, the intention renders the person a trespasser, whether or not their purpose was to act lawfully or wrongfully. As there need be no actual damage to constitute a trespass (*Stoke-on-Trent BC* v. *W J Wass Ltd* [1988] 1 WLR 1406 at 1411) it follows that it is no defence to contend that the trespass was of a trifling nature (*Yelloly* v. *Morley* (1910) 27 TLR 20) though this will go in mitigation of the damages (see 7.5.1).

Consequently it will be trespass for a bailiff to levy distress (*Etherton* v. *Popplewell* (1801) 1 East 139) or to remain on the property after a legal distress has become illegal (*Ladd* v. *Thomas* (1840) 4 Jur 797). The fact that the bailiff either had no right to enter or abused a legal right of entry gives the plaintiff an automatic right to damages (see *The Six Carpenters' Case* (1610) 8 Co Rep 146; *Moir* v. *Munday* (1755) Say 181; *Lamb* v. *Wall* (1859) 1 F & F 503). The sheriff remaining too long in premises is trespass, but it is unclear whether it may be possible to extend this to other bailiffs.

7.5.1 Measure of damages

General damages. As explained in the introductory paragraph if the trespass is proved the client is entitled to damages, even though no loss can be shown. If the trespass caused no identifiable loss damages will only be nominal: see for example *Hogarth* v.

Jennings [1892] 1 QB 907 where an error in using an uncertificated bailiff was held to be technical and occasioning no real loss. If substantial damage can be proved, the damages award will be increased accordingly to compensate for this. The measure of the damages depends on the nature of the trespass.

If there has been physical damage to the land the measure of damages will either be the diminution in value of the property or the costs of replacement or repair. The cost of repair may well be regarded as equal to the diminution in value, but if the cost of repairs exceeds the reduction in value, the higher sum will be paid provided that is is a reasonable amount and even though it may augment the property's value. The costs of repair and replacement should only be allowed where the plaintiff actually intends to do the repair work. The extent of the plaintiff's interest in the land will limit the extent of the damages recoverable, so that a lessee may only recover to the extent of their interest, for diminution in the value of the lease and loss of enjoyment of the property.

If the trespass has involved severance and removal of fixtures, the common law rule is that the plaintiff may elect for the action giving the highest amount of damages – either for trespass to land or for wrongful interference (see *Twigg* v. *Potts* (1834) 3 LJ Ex 336 and 9.26.3).

Consequential damages will also be recoverable under such heads as:

- losses such as loss of profits or expenses may be claimed due to disruption of business;
- alternative accommodation, if necessary, such as a stay in a hotel.

Consequential damages may also be recoverable as aggravated damages.

An example of the extent of both general and consequential damages that may be recoverable is *Munroe & Munroe* v. *Woodspring DC* [1979] CLY 2226. During a levy of distraint for rates the bailiffs forced entry into a garage in the plaintiff's garden. The bailiffs seized and sold a car, but it was held that their actions were unlawful and that the plaintiff was entitled to damages representing the value of the car, general damages for trespass and loss of use of the car and special damages for damage to the garage door.

Aggravated damages may be awarded where the trespass included injury to the claimant's pride and dignity or was accompanied by noise or disturbance (*Chamberlain* v. *Greenfield* (1772) 3 Wils 292). The primary purpose of aggravated damages is to compensate the claimant where the defendant's motive, conduct or manner of inflicting the injury have aggravated the claimant's loss by causing mental distress or embarrassment or by wounding feelings. The court will take into account the circumstances and conduct of the trespasser and an award may be made in respect of malevolent, spiteful, malicious, insulting, aggressive or high handed behaviour. An example may be injury to the reputation of business premises (*Hartley* v. *Larkin* (1950) 155 EG 270), fear at entry or insult suffered by the claimant (*Davis* v. *Bromley UDC* (1903) 67 JP 275 CA).

Additionally the claimant may point to aspects of the defendant's behaviour which aggravated or increased his/her damages or caused additional heads of damage. These are not properly aggravated damages, and will be comprised in the general award, but could include inconvenience. Generally aggravated damages should not be awarded as a mark of retribution or vindictively.

Exemplary damages are a punitive award. In many of the older cases the distinction between aggravated and exemplary damages was not always clearly expressed or appreciated, so the terms used cannot be relied upon: often what are expressed to be exemplary damages are really aggravated damages for wilful acts. Since *Rookes* v. *Barnard* [1964] AC 1129 the rules for such awards have been fixed. Exemplary damages are possible where, in certain specific cases, it is necessary to teach the wrongdoer that tort does not pay:

- if they are expressly permitted by statute (see 9.26.1 later);
- if a public officer can be shown to have acted in an oppressive or arbitrary way (*Broome* v. *Cassell & Co* [1972] AC 1027). The groups affected by the *Broome* judgment are very wide as it has extended the court's ability to punish improper use of power to anyone who, under common law or statute, exercises functions of a governmental character;
- if a desire for personal profit could be shown on the part of the creditor or of the bailiff, where the defendant sought to gain, at the expense of the plaintiff, that which s/he could not otherwise get, or could only get at great expense (*Tufuya* v. *Haddon* [1984] NZ Recent Law 285).

It is likely that cases where exemplary damages are considered appropriate will be rare and the courts will always consider first whether an award of aggravated damages is not on its own sufficient compensation. It will only be inadequate where the defendant's behaviour has been truly 'outrageous' (*Bradford MBC* v. *Arora* [1991] 2 WLR 1377 CA) or where the bailiff acts both maliciously as well as wrongfully – thus a mistakenly excessive levy is wrong but does not justify ememplary damages (*Moore* v. *Lambeth County Court Registrar* [1970] 1 All ER 980).

7.5.2 Trespass ab initio

The doctrine of trespass *ab initio* applies equally to trespass to land, trespass to person (see 7.5.3) and trespass to goods (see 9.26.2). The principle is that if a bailiff enters a property lawfully but, whilst there, abuses his authority by an unreasonable or illegitimate act amounting to trespass, s/he becomes what is termed a 'trespasser *ab initio*' (*Hickman* v. *Maisey* [1900] 1 QB 752). The trespass relates back to render the original entry tortious (Bl. Comm. vol. 3 para. 213). Thus the levy will be trespass from the begining and consequently void ('void *ab initio*'). It will give rise to the normal remedies for trespass, including both actions for damages and replevin (see 9.28).

The rule is based on the legal presumption that if the person acted illegally, s/he entered with that aim in mind and as a result all their actions were illegal (*Dye* v. *Leatherdale* [1769] 3 Wils 20; *Taylor* v. *Cole* [1791] 3 TR 292). The doctrine of trespass *ab initio* has been questioned in recent years – e.g. *Chic Fashions* v. *Jones* [1968] 2 QB 299 – but remains a valid claim.

The bailiff may thus be sued as if the original entry were unlawful. Trespass *ab initio* arises where there is positive misfeasance by a person – mere non-feasance, such as failing to release goods seized on proper tender is not enough (*West* v. *Nibbs* (1847) 4 CB 172). If the tortious act that occurs is not trespass, the tort does not 'relate back' to make the entry illegal (*Shorland* v. *Govett* (1826) 5 B&C 485 – an overcharge by a bailiff was not trespass *ab initio* as the court did not feel it could be reasonably supposed the bailiff had entered solely to extort money from the debtor; see also *Moyse* v. *Cocksedge* [1745] Barnes 459).

Examples of acts that do constitute trespass *ab initio* would be:

- *legal entry followed by illegal seizure* of third party goods – in *Harvey* v. *Pocock* (1843) 11 M&W 740 damages were awarded for seizure of undistrainable goods when others were available. A legal entry followed by illegal seizure of exempt goods would also be trespass *ab initio*: see *Swire* v. *Leach* (1865) 18 CBNS 479. Readers should not overlook the fact that these levies will be both trespass to land and goods, so the damages awarded will be the full value of exempt goods seized;
- *forced entry*: in *Bell* v. *Oakley* (1814) 2 M & S 259 a rates bailiff forced entry into a house, breaking windows in the process, found nothing inside and then removed some timber from the garden. The whole distress was invalid as he was a trespasser *ab initio*; or,
- *remaining in possession too long* (*Gargrave* v. *Smith* (1691) 1 Salk 221).

The courts may be prepared to award higher damages in a case of trespass *ab initio*, such as a sum equal to the whole amount levied (*Shorland* v. *Govett* (1826) 5 B&C 485). Then again the damages may be limited – to the value of a barrel of beer (*Dod* v. *Monger* (1704) 6 MR 215) or for the loss of use of looms (*Harvey* v. *Pocock* (1843) 11 M&W 740).

The wrongful act will not be trespass *ab initio* if the bailiff does that which he is authorised to do as *well* as the tort complained of: thus if only some of the goods seized were third parties', and some were the debtor's and available for distress, the bailiff would not be a trespasser *ab initio* to the land, but only a trespasser to the goods wrongfully taken (*Canadian Pacific Wine Co* v. *Tuley* [1921] 2 AC 417; *Elias* v. *Pasmore* [1934] 2 KB 164: *Owen & Smith* v. *Reo* [1934] 151 LT 274). In such cases it will still be possible to sue for wrongful interference to the goods in question, but the whole levy will not be called into question.

There are certain statutory exemptions to trespass *ab initio* (e.g., rent and local taxes – see 10.8), but not in several other forms of distess. Thus for instance in distress damage feasant abusing an item lawfully seized renders the whole distress void *ab initio* (*Dye* v. *Leatherdale* [1769] p. 109 Wils 20: *Oxley* v. *Watts* (1785) 1 TR 12). A sheriff who enters legally may trespass be remaining too long, but this does not seem to render the execution trespass *ab initio* (*Lee* v. *Dangar* [1892] 1 QB 231).

7.5.3 Trespass to person

The bailiff could also be sued for damages for trespass to person. This covers both assault, battery and unlawful imprisonment. Assault is any intentional or reckless act that causes a person to fear the use of immediate unlawful force or personal violence. It is an overt act indicating an immediate intent to commit battery, combined with an ability to carry that through. Threats, gestures and abuse on their own are not assault, without capacity to carry them out. Battery is the infliction of any unwanted physical contact, force or violence in excess of everyday contact and without the person's consent. It may be a blow, spitting or pushing. There is no need to show that any harm was inflicted or intended. A person cannot sue for shock and fear alone: there must be a physical consequence of the emotion, such as illness arising from shock. Assault must be shown by the plaintiff to be intentional or negligent on the part of the defendant.

As there does not need to be any physical contact or injury in assault, the emphasis being the reaction of the victim, it will be possible for plaintiffs to sue in any situations where there has been a clear physical menace of violence (with the ability to commit it) against them or, it appears, where there has been a simply a verbal intimation of violence. As a form of trespass assault is actionable in all cases without proof of injury. Nominal damages should be recoverable, but substantial damages may be possible where there has been discomfort, inconvenience or injury to dignity, even though there has been no physical injury. If there is physical injury, damages are calculated as in personal injury cases. In addition to general damages for physical or mental injury, consequential damages for specific pecuniary and non-pecuniary losses are recoverable – for example medical expenses, loss of earnings and compensation for pain and suffering and loss of amenities of life. Aggravated and exemplary damages may be possible (see 7.5.1), though any award of aggravated damages may be reduced or eliminated if there was any provocation from the claimant. Aggravated damages will be appropriate where there has been injury and discomfort, embarrassment and injury to dignity and also shock, particularly where there has been physical injury but possibly in other cases too where the distress caused to the person is substantial and directly linked to the assault. The trespass *ab initio* principle should also apply, though see *Smith* v. *Egginton* (1837) 7 A&E 167; *Wiltshire* v. *Barrett* [1966] 1 QB 312.

Assault is also an offence under ss.42-45 Offences Against the Person Act 1861. Criminal proceedings can bar a civil action.

Finally any wilfull act or statement by the defendant, intended to cause physical harm to the claimant, which in fact causes such harm, infringes the person's legal right to personal safety and is tortious and actionable (*Wilkinson* v. *Downton* [1897] 2 QB 57). If proved damages may therefore be recovered for any false statement giving rise to nervous shock or physical illness. Wright J observes in *Wilkinson* at 59 that "this wilful injuria is in law malicious, though no malicious purpose to cause the harm which was caused, nor any motive of spite, is imputed to the defendant." If the acts were unjustifiable there is a good cause of action, and it is no defence to say that more harm was done than was intended. To prove such a wrong the claimant must show an intention to produce the effect produced, having regard to the action's impact on a person of ordinary mental and physical health, and must show that the grave effects produced were not too remote.

7.5.4 Injunctions

Injunctions are available in the county court ancillary to a damages claim. Application can be made before the issue of a summons by the plaintiff in urgent cases and the court may grant an injunction on terms that the action is begun in that court. The courts will take account of several factors when considering applications:

- *other proceedings* having been commenced to restrain the levy, it is generally improper for the plaintiff to also seek an injunction. See *Hilliard* v. *Hanson* [1882] 21 Ch D 69 in which the plaintiff was penalised for costs after applying for an injunction despite interpleader being initiated by the sheriff.
- *legal rights:* in *Carter* v. *Salmon* (1880) 43 LT 490 it was stated that the courts do not favour interference by injunction with the legal right to distrain, even if it is excessive. There are remedies to deal with such a situation and in *Carter* no *prima facie* case could be made out by the tenant for restraining the landlord until trial: he appeared to be in breach of his lease, with no convincing evidence of any defence.
- *protecting the parties:* in *Sanxter* v. *Foster* (1841) Cr & Ph 302 it was held that the court should never interfere in a party's enforcement of a legal right by means of an injunction unless it secures to itself the means of putting any person prevented from enforcing a legal claim in the same position, in the event that the claim turns out to be right, as if the court had not interfered. In Sanxter an injunction was discharged on appeal as the court felt unable, in the circumstances, to set a proper level of security to protect the landlord. The sort of terms that may be set in order to do justice between the parties are illustrated by *Shaw* v. *Earl of Jersey* (1879) 4 CPD 359 in which the court granted an injunction that restrained the landlord for fourteen days, but its continuance thereafter was conditional on the tenant paying all the arrears into court. The landlord was seeking to exercise his legal rights and the court declined to make an unconditional injunction to inhibit these despite the tenants' claims of wrongful and excessive distress. Instead just terms were that payment into court should be made so the landlord could have the rent if he was entitled to it and the tenants could recover it if he were not. In *Walsh* v. *Lonsdale* [1882] 21 Ch D 9 an action was started to recover damages for illegal distress with an interlocutory injunction to restrain sale and the landlord's continued possession. The court held that it was not trying the case, but as the landlord's claim seemed justified he was entitled to retain the security given by his distress so he was ordered to withdraw on payment of the disputed rent into court by the tenant. Thus the utility of the injunction is tempered by its possible expense to the plaintiff.
- *prima facie case: Steel Linings* v. *Bilby & Co* (1993) RA 27 is a recent example in which the plaintiffs sought an injunction against a firm of certificated bailiffs to prevent sale following alleged excessive distress. The Court of Appeal underlined that injunctions would be given only in very exceptional cases where a powerful prima facie case for wrongful distress could be made.

To summarise, injunctions are probably most likely to be granted where there is a bona fide dispute as to whether there are rent arrears at all, whether goods seized are privileged or not (see 9.22) or whether there is a set off or counter claim. As payment into court may be required, from the plaintiff's perspective they be a less favourable remedy than replevin, in which only security is necessary (see 9.28). If application is made to restrain the bailiff, the creditor should at least receive notice of this so that they have an opportunity of being heard (*Hilliard* v. *Hanson* [1882] 21 Ch D 69).

7.6 Complaint to magistrates' court

The regulations for local taxes and child support maintenance give to any person aggrieved by a levy, or an attempt to levy, a right of appeal to the Magistrates' Court. This is done by making a "complaint" and requesting the issue of a summons directed to the creditor. It would appear that no complaint can be made simply because a warrant has been issued to the bailiffs, where no further action has been taken to enforce it (*R.* v. *Justices of London* [1899] 1 QB 532).

If, on hearing the aggrieved person's complaint, the court is satisfied that an irregular levy has occurred, it can order the return of the goods distrained. Although the regulations speak of irregularity alone, it has been held by the courts that this term includes any wrongful act by the bailiff i.e. illegality, irregularity or an excessive levy (*Steel Linings* v. *Bilby* (1993) RA 27).

The court may also, as an alternative to ordering return of goods, order an award of compensation for the goods sold equal to an amount which, in opinion of the court, would be awarded by way of special damages if proceedings had been taken for trespass or otherwise in connection with the irregularity. In assessing the level of compensation the court is required to act reasonably and to give proper attention to any evidence placed before it: *R.* v. *Epping Magistrates ex parte Howard & Leach* (1996) 7 CLY 521. It has been held by the High Court in *Steel Linings* v. *Bilby* , and endorsed in *R.* v. *Hampstead Magistrates Court ex parte St Marylebone Property Co plc* [1995] Legal Action September 1996, p.21 that the reference to special damages has a wider meaning in the regulations than just special damages as opposed to general damages and covers all damages caused by the wrongful levy, including damages for annoyance, injury to credit and reputation. The court can also order the creditor and bailiffs to desist from any levying in an irregular manner.

Several community charge complaints have been reported relating to illegal entry and seizure. Appeal would be by way of case stated.

- *Bates* v. *Northampton City Council* [1990] Legal Action 3/91 – the bailiffs wrote to Bates, never having entered his property, claiming to have levied on his goods. He appealed and the council denied that what had occurred was a levy (as indeed it was not). The magistrates dismissed the case as they held no distress had been attempted. Bates was ordered to pay £1300 costs. A similar case is *Brown* v. *LB Haringey* [1986] noted at [1992] 2 All ER 704. The Divisional Court in an appeal from the Crown Court held that as a draft walking possession agreement was ineffective there was no levy upon which the statutory right of appeal could be founded. By contrast in *R.* v. *Liverpool JJ ex parte Greaves* (1979) RA 119 in which the ratepayer's attempt to appeal to the Crown Court was ignored by the magistrates on the grounds that there can be no appeal before a levy and that no levy had occurred. The bailiffs had made a return of no goods and the High Court held that this was indeed a levy, albeit unsuccessful. The matter was therefore passed to the Crown Court to consider a case stated.
- *H* v. *Sandwell MBC* [1993] Legal Action August p.15: see 8.3.1 for details. On hearing the case the magistrates made an order declaring the attempted levy to be irregular, the walking possession charges unlawful and prohibiting further enforcement against the plaintiff.

7.7 Criminal Remedies

There is no reason why a bailiff acting under a warrant may not commit, or be accused of, a criminal offence (*R.* v. *Beacontree JJ ex parte Mercer* (1970) Crim LR 103). Experience suggests that the police are often reluctant to become involved in anything that may be classed a "civil matter" and, other than a warning against a breach of the peace, they are unlikely to take criminal proceedings.

7.7.1 Forced entry

Under s.6 Criminal Law Act 1977 it is an offence for any person to use or threaten violence, without lawful authority, in order to secure entry into any premises. On summary conviction a person can be fined up to level five and/or be sentenced to up to six months in prison. For the entry to be criminal there must be someone on the premises opposed to the entry and the bailiff seeking to enter must know this. It is immaterial whether the violence was directed against the premises or person. If such an entry is in progress the police may be called by the debtor and under subs. 6 a uniformed constable is empowered to arrest, without warrant, anyone with reasonable cause suspected of committing such an offence. Also under the same act, s.7, an offence is committed if the trespasser excludes a "displaced residential occupier". Though previously aimed at squatters, the provision may be worded in sufficiently broad terms to apply to cases where the bailiff seeks to impound goods by securing the whole premises (see 8.2.2). The section does *not* apply to non-residential premises.

Note also that a criminal entry may also involve criminal damage under Criminal Damage Act 1971. This offence arises wherever another's property is intentionally or recklessly destroyed or damaged without lawful excuse, or threats to that effect are made. The offence is triable on indictment and on conviction the penalty is imprisonment for up to ten years. Self defence or defence of another are lawful excuses for the offence but it is doubtful if the existence of a warrant *per se* would assist the bailiff. There is no power of arrest by constable at the time the offence is being committed, as with forced entry.

7.7.2 Unlawful wounding

Unlawful wounding or other bodily harm can be prosecuted if a bailiff's actions cause any malicious injury. For example, in *ex parte Smith* (1890) 7 TLR 42 a bailiff broke open a door with excessive force whilst trying to levy execution. The bailiff was convicted by the magistrates. The offence is imprisonable. Assault is also an offence for which the court may fine or imprison a person.

7.7.3 Criminal contempt

As described at 5.4.1 it is a misdemeanour and contempt for a civil court bailiff to commit certain offences when in execution of their duty (s.29 Sheriff's Act 1887). It is also contempt for any person to pretend that they are a sheriff's officer (s.29(6)). In both cases the High Court may fine or commit the offender.

7.8 Statutory remedies

There are various remedies unique to distress for rent and related common law forms of distress that are provided by a number of venerable statutes. Partly because of their obscurity, and partly because of their limited application, they are little used today, but are worth brief notice, if only for the sake of completeness. In either case, even though the tenant may settle any arrears due, s/he may still maintain an action as a tort has been committed (FNB 90B; 18 Ed. II).

7.8.1 Distress off demised premises

Under cc.2 & 15 Statute of Marlborough 1267 (confirmed by Statute of Westminster I c.16 in respect of the taking of cattle), if a landlord distrains "out of his fee", in other words not upon the premises in respect of which the rent is due, he is liable to a fine "and that according to the quantity and quality of the trespass". The aggrieved tenant's remedy is to sue upon the statute for trespass. Replevin does not lie (Thel Dig 117; 2 Co. Inst. 101).

7.8.2 Distress on highway

Statute of Marlborough 1267 c15 also makes it unlawful for the landlord to levy distress "in the king's highway nor in the common street". The tenant has the remedy of recaption (see 3.3.2 and *Smith* v. *Shepherd* (1591) Cro Eliz 710) and also the right to bring an action for trespass on the statute. A normal action for trespass does *not* lie (FNB 90A: though see 2 Co. Inst. 131 to the contrary). There is an exception to this rule where the landlord takes goods in 'fresh pursuit' (see 7.3.2).

Chapter Eight

CONDUCTING LEVIES: PROCEDURE

Levies are the crucial stage in the process of either distress or execution as they give the bailiff rights over goods which entitle him to remove and sell them, make further charges and which pressure the debtor into paying. Unfortunately the procedure is uncertain and ill defined: in *Evans* v. *South Ribble* [1992] 2 All ER 695 Simon Brown J remarks "*what constitutes impounding on the premises is . . . unclear, as also is the effect of a walking possession agreement*".

The elements of the levy process are concisely summarised judgment of Simon Brown J in *Evans* (above) that posting "walking possession agreements" to debtors did not amount to seizure: "*the process of distress consists of three stages: the entry into the premises, the seizure of the goods there and the subsequent securing of the goods (generally called impounding) . . . Impounding can take a number of forms*". Entry has been described in the last chapter. The elements of seizure and impounding are analysed in the following sections.

In brief, seizure is taking possession and impounding is keeping possession of the debtor's goods. In respect of these elements of the levy process, there seems no reason for differentiating between the different forms of distress and execution. We may note for example that "Woodfall on Landlord & Tenant" treats the three stages identified in the *Evans* judgment as applicable to distress for rent.[1]

Many of the problems that arise with seizure by bailiffs stem from their failure to adequately distinguish between the separate elements in the procedure. The cause of this seems to be the widespread use of walking possession. As noted in chapter one it was sanctioned by s.10 DRA 1737 but the untility of the process meant that it was quickly adopted as the universal and exclusive means of impounding goods (see for example *Child* v. *Chamberlain* (1834) 5 B&A 1049). The result is that seizure and impounding both occur in the home at the same time, with the result that, in the words of Wightman J in *Johnson* v. *Upham* (1859) 2 E&E 250 at 265, "these acts are very nearly if not quite concurrent". The blurring of these two stages and the resultant problems have been identified as sources of confusion since at least the mid-nineteenth century, as the remarks in the *Johnson* judgment indicate.

8.1 Seizure

8.1.1 Theory

Seizure describes the process of identifying the goods being seized, usually by recording them on an inventory, though the term can also refer to both seizure and

[1] And see Morritt LJ in *Khazanchi* v. *Faircharm Investments* [1998] 2 All ER 901 at para. 5 in which the Evans analysis is taken to apply to both distress for rent *and* execution.

impounding as a process – here levy has been preferred to avoid confusion. The act of seizure of the debtor's goods will involve some process of selecting and securing items: a bailiff is not necessarily entitled to all the goods on the premises and has to select sufficient to cover the debt and costs whilst ensuring this is not excessive. Thus in *Rai & Rai* v. *Birmingham City Council* [1993] unreported, a deputy stipendiary magistrate held that bailiffs have a duty of care to exercise when seizing goods: they must act with discernment and judgment as the power of distraint is not " a dragnet trawling all within it". If put on notice that certain goods do not allegedly belong to the debtor, the bailiffs must act with "caution and circumspection". The goods seized must be available for seizure, that is, not exempt in some way.

In finding items suitable for seizure the bailiff is under a duty to employ "reasonable diligence" in searching premises for goods (*Mullet* v. *Challis* [1851] 16 QB 239). As part of this the bailiff may break open any inner door or cupboard both to find goods (*White* v. *Wiltshire* (1619) 79 ER 476; *Browning* v. *Dann* [1735] Bullers NP 81c) and to escape if he is locked in (*Pugh* v. *Griffith* (1838) 7 Ad & El 827). 'Inner doors' may include chests and trunks (YB 186d, IV fo.4 pl.19) and therefore, presumably, desks and other furniture. In one case it was held that legal entry through an outer door then justified not only the breaking of internal doors, but also windows in the property (*Lloyd* v. *Sandilands* (1818) 8 Taunt 250). Because of the huge inconvenience it could cause to bailiffs, no demand need be made before forcing each inner door, though this precludes the unnecessary use of force where a door is broken despite the debtor's offer to open it (*Hutchison* v. *Birch* (1812) 4 Taunt 619). If force were used despite an offer to open the door, damages would probably be recoverable.

Defining what constitutes seizure can be problematic, but a useful "negative" definition may be found in *Mortimer* v. *Cragg* (1878) 3 CPD 216 CA in which Bramwell LJ considers the basis upon which a sheriff may charge "poundage" (see 11.1.3). Charges may be made if there has been seizure. The test of whether this has occurred is "supposing the sheriff had not the authority of the court, could an action in trespass be brought against him?" As will be seen in chapter 9 trespass to goods can include any disturbance of possession, such as removal (*Wilson* v. *Lombank* [1963] 1 All ER 740), moving goods from one room to another (*Kirk* v. *Gregory* (1876) 1 Exch 55) or securing goods so that they are not in the debtor's control (*Jones* v. *Lewis* (1836) 7 C&P 343; *Hartley* v. *Moxham* [1842] 3 QB 701). Coke (2 Inst 154) defines execution as obtaining actual possession of anything by judgment of law (and see 8.2.1 as well).

8.1.2 Practice

In practice there are two forms of seizure:

- *actual*: as the name suggests this will involve the bailiff actually seeing, even touching, the goods that are to be seized and listed for sale. It may well be coupled with a clear declaration of the bailiff's intention. A good example of this is magistrates' court distraint. If the bailiff levies upon household goods, they cannot be removed from the house before the day of the sale without the person's written consent but must be impounded with a conspicuous mark (r.54(8) MCR). It is an offence, punishable by fine, to remove the goods or remove or deface the mark (s.78(4) MCA). In a bill of sale case effective possession was taken by the plaintiff by marking the goods with his name and taking the keys to the room containing them (*Robinson* v. *Briggs* (1870) 6 Exch 1). It may be that seizure by a distinct act in this manner may relieve the bailiff of the need to do much more in the way of impounding (e.g. *Firth* v. *Purvis* (1793) 5 TR 432, in which the bailiff impounded goods in an unlocked cellar with his mark upon them).

- *constructive seizure* is far harder to define. The bailiff's intentions may be inferred from his actions, e.g. looking through a window, walking round premises, making and presenting an inventory of the goods seized or by some means preventing the removal of goods. The process is summarised by Chisholm J in *Noseworthy* v. *Campbell* (1929) 1 DLR 964: "*. . . to constitute seizure it is not necessary that there should be physical contact with the goods seized . . . Some act must be done to intimate that seizure has been made.*" A good example of this is *Cramer & Co* v. *Mott* (1870) LR 5 QB 357. W lodged in the defendant's house and hired a piano from Cramers. He failed to pay the hire charges therefore two men were sent to collect the piano. They were met by Mrs. Mott who said, in the tenant's presence, that the piano should not be removed until her rent was paid. It was held that there might be a distress without actual seizure and what occurred amounted to distress as it was enough for the landlord to prevent removal: if the firm had ignored her words, Mrs Mott was at the door of W's room and could have barred the way, i.e. her words could have been carried into action. A similar case, cited by counsel for the defendant in *Cramer*, is *Cotton* v. *Bull* (1857) CP, in which a lodging house keeper prevented a tenant in arrears removing personal items from the premises, which detention was held to amount to a distress.

The bailiff can seize one item or part of the goods in the name of all (*Cole* v. *Davies* (1698) 1 Ld Raym 624), but the whole must be in his power: he must know what is distrained and have power to take possession of them (*Re: Meehan* (1879) 6 Nfld LR 172). At least one item must be taken into actual possession it seems – *Re: Henley ex parte Fletcher* [1877] 5 Ch D 809 in which Mellish J states that "it may be by construction of law that his taking of one of the things in deed will amount to possession of all" but there must be actual possession by the bailiff before it can be said that there is formal possession of the rest.

8.1.3 Problems with seizure

Seizure must involve some process of selection before seizure and where this fails to happen the levy may be challenged (*Brintons* v. *Wyre Forest D.C.* [1976] 3 WLR 749). Seizure will fail also where the levying bailiff fails to make his intention to seize clear. Thus in *Nash* v. *Dickinson* (1867) 2 CP 252 the sheriff went to the debtor's house with a warrant and without saying or doing anything more produced the warrant and demanded the debt and costs. It was held that this did not amount to a levy because the bailiff did nothing such as leaving a notice or a possession man to indicate seizure had occurred. Equally in *Re: Williams ex parte Jones* (1880) 42 LT 157 a sheriff went to Williams' house and effected an alleged seizure of a horse and cart. It was held there was no seizure as no warrant was produced, there was no inventory that identified what had been seized and it was insufficient to touch items without informing the debtor that they were being seized by bailiffs. These were cases of execution, but similar principles apply in distress. For example in *Whimsell* v. *Giffard* (1883) 3 OR 1 CAN the landlord made two visits to the house, declaring he had seized everything. He touched nothing and made no inventory. There was no valid seizure. Equally in statutory distraint the same principles of practice are applicable. The court held in *Brintons* v. *Wyre Forest D.C.* [1976] 3 WLR 749 that no valid seizure occurred as, when calling at the plaintiffs' offices, the bailiff simply demanded payment of the rates and costs. He never said that all or any of the goods were seized, no effort was made to inspect or select suitable assets and nothing amounting to the taking of possession was done, e.g. there were no threats to leave a possession man on the premises. See also *Central Printing Works* v. *Walter* (1907) 24 LT 88 which confirms that if all the bailiff does is wait on the premises whilst the debtor seeks to arrange payment of the sum due, without any indication of any seizure, there will be no levy; and see *Ancona* v. *Rogers* (1876) 1 Ex D 285 in which a mere demand for possession after default on a bill of sale failed to alter actual possession.

Even though a valid seizure may have occurred, it must be stressed that the levy process is not yet complete. Seizure gives the bailiff immediate control of the goods, but they must now be impounded for the seizure to have any effect on the debtor, ie: for the bailiff to exert and retain title and control.

8.2 Impounding – theory

8.2.1 Definition

A distinct act of impounding is necessary in order to exert control over the seized goods. Although a bailiff may purport to levy distress by making a list of goods that he has "seized", this alone does not alter the debtor's rights over the property. The bailiff must acquire some legal control over the goods to have the power to return later, break into the premises, remove the goods on the inventory and sell them. This is achieved by impounding.

Impounding is said to be place the goods in the "custody of the law". It effects ownership of the seized goods in the sense that they are still the debtor's, but the his/her rights are now qualified by the rights of the bailiff. The bailiff now has a claim to possession and control of those specific goods against which the creditor's claims have been secured (see for example *Re: Pearce* [1885] 14 QB 966; *Re: Davies ex parte Williams* [1872] 7 Ch 314; *Slater* v. *Pinder* [1871] 6 Exch 228). This protects the goods from interference by the debtor (see 3.3.3) and seizure by other bailiffs (see 6.6.3 and 9.9). The need to give the goods legal protection is especially important for private bailiffs. Unlike officers levying execution (see 8.3.3) bailiffs levying distraint do not have the same legal status and some distinct act is needed to give them greater powers over goods than any other private individual.

This above paragraph gives a practical definition of the effect of impounding. The problem is that there is no coherent or contemporary legal definition of the process. A convenient starting point may be paragraph 490 of volume 17, *Halsbury's Laws*. Here it is stated that the effect of taking possession is:

- goods are no longer in the debtor's "apparent ownership" (see below);
- goods are no longer in the debtor's "order or disposition". This is derived from the

Bankruptcy Acts prior to the present Insolvency Act. The bankrupt's estate included all property in the "possession, order or disposition of the bankrupt . . . under such circumstances that he is the reputed owner thereof". Case law shows that goods seized in execution are no longer in the bankrupt's control such that s/he can be termed the reputed owner and the trustee can claim them (e.g. *Fletcher* v. *Manning* (1844) 12 M&W 571). On examination, we find that the possession referred to is that of a man in close possession on the premises. It is interesting that in a number of cases where this degree of possession was not found to have been achieved or maintained, the seizure failed (see cases discussed at "trading businesses" later at 8.3.1);

- the sheriff gets a special property in the goods, and thus acquires sufficient legal possession as to be entitled to sue in conversion and trespass (*Clerk* v. *Withers* (1704) 6 Mod Rep 290); and,
- the sheriff gets a security over the goods (see *Re: McColla ex parte McLaren* [1881] 16 Ch D 534 and above).

As stated above seizure removes the goods from the debtor's "apparent ownership". This refers to the Bills of Sale Acts – on default by the mortgagor the mortgagee may seize the goods to protect them against the trustees of the grantor and any bailiff levying distress or execution. They may both claim any chattels in the possession or "apparent possession" of the grantor at the time of the bankruptcy or execution. There is considerable bills of sale case law illustrating the nature of the possession required, situations often being brought before the courts when claims of trustee and sheriff conflicted (e.g. *Sales Agency* v. *Elite Theatres* [1917] 2 KB 164). What is apparent is that the sort of possession necessary to defeat claims from either the sheriff, the grantee of the bill or the grantor's trustee will have to be actual physical possession as manifested by a possession man. *In Re: Brenner ex parte Saffery* [1881] 16 Ch D 668 Lush J said of the sheriff's possession "*when I say actual possession, I mean actual visible possession, such a possession that everyone exercising ordinary vigilance can see it*" (see also *Re: Cole ex parte Mutton* (1872) LR 14 Eq 178 or *Taylor* v. *Eckersley* [1877] 5 Ch D 740). Moreover it is clear that something less than a possession man on the premises will not do to displace the debtor's "apparent possession" – see for example the following cases: *Re: Blenkhorn ex parte Jay* [1874] LR 9 Ch App 697 in which Mellish J said "*There must be something done which takes [the goods] plainly out of the apparent possession of the debtor in the eyes of everybody who sees them*" – allowing the debtor to use his furniture in the normal way was not such an action; *Re: Vining ex parte Hooman* (1870) LR 10 Eq 63 in which Bacon CJ commented on similar acts "*nothing has been done to change, in the view of the outer world, the appearance of the ownership which the bankrupt was, and for anything that appears, still is invested with*"; or *Re: Henderson ex parte Lewis* (1871) 6 Ch App 626 in which it is held that more than "mere formal possession" is needed to defeat the trustee, for instance locking up goods in a room on the premises. There are plentiful commonwealth authorities on possession under bills of sale to the same effect (for example *Averill* v. *Caswell & Co* (1915) 31 WLR 953; *Heaton* v. *Flood* (1897) 20 OR 87). On this basis walking possession may not serve to remove goods from the debtor's apparent ownership.

Thus it is clear that are however major problems defining the nature and purpose of impounding. A significant part of this is that practice has converged whilst the stated law has not. Walking possession was developed relatively recently for bailiffs' convenience in retaining possession of seized goods. It has been generally adopted. Despite this, the law on impounding in distress has not acknowledged this change and therefore describes the impact on the parties of a procedure now quite different from that used. It is arguable that impounding in the original sense of the term no longer occurs (see Kruse 1998, 1 and Kruse 1999).

8.2.2 Forms of impounding

Statute recognises four different forms of impounding:

- *immediate removal*: a bailiff may take away the selected goods at the end of the first visit. This is the modern equivalent of medieval impounding when it was customary for the bailiff to remove items to the parish pound and secure them within it. Impounding was thus the physical act of locking the debtor's goods within the stone pound. Nowadays the bailiff will take the items to a store room. Only in distress for rent is the debtor entitled to know where the good have been taken (s.9 DRA 1737). In fact, except against businesses, this method is rarely used because of the expense and trouble involved (when the goods are impounded off the premises the bailiff is liable for them – see *Wilder* v. *Speer* (1838) 8 Ad & El 547);
- *securing in a room on the premises* as a means of impounding is permissible only in distress for rent (s.10 DRA 1737). There is no duty on the landlord to collect goods together in one room to impound them (*Washborn* v. *Black* (1774) 11 East 405) and it is seldom done. It is **not** permissible for a bailiff levying any other form of distraint or execution to lock up goods in a room on the premises. Further, it is illegal for any bailiff to impound goods by locking up the entire premises, thus completing excluding the occupier. This is tantamount to eviction and there is no power to do this. The warrant licenses the bailiff to seize goods, not to seize a property, and to endeavour to take exclusive possession of premises in this way is trespass. See for example *Woods* v. *Durrant* (1846) 6 M & W 149 in which the landlord entered premises by an open door and distrained. The goods were listed on an inventory and impounded in the whole house by locking and bolting the doors and windows and expelling the plaintiff. This lasted until the sale 21 days later. The landlord trespassed by impounding in the whole house when one room would do. The seizure was thus invalid. See also *Watson* v. *Murray* [1955] 1 All ER 350 or *Smith* v. *Ashforth* (1860) 29 LJ Ex 259. It has been held that excluding the tenant in this way can be treated as surrender by operation of law by the courts (*Planned Properties* v. *Ramsdens Commercials* (1984) *The Times* March 2). This of course would terminate the tenant's liability for rent and the right to continue any distress, but it seems a double edged sword with advantages and disadvantages for both parties;
- *close possession*: a bailiff may be left on the debtor's premises guarding the goods as "possession man". Nowadays the cost and staffing problems associated with close possession and the small fees allowed by statute mean that it is virtually never used. Close possession is not trespass if the debtor does not consent

(*Washborn* v. *Black* (1774) 11 East 405) though without any agreement no daily fee for close possession will be chargeable; or,

- *walking possession*: walking possession is a process whereby the debtor agrees (usually in writing) that the goods will remain in his /her premises, subject to the bailiff's possession and right to return and remove them for sale and also subject to payment of a small daily fee to the bailiff. For the debtor the inconvenience of losing the use of items is avoided (and continued use of the goods is not contradictory to them being impounded – see *Dimock* v. *Miller* (1897) 30 NSR 74 and also *ex parte National Guardian Assurance Co Ltd In Re: Francis* [1878] 10 Ch D 408). For the bailiff the inconvenience of leaving a bailiff or removing goods is overcome. Both parties benefit from the breathing space during which arrangements to pay can be explored. As stated earlier seizure is the taking of possession, whilst the walking possession agreement functions as evidence and confirmation of this act and its ongoing effectiveness (e.g. *Husky Oil & Refining Ltd* v. *Callsen Re: Weber & Sheriff of Battlefield* (1964) 45 DLR 396).

  The legal effect of walking possession may be easily characterised by stating that the debtor is appointed as "possession man" by the bailiff, i.e. an agent of the bailiff to supervise his/her own goods (*Federal Bank* v. *Kretschmann* [1886] 7 NSWLR 183). Debtors are effectively appointed as custodians of the goods and as agents for the creditor (*Dimock* v. *Miller* (1897) 30 NSR 74). Davies LJ at para. C p.601 in the judgment in *National Commercial Bank of Scotland Ltd* v. *Arcam Demolition & Construction Ltd* [1966] 2 QB 593 suggested that the wife who signed a walking possession agreement was appointed as the sheriff's agent and remained in possession as "a sort of bailee". If this is so, care must be taken by bailiffs when agreeing to such bailment that the debtor must be left in possession as "mere servant" of the bailiff and not left in full, independent possession (*McIntyre* v. *Stata & Crysler* (1854) 4 CP 248).

  As seen, the exact effect and status of the walking possession agreement is uncertain, and it is at least arguable that it is not permissible at common law and therefore not applicable to any form of distress where statute has not sanctioned its use – which has implications for statutory distraint (see for instance Co Litt 47b and the more recent rates case *Peppercorn* v. *Hofman* [1842] 9 M&W 618). Despite these theoretical concerns it has been recognised by custom and practice and by the courts for at least one hundred years (see for example *Berry* v. *Farrow* [1914] 1 KB 632, in which it was acknowledged that walking possession could not constitute either abandonment or withdrawal). Most of the relevant regulations provide for walking possession and for the debtor to pay for this (though the fee may be small and its duration limited), though some are less specific, instead requiring goods to be either deposited by the bailiff in some fit place, left in the custody of a fit person or safeguarded by some other fit manner(s.90 CCA; art. 11 ERTDO). Some regulations also provide either a definition of the nature of walking possession (see local tax charge scales in the schedule to the regulations) or a standard form of agreement that bailiffs should use (see for example DRR 1988; county court form N334 or Sheriff's Fees (Amendment) Order 1956). However the definition of the effect of walking possession can differ from one form of distress to another – a point to be returned to at 8.4.2.

8.3 Impounding: practice

8.3.1 Walking possession

Walking possession is the form of impounding used almost exclusively and attention must therefore be concentrated on its operation in more detail. If the premise behind distress or execution is borne in mind – that the tenant is made to pay through the inconvenience of being deprived temporarily or permanently of his/her goods – for a possession arrangement made for the parties' convenience to have any meaning, an agreement to impound must be made (*Black* v. *Coleman* (1878) 29 CP 507). An explicit agreement is also important to permit the bailiff to charge for this form of impounding, to secure the creditor's rights and provide evidence of the continuing existence of the levy in the bailiff's absence. However once goods are impounded by leaving them in situ in the debtor's house, for his/her benefit, it will not be possible for him/her later to complain that there has been no impounding (see Macnaghten J at 207 in *Lavell* v. *O'Leary* [1933] 2 KB 200).

In respect of the making of these agreements, the following principles may be elaborated. The effect of failure to comply with these is discussed at 8.4.2.

- *any responsible person* on the premises, including the spouse, partner or adult relative of the debtor, can in most cases make the agreement. See *National Commercial Bank of Scotland Ltd* v. *Arcam Demolition & Construction Ltd* [1966] 2 QB 593 in which the sheriff's officer obtained the signature of the debtor's wife. It was argued that she was not authorised to sign and thus the goods had been abandoned. On appeal it was decided that she was a responsible person capable of signing even without her husband's authority and against his will. The debtor's authority or consent is not necessary and "responsible" was defined as knowing the goods shouldn't be moved by anyone else, stopping them being removed and telling the bailiff if they are.

  The relationship between signatory and debtor is not important so long as that person is capable of understanding the implications of the agreement and being able to transmit that information to the debtor (or any other bailiff who might call) should they wish to remove the seized goods from the property. Finally it is interesting to speculate whether a walking possession agreement made by a "responsible person" can be a contract held to commit the debtor to pay walking possession charges.
- *children* cannot make such agreements, nor, arguably, can individuals only temporarily present in the property at the time the bailiff calls (*Lumsden* v. *Burnett* (1898) 2 LRQB 177).
- *for local taxes* much stricter requirements are laid down in the regulations. The only acceptable signatory is the debtor named on the liability order, and s/he must sign at the time of the levy. If the debtor does not sign, no charges may be made This provision needs to be read in conjunction with the decision in *H* v. *Sandwell MBC* (1993) Legal Action August p.15. Here a husband and wife were both in arrears with community charge. The husband signed a walking possession agreement in respect of a levy for his debt. The bailiff later sought to remove goods under this in respect of the wife's debt. A complaint was made to magistrates'

court. At the hearing the council conceded that there was no valid walking possession agreement in respect of the wife and the magistrates made an order declaring the attempted levy to be irregular, the walking possession charges unlawful and prohibiting further enforcement against the plaintiff.

- *trading businesses*: where distress is levied upon a business that continues to trade the stock and materials seized and subject to walking possession must, if the business is to continue, be sold by the firm. In theory this would be a breach of the possession agreement by the debtor (see 3.3.2) and to allow it would be abandonment by the bailiff (see 8.4.1). At the same time, to permit the firm to trade is likely to raise income to satisfy the debt. The bailiff must therefore find a means of taking possession that is both apparent and yet permits the business to continue to operate.

  A solution to this is allowing the trader to dispose of seized items so long as they are replaced immediately. The bailiff must make any such arrangement very carefully or else he risks abandonment of the goods. Upon initial seizure a detailed inventory should be taken and the fact that stock will change noted on it. Limits on the amounts of stock that may be sold over a given period may be imposed. Regular repeat visits will need be made to the premises to check on the goods. On such occasions it will be necessary for the bailiff to either up date the inventory by seizing more goods or receive the proceeds of sale of the items that have been sold by the trader. If sold stock is not being replaced by the trader, it will be necessary for the bailiff to consider removal if no funds are available to make payment to cover the value of the missing goods. Such successive levies may be permissible for execution and distraint, but it is doubtful that the procedure could be legal in distress for rent (see 10.7).

  This kind of approach has been sanctioned by the courts in *Re: Dalton ex parte Herrington & Carmichael* v. *Trustee* [1963] Ch 336. See also *Re: Hunter* (1912) 8 DLR 102 in which the sheriff, instead of seizing and selling the assets of a liquor business, placed a bailiff in possession to receive the daily receipts of the business as a going concern. Where the receipts were handed over on a daily basis, the court was prepared to place on this the legal construction that each taking was a levy of execution. However where the debtor is allowed to trade with no indication of any alteration in possession, and no accounting for proceeds to the man in possession, the seizure is voided and the goods are abandoned (*Paget* v. *Perchard* (1794) 1 Esp 205).

  See also *Toussaint* v. *Hartop* (1816) Holt NP 335 in which the sheriff was in possession but the seizure and possession were both "concealed from the world" by the fact that the debtor was allowed to keep trading with the seized goods over an extended period of five months. When the trader went bankrupt the trustee's claim to the goods defeated that of the sheriff. A similar conclusion was reached in *Jackson* v. *Irvin* (1809) 2 Camp 48 – the debtor's employee acted as possession man of his stock and carried on the business as normal. When the debtor went bankrupt the trustee's claim to the goods defeated that of the execution creditor. In *Edwards* v. *Edwards* [1876] 2 Ch 291 a receiver failed to take effective possession of a business when trade was continued ostensibly by the debtor and the change of possession was not publicised. Such a "mere nominal possession" was not enough to defeat a later execution. These cases suggest that walking possession will not operate to remove the goods from the "order and disposition" of the debtor. In contrast two bills of sale cases show that publicly apparent possession of business assets will be effective seizure (see *Re: Basham* (1881) WN 161; *Gibbons* v. *Hickson* [1885] 55 LJQB 119). Numerous commonwealth cases give the same impression. It seems that such apparent possession is not necessary in respect of domestic assets (*Meggy* v. *Imperial Discount Co Ltd* [1878] 3 QBD 711). It was held that a person with claims to the property of a business could lose priority in those claims if the trader is allowed to continue to act as if s/he is entitled to them for all purposes and may sell or borrow against them, but no such inference about absolute ownership can be drawn from continued possession of household effects as they are being properly employed for their normal purpose if they are permitted to remain in the home.

8.3.2 Constructive walking possession

The passing of s10 DRA 1737 initiated (or endorsed) the practice of securing goods on the debtor's premises. From this point the link between impounding and real possession began to weaken, and it is clear from authorities already quoted that by the late eighteenth century the need for ongoing physical possession had diminished to a point where impounding could be achieved by quite simple steps on the part of the bailiff. Thus, even if there is no written possession agreement, a valid impounding will have occurred if the debtor, or a responsible person, is present during the levy and it is made quite clear to them what is happening.

So it is now that any act or word expressive of the intention to assume control of the goods is likely to be sufficient to take goods into (using the words of Sir John Allen CJ spoken with prescience in *De Grouchy* v. *Sivret* (1890) 30 NBR 104) the "virtual control" of the bailiff. This form of possession may be taken because of the inconvenience or impossibility of seizing items more fully. Nevertheless if the bailiff does act in this way, he has a valid possession of goods and all the rights that spring from that even though there is no signed agreement. The following cases give examples of how this form of possession may be taken:

- *seizure with written notice of impounding:* Service of a notice confirming a seizure amounts to impounding. In *Thomas* v. *Harries* (1840) 1 Man & G 695 a bailiff had entered a field and touched one of the cattle in it stating that it was distrained for rent as a representative of all the cattle. A list was made but the cattle were not moved or the gate locked. Notice that the cattle were impounded was then given to the tenant. This was held to be valid distress. Tindal CJ at 703 cited *Firth* v. *Purvis* (1793) 5 TR 432 in support of his judgment that giving notice amounted to impounding (however Lord Hanworth MR in *Lavell* v. *O'Leary* [1933] 2 KB 200 at 215 treats the marking of the goods by Firth as the act impounding – see 8.1.2). Furthermore we may note that Maule J dissented from the judgment *Thomas, supra,* as he felt that impound and secure were equivalent terms and that in this case the seizure thus fell short of this.

  Similarly in *Swann* v. *Earl of Falmouth & Jennings* (1828) 8 B&C 456 it was held that an effective levy occurred as notice to the tenant indicated an intention to leave the goods on the premises in the custody of the law without abandoning them: on arrival at the rented premises the bailiff announced his intention to levy for rent arrears, walked round the wharf and departed, leaving a notice listing the goods that had been seized, although they were left behind on the premises.

It seems that any notice will be valid whether given to the debtor or to a third party or agent. In *Re: Cooper* [1958] Ch 922, a dispute arose as to whether the sheriff's officer had indeed conducted a levy and was therefore entitled to reimbursement for the costs of execution from the bankrupt's estate. The sheriff levied by leaving with one of the bankrupt's employees forms stating that two tractors had been seized in execution. The bankrupt was asked to sign two walking possession agreements (though it appears he did not). One week later (after the Bankruptcy Order) the tractors were removed. Danckwerts J held "*it is not necessary that the actual goods be taken into possession by the sheriff's officer. Also it is not necessary that he should retain possession of the goods . . . There is certainly one authority (Lumsden* v. *Burnett* – see 8.4.2*) which shows that very little in the way of actual seizure would be sufficient to satisfy the requirements of delivery in execution . . . it does indicate the way in which very simple acts would be sufficient to satisfy the requirements of taking and retaining possession. But it is, in each case, a question of fact . . . events (in this case) entirely negatived an intention to abandon possession because everything was consistent with completing the process of execution*". In addition to leaving the four documents at the debtor's premises, the sheriff had taken all the necessary steps to arrange removal, again indicating his intentions.

- *verbal notice of impounding:* a landlord, hearing a tenant and a stranger disputing ownership of a lathe on the rented premises entered, touched the item and said "the article shall not be removed until my rent is paid". It was held that from the time of this declaration the lathe was in the custody of the law, so removal later by the stranger was wrongful (*Wood* v. *Nunn* (1828) 5 Bing 10).

  It seems that this will apply even where the notice is given for the creditor by a third party or agent. See *Werth* v. *London & Westminster Loan and Discount Co* (1889) 5 TLR 520 in which a tenant had given a bill of sale over his furniture to the defendant company, who then seized the furniture and left a man in possession. The landlord, Werth, heard of this and claimed his rent arrears by requiring the tenant, on his behalf, to hand a letter in respect of the arrears to the man in possession. The tenant declared "I distrain for rent due to my landlord". Later the defendants removed the goods. The landlord claimed wrongful removal, which was upheld on appeal as it was held that the landlord's actions constituted valid seizure against the company

- *assent by debtors*: In *Finn* v. *Morrison* (1856) 13 UCR 568 CAN the bailiff went to a shop and the owners told him to proceed as they would replevy. He listed some barrels at their request, but did not touch them or leave a possession man, relying on the tenants' assent and their stated intention to replevy. This was held to be a valid levy. A similar case in the same year is *Tennant* v. *Field* (1856) 8 E & B 336: the landlord entered to distrain and with the tenant's assent made up an inventory from a list provided by the tenant. The landlord did not enter any of the rooms in which furniture was situated, but handed the inventory to the tenant before leaving. This was held to be a valid impounding as the agreement with the tenant made a pound of the rooms in which the goods were located. In *Washborn*

v. *Black* (1774) 11 East 405 the courts held that there is no duty on a landlord to collect goods together in order to impound them and that they will still be impounded though not collected together by consent between the parties. See also *Kemp* v. *Christmas* (1898) 79 LT 233 where a comparable process of impounding seems to have been used, or at least implied by the court, so that the plaintiff could maintain an action for poundbreach. Note may also be taken of *Vicarino* v. *Hollingsworth* (1869) 20 LTNS 780 or *ex parte National Guardian Assurance Co Ltd In Re: Francis* [1878] 10 Ch D 408: the fact that possession is "friendly", in the sense that the debtor does not object (and may even find it convenient) does not make it any less real and absolute.

- *during interpleader proceedings:* a more modern example of the possibility of the bailiff's possession being deemed to continue whilst he was out of possession is found in *PB Manufacturing* v. *Fahn* [1967] 2 QB 1059 in which the court held that possession held before interpleader claims were made was restored without any need for a new writ once the claims were dismissed.[2]

Recently this form of walking possession has been termed possession by "operation of law" – Cooke J in *McLeod* v. *Butterwick* [1996] 1 WLR 995. However, as it is by its nature implied, rather than either agreed in writing or physically apparent, regular steps must be taken by the bailiff to ensure that possession continues, otherwise it will be "abandoned". This may be by return visits to the property, letters, phone calls etc (e.g. *Lloyds & Scottish Finance* (1966) – see 8.4.3). It is not uncommon to encounter this sort of impounding. Bailiffs prefer to make written possession agreements so that they may charge the statutory fee for the impounding, but if this cannot be done, they may still retain their rights by this route.

8.3.3 Execution

Execution by the sheriff's officer or county court bailiff is seizure by officers of the court. Because of their status, the goods are in the custody of the law as soon as, and at the same time as, they are seized by such a bailiff. An individual such as a landlord needs to undertake a further distinct act to achieve the same effect. Thus a bailiff levying execution who looks through a window may validly and legally seize and impound the items seen (*Giles* v. *Grover* (1832) 1 Cl & Fin 72 at 77 and *Wilbraham* v. *Snow* (1670) 2 Saund 47). However despite this, court bailiffs generally choose not to exercise this power and will, like private bailiffs, prefer possession agreements to evidence what has occurred so that no disputes can arise. What an officer levying execution must do to validly seize goods is very unrestricted:

- *an officer remains with warrant:* It was held that if a man enters under a warrant, not as a trespasser, with the intention of seizing, then the entry and his remaining must be held to be seizure (*Bird* v. *Bass* (1843) 6 Scotts NR 928). The sheriff attended to execute and, as the defendant was out, the officer, without saying anything, left a man with the warrant to wait.

[2] The same was held by Morritt LJ in *Khazanchi* v. *Faircharm Investments* [1998] 2 All ER 901 at para. 77.

- *verbal seizure:* In *Gladstone* v. *Padwick* (1871) LR 6 Exch it was held that "*It is clear that it is not necessary for the sheriff to lay his hand on a single article . . . I am of the opinion that . . . if the sheriff gives and makes known that he has come to seize and does, as far as words and intention go, seize all the goods . . . he has done enough*". The court also held that seizure in one part of a property is equivalent to seizure of goods in the whole property. This verbal seizure may be accompanied by production of the warrant as in *Balls* v. *Pink* (1845) 4 LTOS 356. The sheriff attended and stated that all chattels were in his possession, so that subsequent removal was at the debtor's peril, produced the warrant and then left. This amounted to seizure as the debtor understood his intentions.

The officer who is seeking to levy execution must totally fail to make his intentions clear to render the process ineffectual, such as a lack of any indication of seizure as in *Nash* v. *Dickenson* (1867) 2 CP 252 or a failure to indicate his purpose as in *Re: Williams ex parte Jones* (1880) 42 LT 157 (see 8.1.3 earlier for details). In levying under a second writ there is no need for actual seizure as the second writ's issue binds the goods already seized under a prior writ (*Jones* v. *Atherton* (1816) 7 Taunt 56).

8.4 Impounding: problems

8.4.1 Abandonment

Abandonment occurs when the bailiff fails to remain adequately in possession or delays his return and thus loses any right to return and remove goods seized. Any abandonment, however urgent and necessary, must be satisfactorily accounted for if the bailiff is to retain his rights (*Ackland* v. *Paynter* (1820) 8 Price 95). Any sort of agreement or arrangement with the debtor is likely to be evidence of impounding contrary to a claim of abandonment (*Anderson* v. *Henry* (1898) 29 OR 719; *Black* v. *Coleman* (1878) 29 CP 507). However four situations where the bailiff leaves will not be held by the courts to be abandonment:

- withdrawal under false representation by the debtor to the bailiff does not amount to abandonment (*Wollaston* v. *Stafford* (1854) 15 CB 278).
- *temporary withdrawal*: it is not abandonment to go out of possession briefly with the intention of returning: e.g. the bailiff goes out to get a drink of beer (*Bannister* v. *Hyde* (1860) 2 E & E 627). The bailiff was held to retain a "constructive possession" during his brief absence from the premises. Another example is *Coffin* v. *Dyke* (1884) 48 JP 757 – Coffin was left as a "possession man" in premises under a warrant of execution. No refreshment was provided for him therefore he went to a pub one mile away taking the warrant with him. His absence was only temporary. On return he was assaulted by Dyke to prevent re-entry. The court found that Coffin was in execution of his duty in re-entering and Dyke could be convicted for assault on a court officer.
- *walking possession:* the courts have been prepared to treat walking possession, whether by agreement or not, as a form of ongoing constructive possession that survives the bailiffs' absence from the premises, even though that may be prolonged. However in one case where the bailiff withdrew simply on receiving

from the debtor a letter (rather than signed agreement) acknowledging the possession and permitting him to re-enter as and when he wished it was held that the bailiff went out of possession and did not retake it, so that the goods were abandoned (*Bower* v. *Hett* [1895] 2 QB 337).

- *payment*: there may be no abandonment where there is an arrangement to pay, such as by instalments. If distress is then withdrawn such abandonment at the debtor's request is not voluntary (*Thwaites* v. *Wilding* [1883] 12 QBD 4).

To conclude, whether goods have been abandoned is a question of fact (*Eldridge* v. *Stacey* (1863) 15 CB NS 458), and depends on the court deciding whether there has first been impounding and secondly whether there has been an intention to remain in possession (*Jones* v. *Biernstein* [1900] 1 QB 100).

8.4.2 Ineffective agreements

To be valid a possession agreement must be in accord with the minimum statutory and common law requirements. If it is not, the bailiff may fail to retain possession and may abandon the goods. There are three main ways in which an agreement may be invalid.

Wrong place and time: A possession agreement must be made at the correct stage in the levy process and in the correct circumstances in order to be valid. Thus the following agreements will be vulnerable to challenge by the debtor:

- *posted to the debtor* – an agreement must follow a legal entry and levy and that paperwork dropped through the door for signature and return by the debtor is unacceptable and ineffective (*Evans* v. *South Ribble Borough Council* [1992] 2 All ER 695). *Evans* was an appeal by a community charge payer against the magistrates' court decision dismissing her complaint against bailiffs levying for S. Ribble B.C. The bailiffs attended for £341 arrears and as Evans was out, posted an envelope through her letter box containing a notice of distress, a draft walking possession agreement signed by the bailiff which required her signature and return plus various documents explaining methods of payment, the level of the debt etc. Evans ignored this and instead sought advice, leading to her complaint as to the method of seizure. In his judgment Mr. Justice Simon Brown reviewed the law as described earlier and concluded "*once entry is made, little in the way of seizure and impounding is required . . . (but) there must in the first instance be an entry*" thus "*it is my clear conclusion that external inspection and posting through the letter box is a course of action insufficient to bring about the legal consequences of distress*". Note also the case *Davidson* v. *Roach & Co* (1991) heard in Bristol County Court on May 30th and reported in Legal Action: goods were removed on the basis of notices posted through the door without any entry being gained. An injunction was granted by the court to prevent sale and the case was settled by the bailiffs and the local authority, apparently acknowledging that the seizure was invalid.

  It is clear therefore that the mere posting of documents by bailiffs levying distress has no effect whatsoever on the debtor's goods. A person cannot retrospectively make an agreement transferring rights over their property. A "walking possession" agreement signed by the bailiff alone and posted to the debtor cannot be an agreement binding on the debtor. Even if s/he subsequently signs and returns the document, as is usually requested, the debtor does not waive any irregularity in the manner of levy or adopt the agreement. Signing the agreement retrospectively will not estop the debtor from any subsequent objection to its legality. Even if the documents constitute a valid agreement it may be a voidable contract which could be set aside by the court because of fraud or misrepresentation by the bailiff. Even if distress had been successfully levied it would effectively be abandoned by the procedure (see *Dod* v. *Monger* (1704) 6 Mod 215; *Spice* v. *Webb & Morris* (1838) 2 Jur 943). If the agreement is invalid or there has been abandonment, no walking possession fee may be charged and the goods are not effectively seized. The debtor may thus may continue to deal with goods as s/he wishes as they are not in the custody of the law and cannot be until the bailiff has at least entered the property.

Readers should note one case that appears to suggest that "constructive impounding" after external inspection is a valid levy. This is *United Counties Trust Ltd & Duncombe* v. *Swaffield* (1939) 6 LJCCR 79 – this case is of great interest as it is the only recorded case where a bailiff has successfully impounded by looking through a window. However, the circumstances are significant. Duncombe was in rent arrears therefore Swaffield, a bailiff, was sent to distrain. He entered through an open window and legally seized furniture in the house. He then entered the garden. A motorbike was parked in a glass-house, the door of which was locked. Swaffield therefore read the number plate through the glass and added it to the inventory. The bike was later sold but Duncombe declared no effective seizure had been made. It was held that "*it is not necessary for the bailiff physically to seize every chattel on which he distrains; constructive seizure is enough and may be effected by taking any chattel on the premises and making clear an intention to seize everything there, or so much as will satisfy the rent. In this case the defendant seized some chattels and made an intention to seize the bike clear by including it on the inventory. The true test therefore seems not to be . . . whether the bailiff can physically seize if so minded, but whether he can impound them in the sense that he can prevent the tenant removing or dealing with them*". Clearly constructive seizure can be valid following an entry and as part of a more normal impounding, but will not be effective as the only means of taking possession of goods at a property.

- *made at the office* – "walking possession agreements" signed at an office without entry or even visits to premises are, by the same token, void (see 8.4.7).
- *local tax and child support* agreements must be made " at the time that distress is levied". If this is not done, there is no valid agreement as defined by the law.

W*rong signature* As seen at 8.3.1 in most forms of distraint and execution any "responsible person" may sign. If a suitable person cannot or will not sign, no walking possession fee may be charged. However the goods may still be impounded constructively (8.3.2) and the agreement with the "third party" is evidence of this, provided that it is left on the premises. If the bailiff endeavours to take possession and does so by means of an arrangement that is defective, it still demonstrates an intention to remain in possession and not to abandon the impounded goods. In *Lumsden* v.

Burnett (1898) 2 LRQB 177 the plaintiff's goods were distrained by collector of taxes but the bailiff went out of possession after getting the plaintiff's thirteen year old daughter to sign the walking possession agreement without authority from her father. However the bailiff did not abandon distress as he returned daily to the property to ensure nothing was removed. The seizure was valid and the agreement (though not binding on L) showed the bailiff's intention not to abandon possession and his return visit showed the goods were not abandoned. However as the possession was "constructive" rather than "real", no charges for a possession man could be made.

However for local taxes only the signature of the person named on the liability order will be acceptable. The signature of a spouse or partner will not do as a substitute. Because of the difficulty of always getting the liable person's signature, bailiffs often get someone else to sign. It is arguable that, in such cases, as an agreement not signed by the debtor is not an agreement made in line with statute, it will be completely void.

Wrong wording: The wording used on the walking possession agreement is crucial. This is because of the different phraseology used in the legislation.

- *distress for rent and road traffic penalties*: the DRR 1988 state that walking possession is "*in consideration of [the bailiff] not leaving a man in close possession*". This wording is on form 8 provided in the appendix to the rules.
- *statutory distraint for local taxes and child support*. The regulations state that walking possession is "*in consideration of the [bailiff] not immediately removing the goods*". Some bailiffs firms use the standard distress for rent agreement in all contexts. As the local tax and child support regulations state that the purpose of walking possession is quite different to that in rent distress, the agreement is likely to be void. No charges could be made and no removal could follow from it. All the bailiff could do is reword the form and start the levy again.

8.4.3 No written agreement

If it is not possible to find, or persuade, the debtor or another person to sign, it may still be possible for a bailiff to impound the goods by an oral agreement, though there is no clear authority on this. Charges could not be made for such an arrangement. However, despite the oral agreement being evidence of an intention not to abandon, in the absence of a written agreement as evidence of this impounding, the bailiff's rights will be quite short lived. If steps are not taken to keep the possession in existence, e.g. follow up visits, letters or telephone calls, or of course prompt removal, within a relatively short time the bailiff's rights will be lost. The goods are then abandoned and the seizure process will have to be begun again from the start.

If no agreement is made at all, either written or oral, the bailiff can leave notice on the premises that seizure has occurred and this will operate to adequately impound the goods for a brief period. The notice and the debtor's presence during the seizure will be enough for the bailiff to have asserted his legal rights and for the debtor to understand what was intended. However the right to return and remove will be transitory and soon lost unless the levy is quickly followed through by the means described above. Of course, no charges can be made for possession in this situation.

A good example of this sort of procedure is *London & Scottish Finance Ltd* v.

Modern Car & Caravans (Kingston) Ltd [1964] 2 All ER 732. The sheriff's officer went to a caravan occupied by the judgment debtor to execute a writ of fi fa. The sheriff gained entry and informed the debtor of his purpose, saying the caravan should not be moved. The debtor refused to sign any walking possession agreement so the sheriff restated the position, left a notice and departed. The sheriff left but did not abandon the goods as he could demonstrate he had returned to the site nine times in one month to check that the caravan was still there. Note that the courts have emphasised that possession should be actually, visibly retained wherever possible (i.e. even walking possession might not be enough – see discussion earlier at 8.2.1) but a notice left at the premises may be sufficient if the bailiff cannot remain *(Young* v. *Dencher; Bank of Toronto* v. *Adames, Sheriff of Acadia* (1923) 1 DLR 432).

This case may be contrasted to *Blades* v. *Arundale* (1813) 1 M & S 711 in which a sheriff's officer seized a table by touching it and saying "I take this" but then locked the warrant in the drawer, removed the key and left. The court held that although the seizure was good, the sheriff did not then remain in constructive possession: locking the writ up could not amount to continuance of possession. Readers may also wish to note the judgment of the Divisional Court in *Brown* v. *LB Haringey* (1986) cited by Simon Brown J at 704 in *Evans* v. *South Ribble BC* [1992] 2 All ER 695. In this case bailiffs had been allowed to enter to levy for general rates by the appellant's wife. They left a draft walking possession agreement with her. The Court found this agreement to be unsigned and therefore ineffective.

8.4.4 Conduct of impounding

A bailiff should not remain in possession an unreasonable period or without the debtor's consent (*Re: Finch* (1891) 65 LT 466, where possession for a period of ten days was felt more reasonable than five months). The circumstances of the possession should not be unreasonable (*Griffin* v. *Scott* (1726) 1 Barn KB 3 – eight bailiffs in possession for six days led to an award of damages for trespass).

Where ever goods might be impounded, a definite place must be chosen and must be fit, as the bailiff is responsible for taking care of seized goods and can be sued for any damages caused by the pound's unfitness. The place chosen must not only generally be fit, but must be fit at the particular time in question i.e. it should be checked before hand and regularly during impounding (*Wilder* v. *Speer* (1838) 8 Ad & El 547). If it becomes unfit the distrainor must find an alternative location (*Bignell* v. *Clarke* [1860] 5 H&N 485). Note that in distress damage feasant there is no duty to inform the owner of either the fact or the place of impounding. A distrainor can choose what pound to use, but has a duty of care for impounded chattels.

8.4.5 "Doorstep levies"

There has been recent evidence of the development of a practice by bailiffs which appears to aim to get around the not infrequent tendency of debtors to refuse entry to their homes. The bailiff, not to be deterred by the refusal, instead levies upon some item of value that they are wearing – typically a watch or jewellery – and then obtains a walking possession agreement for this. Sometimes an inventory of household is prepared on the doorstep, in conversation with the debtor. This may be termed a "doorstep levy". It is necessary here to determine whether this a proper and valid procedure. Furthermore we must ascertain whether a standard endorsement on any inventory referring to "all other goods on the premises" means that the bailiff has in fact seized the goods in the house as well, despite being refused entry.

- *A valid levy?* The bailiffs concerned tend to be collecting local taxes. These, and most other debts, may be levied upon the debtor's goods wherever they are in England & Wales, so the mere fact that they are not within the home is not of itself a problem. The seizure of a watch or ring would thus be legal, unless it could be argued that the item seized was exempt as basic clothing, wearing apparel in use or, perhaps, valueless (see 9.1.1).
- *Household goods too?* This question can appear more problematic, especially where, as sometimes happens, the inventory includes a list of items inside the home drawn up by the bailiff in conversation with the debtor on the door step. A glance at the authorities might appear to support the legality of this. In *Tennant* v. *Field* (1856) 8 E&B 336, the bailiff attended to levy at the debtor's premises and, in order to avoid disturbing lodgers in certain of the rooms, based the seizure on an inventory of goods drawn up in consultation with the debtor's spouse. The court held this to be a valid seizure and impounding. This appears to support the practices described above. There is, however, one crucial difference. In *Tennant* the bailiff gained entry to the property and could have gone into every room if he had wished. What was done was done partly out of courtesy and partly out of convenience. A way of proceeding was agreed, to which the debtor later assented, that avoided doing unnecessary injury to the plaintiff by leaving the goods in place so that lodgers were not disturbed, and avoided any risk of damage to the goods that might arise during removal. In the examples under discussion, there has of course been no entry. On the basis of the decision in *Evans* v. *South Ribble Borough Council* [1992] 2 All ER 695 (see earlier), it may be concluded that without prior entry, the bailiff cannot purport to seize household goods – regardless of any transaction with the debtor on the doorstep. The wording of the inventory implies nothing. Whilst the debtor refusing to sign a walking possession agreement after entry and seizure cannot defeat the bailiff's rights, signing walking possession before any such entry cannot, conversely, expand or create any rights.

To summarise, seizure of an item on the doorstep cannot be extended to the property inside which was never seen and to which access was not obtainable. Further, even though the debtor may provide details of property inside the house, without actual entry to the premises, it has still not been seized.

8.4.6 Clamping

The use of clamping to immobilise motor vehicles may be encountered in a number of contexts. Clamps may be applied:

- *to an illegally parked car* by a police officer under s.104 Road Traffic Regulation Act 1984;
- *to a car with no valid vehicle fund licence* (tax disc) by agents appointed by Customs and Excise under s.32A and sch. 2A Vehicle Excise and Registration Act 1994;
- *to a car wrongfully parked* on private property (see 8.4.8); and,

- *to car being seized* by a bailiff levying distraint. It is now very common for bailiffs levying distraint, especially for fines and road traffic penalties, to seize and clamp motor vehicles.

In the case of distraint no statutory provision exists to confer the power of clamping on the clamper. The activity must be set within the broader context of enforcement law to question whether or not it is a legal process. The case law on distress damage feasant (see 8.4.8) cannot be of much assistance, particularly where prior trespass by the car owner is absent.

Clamping must be regarded as an effort to impound or take possession of seized goods. Immobilisation secures and continues the bailiff's rights and purports to place the goods in the custody of the law. It is clear that clamping is neither close possession nor immediate removal to a pound. Some within the bailiffs' profession have argued that clamping is part of the removal process. If this is so, then justifying the practice may face less of the problems to be outlined below, but one would expect it to be preceded by some separate act that constitutes impounding. Usually such an act is not identifiable, and as there is often a delay between clamping and actual removal by tow truck of normally at least a day, it seems more realistic to define clamping as the earlier act of impounding, rather than to suggest that both clamping and towing away are one part of a (protracted) act of "immediate" removal.

By process of deduction, therefore, if clamping resembles any form of impounding it must be walking possession. Walking possession is often defined as a way of avoiding both close possession or immediate removal. In distress for rent it is explicitly stated that walking possession is for the "convenience" of the debtor (see form 8, DRR 1988). Clearly a clamped vehicle is not convenient to the debtor. Whilst walking possession most closely resembles clamping, there are significant differences between the two processes.

Both walking possession and clamping seem similar in that they are "remote" forms of control – the bailiff need not remain in possession of the goods in order to maintain the possession/impounding. Indeed, clamping may seem superior as it is more secure and obvious than walking possession. The similarity is deceptive. What makes walking possession acceptable as form of impounding is that is a derivation of close possession. Essentially the debtor is appointed as "possession man" to guard his/her own goods (*Federal Bank* v. *Kretschmann* [1886] 7 NSWLR 183). This is the root of the efficacy and validity of walking possession. To be clear about the nature of walking possession is to see the difficulties in endorsing clamping within the present law. Clamping is a new means of taking possession which cannot be reconciled with the previous authorities and practices. Of course the law can change, but the only recent extension in the practice of impounding by walking possession has been for the courts to acknowledge, albeit implicitly, that walking possession may often be taken without any agreement with the debtor i.e. goods may be impounded on the premises in his/her absence or without his/her explicit consent (*McLeod* v. *Butterwick* [1996] 1 WLR 995; see 8.3.2). To extend the principle beyond this would seem to be going too far. Note that distress for rent may be an exception to this statement – s.10 DRA 1737 grants to the landlord the power to "impound, *or otherwise secure*" seized goods on the debtor's premises. This phrase could include clamping.

Thus though the right to clamp may be useful, especially if the alternative for the debtor is the expense and inconvenience of removal, and the risk for the bailiff is poundbreach by the debtor removing a highly mobile and valuable asset, this cannot justify the current use of a procedure that lacks Parliamentary sanction and which as a result must be treated as trespass *ab initio* to the debtor's vehicle (see *Welsh* v. *Bell* (1669) 1 Vent 37 and 7.5.2). The act of clamping is initially trespass when wrongful possession of the car is taken, and its continuing immobilisation is a wrongful detention of goods (see 9.26). Faced with such torts, the debtor has four possible remedies. Recaption would be one: self help measures may be employed to release the car (see 3.3.2). The clamp may be removed by taking "reasonable" steps, including the use of "reasonable" force. This should only be done if it can be achieved without any damage to the clamp e.g. letting down the tyre. The criminal case law on this subject arose because drivers failed to take such care and were guilty of criminal damage. One levered off the clamp with a crow bar and dropped it over a 12 foot high parapet (*Stear* v. *Scott* [1984] unreported), the other set about the clamp with a disc cutter (*Lloyd* v. *DPP* [1991] *Independent* 21/6/91). *If*, however, the clamp can be freed without marking or injuring the clamp, and *if* it can be put in a safe place for the bailiff to collect, there seems to be no problem with a self help remedy. The vehicle has been wrongfully immobilised, and one may properly remove that restriction. It is even possible to use reasonable force to resist a bailiff found in the act of trying to apply a clamp. In either case, as defining "reasonable force" is difficult and such situations may easily escalate, self help is best avoided (see also 3.3.1). Other remedies would include suing for wrongful interference (see 9.26), paying the debt and then suing (see 9.32) or replevin (see 9.28).

8.4.7 "Counter levies"

Walking possession should normally be agreed at the time of a levy of execution but Court Service permits county court bailiffs to either leave an agreement for signature at the debtor's premises or even, in some cases, invite the debtor to attend the court at a later time to sign. This latter practice has developed into a procedure that may be very prejudicial to the judgment debtor's rights. If the person wishes to file an application to suspend the warrant on N245 they are required to first sign what purports to be a walking possession agreement. Some of the difficulties with court staff refusing to accept N245 applications were discussed earlier at 3.1.2. The particular aspect requiring attention here is the validity of this "possession agreement". As these are signed generally without any visit to the premises having occurred, it will be apparent from what has gone before in this chapter that these agreements will be of no effect. Like the posted possession agreements rejected by the court in *Evans* v. *South Ribble BC*, an agreement that purports to take possession without the bailiff having visited, let alone entered the debtor's property, clearly does not comply with the minimum elements of a valid levy as laid down in *Evans* (and recently confirmed in *Khazanchi* v. *Faircharm Investments* [1998] 2 All ER 901) and cannot alter the property in the debtor's goods at all. Generally there will be no prejudice to the debtor in signing such an agreement as it will enable the warrant to be suspended on reduced terms of payment. The only concern is where the debtor once again defaults and the warrant is reissued with the intention of following through the alleged levy. It would then be necessary to challenge the validity of the execution. An injunction, perhaps from the High Court, might be needed and it would then be necessary to challenge the procedure. As they seem to arise from District Judge's directions to the bailiffs, it is not clear if this is by judicial review or by appeal.

8.4.8 Distress damage feasant impounding

As has already been mentioned, distress damage feasant is typically used as a justification for clamping cars in private car parks. Until recently English courts have only considered the legalities of clamping in the context of criminal law (e.g. *Lloyd* v. *DPP* [1992] 1 All ER 982; see 8.4.6 earlier). However in *Arthur* v. *Anker* [1996] 3 All ER 783 the Court of Appeal specifically considered the application of distress damage feasant to private parking control. The majority decision of the court was that clamping could only be justified under distress damage feasant if actual damage was suffered. This might be physical damage to the land or might be the loss or obstruction of its use by the owners. In the instant case there was no evidence of any actual loss either to the owners of the land in question or to the defendants, the private security firm. Hirst LJ however dissented from this judgment, the difference in judicial opinion centring on the existing case law on the use of distress damage feasant in parking cases, which is mostly from commonwealth jurisdictions.

In the leading judgment in *Arthur* v. *Anker*, Sir Thomas Bingham MR analysed the applicability of distress damage feasant in three ways, which it will be convenient to follow. First, the purpose of the distress is to prevent ongoing damage by a trespassing chattel. In cases of illegal parking impounding cars by means of clamping actually prolongs the trespass by immobilising the vehicle on the private land. The Master of the Rolls' objection to this use of the remedy was thus conceptual – it seemed "anomalous that a self help remedy should amount in effect to a self inflicted wound." The true purpose of clamping is to deter wrongful parking rather than to terminate it.

Secondly, it was felt that proof of actual damage was essential and that Canadian authorities supported this (*R.* v. *Howson* (1966) 55 DLR 582; *Controlled Parking Systems* v. *Sedgewick* (1980) 4 WWR 425). None was proved in *Arthur* v. *Anker*, and the argument that the cost of clamping constituted damages was rejected.

On this point Hirst LJ dissented. He felt that as distress damage feasant is a remedy for trespass, in an action for which no damages need to be proved, the same should apply to the self help redress. It must be noted that Canadian authority on the use of distress in a case of bare trespass by a car does not support this (*Forhan & Read Estates* v. *Hallet & Vancouver Auto Towing Service* (1959) 19 DLR 756). Even if this point were wrong, Hirst LJ continued, it could still be argued that sufficient damage could be shown by the impending threat of loss (e.g. the owner not being able to use the car park) even though this might not be imminent. Finally, even if this were wrong, Hirst LJ argued that an obviously foreseeable expense such as the cost of clamping and removing a vehicle could be held to be actual damage. In this he followed *Jamieson's Tow & Salvage Co Ltd* v. *Murray* [1984] 2 NZLR 144, an authority that the rest of the court rejected as they felt that, in the absence of actual damage, "it would defy logic to allow the distrainor to rely on the cost of the distress alone to justify the distress . . ." as this would be the landowner creating his own damage.

Thirdly the court rejected distress damage feasant as applicable to the case as the fee payable to the clamping company for release contained no element of compensation for the trespass at all. Rather it simply augmented the profits of the security firm, who rendered their services to the owner of the car park free of charge. Conversely Hirst LJ felt that if the charge could be equated exactly with the damages suffered, as long as the charge was reasonable, it could be recovered.

This disagreement in the Court of Appeal is unsatisfactory. Where does it leave advisers confronted with claims of illegal distress damage feasant? The court accepted that the remedy survives and is applicable to chattels, though it was felt that it was undesirable to encourage its application to modern parking problems (here again Hirst LJ differed, seeing this development not as "some outlandish extension of an antiquated remedy, but rather another valuable instance of the strength and flexibility of the common law in adapting itself to new circumstances in an ever changing world"). We may conclude in summary:

- Distress damage feasant will continue to be used as a justification of car clamping. The decision in *Arthur* v. *Anker* does not forbid it in principle. However its application may henceforth be limited. Ideally distress should only be employed to prevent actual loss or damage to the property owners: in other words to deal with a situation of obstruction of access or parking, or if there is physical damage to the car park and there should be notice to the driver of the potential risk involved;
- If the compensation payable is to be solely based on the costs of the distress, it will be more likely to be accepted by the court in circumstances where there is some actual cost to the owner of the land. In *Arthur* v. *Anker* the security firm supplied its services as agents free of charge, making its money from the fees imposed on errant motorists. The Court of Appeal could not regard this as discharging any liability to the principle, but a retainer paid to a security firm, or costs incurred directly by the landowner in levying their own distress may be permissible; and,
- The remedy is more appropriate in cases where vehicles are towed away rather than clamped. The inherent contradiction in clamping and immobilising the vehicle causing the obstruction was highlighted by the court, and it is worth noting that the commonwealth authorities cited all concerned impounding by removal of cars from the premises. Indeed, the older English cases concerning distress of chattels also involve similar impounding: for example see *Ambergate, Nottingham & Boston & Eastern Junction Co* v. *Midland Railway Co* (1853) 2 El & Bl 792, or *Reynell* v. *Champernoon* (1631) Cro Car 228.

8.4.9 Permitted interference

Permitting sale or removal of goods by the debtor may constitute abandonment. In the first case to be considered (*Bagshawes* v. *Deacon* [1898] 2 QB 173) the sheriff seized goods from Bagshawes Bros. but was persuaded to withdraw from possession on learning that the business's goods were to be sold to a limited company. He received part payment and a written promise from Bagshawes to allow him to re-enter. The sale took place and then eight days later the sheriff once more seized the goods but the limited company initiated interpleader (see 9.24). The court held that as the sheriff withdrew to enable the goods in the custody of the law to be sold, without being able to demonstrate any urgent necessity to do this, he had abandoned the goods. Secondly in *Re: Dalton* [1963] Ch 336: a sheriff levied on the stock of a shop and took walking possession but gave limited permission to allow the trader to sell goods as long as they were replaced. The court held that the goods sold under that agreement were abandoned and the value of the execution thus reduced. It went on to make recommendations as to how such levies should be conducted.

However allowing temporary removal need not be abandonment (*Kerby* v. *Harding* (1851) 6 Exch 234). The bailiff permitted a person to take seized goods off the premises for a temporary purpose, with the intention on the part of the bailiff that they should be returned, which was done. It was held that there was no abandonment if the plaintiff restored goods to the bailiff voluntarily.

Commentary

It will be clear from the foregoing that the current state of the law on impounding is unsatisfactory (Kruse 1998, 1) and it is even arguable that in many cases impounding is actually unlawful (Kruse, 1999, 1) and that, largely as a consequence of this but partly as a result of bailiffs' own failure to follow strict procedures with care, many seizures are potentially invalid, normally as a result of failure to impound seized goods adequately. Possession agreements should always be checked and the circumstances in which such agreements were made should be investigated in detail. To summarise the basic steps that the bailiff should take – the predicating element is a legal entry to the premises. Once inside little need by done to effectively seize the goods, nor to impound them. There can be a pound whilst the goods remain in situ i.e. walking possession (*Washborn* v. *Black* (1774) 11 East 405); this impounding serves to secure the goods against both the occupier and strangers (*Lavell* v. *O'Leary* [1933] 2 KB 200) and there does not need to be any ongoing real or actual possession (*Jones* v. *Biernstein* [1899] 1 QB 470). However failure to enter, failure to indicate that seizure is intended and the use of procedures too much at variance with established authority will mean that the levy may be invalid.

8.5 Remedies for wrongful seizure

If seizure itself is not rendered illegal by any earlier unlawful act, such as forced entry, it will be the nature of what is seized that makes a levy wrongful. These issues are discussed in the next chapter at Part Four, 9.24 *et seq*. Remedies will arise in respect of the illegal taking of the goods and further may follow if removal or sale occur.

Chapter Nine

CONDUCTING LEVIES: GOODS

PART ONE – DEBTOR'S PROPERTY

9.1 Saleable goods

9.1.1 Goods with value

The bailiff can only seize such things "where the valuable property is in somebody" (Coke Litt 47) and that can be sold (*Francis* v. *Nash* (1734) 95 ER 32). As a consequence items that cannot be sold, such as deeds or personal papers, should not be the subject of a levy. Equally personal effects of minimal worth (and very likely not attractive at public auction, as is the case with much jewellery) should not be taken. A further relevant principle that is applicable in execution and of relevance to distraint is that where the only goods available are of insufficient value to even cover the costs of the process, the proper course of action for the bailiff is to notify the creditor of this and to return the warrant unexecuted (*Dennis* v. *Whetham* [1874] 9 QB 345 at 349). Where inexpensive jewellery or other personal items are taken, they will very likely not even cover the standard visit and levy fees, and a return of no goods is the appropriate response by the bailiff.

The sort of goods typically worth seizing are office furniture, cars, high quality domestic furniture, garden equipment and antique and "art" items. These will be seized based on a valuation of their sale price at auction. Only enough to cover the execution can be seized (*Pitcher* v. *King* [1844] 5 QB 758). However it is difficult to sell many second hand goods by auction because of controls, such as Consumer Protection Act 1987, over the electrical safety of audio visual and white goods, the fireproofing of furniture and safety of children's items. The effect of this is that it may often not really be worth removing any items from the average home.

9.1.2 Equitable interests

As they cannot be sold, equitable interests should not be seized (*Scarlett* v. *Hanson* [1883] 12 QBD 213; *Miller* v. *Solomon* [1906] 2 KB 91 at 96). In *Scott* v. *Scholey* [1807] 8 East 467 the court reasoned that whilst a legal interest in property such as a lease could be seized and sold, the same could not apply to equitable interest through simple practical considerations of inconvenience – for example the difficulty of valuation and the impossibility of delivery of possession (*In Re: Duke of Newcastle* (1869) 8 Eq 700). Although the court in Schott did question if the case might be different for equitable interests in goods rather than land, the case law is that any equitable interests, whether under an equitable mortgage (*Re: Lusty* (1889) 60 LT 160), under a bill of sale (*Holroyd* v. *Marshall* [1862] 10 HL Cas 191) or otherwise, are protected from seizure and may be protected by interpleader etc. Nonetheless "Halsbury's Laws" vol. 17, para. 480, note 3 states that ancient Chancery practice was to grant an order to the sheriff allowing seizure of an equitable interest or validating a prior seizure, for example from a trustee (*Pit* v. *Hunt* (1681) 2 Cas in Ch 73). The note continues to the effect that the High Court may therefore still have the power to grant leave to seize such property (see also *Horsley* v. *Cox* [1869] 4 Ch App 92 at 100).

9.2 Financial assets

9.2.1 Money

Bailiffs are granted the power by statute to seize money, in the sense of cash, in the following cases – execution, and distraint for child support maintenance, road traffic penalties, magistrates' courts orders and for income tax (*E India Co* v. *Skinner* (1695) 1 Botts PL 259). Note that case law suggests that this power may exist for local taxes as well (*Hardistey* v. *Barney* (1696) Comb 356). In the case of distress for rent loose money cannot be taken – that is, money not in a wallet, purse or other container (*Wilson* v. *Ducket* (1675) 2 Mod Rep 61). This is because, as distress was originally held only as security for the debt and had to be returnable in the same condition, any cash seized had to be distinguishable from the seizor's own. In other cases the money is of course simply paid over to the creditor.

The sums seizable must be in the debtor's actual possession, but this will include the daily takings of a business (see 8.3.1 earlier) and bank notes on a bank counter being paid out to a customer (*Hall* v. *Hatch* (1901) 3 OLR 147). Thus proceeds of sale of a property held by a third party cannot be taken (*Robinson* v. *Peace* (1838) 7 Dowl 93), nor can sums paid into court for the debtor (*France* v. *Campbell* (1841) 9 Dowl 914) or cheques written out by HMPG but not yet issued to the debtor (*Courtoy* v. *Vincent* (1852) 15 Beav 486), proceeds of sale held by the sheriff's officer or county court bailiff for the debtor (*Padfield* v. *Birne* (1822) 3 Brod & Bing 294) nor money held by an agent of the debtor (*Bell* v. *Hutchinson* (1844) 8 Jur 895; *Re: Fort Frances Pulp & Paper Co* v. *Telegram Printing Co* (1923) 4 DLR 204). As any goods seized do not become the judgment creditor's, neither does this happen to money seized, so a bailiff holding money taken in execution cannot in turn set that against a judgment debt of the execution creditor (*Collingridge* v. *Paxton* (1851) 11 CB 683). If the sheriff is holding proceeds of sale for a judgment creditor, if he has appropriated and set apart sums to pay over to that creditor, they may be seized under a writ issued against that party (*Wood* v. *Wood* (1843) 4 A&E 397).

9.2.2 Bills of exchange etc.

Some provisions also allow bailiffs to seize bills of exchange, promissory notes, specialties, bonds, cheques and other financial securities. Such instruments may be seized in execution and by the CSA. In road traffic distraint bills can be seized (art 9) but promissory notes, bonds, specialties and securities cannot (art. 9(b)).

Bills of exchange and the like partake of the nature of money, but have the character of chattels and choses in action as well. It is as chattels that they may be seized by bailiffs. It is as choses in action that they may be converted into the proceeds of execution. At common law negotiable instruments and cash were not seizable, and it is only by statute that this situation has been changed. This was done originally for sheriffs by means of s.12 Judgments Act 1838. This section provides a model for the later civil court provisions (e.g. s.91 CCA) and, it is suggested, for the procedure to be followed by other bailiffs in this position.

The instruments (or sufficient as are necessary to cover the judgment debt) may be seized and held as security by the bailiff. When the time for payment on the bill, bond etc arrives, the bailiff may sue upon it in his/her name to recover the sums due (and may even issue execution upon such a judgment). The sums raised are paid over to the original creditor. Any surplus after the expenses of the execution shall be returned to the debtor. Note however that the sheriff is not bound to sue on the instruments unless indemnified for all the costs of the action by the execution creditor.

9.2.3 Other assets

A life assurance policy has been held not to be security for money and thus not seizable (*Re: Sargent's Trusts* (1879) 7 LR Ir 66), nor is any money payable under it (*Re: New York Life Assurance Association & Fullerton* (1919) 45 OLR 606). The common law principle that choses in action cannot be taken in execution has not been altered by statute other than in respect of bills of exchange (*Dundas* v. *Dutens* (1790) 1 Ves Jnr 196) so it seems that it is not possible to seize the debtor's debts (eg *Willows* v. *Ball* (1806) 2 Bos & Pull 376), stocks and shares (*Dundas* v. *Dutens* above; *Taylor* v. *Jones* (1734) 2 Atk 600; *Nantes* v. *Corrock* (1802) 9 Ves Jnr 182), dividends (*Evans* v. *Stephen* (1882) 3 NSWLR 154), patents (see *Brown* v. *Cooper* (1870) 1 VR(L) 210; *British Mutoscope & Biograph Co Ltd* v. *Homer* [1901] 1 Ch 671) or trade marks and copyright (*Re: Baldwin* (1858) 2 De g & J 230 at 237).

9.3 Jointly owned goods

Only those goods belonging to the debtor may be taken (*Glasspoole* v. *Young* (1829) 9 B & C 696). This means that jointly owned goods may also be seized (*Farrar* v. *Beswick* (1836) 1 M&W 682) though the proceeds must be divided between the owners according to their shares (*The James W Elwell* [1921] P.351). Most regulations for statutory distraint refer to seizure of the "goods of the debtor" so that it is possible that jointly owned goods cannot be seized in such cases. The Inland Revenue can seize joint goods but choose not to do so.

9.4 Chattels

In income tax and VAT distraint and in execution the bailiff may seize not only goods but chattels (for tax see *Earl of Shaftesbury* v. *Russell* (1823) 1 B&C 666). Chattels can include more than just tangible property and the term covers leases (but not interests in leases – *Scott* v. *Scholey* [1807] 8 East 467) and rights under contracts. Where this wording is found in the relevant legislation the bailiff may seize the debtor's interest in goods on hire or hire purchase (see 9.16 and 9.17). Most regulations for statutory distraint refer only to the "goods of the debtor" so such property may not be taken.

9.5 Fixtures

The case law on fixtures differentiates between execution and distress for rent. For the latter see 9.21.2. This section will describe the rules for execution and assume that these are likely to also apply to statutory distraint.

9.5.1 Basic rules

The basic principle is that as execution cannot be levied on real property, fixtures which are attached to the property have ceased to be chattels and as a result cannot be taken (*Hulme* v. *Brigham* [1943] 1 KB 152). In *Boyd* v. *Shorrock* (1867) 5 Eq 72 the definition given in *ex parte Barclay* (5 DM & G 410) was quoted with approval – fixtures are "things ordinarily affixed to the freehold for the convenience of the occupier, and which may be removed without material injury to the freehold", for example machinery and cupboards. Chattels actually built into the structure of a property become part of it, such as doors, windows, hearths and chimney pieces (*Boswell* v. *Crucible Steel Co* [1925] 1 KB 119). Help may also be derived from the definition found in *Hellawell* v. *Eastwood* [1851] 6 Exch 295. Whether an item is a fixture is a question of fact. The court must firstly consider the mode of annexation and the extent of annexation – whether an item can be removed easily, safely and without damage to itself or the building; secondly the court must examine the object and purpose of the annexation and the intention of the person fixing them – whether it was for the permanent and substantial improvement of the property or for a temporary purpose. These elements may be examined in detail:

- *degree of annexation*: articles simply resting on the ground by their own weight are not normally regarded as fixtures. This is so even though the ground may be specially prepared to receive them or though a base is built (see *Re: Richards ex parte Astbury & Lloyds Banking Co* [1869] 4 Ch App 630 later) and even though they may sink into the ground by their own weight (*Wood* v. *Hewett* [1846] 8 QB 913). If an item can be removed without great damage, even though it may be well attached and the process of removal may involve digging, it is not a fixture (*Provincial Bill Posting Co* v. *Low Moor Iron Co* [1909] 2 KB 344). Items screwed, bolted or nailed down are generally fixtures, but the *purpose* can be a very important factor. Consequently even if the chattel is cemented it will not be a fixture if the purpose is not permanent (*Snedeker* v. *Waring* (1854) 12 NY 170 approved in *Elitestone* v. *Morris* [1997] 1 WLR 687). The importance of degree as a factor will vary also with the size of the item in question, so that a house, though not fixed, will probably be a fixture. Unfixed articles essential for the use of the property may be treated as fixtures, such as keys (*Liford's Case* (1614) 11 Co Rep 46b; *Hellawell* v. *Eastwood* [1851] 6 Exch 295). Items simply plugged into a power supply are not fixtures (*Vaudeville Electric Cinema Ltd* v. *Muriset* (1923) 2 Ch 72) but light fittings wired in probably are (*Gray* v. *Fuller* [1943] 1 KB 694; *Young* v. *Dalgety* (1987) 1 EGLR 117).
- *purpose of annexation*: increasingly in modern cases degree has been replaced by purpose as the important factor in determining the nature of a chattel (*Berkley* v. *Poulett* (1976) 241 EG 911). If the purpose of the annexation of a chattel is its better enjoyment as a chattel, it is not a fixture. An item affixed for permanent improvement of a property is a fixture (*Walmsley* v. *Milne* (1859) 7 CBNS 115). Thus items such as paintings, tapestries and antique panels are not fixtures, but a wall, though simply resting by its own weight, is a fixture if the intention is to make it part of the realty (*Holland* v. *Hodgson* (1872) 7 CP 328). The purpose of annexation is to be ascertained not from the motives of the person fixing the

chattels but from the circumstances of the case (*Re: De Falbe* [1901] 1 Ch 523). The circumstances can include current tastes and fashions as well as the property interest of the person (*Leigh* v. *Taylor* [1902] AC 157). Direct evidence of intention is inadmissible, instead the court's test should be objective.

This analysis was adopted in the modern case *TSB ex parte Botham* (1996) EGCS 149 in which the Court of Appeal repeated that the two main factors to be considered when determining whether items were fixtures were method and degree of annexation, and object and purpose of annexation. On this basis it was concluded that fitted carpets, curtains, gas fires and white goods are not fixtures, whilst, on the facts of the case in question, light fittings, bathroom fittings and fitted kitchen units had become fixtures. The existence of a hire purchase agreement in respect of a chattel, or an agreement that it will not become a fixture, does not prevent it becoming one.

We may therefore identify the following as classes of fixtures:

- *barns, sheds & greenhouses:* these are not fixtures even if they are bolted down (*Billing* v. *Pill* [1954] 1 QB 70). A conservatory however will be a fixture;
- *machines:* engines and parts fitted to them are fixtures. Looms nailed to the floor are affixed (*Boyd* v. *Shorrock* (1867) 5 Eq 72) as are beer machines in a pub (*Dalton* v. *Whittem* [1842] 3 QB 961), but a printing machine simply standing on a floor remains a chattel (*Hulme* v. *Brigham* [1943] KB 152). Freestanding equipment does not become a fixture solely because another machine supplying power to it is affixed (*Hulme* v. *Brigham*);
- *other business equipment*: fixtures may include stills set in brickwork, fixed ladders, swimming pool equipment, an alarm and video door entry system and a lift (*Melluish* v. *BMI (No. 3)* [1994] 2 WLR 795); a cinema screen fixed to a wall, advertising boards and tip up seats fixed to the floor, all equipping a cinema (*Vaudeville Electric Cinema Ltd* v. *Muriset* [1923] 2 Ch 72); millstones (*Wystow's Case* (1523) YB 14 Hen VIII fo 25 pl 6); a skating rink floor especially installed by the tenant (*Howell* v. *Listowel Rink & Park Co* (1886) 13 OR 476); items, such as an emulsifier, cream separator and ice chopper, used in a dairy ice cream business (*Assiniboia Land Co* v. *Acres* (1915) 25 DLR 439); an inn signboard (*Re: Thomas* (1881) 44 LT 781); post office fittings such as lockable letter boxes (*Bruce* v. *Smith* (1923) 3 DLR 887), and railway tracks (*Turner* v. *Cameron* [1870] 5 QB 306). By contrast chairs lent on hire for a limited period but screwed to the floor for safety reasons (*Lyon & Co* v. *London City & Midland Bank* [1903] 2 KB 135), a machine fixed by brickwork to a factory floor (*Parsons* v. *Hind* (1866) 13 WR 860) and a railway laid on piles (*Chamberlayne* v. *Collins* (1894) 70 LT 217) are not fixtures. Nor are horses, and by extension motor vehicles, used by a firm off their premises (*London & Eastern Counties Loan & Discount Co* v. *Creasey* [1897] 1 QB 768).
- *fuel meters and fittings* are fixtures (*Lee* v. *Gaskell* [1876] 1 QBD 700); light bulbs are not (*British Economical Lamp Co* v. *Empire, Mile End* (1913) 29 TLR 386);
- *shop fittings*:a counter and rack lightly screwed to a wall are not fixtures (*Horwich* v. *Symond* (1915) 84 LJKB 1083);

- *domestic fittings*: kitchen units are fixtures, but appliances within them such as fridges and gas cookers are not (*Allan* v. *Lavine* (1942) 1 DLR 731). However items such as ranges and ovens are fixtures (*Winn* v. *Ingilby* (1822) 5 B & Ald 625). Bathroom fittings in a fitted bathroom are fixtures (see *TSB* v. *Botham* above) as are fitted wardrobes and cupboards, mirrors, shelves and towel rails (*Gray* v. *Fuller* [1943] 1 KB 694). The same case also indicates that parquet floors and linoleum or vinyl flooring are also likely to be treated as fixtures (see du Parcq LJ at 712).

In summary items simply resting on the premises or lightly attached are unlikely to be fixtures but once an item is a fixture, any other article which is an integral part of it also becomes annexed, even if not attached to the fixed item (such as the drive belt on a machine) and the whole assemblage then remains a fixture permanently and cannot be seized in distress or execution. A bailiff can be sued for trespass to land for removing fixtures (*Moore* v. *Drinkwater* (1858) 1 F&F 134), but mere constructive seizure without severance or removal is not enough to found an action (*Beck* v. *Denbigh* (1860) 29 LJCP 273).

9.5.2 Other examples

The above examples can be supplemented by case law looking at various situations in which claims are made to property affixed to the freehold by the owner – for example, between mortgagor and mortgagee or tenant for life and remainderman (*In Re: Sir Edward Hulse* [1905] 1 Ch 406).

The principle in mortgage case law is that items annexed by the mortgagor pass as fixtures with the freehold to the mortgagee (see for example *Meux* v. *Jacobs* [1875] 7 App Cas 481; *In Re: Yates* [1888] 38 Ch D 112; *Gough* v. *Wood* [1894] 1 QB 713). This seems to apply even when partnership property is annexed to the premises of one partner (*Sanders* v. *Davis* [1885] 15 QBD 218). Thus from mortgage cases we gather that if machines are fixtures which pass automatically with the land, so is every part of them, such as drive belts (*Sheffield & South Yorkshire Permanent Benefit Building Society* v. *Harrison* [1885] 15 QBD 338); that the degree of annexation is an important factor to consider – so even an item on HP secured by bolts to prevent rocking ceases to be a chattel and becomes a fixture (*Hobson* v. *Gorringe* [1897] 1 Ch 182); that even if fixtures are intended only as temporary improvement, they can still become part of the land but the onus of arguing this lies with the person seeking to protect them (*Holland* v. *Hodgson* (1872) 7 CP 328); that items set into, but not attached to property, are not fixtures – nor are spares for machines that are not actually attached to them (*In Re: Richards ex parte Astbury & Lloyds Banking Co* [1869] 4 Ch App 630); that all machinery affixed in a "quasi-permanent" manner becomes part of the property (i.e. the items are intended to remain on the premises for their better use and enjoyment), even though the purpose of annexation was steadying the items and that they could be removed without injury to them or to the freehold (*Longbottom* v. *Berry* [1869] 5 QB 123); and that even if goods are simply annexed for their more convenient use, not to improve the property, and may be removed without any appreciable damage to the freehold, they are fixtures (*Climie* v. *Wood* [1868] 3 Exch 257 – in this case an engine screwed to thick planks laid on the ground and set in brickwork).

Note that items do not need to be separately mentioned to pass as fixtures with a mortgage (see *Re: Yates* above). If they are separately described, it will not make the mortgage a bill of sale (*Re: Armytage* [1880] 14 Ch D 379), nor will the right of a mortgagee of a leasehold to remove fixtures as against the lessor – for which see below (*In Re: Rogerstone Brick & Stone Co Ltd* [1919] 1 Ch 110). However if the mortgage allows the mortgagee to sever and sell fixtures apart from the land, it is a bill of sale – for which see 3.4.3 (*Small* v. *National Provincial Bank of England* [1894] 1 Ch 686).

The above rules are complicated by the further principle that, in execution against a tenant, whatever the tenant could sever, as between landlord and tenant, can be seized by the bailiff (*Day* v. *Bisbitch* (1595) 78 ER 622; *Poole's Case* (1703) 1 Salk 368). Therefore, having determined that an item is a fixture, in some cases it will be necessary to move onto consideration of the separate issue of whether it is a fixture removeable by a tenant.

9.5.3 Tenant's fixtures

Generally tenants are permitted to remove those chattels that they have affixed for the purposes of trade, and those put up for ornament or domestic use, and which are physically capable of removal without substantial damage to the land or to the chattel (*Webb* v. *Frank Bevis* [1940] 1 All ER 247). All such items may be seized in execution (*Dumergue* v. *Rumsey* (1863) 2 H&C 777). However these rights may be modified by the lease, in which case the sheriff cannot remove if the tenant cannot (*Duke of Beaufort* v. *Bates* [1862] 6 LT 82). The rules on tenant's fixtures apply to licensees just as much as tenants (*Never Stop (Railway) Ltd* v. *British Empire Exhibition (1924) Inc* [1926] Ch 877). The authorities on landlord and tenant fixtures give a contrasting picture of what can be removed from premises, but the case law may be summarised as follows. Trade fixtures include:

- *business equipment* such as machines, plant, vats and utensils (*Whitehead* v. *Bennett* (1858) 27 LJ Ch 474) but not chemical plant; engines for collieries (*Lord Dudley* v. *Lord Ward* (1751) Amb 113); petrol pumps – though bolted down and linked to underground petrol tanks (*Smith* v. *City Petroleum* [1940] 1 All ER 260); pub fittings (*Elliott* v. *Bishop* (1854) 10 Exch 496); brewing equipment (*Lawton* v. *Lawton* (1743) Atk 13);

- *small buildings* such as sheds built on brickwork in the ground (*Penton* v. *Robert* (1801) 2 East 88), glasshouses in a market garden (*Mears* v. *Callender* [1901] 2 Ch 388) and pre-fabricated buildings;

- *electrical & gas fittings* including fluorescent light boxes screwed to a ceiling (*Young* v. *Dalgety*, *Elliott* v. *Bishop*, *supra*);

- *shrubs & trees* which are the stock of a market garden (*Mears* v. *Callender* [1901] 2 Ch 388), but not fruit bearing trees in an orchard or trees which would be destroyed by removal;

The purpose of this right of removal is the protection of trade. Accordingly it has been held that locks, keys, bolts and bars to secure premises are not fixtures that can be taken by a tenant.

There is also a right to remove fixtures installed for ornamental purposes or for the domestic convenience and utility of the tenant. In determining whether the fixture is removable a number of considerations should be taken into account. Has the method of fixing made it permanent, as a more secure method of annexation may indicate that purpose of affixing was improvement of the premises? Would the chattel still be usable after removal? Would removal do serious damage to the structure of the property, rather than just the decoration? Ornamental items should be specifically ornamental and not an ordinary accessory of the property. Thus a conservatory was not a removable fixture (*Buckland* v. *Butterfield* (1820) 2 Brod & B 58). This class of fixtures includes such items as: panelling, suspended ceilings and chimney pieces installed by a tenant in a flat (*Spyer* v. *Phillipson* [1930] 2 Ch 183); bookcases and ornamental fireplaces (*Bishop* v. *Elliot* (1885) 11 Exch 113); pictures and frames screwed to walls (*Buckingham* v. *Pembroke* (1672) 3 Keb 74; blinds (*Colegrave* v. *Dias Santos* (1823) 2 B&C 76); cupboards (*R.* v. *St Dunstan (Inhabitants)* (1825) 4 B&C 686; *Re: Gawan ex parte Barclay* (1855) 5 De G M & G 403); bookshelves (*Birch* v. *Dawson* (1834) 2 A&E 37); cornices, wainscotting and stoves, ranges, ovens and boilers (*Grymes* v. *Boweren* (1830) 6 Bing 437).

The sheriff may also seize any interest that the tenant has in fixtures which are included in the lease. All fixtures removeable by a tenant may be taken, whatever their description (*Place* v. *Flagg* (1821) 4 M&R 277) unless they are simply too unwieldy to remove. Upon seizure fixtures should be separated from the rented property and sold (*Barnard* v. *Leigh* (1815) 1 Stark 43).

The sheriff cannot seize fixtures unlawfully severed by the tenant (*Farrant* v. *Thompson* (1822) 5 B&Ald 826). A tenant's right to remove items as against the landlord ceases on termination of the lease (*Pugh* v. *Arton* (1869) 8 Eq 626) and on disclaimer by the tenant's trustee in bankruptcy (*In Re: Lavies ex parte Stephens* [1877] 7 Ch D 127; *In Re: Roberts ex parte Brook* [1878] 10 Ch D 100) – though it has been held that the tenant (and his/her trustee) has a reasonable time to remove after termination (*In Re: Moser* [1884] 13 QBD 738). At the time of termination of the lease, property in the tenant's fixtures vests in the landlord (*In Re: Maryport Haematite Iron & Steel Co Ltd* [1892] 1 Ch 415). The tenant may still remove fixtures if s/he is holding over at the end of the term (*Weeton* v. *Woodcock* [1840] 7 M&W 14).

Remember that these categories are only of relevance to execution. In distress tenant's fixtures, and fixtures in general at common law, cannot be seized (*Darby* v. *Harris* [1841] 1 QB 895).

9.5.4 Agricultural fixtures

One class of tenant's fixtures requires separate consideration, that of chattels affixed to premises by tenants of agricultural holdings. At common law such fixtures were not removeable, but statute has intervened to alter this, with the consequence that these items will be seizable in execution. Two statutory codes apply, depending on the nature of the tenancy.

If the tenancy is of an agricultural holding regulated by Agricultural Holdings Act 1986, the rights of tenants to remove fixtures are controlled by s.10. The basic rule is that a tenant farmer may remove:

- any engine, machinery, fencing, or other fixture of any description fixed to the holding by the tenant, whether for agricultural purposes or not; and,
- any building erected by him on the holding (s.10(1)).

These rights apply to any fixture or building acquired by the tenant as well as erected by him/her (s.10(7)), but do not apply to any buildings or fixtures put in place as a result of an obligation; any fixture or building replacing one belonging to the landlord; a building in respect of which the tenant is entitled to compensation under the Act or a building or fixture dating to before 1884 (s.10(2)). The tenant's common law right to remove trade or ornamental fixtures is unaffected (s.10(8)).

If the tenancy is a farm business tenancy regulated by Agricultural Tenancies Act 1995, the Act provides a complete code relating to all tenant farmers' fixtures (s.8). The basic right to remove applies to:

- any fixture of whatever description affixed to the holding by the tenant, whether for agricultural purposes or not; and,
- any building erected by him on the holding (s.8(1)).

As under the 1986 Act these rights to remove do not apply to certain fixtures – specifically any buildings or fixtures put in place as a result of an obligation; any fixture or building replacing one belonging to the landlord; a building in respect of which the tenant is entitled to compensation under the Act or a building or fixture to which the landlord gave consent on the condition that it was not removed by the tenant (s.8(2)). These provisions apply to any buildings or fixtures acquired by the tenant as they apply to items fixed by him/her (s.8(5)). Tenants of farm business tenancies are deprived of their common law rights regarding fixtures (s.8(7)).

There is also a common law right for tenants of agricultural properties to remove certain items which may at first glance appear to be fixed buildings. These are Dutch barns (*Dean* v. *Allalley* (1799) 3 Esp 11); barns resting on the soil (*Culling* v. *Tufnal* (1694) Bull NP (5th edn) 34; *Wansborough* v. *Maton* (1836) 4 A&E 884) and barns resting on staddles (*Wiltshear* v. *Cottrell* (1853) 1 E&B 674). These structures are not regarded as fixtures as normally soil is not displaced in their erection, nor is there any cementing or fastening of them to existing structures in the soil. Readers should however note that the Court of Appeal felt it could derive little assistance from these cases because of their age in determining *Elitestone* v. *Morris* [1997] 1 WLR 687.

9.6 Statutory exemptions

Since the early 1990's Parliament has deliberately increased the protection given to basic tools and household items (eg for road traffic penalties by ERTDO art. 9(a) applying CCA s.89(1)(a)(i)&(ii)). The categories of assets exempt from seizure in bankruptcy have been extended to all but the following:

- *magistrates' court distraint*. Under r.54(2) MCR thc bailiff may seize the money or goods of the named person, but must leave beds and clothes of the person and family and also tools of the trade (r.54(4)). The term beds may be construed to include bedclothes as well as the bed frame (*Davies* v. *Harris* [1900] 1 QB 729). It is probable that the phrase "tools of the trade" should be construed quite narrowly. There is little English authority on this, but there are a number of helpful commonwealth cases. In *Burns* v. *Christianson* (1921) 60 DLR 173, a chauffeur claimed that the car he used for his business was exempt from seizure. The court held against him on interpleader by strictly interpreting the words of the legislation: trade is not synonymous with business, occupation or employment and includes only the occupation of one who is a mechanic and works at manual labour with the aid of tools, and is not one who conducts the business of contractor, manufacturer or merchant. Tools applies to instruments used by a carpenter, mason or blacksmith. Thus in the case of the claimant, the occupation of chauffeur was not a trade and a car was not a tool. The court also added that the aim of the exemption was not to protect expensive chattels. See also *McLeod* v. *Girvin Telephone Association* (1926) 1 DLR 216 in which a telephone line repair man claimed that his car was an exempt tool of his trade. The court refused his claim partly because he could not show he was actually following the trade at the time of seizure (having been sacked by the defendants and working part time as a farmer) and because, even assuming his work was a trade, a car is not a tool (see also 9.10 later). It seems that the exemption of tools of the trade extends to record books and ledgers (*Gauntelett* v. *King* (1857) 3 CBNS 59), though readers should note that "Halsbury's Laws" doubts this (vol. 13 para. 249 n.4) and "Woodfall" is cautious on the point (para. 9.059). The authority in question is an appeal which proceeds on the basis that the exemption was accepted by the parties and the earlier judge and jury – an assumption that is questioned but not overturned in the judgment. The exemption of tools also extends to materials (Co. Litt. 47);

- *income tax distraint* All goods and chattels may be seized, including tools of the trade (*MacGregor* v. *Clamp & Son* [1914] 1 KB 258). The plaintiff in this case tried to extend the distress for rent exemptions under LDAA 1888 to a distraint for tax. The court rejected this partly because common law rules do not apply to statutory distraint (see chapter 2) and partly because the rights of the crown are unaffected by statute unless expressly provided. See also *Swann* v. *Sloan* (1895) 29 ILT 109: in an action against a poor rate collector for seizing a plough horse HHJ Fitzgibbon stated that "*the contention that distress [for rates] is analogous to distress for rent is not correct: the rule of law which exempts instruments of husbandry from distress for rent does not extend to cases where the distress is given in the nature of an execution by a particular statute*"; and,

- *VAT distraint* All "goods and chattels" that belong to the debtor may be seized except those exempted by reg. 6 and sch. 1 of the Distress for Customs & Excise Duties Regulations 1997. These apply to any of the following which are located in the home at which distraint is levied and which are reasonably required to meet the domestic needs of any person living there. The exempt goods are beds and bedding; household linen; chairs and settees; tables; food; lights and light fittings; heating appliances; curtains; floor coverings; furniture, equipment and utensils used for cooking, storing and eating food; refrigerators; articles for cleaning, pressing and mending clothes; articles for cleaning the home; furniture used for storing clothing, bedding or household linen; cleaning articles or utensils for cooking and eating food; articles used for safety in the home; toys for the use of any child in the household and medical aids and equipment. On business premises the exempt goods are fire fighting equipment for use on those premises and medical aids and equipment for use there.

Note also that the statutory exemptions are modified in two cases:

- under NNDR distraint the only goods protected are basic household items, **not** tools of the trade (reg. 14(1A)); whilst,
- under CSA distraint it is provided that the goods needed to satisfy the basic domestic needs of the debtor include those needed by any member of the family with whom s/he resides (s.35(4) CSA). This unique provision presumably is intended to protect any new spouse and children the liable person may have. Considerable additional items are exempted by defining the phrase "basic domestic needs" in the CSA code of practice (see below).

The statutory exemptions are:

- "such tools, books, vehicles and other items of equipment as are necessary for use personally in business, employment or vocation". Attempts to limit this exemption to tools only capable of being carried by the debtor are incorrect. However in *Sheriff of Bedford & Toseland Building Supplies Ltd* v. *Bishop* [1993] CA (unreported) it was held that if a tool was occasionally used by another, it was not protected; and,
- "such clothing, bedding, furniture, household equipment and provisions as are necessary for satisfying the basic domestic needs of the person and family". It may be difficult to argue that personal jewellery or watches are protected as basic items of clothing.

These exclusions are both phrased very broadly. Naturally there have been various attempts to define what is meant. The Lord Chancellor's Department has provided guidance on these categories for county court bailiffs. For example it is suggested that:

- *tools* will only be protected if they are so essential that without them there is no way that the debtor's present business or job could continue. It has been held under the bankruptcy legislation that this protection was intended for the tools of a workman's trade so that he might not be prevented from earning a living, and does not extend to items that are not implements, such as documents, patents, address books and references (*Re: Sherman* (1915) 32 TLR 231). It has been held that a trader's stock includes the safe, cash register and counter of the business, so that these items are not exempt from seizure (*Endrizzi* v. *Peto & Beckley* (1917) 1 WWR 1439). Tools of the trade do not include samples held by a commercial traveller or representative (*Addison* v. *Shepherd* [1908] 2 KB 118). Having these is helpful to the individual but not essential to their business, so they are not exempt.
- *motor vehicles* will only be treated as a necessity in exceptional cases. Either the vehicle will be needed to continue a job or business or to get to work, and there will be no reasonable alternative (see 9.10);
- *household necessities* are not likely to include stereos, televisions, videos and microwaves. A fridge has been held to be household furniture (*Canadian National Railways* v. *Norwegian* (1971) 1 WWR 766).

Another approach to the problem of definition has been through codes of practice which often list specific exempt items. For example the CSA code suggests, amongst other things, that toys, curtains, cooking utensils, cleaning equipment and basic household tools may be included in the definition. The problem with any of these is that they can come to be seen as definitive lists. In fact each case must be decided on its individual facts and merits. The bailiff will have, at each levy, to exercise discretion in weighing up the interests of the debtor and family and the creditor for whom they are enforcing.

The previous statutory exemptions were based partly on the value of the protected goods. This no longer applies and there is no reason why assets of considerable value might not be protected by the above categories. See for example *Brookes* v. *Harris* [1995] *The Times,* April 22 in which the defendant successfully argued that, as a presenter of musical programmes on television and radio, his collection of records, cassettes and compact discs was exempt from seizure because it was a tool of his trade. The High Court accepted this, irrespective of the fact that the total collection was valued by the defendant at between £10,000 and £20,000.

In the High Court if a dispute arises as to whether goods fall within the exempt categories under s.138(3A) SCA, the sheriff may apply for directions from the Court by way of interpleader (see O.17 r.2A & 9.25). The procedure is for the debtor to give written notice of the claim that the goods are exempt within five days of their seizure. The sheriff must then serve notice of this claim on the execution creditor, who has seven days to accept or dispute the exemption. If the creditor does not respond or admits that the items are exempt, the sheriff withdraws from possession. If the claim of exemption is disputed, the sheriff seeks directions from the High Court and may also apply for an order protecting himself from any action. The Court will normally hear and determine the claims summarily. In the county court in the event of any dispute the matter is referred to the bailiff manager and ultimately a district judge's directions could be sought. The High Court provisions do not apply to the county court, or to road traffic distraint, but under s.76 CCA and O.1 r.6 CCR the county court could adopt similar procedures to resolve such disputes.

The burden of making and proving the claim lies on the debtor *Moffatt* v. *Lemkin* (1993) (unreported). It would seem reasonable to insist that any claim to exemption should be made within a reasonable time of seizure, and certainly before sale takes place. Otherwise the exemption will be presumed to have been waived (*Pilling* v. *Stewart* [1895] 4 BCR 94; *Roy* v. *Fortin* [1915] 26 DLR 18 – in which a delay of several months before making a claim was held too long). It is probable that only the debtor can make such a claim for exemption (*Young* v. *Short* (1883) 3 Man LR 302).

9.7 Personal items

Wearing apparel in use, in the sense of clothing, may not be seized (*Wolfe* v. *Summers* (1811) 2 Camp 631; *Sunbolf* v. *Alford* (1838) 3 M & W 248). Whether this exemption extends to items such as jewellery and watches is unknown. Nevertheless the courts may be prepared to extend these authorities as their primary purpose was not to protect specified items but to avoid levies which would almost necessitate an assault and breach of the peace in order to realise them. However if the clothes have been removed, for instance in getting ready for bed (*Bissett* v. *Caldwell* (1791) 1 Esp 206) or for the purpose of washing them (*Baynes* v. *Smith* [1794] 1 Esp 206), they may be seized.

9.8 Assets of deceased debtors and their personal representatives

Introduction

If the debtor dies a number of extra rights and liabilities come into effect. In execution, if the debtor dies after the judgment, but before issue of a writ or warrant, leave of court is needed to issue (see 6.3 earlier). If the judgment debtor dies after the writ is issued the bailiff may proceed and seize the debtor's goods, whoever may be holding them. Goods of a testator in the hands of an executor or administrator can be taken in execution against that person as executor/administrator. Presumably something similar to the latter principle will apply to statutory distraint. Note that money belonging to the late debtor is not bound by the writ (see 6.1.3) and therefore cannot be seized in execution against the judgment debtor who dies pending the levy (*Johnson* v. *Pickering* [1908] 1 KB 1).

9.8.1 Trustees

Execution against a trustee cannot be levied on the trust estate (*Duncan* v. *Cashin* (1875) 1 CP 554). Note also that in this case the settlee had replaced some of the items left in trust for her by her father. It was suggested that these were bought by her with her own money as agent for the trustees and also could not be seized. The same rules will no doubt apply in statutory distraint. If a trustee runs up debts whilst administering the business of the assignor, the trust property cannot be seized (*Jennings* v. *Mather* [1901] 1 QB 108). However the trustee has a right and interest in the goods and has a right of indemnity in the nature of as lien. A creditor of the trustee can in turn demand an indemnity for trade debts out of the business estate held on trust (*Re: Johnson* [1880] 15 Ch D 604).

9.8.2 Personal Representatives

Where execution is levied against a debtor acting as personal representative for a deceased third party, the bailiff cannot seize the deceased's goods in the debtor's hands (*Farr* v. *Newman* (1792) 4 TR 621; *In Re: Morgan* [1881] 18 Ch D 93). In the latter case, the fact that the executor carried on the deceased's business as his own was held not to entitle the judgment creditor to seize the deceased's assets. However, it was stressed that lapse of time and enjoyment of assets in a manner inconsistent with the trusts in the will, coupled with the consent of the beneficiaries, may raise an inference of a gift of assets to the executor by them, thus entitling the judgment creditor to seize them. If the business is carried on in line with trusts in the will, the lapse of time will not be relevant (*Ray* v. *Ray* (1813) Coop 264). If the business is continued for the benefit of the estate, but debts are accrued, it appears that creditors of the business may enforce against the assets of the estate (*Moseley* v. *Rendell* [1871] 6 QB 338; *Abbott* v. *Parfitt* [1871] 6 QB 346). If the personal representative and spouse treat the testator's goods are if they were their own, they may be seized in execution against the spouse (*Quick* v. *Staines* (1798) 1 B&P 293). If the executor incurs debts in the course of such trading, these are his/her personal debts, and execution must be against his/her own property (*In Re: Evans* [1887] 34 Ch D 597). Evans also makes it clear that the creditors have a lien on the personal representative's interest in the estate, so as s/he is entitled to be indemnified out of the estate (*Dowse* v. *Gorton* [1891] AC 190), they may also claim the benefit of that right (*In Re: Johnson* [1880] 15 Ch D 548). Creditors are also entitled to an indemnity if the assets of the testator are used for the benefit of the executor (*In Re: Oxley* [1914] 1 Ch 602). Goods in the hands of an agent of the executor cannot be seized (*Sykes* v. *Sykes* [1870] 5 CP 113). Where a receiver or manager is appointed in an administration action to carry on the business in succession to the executor, the same principles apply (*In Re: Brooke* [1894] 2 Ch 600).

9.8.3 Heirlooms

Heirlooms require special mention apart from fixtures, for which see 9.5. They are chattels which are so associated with real property that they are regarded as an essential feature of its ordinary enjoyment and use, and are accordingly treated as inseparable from the land in any settlement. A settlement may thus annex furniture and household chattels, goods and effects to a house as heirlooms and give them a heritable character which they would not otherwise possess. Because of this nature as real property, heirlooms cannot be seized.

9.9 Goods subject to prior levies

Those items already seized in execution or distress cannot normally be seized again (*eg: Grant* v. *Grant* (1883) 10 PR 40; *Kingston City* v. *Rogers* (1899) 31 OR 119) as an interest in the goods has been vested in a third party by the prior seizure. For instance goods seized in distress for rent cannot be seized in execution (*Haythorn* v. *Bush* (1834) 2 Cr & M 689) though the landlord could consent to waive his rights (*Belcher* v. *Patten* (1848) 6 CB 608). There is an exception to this general rule for the Crown, for which see 6.6.2. There is also an exception in respect of execution, as later writs bind earlier (see 6.1.3), even though the goods are already seized and in the custody of the law under a prior writ (*Belcher* v. *Patten*, *supra*). Goods already distrained cannot be seized in execution whether for rent (*Edmunds* v. *Ross* (1821) 9 Price 5) or for taxes (*Dicas* v. *Warne* (1833) 10 Bing 341). Goods already seized in execution cannot be seized unless the execution has been abandoned (*Crowder* v. *Long* (1828) 8 B&C 598), the levy was irregular (*Blades* v. *Arundale* [1813] 1 M&S 711) or the execution has been satisfied (*Harwell* v. *Burwell Sir W Jones* (1641) 456). An illegal seizure does not disturb the debtor's possession (*Barrow* v. *Bell* (1855) 5 E&B 540; *Re: Cuthbertson ex parte Edey* [1875] LR 19 Eq 264) so they may still be seized in subsequent levies. If goods already subject to a levy are seized again it is pound-breach, for which see 3.3 and *Reddell* v. *Stowey* (1841) 2 Moo & R 358.

9.10 Motor vehicles

Motor vehicles are available for seizure like any other asset, and are obviously the most valuable and easily accessible of most debtors' possessions. There is almost no legal guidance as to the procedure to be followed in seizing vehicles.

It would appear that the same rules of location and entry apply as in any other levy. Whilst the vehicle itself may be levied upon, it does not seem safe to assume that items within it may be taken if that involves forced entry. Impounding may be by notice, walking possession or removal as already described (see 8.4.6 earlier in respect of clamping).

It may be possible for the debtor to successfully claim that his/her vehicle is an item exempted by statute as necessary for his/her trade or employment. Again there is little English authority on the matter, but Canadian cases are very instructive. Vehicles have been held to be exempt in the following instances:

- when used by a pedlar for travelling around selling goods – even though the car was bought for a different business – for use in connection with the debtor's shop (*Re: Bell* (1938) 2 DLR 754);
- when used by a self employed person to transport his/her equipment and materials – see *York* v. *Flatekval* (1971) 3 WWR 289 (a musician) and *Hayward Builders Supplies Ltd* v. *Mackenzie* (1956) 2 WWR 591 (the debtor was a floorer and the car was held exempt, even though it was not registered as a commercial vehicle and was used as a "pleasure car" for the debtor and family at weekends);
- if the vehicle itself is the sole source of the debtor's income – such as a car equipped as a taxi and used by a one man taxi service (*Metro Cab Co Ltd* v. *Munro* (1965) 48 DLR 701); or,
- where owning a vehicle is a condition of the person's employment and it would be virtually impossible for them to do the job without: see for instance *Bank of Nova Scotia* v. *Jordison* (1963) 40 DLR 790 (the debtor was a salesman) or *Armstrong* v. *Terry* (1967) 1 OR 588 (the debtor was an estate agent).

  Note that in these cases the wording of the exemption in the relevant statutes referred to tools or "necessaries" required in a person's trade or "calling", which latter term was interpreted as meaning a person's ordinary occupation or business.

  A motor vehicle will not be regarded as exempt from seizure where:

- it is used for convenience and not as a necessity (such as, to carry a salesman's samples) and car ownership is not a condition of employment (*Langdon* v. *Traders' Finance Corporation Ltd* (1966) 1 OR 655; see also *Re: General Steel Wares Ltd* v. *Clarke* (1956) 20 WWR 215);
- the debtor's contract of employment neither requires the employee to have a car nor defines the person's duties as involving the use of one. See *Goldsmith* v. *Harris* (1928) 3 DLR 478: the claimant was a manager in a house building firm, and used his car to travel from site to site within the city where he supervised the construction work. The vehicle was claimed as a necessary, but it was not required by the terms of his contract, nor was it essential because of the nature of his occupation. Denniston JA held "*A saw, a plough, an anvil, a fishing net, a truck are necessary to a carpenter, farmer, blacksmith, fisherman or carter if he is to follow his occupation at all. A vehicle for a country doctor, books of account for a business man . . . are recognised as necessaries as soon as mentioned, for without them pursuit of their respective occupations is impossible. The mere statement that a person is a manager of a building company does not import that a private motor*

> *car is necessary; it is only after special evidence is given to show special circumstances relating to a particular position, which involves special duties, that one may say that the work cannot be done without a motor car.*" In this case there was no such evidence that the person would be unable to hold his position or performing his duties. The debtor may have suffered inconvenience, and may have had to curtail his activities, but that was a matter for arrangement between him and his employer and was not the concern of the judgment creditors.

Issues of ownership are very likely to arise in respect of cars as they may be subject either to HP or leasing agreements. Before removal therefore, the bailiff should check ownership with HPI and DVLA and if the results of this are satisfactory is then likely to remove promptly. One issue to note in respect of road traffic penalties is the difference between who may be held liable for such a penalty, and ownership of a vehicle. Under s.82 RTA the registered keeper of the vehicle can be regarded as the owner for the purposes of imposing a penalty (see also *R.* v. *The Parking Adjudicator ex parte London Borough of Wandsworth* [1996]). It is submitted that these provisions apply solely to liability for the penalty and cannot be held to alter the rights of a person with legal title to a vehicle.

When removing a vehicle any personal contents in the vehicle should be either returned to the debtor or listed in the presence of a witness. If possible the registration documents and keys will be obtained from the debtor or another responsible person. Forced entry may be possible in order to remove the vehicle, but the use of force is probably not justifiable as other means exist for transporting cars and vans – i.e. by towing or loading on transporter. The only English case law on the subject of cars relates to this matter. It indicates that the bailiffs should use reasonable care when arranging a contractor to move the vehicle, but, provided this is done, they are not liable generally for any negligence on the part of the contractor. Arranging removal by a reputable garage or haulage firm should be seen as discharge of the duty of care (*Rivers* v. *Cutting* [1982] 3 All ER 69 CA).

9.11 Partnership assets

The rule in the civil courts is that execution under a judgment against a firm can be levied against any property of the firm, against the property of any person who admitted to being a partner or was held by the judgment to be a partner, and against the property of any person who was served with the writ or summons and who failed to respond to the action or to attend hearings (RSC O.81 r.5; CCR O.25 r.9). The fact that membership of a partnership has changed is no bar to enforcement. By analogy from *Re: Frank Hill ex parte Holt & Co* [1921] 2 KB 831 retirement will not prevent execution, nor will death of a partner after issue of the originating process (*Ellis* v. *Wadeson* [1899] 1 QB 714). Each individual partner can be separately pursued by execution (*Clark* v. *Cullen* [1882] 9 QBD 355) but an action against a firm must lead to a judgment against the firm, not just one partner (*Jackson* v. *Litchfield* [1882] 8 QBD 474). In this case an action for wrongful execution and detention of goods was successfully taken. Similarly if judgment is obtained against several named individuals, the warrant must also be issued against them all (*Penoyer* v. *Brace* (1697) 1 Ld Raym 244; *Clark* v. *Clement* (1796) 6 TR 525). That said, it does not have to be levied on all or any one or more of those joint judgment debtors (*Herries* v. *Jamieson* (1794) 5 TR 556). If execution against one partner clears the debt, the others may not of course be pursued. There is no requirement that partnership property be seized before the private property of partners, or vice versa.

Execution may not be issued against a person who was out of the country when the writ or summons was issued unless he or she was served within England & Wales; who with leave was served outside the jurisdiction, or (High Court only) who responded to the writ as a partner. Partners who were out of England & Wales when the action commenced are not otherwise effected. Permission can be sought to issue execution against a person claimed to be a partner, this being on notice under CPR Part 23 (O.81 r.5(4)); (CCR O.25 r.9(4)). This gives the alleged partner an opportunity to contest the claim of liability, and the dispute may be tried as the court directs. Permission cannot be given to issue execution against a person who leaves the firm before an action begins (*Wigram* v. *Cox* [1894] 1 QB 792). Permission may be given where a person has "held themselves out" to be a partner (*Davis* v. *Hyman & Co* [1903] 1 KB 854).

Execution made not be made against partnership property for the separate debt of a partner (s.23(1) Partnership Act 1890). If this were to happen the partners could interplead – see 9.25 later (*Peake* v. *Carter* [1916] 1 KB 652). Note that in *Flude Ltd* v. *Goldberg* [1916] 1 KB 662 a person interpleaded over goods claimed as his sole property. On hearing the case it was decided that the goods were in fact partnership property of the claimant and the defendant, but as the claimant had not claimed on this basis the claim was barred.

These basic principles will apply in statutory distraint as well. In road traffic distraint O.48B CCR applies O.25 r.9 dealing with enforcement against partnerships. The situation is different in distress for rent, for which see 9.22.3 – no protection is given to goods of a business partner.

9.12 Business assets

There are a number of specific provisions dealing with different items of equipment or stock that may be liable to seizure from a business or farm (NB greater protection existed until recently in the textile industry – however the Hosiery Act 1843 which contained protections against distress and execution was repealed by Statute Law (Reform) Act 1993). These provisions are in addition to the exemptions for tools of the trade by statute (see 9.6), for motor vehicles used in trade (see 9.10) and for items subject to third party interests such as debentures and reservation of title clauses (see respectively 9.20 & 9.21).

9.12.1 Railway rolling stock

Under s.4 Railway Companies Act 1867 the "engines, tenders, carriages, trucks, machinery, tools, fittings, materials and effects constituting the rolling stock and plant" used by a company on its railway for the purposes of public traffic cannot be taken in execution (though the judgment creditor may obtain the appointment of a receiver). If a dispute arises as to whether items are covered by this exemption, application may be made on summons for summary determination in the county court or to a Judge in the High Court (s.5).

Under s.3 Railway Rolling Stock Protection Act 1872 rolling stock (which is defined in s.2 as waggons, trucks, carriages of all kinds and locomotive engines) may not be taken in distress for rent if they are found on any rented premises, such as a colliery, quarry, mine factory, warehouse or wharf, and they are not the tenant's property (see *Easton Estate & Mining Co* v. *Western Waggon & Property Co* (1886) 50 JP 790). If stock is seized, application may be made to the magistrates' court for an order against the landlord to restore the goods or pay their value and costs. If the tenant has an interest in any rolling stock, this may be distrained for rent and disposed of. If a disagreement arises between landlord and tenant as to the best way of disposing of the tenant's interest, application may be made to the magistrates' court for directions (s.5). Any order of the magistrates' court may be appealed to the Crown Court (s.6).

9.12.2 Farming Stock

Special provision is made for officers levying the "process of any court of law" (which presumably must include warrants issued by magistrates' courts) against a farm by Sale of Farming Stock Act 1816 (*NB* the Act does not affect levies by the Crown – *R.* v. *Osbourne* (1818) 6 Price 94).

Generally the officer levying execution can seize any "*fructus industriales*" – that is, any crops which are reaped at maturity (*Cameron* v. *Gibson* (1889) 17 OR 233). This includes such crops as corn and similar produce such as potatoes (*Evans* v. *Roberts* (1826) 5 B&C 829). It does not include trees (*Scorell* v. *Boxall* (1827) 1 Y&J 396), grass (*Late* v. *McLean* (1870) 8 NSR 69), seeds unsprouted in the soil (*Bagshaw* v. *Farnsworth* (1860) 2 LT 390) or fruit on trees (*Rodwell* v. *Phillips* (1842) 9 M&W 501). Standing crops are bound by the issue of a writ (*Belair* v. *Banque d'Hochelaga* (1923) 2 WWR 771) though they cannot be sold until they have been harvested (*Kidd & Clements* v. *Docherty* (1914) 27 WLR 636).

However under s.1 of the 1816 Act an officer cannot in any levy seize any straw, chaff, turnips, manure, compost, ashes or seaweed. Also under s.1 if the terms of a tenant farmer's lease require that any hay, grass, tares, vetches, roots and vegetables are not to be removed from and consumed off the premises, the execution must be conducted subject to these conditions provided that the sheriff's officer or county court bailiff has been given notice of such covenants before sale takes place. The tenant is required to give written notice to the bailiff of the terms of the lease and of the landlord's name and address (also it is the bailiff's duty to make enquiries on this – s.5) and the bailiff should then notify the landlord of the seizure and delay sale until a reply is received (s.2).

Produce may be disposed of by the sheriff provided that the purchaser agrees in writing to use them on the premises in accordance with the lease (or in accordance with the "custom of the country" if no such conditions apply) and that person shall be entitled to have barns etc on the premises allocated to their use by the bailiff (s.3). The requirement to respect the terms of the farm lease as to the use of such produce as hay, straw, grass, turnips, roots, manure, compost or seaweed is repeated by s.11, which applies to any sale of farming stock contrary to the lease, not just those in execution (*Wilmot* v. *Rose* (1854) 3 E&B 563), for instance by the trustee of a bankrupt tenant farmer. Neither the bailiff nor the purchaser shall be liable in trespass for coming onto the premises in order to use produce (s.10). Furthermore, the landlord may not levy distress upon any of the corn, hay, straw or other produce sold under the execution, nor any horses, sheep, cattle, carts, waggons or other implements of husbandry brought onto the premises by the purchaser (s.6).

If the terms of the lease are breached, the landlord may sue in the name of the bailiff having provided an indemnity for any costs or losses that may be incurred (s.4). The sheriff is not liable to damages under the Act except for any wilful breach or omission (s.9). If under any contract a tenant farmer may remove straw, turnips etc. the Act will not apply (s.8).

There is also exemption for plough beasts under the statute 51 Hen 3. Coke states (2 Inst 131 *et seq.*) that this provision applies to *all* distresses, not just those between landlord and tenant but also the Crown's and to executions (but contrá, see *Swaffer* v. *Mulcahy* [1934] 1 KB 608). To be exempt, there must have been sufficient other goods available at the time of the levy (29 Ed III 17; 4 Hen VI 86).

9.12.3 Ships and aircraft

Ships may be seized in execution, as may debtors' shares in ships (at least, foreign ships – see *The James Elwell* [1921] P 351, particularly at 368). Various claims may have priority to such a seizure, such as claims by a mortgagee. The disposal of a ship is a complex matter, for which see "Mather" pp.98-100. Aircraft may also be seized, but again special procedures must be followed (see Keith, Podevin & Sandbrook at pp.38–40).

PART TWO – THIRD PARTY GOODS

Other than jointly owned and partnership property, other third parties' goods cannot be taken as a rule. However, the third party may be estopped from recovering damages if s/he intentionally induced the bailiff to seize the goods, either by expressly or impliedly representing that the goods were the debtor's (*Pickard* v. *Sears* (1837) 6 A&E 469). There must be something equivalent to a licence from him/her (*Freeman* v. *Cooke* (1849) 4 Exch 654; *Dawson* v. *Wood* (1810) 3 Taunt 256). However once notice of the true situation is given, the bailiff will be liable for any subsequent wrongful acts such as proceeding to sell (*Dunstan* v. *Paterson* (1857) 2 CBNS 495).

9.13 Utility fittings

There are statutory exemptions from seizure for fixtures and other property belonging to utility suppliers. The details are as follows:

- Gas Act 1986 sch. 2B, para. 29(1)(a): any gas meter connected to a service pipe and any gas fitting in a consumer's premises which is owned by a gas transporter or gas supplier and is sufficiently marked with an indication of ownership shall not be subject to distress or execution. Fittings for gas include hired cookers (*Gas Light & Coke Co* v. *Hardy* [1886] 17 QBD 619; and *Gas Light & Coke Co* v. *Herbert Smith & Co* (1886) 3 TLR 15). It is also an offence under para. 10 sch. 2B to injure, or allow to be injured, any gas fitting or service pipe, whether intentionally or by culpable negligence;

- Electricity Act 1989 sch. 6 para. 9: any electrical plant, line or meter owned or hired by a supplier to a customer and marked with a sufficient indication of their ownership shall not be deemed to be landlord's fixtures, notwithstanding that they may be affixed to any part of the premises in which they are situated and shall not be taken in distress or execution. As with gas fittings, it is an offence to damage electrical fixtures (para. 4); and
- Water Industry Act 1991: s.179(4) provides that any water fittings let for hire by a water undertaker shall, if they are properly marked, continue to be the property of the undertaker even if they are fixed to some part of the premises and shall not be taken in distress or execution. Water fittings are defined by s.93 as including pipes, taps, cocks, valves, ferrules, meters, cisterns, baths and toilets.

These exemptions may be referred to in specific legislation (reg. 45(8) CT and reg. 14(8) NNDR state that the "provisions shall not affect the operation of any enactment which protects goods of any class from distress") but will apply generally to all forms.

9.14 Children's goods

Children may be given personal property in any manner – for instance by will or by gift. Thus "*if property be put up on a boy, this is a gift in the law, for the boy hath capacity to take it*" (*Hayne's Case* (1614) 12 Co Rep 113). Whenever property is given to a child, it becomes the child's as soon as the gift is made (*Hunter* v. *Westbrook* (1827) 2 C&P 578). At common law there is a presumption in favour of the validity of a gift by a parent or grandparent to a child (*Garrett* v. *Wilkinson* (1848) 2 De G & Sm 244 at 246; *Beanland* v. *Bradley* [1854] 2 Sm & G 339 at 343) provided that the gift is complete, such as by delivery (*May* v. *May* (1863) 33 Beav 81 at 87).

Purchase of property by a child is valid and effectual (*Holmes* v. *Brigg* (1818) 8 Taunt 508). Children can deal with property in the same manner as adults, whether disposing of it by gift or by sale of goods in the normal fashion (*Manby* v. *Scott* [1663] 1 Mod Rep 124).

In consequence, therefore, items bought by children, or for children, and presents to them, should not be taken in distress or execution unless the bailiff can successfully challenge any of the above principles or show a particular transaction to be invalid. Subject to special procedural provisions (RSC O.80; CCR O.10), the child may take court proceedings to protect his or her property.

9.15 Spouses' goods

It is not unusual for bailiffs to seek to seize the property of one spouse to satisfy the debts of the other. The existing case law relates to the rights of a married woman, but the general principles will apply to cohabitees as well.

A married woman is capable of acquiring, holding and disposing of any property in all respects as if she is a single woman (s.1(a) Law Reform (Married Women & Tortfeasors) Act 1935. All property belonging to woman at marriage or acquired by or devolving upon her after that date belongs to her as if she is a single woman (s.2(1)).

Clearly such goods cannot be seized. However s.4(2)(c) provides that none of the above stops couples jointly owning goods, which could be seized (see 9.3 above).

In respect of gifts from one spouse to another, it used to be a presumption that a gift had been made where the husband bought property in his wife's name. This is not now presumed. It will be assumed to be owned jointly if bought with joint money. If the wife buys property in her husband's or joint names, there is no presumption of a gift if it is acquired with her money. If the items are bought by the husband for the wife's own personal use (e.g. for birthdays, anniversaries or Christmas), they will be gifts. Note however the arrangement made by the spouses in *Rondeau Le Grand & Co* v. *Marks* [1918] 1 KB 75 where execution creditors against a wife were unable to seize her personal effects because she had made a valid agreement with her husband that he would purchase items for her in his own name and simply lend them. Jewellery etc given to the wife by relatives and friends are her property. Wedding presents from the wife's family are hers, and those from the husband's family are his, unless there is evidence of the donor's intentions. Gifts to the couple give each a separate share. If the one spouse makes a gift to the other, the items become the other's absolute property. In *French* v. *Gething* [1922] 1 KB 236 the gift was by means of a post nuptial deed. Although the chattels transferred were furniture in the marital home which both continued to use, the goods were the wife's.

If one spouse purchases chattels from the other there is no reason not to treat this as a valid transfer that would defeat an execution creditor. In *Ramsay* v. *Margrett* [1894] 2 QB 18 the husband sold furniture and personal chattels to his wife. She received a receipt for them, though there was no formal delivery of the goods as they remained in the marital home. The wife succeeded in an interpleader claim against an execution as the court held that the intention of the deal had been to pass her absolute title which was demonstrated by her separate dealings with the goods (some were removed prior to the execution) and which was combined with sufficient possession.

The above principles do not just apply to married couples but could apply to any parties living together or sharing accommodation. See for example *Koppel* v. *Koppel* [1966] 2 All ER 187 in which the court upheld an interpleader claim by Mrs Wide the housekeeper to the contents of Koppel's house. They had been made over to her in return for her coming to live in the property to care for his two children and to replace items of her own that she disposed of before moving in. In this case the court held that there was no need for delivery to be demonstrated as the transfer was not a gift but was for money or money's worth. See also *Antoniadi* v. *Smith* [1907] 2 KB 589 – a case of a man and his mother in law.

The real problems arise in respect of items bought by the couple after marriage (or after beginning to live together). The courts generally assume an intention to share any property acquired, and allocate interests in it equally. Housekeeping money or property acquired with that will be treated as shared equally unless it is clearly intended to be shared otherwise (s.1 Married Women's Property Act 1964). Where there is a joint bank account or other common pool of income, the wages of one spouse are generally seen as being earned on behalf of both and to be joint property, and the sums paid in or withdrawn by each are irrelevant. For instance see *Jones* v. *Maynard* [1951] Ch 572 – the husband withdrew sums from a joint account to buy investments in his sole name. The court held the wife to be entitled to half their value. Joint ownership of assets is also not the case where one spouse provides all the income in a joint account, which is simply used as a matter of administrative convenience. The money (and thus the acquisitions) belong to the person providing it (*Heseltine* v. *Heseltine* [1971] 1 All ER 952 at 956). By way of contrast see *Re: Bishop (deceased)* [1965] Ch 450 in which a husband and wife opened a joint account to which each contributed in unequal amounts. Money was withdrawn for housekeeping purposes and for investment, in both their sole and joint names. On his death the trustees sought to determine the wife's interest and it was held that as the account had been opened on terms that either could withdraw from it, with no evidence of any specific or limited purpose, then any item bought in sole name was for that person alone. (Items bought from such an account therefore would be regarded as jointly owned and seizable.)

9.16 Hired goods

Goods subject to a hire or leasing agreement are not the property of the debtor and on the face of it are not available for seizure. In distress for rent, though, they were not regarded as exempt until a recent Court of Appeal decision (see 9.22.2 later). As described at 9.4 in execution where the bailiff is permitted to seize the goods and *chattels* of the debtor, the debtor's interest in the goods may be seized if it is saleable. See for example the notes to the "White Book" at RSC 45/1/19 which state that "where two persons have separate and different interests in a chattel (e.g. one is owner subject to another's charge or lien) the sheriff may seize if the judgment debtor is entitled to possession, but may only sell the debtor's interest". In those cases of statutory distraint where chattels cannot be seized rented or hired goods are exempt (see for example the rates cases of *Prudential Mortgage Co* v. *St. Marylebone (Mayor)* [1910] 8 LGR 901; *Carter* v. *Vestry of St. Mary* [1900] 64 JP 548) The owner's interest may not be seized.

Thus the debtor's interest for a term (i.e. the remaining rental period) may in theory be seized and sold. The owner can not sue the bailiff for conversion for selling (*Gordon* v. *Harper* [1796] 7 Term Rep 9; *Pain* v. *Whittaker* [1824] 1 Ry & M 99) or for simply seizing them (*Duffil* v. *Spottiswoode* [1828] 3 C&P 435) as the owner has no right to immediate possession (see 9.26.2). The *Duffil* case also determined that the hirer is under a duty to notify the bailiff of his/her limited interest in the goods. However, if after notice from the owner, the bailiff purports to sell the absolute property in the goods, s/he may be liable for damages in conversion (*Ward* v. *Macauley* (1791) 4 D&E 489; *Lancashire Waggon Co Ltd* v. *Fitzhugh* (1861) 6 H&N 502) though an action for trespass would fail for lack of possession by the owner (9.26.2). To succeed in such an action the owner would have to show that as soon as the goods were seized the bailiff was notified that the goods were on hire so that the bailiff knew only a qualified property could be sold (*Dean* v. *Whittaker* (1823) 1 C&P 347). If the hire is of such a nature that the debtor has no saleable interest (*Cooper* v. *Willomatt* (1845) 1 CB 72) or if the interest is determined by the seizure, the bailiff cannot legally seize (*Manders* v. *Williams* (1849) 4 Exch 339) and could be sued for conversion for so doing. If goods are sold, the owner can recover a proportion of the proceeds of sale paid to the creditor (see *Jones Bros (Holloway) Ltd* v. *Woodhouse* [1923] 2 KB 117). Another remedy for the hirer would be interpleader (*Ford* v. *Baynton* (1832) 1 Dowl 359 and 9.25 later).

Goods hired out by the debtor to a third party cannot be seized and the hirer's quiet possession cannot be disturbed (*Garstin* v. *Asplin* (1815) 1 Madd 150; *Izod* v. *Lamb* [1830] 1 Cr&J 35).

9.17 Hire purchase goods

The same principles that apply to the seizure of hired goods also apply to those subject to hire purchase (HP) agreements, i.e. the debtor's interest can be sold if the bailiff is entitled to sell chattels as well as goods. In respect of HP this would be the debtor's "equity" in the goods – the difference between its present value and the outstanding balance on the agreement. Distress for rent is again a special case (see 9.22.2).

Only the debtor's interest, not the finance company's, may be sold. Where the bailiff does sell the absolute property the finance company may sue the creditor for a proportion of the proceeds relative to the proportion that their goods formed of the total value of the goods seized (*Jones Bros (Holloway) Ltd* v. *Woodhouse* [1923] 2 KB 117). If, by a term of the contract, any distress or execution ends the agreement, the goods cannot be seized. The bailiff may be sued for conversion for seizing goods in such circumstances (*Jelks* v. *Haywood* [1905] 2 KB 460) even if the finance company only makes a claim *after* sale has occured. A delay of up to a year has not estopped an owner's claim (*Jones Bros.*). However in *Times Furnishing* v. *Hutchings* [1938] 1 KB 775 the HP company was defeated in its claim as, despite the fact that the agreement terminated automatically on the issue of distress by the landlord, as no steps were taken to recover the goods they remained in the possession of the debtor with the owner's consent and were seizable under s.4(1) LDAA 1908. Interpleader would be another remedy available to the finance company (see 9.25 later and *Green* v. *Stevens* [1857] 2 H&N 146). The Inland Revenue is entitled to seize goods on HP but chooses not to exercise the right.

9.18 Goods subject to liens and pledges

Since at least 1483 it has been settled that goods subject to pledges and charges may be seized in execution, but subject to those claims (22 Ed IV 11). Thus goods subject to a lien for work done upon them are seizable, in execution at least, subject to that lien (*Duncan* v. *Garrett* (1824) 1 C&P 169). The lien has priority to both the debt and the bailiff's fees (*The Ile de Ceylon* [1922] P 256). If such goods are sold, the bailiff is liable for the amount of the lien (*Proctor* v. *Nicholson* (1835) 7 C&P 67). An lien cannot have any effect if it has not yet come into effect. In *Byford* v. *Russell* [1907] 2 KB 522 it was agreed between builder and client that if work was not completed quickly enough notice would be served and a lien would be created on the builder's plant. The sheriff levied on the plant before the notice was served and the court held the client had no lien or interest and could not defeat the judgment creditor. Goods held by a debtor subject to a lien that s/he claims against a third party cannot be seized in execution (*Legg* v. *Evans* (1840) 6 M&W 36).

Goods given in pledge by the debtor to a third party cannot be seized in execution against the debtor, and the pawnbroker could sue the bailiff in conversion (*Rogers* v. *Kenmay* [1846] 9 QB 592). Mather however speculates that pawn tickets, though not seizable or saleable as such, could be taken in execution in order that the bailiff could redeem the goods and sell them (para. 9, p. 96). If execution is levied against a pawnbroker, pledged goods can be seized. The sheriff has a right of possession in the pledges arising from the pawnbroker's qualified property, and when the redemption period has passed the sheriff's interest permits him to sell. If the pledges redeem their goods the sheriff may receive the redemption monies: if the pledges are not redeemed, the sheriff may sell the goods (*Squire* v. *Huetson* [1841] 1 QB 308; *In Re: Rollason, Rollason* v. *Rollason* [1887] 34 Ch D 495).

9.19 Bills of Sale

Bills of sale are unlikely to be encountered as commercial arrangements very frequently. This is because the technicalities of the procedure mean that they are not a widely used form of security, and conditional sale or HP will be a preferred arrangement. Bills of sale may still be encountered in respect of loans on motor vehicles as a way of avoiding some aspects of Consumer Credit Act regulation. As discussed in chapter 3, they may also be encountered as a way of trying to avoid the impact of seizure.

9.20 Reservation of title clauses

There are a number of modes in which title to goods being sold may be subject to provisions reserving title in the seller. For instance, if goods are supplied to a prospective buyer on approval or on "sale or return", the property only passes to the buyer when s/he signifies approval or acceptance to the seller, or does any other act adopting the transaction – this may be by retaining the goods for a reasonable period of time (see rule 4, s.18 Sale of Goods Act 1979 but note that the mere fact of seizure of the goods in execution is not such retention to render the property passed – *Re: Ferrier* [1944] Ch 295). The most common means of reserving title are the so called "Romalpa clauses".

The rule regarding sale of goods is that title of the goods passes only when the parties want it to. Consequently, by agreement, title is often reserved until certain conditions are satisfied, typically that the goods (and sometimes others) are fully paid for, rather than passing when the contract is made or when the goods are delivered. Such agreements are often called "Romalpa clauses" (see *Aluminium Industrie Vaassen* v. *Romalpa Aluminium Ltd* [1976] 2 All ER 552) but such clauses are sanctioned by s.19 Sale of Goods Act 1979.

In any of these situations if property in the goods has not passed to the purchaser who is then subject to distress or execution, the relevant goods will not be seizable. This will even apply in distress for rent as they are either held "in the course of business" or as "third party goods" (see 9.22.2 later). In reality it is often difficult for the seller claiming under a retention of title clause to identify which specific items are covered. When a firm is supplied with stock in the course of business invoices rarely specify serial numbers or even models. Furthermore where the goods being supplied subject to the reservation of title clause are materials rather than finished items, successfully asserting any claim may be even more difficult for the seller as the goods to which they claim title may no longer have any identifiable separate existence

(*Borden (UK)* v. *Scottish Timber Products Ltd* [1979] 3 All ER 961 CA). In all cases the exact terms of the sales contract will need careful scrutiny to see if it does in fact protect the vendor against the enforcement being levied against the customer (see also *Re: Bond Worth* [1979] 3 All ER 919 CA).

9.21 Floating charges

Bailiffs may, in the course of levies against limited companies, endeavour to levy on goods subject to floating charges. Such a charge is created by a debenture – a document acknowledging the company's indebtedness and giving security over some or all of the present and future assets of the firm. The assets will change over time as the company trades in the normal fashion but the charge will apply to the changing plant and goods in stock. However, if the firm defaults in payment of its debt, an administrative receiver can be appointed and the floating charge "crystallises" and becomes fixed, giving the creditors the power to recover their money. If the property charged is far less in value than the sum charged, it can mean that property loses the protection of the debenture and may be distrainable. This is because effectively the firm loses any interest in the goods and they cease to be the firm's assets (*Re: New City Constitutional Club Co ex parte Russell* [1887] 34 Ch D 646). The effectiveness of a floating charge in protecting goods against distress depends on the stage that has been reached in the process of making and enforcing the charge when distress or execution begins. The debenture will be regarded as valid and will defeat execution even if it was issued without authority (*Duck* v. *Tower Galvanising Co Ltd* [1901] 2 KB 314).

9.21.1 Contract to issue

Where a firm has contracted to issue debentures but, before this is done, goods are seized, the intended debenture holder is in the same position as if the debenture had been issued, i.e. the goods are seized subject to all equities upon them (*Simultaneous Colour Printing Syndicate* v. *Foweraker* [1901] 1 KB 771).

9.21.2 Prior to crystallisation

Prior to crystallisation of the charge execution or distraint on the charged goods cannot be prevented as they are still the company's property (*Re: Roundwood Colliery Co* [1897] 1 Ch 373). If goods are charged to a value far in excess of their worth, the rights of the debenture holders will defeat those of the execution creditors if the debentures are valid, even though the charge has not crystallised (*Davey & Co* v. *Williamson & Sons* [1898] 2 QB 194) and the debenture holder may interplead to safeguard the security. If the debenture holder fears that their goods are in jeopardy, they may appoint a receiver if it is reasonable – this could be because a judgment creditor is in a position to issue execution (*Wildy* v. *Mid-Hampshire Railway Co* (1868) 16 WR 409; *In Re: London Pressed Hinge Co Ltd* [1905] 1 Ch 576). This intervention must be in such a way as to crystallise the whole security: a particular asset cannot be claimed from the enforcing creditor whilst the security remains a floating charge against the other assets (*Evans* v. *Rival Granite Quarries* [1910] 2 KB 979). If goods are seized in execution prior to crystallisation, the debenture holder may interplead if the sheriff is disputing the validity of the charge (*Taunton* v. *Sheriff of Warwickshire* [1895] 2 Ch 319 and see 9.25 later). If the bailiff has levied and completed execution by sale the debenture holders cannot compel the creditors to restore the money (*Re: Opera* [1891] 3 Ch 260). If the company pays the bailiff to get rid of a man in possession or a threat of removal and sale, but before the money is passed to the creditors the debenture holders appoint a receiver, as the company has an implied power to settle its debts the creditors may receive the money from the bailiff (*Heaton & Dugard Ltd* v. *Cutting* [1925] 1 KB 655; *Robinson* v. *Burnell's Vienna Bakery Ltd* [1904] 2 KB 624). It does not make any difference whether the agreement reached over payment is for instalments or for a lump sum (*Heaton* v. *Dugard Ltd & Cutting Bros Ltd* [1925] 1 KB 655).

9.21.3 After crystallisation

Where a floating charge has crystallised on the appointment of a receiver, the goods are no longer the company's goods and are not available for seizure (*Re: ELS* [1995] Ch 11). There is one case at variance with this – *Cunliffe Engineering* v. *English Industrial Estates* [1994] BCC 974. Here a landlord was held to be entitled to seize goods from a receiver partly because the debenture holder was held to have an interest in the tenancy and partly because the goods were in the reputed ownership of the firm and thus excluded from protection under s.4 LDAA 1908 (see 9.22.2 later).

Generally the bailiff will not be able to levy and if he does, for instance, in ignorance of the receiver's appointment, he will have to withdraw (*Edwards* v. *Edwards* [1875] 1 Ch D 454). See also *Re: Marriage, Neave & Co* [1896] 2 Ch D 663 which until recently was cited as an authority on this matter. In *Re: ELS* it was explained that the ruling in this case that a rates distraint *could* proceed after a receiver had been appointed as manager by debenture holders was distinguishable because there had been no change of occupation for rating purposes and no assignment of the chattels under the deed creating the equitable charge. The firm's creditors had a right to action under the agreements but, not a right to possession of any of the goods. Normally, as in *Re: ELS,* the charge crystallising will result in transfer of the goods to the debenture holders' receiver, thus preventing most distraint. A creditor may appoint a receiver and begin winding up proceedings after seizure and before sale by a bailiff and assert his/her priority over that bailiff against the proceeds of sale of the goods by the liquidator (*Re: Standard Manufacturing Co* [1891] 1 Ch 639).

If there has been a change of occupation of the premises as a result of the receiver's appointment, s/he will become liable for any rates and may be subject to distraint for them (*Richards* v. *Overseers of Kidderminster* [1896] 2 Ch 212). Normally, though, the terms of the debenture will not make the receiver an agent of the company and thus s/he is not liable for any rates due after the date of the appointment (*Taggs Island Casino Hotel Ltd* v. *Richmond upon Thames Borough Council* [1967] RA 70). The company will remain liable, though possessing few seizable assets.

9.21.4 Agricultural charges

Assets on a farm may be subject to charges that may be either fixed or floating. These are created by banks with tenant or owner farmers, charging all the livestock, crops, machinery, seeds and manures, fixtures and other produce of the farm as security for short term credit, under s.5 Agricultural Credits Act 1928. Such charges, whether crystallised or not, do not prevent distress on the charged items for rent, rates and taxes (s.8(7)).

However these charges, even if uncrystallised, do prevent execution (according to Keith, Podevin & Sandbrook at p. 44 – but contrast "Mather" pp. 100–102 which follows s.7(1) of the Act and which treats agricultural charges like charges under debentures i.e. they are not effective against execution or distraint whilst they are still floating and have not crystallised – see the previous subsections above). In the county court, the execution creditor may be required by the court to conduct a search at the Land Registry to ascertain whether any charges are registered under the 1928 Act prior to seizure taking place (CCR O.26 r.3). This will enable the court to determine whether there are any sufficient goods available for seizure, and is it obviously important for the debtor farmer to alert any bailiff levying execution to such charges. A similar procedure is followed by sheriff's officers.

PART THREE – COMMON LAW DISTRESS

9.22 Distress for Rent

There are many detailed rules applying to what may be taken in distress for rent. There has been a tendency to seek to extend these categories to other forms of distress. However in chapter 2 it was shown why this should not be done. Over and above this, it should be noted that in statutory distraint the legislation usually only ever speaks of the debtor's goods alone and there is no suggestion that anything broader than that is intended. In the absence of such indications, the rent classifications should not be applied.

The basic common law rule is that any item on the premises may be taken to a value sufficient to cover the rent arrears and costs (see Blackburn J in *Lyons* v. *Elliott* [1876] 1 QBD 210 at 213). This right to seize in distress is regardless of ownership (*Gorton* v. *Falkner* [1792] 4 Term Rep 565) and, it would seem, regardless of the fact that the occupier is now a person such as a squatter who has disseised the tenant (*Humphry* v. *Damion* [1612] Cro Jac 300). This right has been modified by statute and some goods are now exempted, or privileged, as the following sections describe. The rules often seem inexplicable as Phillimore J observed "*It is a strange thing, and I see no principle in it, . . . That, however, appears to be the law, and it is due partly to the fact that the law of distress is partly archaic and very technical.*" *Crossley Bros. Ltd* v. *Lee* [1908] 1 KB 86. The courts, when an opportunity presents itself, attempt to modernise the privileges.

Readers should note that all the categories of exemption (or privilege) are separate exclusive clauses i.e. tools are protected even if they are not in use. It is however possible for a lease to vary the protection afforded by the various privileges, either by permitting distress on privileged goods, as *In Re: The River Swale Brick & Tile Works Ltd* [1883] LJ Ch 638 (but only after a delay of a certain period, during which the right to exercise the common law remedy was unaffected), or by agreeing not to distrain on certain goods such as cattle (*Horsford* v. *Webster* (1835) 1 CM & R 696) or third parties' goods (*Welsh* v. *Rose* (1830) 6 Bing 638).

9.22.1 Qualified privilege

The items granted conditional privilege can only be taken if there are insufficient other goods. If it appears that nothing else seizable is present on the property the landlord may take items with qualified privilege, as he is by right entitled to whatever distrainable items there are actually available at the time of the levy (*Piggott* v. *Birtles* [1836] 1 M&W 441). The landlord may be sued for seizing goods with qualified privilege unless s/he genuinely believed that there were no alternative items (*Jenner* v. *Yolland* (1818) 6 Price 3). The privileged items include:

- *tools of the trade* in excess of the limit of absolute privilege (see 9.22.2 below) (*Nargett* v. *Nias* (1859) 1 E & E 439);
- *sheep and beasts* which "gain" the land (i.e. plough beasts) (*Simpson* v. *Hartropp* (1744) Willes 512). However if the beasts are too young to be used for this purpose, they are not privileged (see also 9.12.2);
- *agisted beasts* i.e. livestock belonging to a third party taken in commercially by the tenant for grazing. These are protected under s.18(2) Agricultural Holdings Act 1986. The agistment must be for a fair price, but this need not be in cash-payment in kind will be sufficient to give the privilege (*London & Yorkshire Bank* v. *Belton* [1885] 15 QBD 457) but cattle taken under a contract for the grazing of land will not (*Masters* v. *Green* [1888] 20 QBD 807). Under s.18(3) a ceiling is placed on how much the landlord can realise by the seizure of agisted beasts. He or she cannot recover more than the (balance of the) sum agreed to be paid for the feeding of the stock. If, before sale, the owner of any such agisted stock pays to the landlord a sum equal to the above amount, the animals can be recovered and any amount due from the third party to the tenant is released (s.18(4)).
- *growing crops already seized in execution* (s.2 Landlord and Tenant Act 1851). A landlord may seize growing crops seized and sold by the sheriff if they are still on the farm and if there is insufficient distress to cover any rent due after the date of the sheriff's seizure and sale of those crops. The crops lose all privilege if the purchaser from the sheriff allows them to remain an unreasonable time on the premises after they are ripe (*Peacock* v. *Purvis* (1820) 2 B&B 362).

9.22.2 Absolute privilege

Items given absolute privilege are totally exempt from seizure. They include:

- *incorporeal chattels* – such as the rights of an owner of a patented chattel under letters patent to make and use the chattel and to license others to do so (*British Mutoscope & Biograph Co Ltd* v. *Horner* [1901] 1 Ch 671). This is because the right to distrain arises out of the demised premises and distress can be levied on goods on such premises. Just as distress cannot be levied under a demise of an incorporeal hereditament, it cannot be levied on chattels that have no local position and that cannot be physically seized.
- *wild animals* and other items of no value (*Davies* v. *Powell* (1738) *Willes* 46);

- *perishable items* – those which cannot be returned to the tenant in the same condition (*Wilson* v. *Ducket* (1675) 2 Mod Rep 61). This will exempt such items as fruit and meat, but extends also to items that will be scattered by an attempt to remove, such as corn in a sheaf, or items whose exact quantity may not be easily ascertained at the time of seizure, such as removing some grain or flour from a sack. Wine in bottles are not protected by this privilege (*Re: Russell* (1870) 18 WR 753), so "Woodfall on Landlord & Tenant" speculates at para. 9.055 that food in tins, jars or vacuum packs similarly will not be exempt. The item containing the privileged goods is also privileged e.g. a lorry transporting fresh fruit (*Muspratt* v. *Gregory* [1838] 1 M&W 633);
- *fixtures* – as described at 9.5 the courts have recognised two categories of fixtures: those that are irremovable (which are never distrainable) and those that may be removed by the tenant but are otherwise part of the freehold (*Turner* v. *Cameron* [1870] 5 QB 306). The basic rule is that the latter category of fixtures (items such as kitchen ranges and stoves) which the tenant may sever from the freehold and remove during the term cannot be seized in distraint (*Darby* v. *Harris* [1841] 1 QB 895). This seems to apply even if the fixed item is removed for some purpose at the time of seizure (*Gorton* v. *Falkner* [1792] 4 TR 567). The landlord can only seize items which may be restored in the same condition as before seizure, and the ability of the tenant to remove and the landlord to restore are different questions. It is irrelevant that the goods were, or may become, the tenant's chattels. If they are affixed to the premises for the purposes of the tenant, they may not be seized (*Provincial Bill Posting Co* v. *Low Moor Iron Co* [1909] 2 KB 344). Those fixtures that are removable by the tenant become the landlord's if the tenant does not take them at the end of the lease, but despite the curious feature that the latter will ultimately become the landlord's they still may not be seized (*Crossley Bros Ltd* v. *Lee* [1908] 1 KB 86);
- *public utility fittings* see 9.13;
- *loose money* (i.e. not in a purse or wallet) which cannot be kept separate;
- *things in actual use* (*Read* v. *Burley* (1597) Cro Eliz 549) including clothes being worn (*Baynes* v. *Smith* [1794] 1 Esp 206) and machinery (*Simson* v. *Harcourt* (1744) Esp NP);
- *household goods and tools of the trade* as protected in the county court (see 9.6 earlier) as s.4 LDAA 1888 exempts from distress the same goods that are protected from execution. Tools of the trade can include items hired or on HP in the spouse's name so that the other spouse can earn a living for the whole family e.g. a sewing machine (*Churchward* v. *Johnson* (1889) 54 JP 326; *Masters* v. *Frazer* (1901) 85 LT 611). Even if there is only one tool of considerable value, it is still privileged (*Lavell* v. *Richings* [1906] 1 KB 480). By the proviso of s.4 this protection does **not** apply to any case where the lease, term or interest of the tenant has expired, where possession of the premises in respect of which the rent is due has been demanded and where the distress is levied not later than seven days after that demand. It seems that these conditions are cumulative rather than separate. The proviso relates to those tenancies where the landlord may distrain under ss.6 & 7 L&TA 1709 (see 3.2.2). Coke also states (2 Inst 133) that apparel, jewels and "vessels" are exempt at common law;

- *goods already seized* in execution (*Eaton* v. *Southby* (1738) 7 Mod Rep 251);
- *Crown property* – there is almost no authority on this privilege, which was interpreted by Wills J as an argument in favour of the long established and undisputed exemption of the Crown (*Secretary of State for War* v. *Wynne* [1905] 2 KB 845);
- *goods in the mail* under s.64(1)&(3) Post Office Act 1969;
- *goods held in the course of business* on trade premises as a direct part of the tenant's business (*Challoner* v. *Robinson* [1908] 1 Ch 490). This exemption is based on the need to protect trade by not allowing distress to close businesses down see Co Litt 47 citing authorities that this protection is for the good of the "commonwealth". The trade must be "public" i.e. anyone can approach the trader to use his/her services. Thus in *Tapling & Co* v. *Weston* (1833) Cab & El 99 a sales agent acting for one firm alone was not held to be in public trade. Public trade will include a butcher (*Brown* v. *Shevill* (1834) 2 Ad & El 138), a wood mill (*Guy* v. *Rankin* (1883) 23 NBR 49), a book binders (*Munster* v. *Johns* (1850) 16 LTOS 245) and a restaurant or shop where the business is open to any customer.

  The exemption covers all goods delivered to the tenant to be "carried, wrought or managed in the way of trade or employ" (*Simpson* v. *Hartopp* (1744) Willes 512). There is no need for the goods to be physically altered whilst in the trader's hands, but for the goods to be privileged it must be necessary for them to be on the premises for the trade to be conducted (*Parsons* v. *Gingell* (1847) 4 CB 545). Goods left at the premises for the owner's convenience, and not to be worked upon by the tenant, are not privileged (see *Joule* v. *Jackson* (1841) 7 M&W 450 – beer barrels left at a pub until the beer was drunk; or *Mitchell* v. *Coffee* (1880) 5 AR 525 – machine left a hotel by customer in his absence).

  The privilege will cover the following categories of goods:

  - items left for repair or alteration (*Clarke* v. *Millwall Dock* [1886] 17 QBD 494);
  - goods in the hands of a public carrier (*Gisbourn* v. *Hirst* (1710) 1 Salk 249);
  - furniture held in store (*Miles* v. *Furber* [1873] 8 QB 77);
  - goods on pawn or at an auctioneer's (*Findon* v. *M'Laren* [1845] 6 QB 891; *Adams* v. *Grane* (1833) 1 Cr & M 380);
  - goods held by a sale agent acting on commission (*Gilman* v. *Elton* (1821) 3 B&B 75; see also *Thompson* v. *Mashiter* (1823) 1 Bing 283);
  - goods held by a shopkeeper on sale or return, as the arrangement is a "notorious" trade practice which will prevent any claim that the goods are in the reputed ownership of the tenant (*Re: Florence ex parte Wingfield* [1879] 10 Ch D 591). See also *Perdriau Rubber Co Ltd* v. *Sadek* (1928) SRQ 114.

  The protection does not apply to:

  - goods purchased by a retailer from a wholesaler;
  - goods on sale in a shop rather than in a public market (*Bent* v. *McDougall* (1881) 2 R&G 468); or,
  - second hand goods sold on commission by a dealer (*Lawrence* v. *Turner* (1934) 3 WWR 353).

  There must be delivery of goods to the tenant's own premises to attract the privilege, so if goods happen to be on premises for use in the manufacture of products, they will not necessarily be privileged, nor will goods being worked on at the owner's own premises. Although materials sent to be worked upon may be privileged (*Gibson* v. *Ireson* [1842] 3 QB 39), machines delivered with them will not, nor will the vehicles in which they were delivered (*Joule* v. *Jackson* (1841) 7 M&W 450), unless there are sufficient other distrainable goods on the premises (*Wood* v. *Clarke* (1831) 1 C&J 484).

The premises upon which the goods are seized must be occupied by the trader. Goods are privileged if they are on premises which the trader is hiring temporarily for the purposes of trade (*Brown* v. *Arundell* (1850) 10 CB 54). The goods to be worked on by the trader may be stored on his/her premises (*Williams* v. *Holmes* (1853) 8 Exch 861) or in a warehouse without losing their privilege (*Matthias* v. *Mesnard* (1826) 2 C&P 353) as long as they are also worked upon and not just stored (*Re: Russell* (1870) 18 WR 753). Goods held for trade may also have protection from their third party status (see below).

- *agricultural items* – various items that a bailiff may find on an agricultural holding or farm are completely exempt from seizure. These include:
  - *agricultural machinery* owned by someone other than the tenant or left on the premises under a hire agreement or for use in the farming business (s.18(1) Agricultural Holdings Act 1986);
  - *livestock of all descriptions* belonging to a third party and present on the farm solely for the purposes of breeding (s.18(1)(b) 1986 Act);
  - *cattle* belonging to a third party and consuming "eatage" which, with the landlord's consent, have been sold to a third party on condition that rent is paid from the proceeds of that sale (*Horsford* v. *Webster* [1835] 1 Cr M & R 696);
  - *cattle pastured overnight* on the demised premises, whilst being driven to market (*Tate* v. *Gleed* [1784] 2 Wms Saund 290a; *Nugent* v. *Kirwan* (1838) 1 Jeb & Sy).
  - *certain produce and implements* subject to execution (ss.3 & 6 Sale of Farming Stock Act 1816 – see 9.12.2 earlier).
  - *certain basic items exempt at common law,* such as ploughs, poultry, saddle horses and fish (2 Co Inst 133).
- *goods on hire purchase or conditional sale* subject to a Consumer Credit Act 1974 default notice (s.4A(2) LDAA 1908), a suspended delivery order or a termination notice (*Smart Bros* v. *Holt* [1929] 2 KB 303). If the goods are subject to an agreement in the tenant's spouse's name, they are protected (*Rogers, Eungblutt & Co* v. *Martin* [1911] 1 KB 19), but not if they are in joint names (*Shenstone & Co* v. *Freeman* [1910] 2 KB 84; *AW Garnage Ltd* v. *Payne* [1925] 134 LT 222). In some cases goods may be protected without the need to serve any form of termination notice (*Perdana Properties* v. *United Orient Leasing* (1981) 1 WLR 1496). A written notice clearly indicating that consent to continued possession has been withdrawn by the finance company takes the goods out of "reputed ownership" (see 9.22.3 below) and will be sufficient to protect them from seizure (see also *Hollinshead* v. *Egan* [1913] AC 564 – a bills of sale case). Any such notice is operative from the date that it is posted by the finance company, and from this date

the goods will be exempt from distress (*Drages Ltd* v. *Owen* [1935] All ER Rep 342).

- *hired and leased goods:* In *Salford Van Hire (Contracts)* v. *Bocholt Investments* [1996] RTR 103 the Court of Appeal ruled that changes in commercial and financial practice meant that goods hired or leased by firms can no longer be regarded as being in their "reputed ownership" and were to be regarded now as exempt from distress for rent. It is likely that these same principles will apply to goods on hire purchase or conditional sale, thus offering a more complete protection for such items than the above paragraph, and overruling earlier cases such as *Chappell* v. *Harrison* [1910] 103 LT 594 in which a piano on HP was seized as the existence of an HP agreement did not prevent "reputed ownership" of the goods by the tenant.

  The courts have also held that, on the terms of some agreements, even after default and termination and until further steps were taken to recover the goods, they still remained in the order and disposition of the debtor (*Times Furnishing Co* v. *Hutchings* [1938] 1 KB 775) or even subject to the agreement (*Hackney Furnishing Co* v. *Watts* [1912] 3 KB 225), so that no action would lie against the landlord for, respectively, damages for illegal distress or for the recovery of sums paid to release the hired goods as money had and received. Conversely, it has also been held that consent to possession of goods under a hire purchase agreement may be withdrawn without the need to terminate the agreement itself (*Perdana Properties* v. *United Orient Leasing* (1981) 1 WLR 1496 – see above).

- *third party's goods:* The property of lodgers and sub-tenants and strangers (i.e. "*any other person whatsoever not being a tenant of the premises or any part thereof and not having any beneficial interests in any tenancy of the premises or any part thereof*") is absolutely privileged under s.1 LDAA 1908. Also case law provides some protection e.g. strangers' goods cannot be seized if brought onto the premises by the stranger personally (*Paston* v. *Carter* [1883] Cab & El 183). These individuals must make a written declaration to the landlord in a set form accompanied by an inventory stating that items levied upon are theirs. On receiving a declaration the landlord should return the goods and to continue to distrain would render it illegal. If this is not done the person may apply before two JPs for a restoration order (for more detail on this procedure see 9.29.2 *infra*).

  The protection only applies to subtenancies where the sub-tenant is liable to pay a rent not less often than quarterly which represents the whole annual value of the property or such proportion of it as he or she occupies (s.1(a) LDAA 1908). The protection also does not apply to sub-tenants whose tenancy has been created in breach of a term of their landlord's lease or tenancy agreement (s.5 LDAA 1908). Lodgers and licensees are not effected by this exclusion.

  One considerable problem with the protection given by the LDAA 1908 is that "lodger" is not defined within it. A lodger is clearly not a tenant, sub-tenant or stranger, and is probably being referred to in the ordinary sense of a person living and sleeping on the premises (see *Heawood* v. *Bone* [1884] 13 QBD 179). This question of status is for the person claiming the Act's protection to prove. There is considerable authority on the meaning of the expression, which it may be helpful to note for both residential and business licensees.

- if the user of the premises does not have exclusive possession, for example, accommodation can be used by others in their absence, and if possession is given on sufferance and is provisional, at the owner's pleasure, even though a rent is paid for it, the user is not a tenant (*Allan* v. *Overseers of Liverpool* [1874] 9 QB 180);
- though an arrangement may be termed a sub-tenancy and involves the letting of nearly an entire property, if the landlord retails possession of part of the property, the "sub-tenant" is a lodger (*Phillips* v. *Henson* (1877) 3 CPD 26);
- if the tenant shares accommodation with the landlord, even though no service or attendance is provided, s/he is a lodger (*Bradley* v. *Bayliss* [1881] 8 QBD 195);
- where the landlord let all the property except for ground floor shop accommodation which he retained and used for trade, the tenant was held to be a lodger under the Act. The landlord does not have to be resident and the tenant's power of separate and unrestricted access will not have an impact. The important point is control: if the landlord retains some control of occupation and access, the tenant is a lodger. Control is, however, not retaining common parts or the right to enter to do repairs (*Ness* v. *Stephenson* [1882] 9 QBD 245);
- in contrast to *Allan* above, it was held that a person occupying business premises is not a lodger, even where they do not occupy the whole premises and access is given by the landlord who holds the key (*Heawood* v. *Bone* [1884] 13 QBD 179);
- if the landlord occupies a separate flat in the same building, the occupier is not a lodger (*Kent* v. *Fittall* [1906] 1 KB 60); and,
- even if accommodation is shared with others, if the landlord does not reside but calls weekly to collect rent from the tenants, each of whom occupies individual rooms with their own keys and rent books, the person is not a lodger (*Honig* v. *Redfern* [1949] 2 All ER 15).

Additionally, the goods of a third party are protected if that person is agent of the landlord and occupies the demised premises as such, for instance as a caretaker (*Wheeler* v. *Stevenson* (1860) 6 H&N 155).

9.22.3 No privilege

No privilege is given to the goods of the following:

- *the tenant's spouse* (s.4(1) LDAA 1908);
- *a person who has lent goods* to the tenant, but note the absolute privilege of agricultural machinery and the recent exemption of hired and leased goods (see 9.22.2).

  This exclusion from privilege is provided by s.4(1) LDAA 1888 which refers to "*goods in the possession, order or disposition of such a tenant by the consent and permission of the true owner under such circumstances that such tenant is reputed owner thereof*". Reputed ownership is a question of fact. It is to be inferred in situations where, by exercise of reason and judgment on the facts capable of being found on enquiry, a reasonable person would have to conclude that the goods in the possession of the debtor were fully owned by that person (*Re: Fox* [1948] Ch 407).

Equally if it is to be disproved, the real owner must show that steps had actually been taken to terminate ownership and recover the goods so that no grounds could exist on which to form such an impression. Goods on HP are exempted from this section, even if both the agreement and the bailment to the tenant has been terminated so long as a right to repossess the goods remains under the agreement *(Jays Furnishing Co* v. *Brand & Co* [1914] 2 KB 132). Goods on "permanent loan" with no conditions attached would be seizable. Property held on trust is not in a person's reputed ownership (*Re: Sibeth ex parte Sibeth* [1885] 14 QBD 417).

Traders with goods on "sale or return" will be able to rebut any claim of "reputed ownership" provided that they can demonstrate that such terms of trade are a "notorious custom" in their business (*Ex parte Wingfield In Re: Florence* [1879] 10 Ch D 591). A person who receives goods on sale or return receives them with the option of becoming owner, which can be exercised by buying the goods at the vendor's price, by selling to a third party or by keeping the goods so long that it would be unreasonable to return them. If he sells or attempts to sell, he does not do so as owner, but as having the option to take the goods if they are sold. The trader needs to show that customers would understand that possession does not necessarily indicate ownership.

- *a business partner* (s.4(2)(a) LDAA 1908). Their separate property, if on the rented premises, may be seized. Application may be made by a claimant to magistrates' court for a determination as to whether goods are covered by this subsection. Readers should however note the decision in *Re: Potter* (1874) 18 Eq 381 in which it was held that a landlord may seize chattels, but not a partner's potential interest in chattels. The distress had to be limited to property of the debtor solely as their joint property was subject to payment of their joint debts, until satisfaction of which, it was impossible to quantify the interest of each partner in the chattels.
- *various goods on business premises*: under s.4(2) LDAA 1908 no privilege is given to goods jointly owned by a tenant and sub-tenant found on trade premises; goods left in offices and warehouses one month after notice from the landlord to remove them, and goods belonging to, and in the offices of, any company which are located in premises rented by a director, officer or employee of the company. Application for a declaration as to protection may be made to the magistrates' court.
- *a farmer or smallholder* may have any of the following items seized in distress for rent:
  - *sheaves of corn and hay* if it is in a barn or granary, and not subject to replevin (s.2 DRA 1689). In light of this provision Gilbert (at p. 213) questions whether the common law privilege of goods liable to deterioration no longer applies to goods which will not be ruined during the five day delay before sale. Such produce must be impounded on the farm and, it would appear, must be sold after an optional appraisement;
  - *cattle or stock* feeding on the commons or roads on the premises (s.8 DRA 1737). Once the landlord has entered to seize such beasts, the tenant may not drive them off (*Clement* v. *Milner* (1800) 3 Esp 95). Horses being kept by a third party in a stable let by the tenant may also be seized (*Crosier* v. *Tomkinson* (1759) 2 Keny 439);

- *all produce* (i.e. corn, grass, hops, roots, fruits and pulses) growing on the holding (s.8 DRA 1737). This right does not apply to trees, shrubs and bushes, but only such crops as ripen and are harvested (*Clark* v. *Gaskarth* (1818) 8 Taunt 431). The landlord may both seize the crops when growing (*Glover* v. *Coles* (1822) 1 Bing 6) and also cut this produce when it has ripened, but not before (*Owen* v. *Leigh* (1820) 3 B & Ald 470) and store it either on the holding or off the holding in suitable premises as close by as possible if there are no adequate storage facilities in the farm. A cart loaded with sheaves may also be seized (*Horton* v. *Arnold* (1731) Fortes Rep 361). The produce must be appraised and must be sold. However, if the tenant makes payment or tender of the full rent and costs due before the produce has ripened and been cut, the distress shall cease (s.9 DRA 1737). If produce is sold before it is in ripe, but the tenant can show no loss to have been caused by this, no damages may be recovered (*Rodgers* v. *Parker* (1856) 18 CB 112). This power to seize growing crops does not extend to the grantees of rentcharges unless there is an express power in the grant (*Miller* v. *Green* (1831) 2 C&J 142). Grantees may however distrain on oats and hay in stacks under DRA 1689 s.2 mentioned above (*Johnson* v. *Faulkner* [1842] 2 QB 925);
- *a stranger's cattle* that have been allowed on the premises or have strayed onto the farm by breaking through sound fences or unsound fences if the tenant was not responsible for their repair (*Jones* v. *Powell* (1826) 5 B&C 647). If however they enter through defective fences that the tenant should have repaired, they may not be seized until they have been on the premises for a day and a night ("levant et couchant") and notice to remove has been given to the owner, to which he has not responded (*Kempe* v. *Crews* (1697) 1 Ld Raym 167). If they are removed after notice, it is not rescue (*Fowkes* v. *Joice* 2 Vern 131).

9.23 Distress damage feasant

As was originally the case at common law with distress for rent, before statutory modifications were made, in distress damage feasant all chattels (and animals) except those in actual use are seizable. As with distress for rent this last exemption is purely to avoid potential breaches of the peace, and reflects no deeper principle (*Collins* v. *Renison* (1754) Say 138). The case law distinguishes between those items in the personal possession of the debtor and those in actual use (*Bunch* v. *Kennington* [1841] 1 QB 679). Thus sheep in a shepherd's care are not "in use" (*Brough* v. *Wallace & Affleck* (1863) 2 W&W 195). No actual danger of a breach of the peace need be shown by a person seeking to benefit from this exemption (*Field* v. *Adams* (1840) 2 Ad & El 649), but if the item allegedly in use is nowhere near the plaintiff, the case will fail – it must be shown that a breach of the peace was possible, and nothing but actual use that may lead to a personal struggle will support this plea (*Bunch* v. *Kennington* [1841] 1 QB 679). There is a query as to whether a horse being ridden, and one presumes therefore, a car being driven, can be seized (see footnote c on page 49 of "Gilbert" for discussion, but see also *Storey* v. *Robinson* (1795) 6 Term Rep 139). A horse and cart being driven by a servant of the debtor has been held to be exempt as it was in use (*Welsh* v. *Bell* [1669] 1 Vent 37 citing 3 Cro 549 & 598). Certainly tools of the trade are not exempt (Com Dig Distress B4).

Nowadays, as already stated, the almost exclusive subject of distress damage feasant is likely to be motor vehicles. Whether an argument can be constructed to protect those in use in the sense of having the engine running with the driver at the wheel – whether parking or preparing to leave the car park remains to be seen. Note also that chattels may be severed from others to which they are attached or form a part (e.g. a horse from a cart). This is because each may trespass individually (*Tunbridge's Case* [1582] Cro Eliz 8). Thus a trailer may be separated from the vehicle towing it.

Chattels that are perishable may be seized, as may those in legal custody, so it would appear that a vehicle seized in distraint by another bailiff may be seized in distress damage feasant if it is allowed to trespass on private property.

PART FOUR – REMEDIES TO WRONGFUL SEIZURE OF GOODS

If any exempt goods are seized, the onus of proof in any case is on the debtor to show that they are exempt because they fall in any particular category or below any financial limit and that insufficient goods were left (*Gonsky* v. *Durrell* [1918] 2 KB 71). However note that in *Rai & Rai* v. *Birmingham City Council* (1993) unreported, on appeal under reg 40 of the community charge regulations, a deputy stipendiary magistrate held that bailiffs have a duty of care to exercise when seizing goods and must act with discernment and judgment. If, during a levy, the bailiffs are put on notice that certain goods do not allegedly belong to the debtor, they must act with due caution and circumspection. As they did not in this case an illegal levy occurred. See also *Dunstan* v. *Paterson* (1857) 2 CBNS 495 – the sheriff may be justified in seizing the wrong person (or goods) if he is misinformed or misled as to their identity, but they must be released as soon as the true state of affairs is known.

The remedies to be described apply to most forms of distress. Thus, if unlawful distraint for income taxes takes place, the debtor can sue for damages in the county court and return of the goods (*Berry* v. *Farrow* [1914] 1 KB 632) or seek replevin. Equally where a remedy is provided by the relevant statutes, this does not exclude the general remedies. It was noted in *R.* v. *Hampstead Magistrates Court ex parte St Marylebone Property Co plc* [1995] Legal Action Sept 1996, p.21 that "*the statute clearly incorporated distress as a well established remedy. It can be assumed that it was intended that the established incidents of the remedy would apply except as specifically provided.*" Hence there is a right to sue for damages as much as the statutory right of complaint.

9.24 Complaint to magistrates' court

Under the regulations for local taxes (reg. 46 CT & reg. 15 NNDR) and child support maintenance (reg. 31) any person aggrieved by a levy, or an attempt to levy, can appeal to the magistrates' court. The existence of this statutory remedy does not however exclude the right to sue for wrongful distress (*Governor of the Poor of Bristol* v. *Wait* (1834) 1 Ad & El 264) and the local authority may be liable for trespass for any distraint levied in unlawful circumstances (*London & North Western Railway Co* v. *Giles* (1869) 33 JP 776).

The case is commenced by making a "complaint" and requesting the issue of a summons directed to the creditor. The complainant need not specially argue that the distraint was wrongful, as the onus lies on the defendant to show the legality of their actions (*R.* v. *Justices of Devon* (1813) 1 M&S 411). At the hearing, if the court is satisfied that the levy was irregular, it can order the return of the goods distrained. Although the regulations speak of irregularity alone, it has been held by the courts that this term includes any wrongful act by the bailiff i.e. illegality, irregularity or an excessive levy (*Steel Linings* v. *Bibby* (1993) RA 27).

As an alternative to ordering return of goods the court may order an award of compensation for the goods sold equal to an amount which, in opinion of the court, would be awarded by way of special damages if proceedings had been taken for trespass or otherwise in connection with the irregularity. (NB in assessing the level of compensation the court is required to act reasonably and to give proper attention to any evidence placed before it: *R.* v. *Epping Magistrates ex parte Howard & Leach* (1996) 7 CLY 521.) It has been held by the High Court in *Steel Linings* v. *Bibby* , and endorsed in *R.* v. *Hampstead Magistrates Court ex parte St Marylebone Property Co plc* [1995] Legal Action Sept 1996, p21 that the reference to special damages has a wider meaning in the regulations than just special damages as opposed to general damages and covers all damages caused by the wrongful levy, including aggravated damages for annoyance, injury to credit and reputation. The court can also order the creditor and bailiffs to desist from any levying in an irregular manner.

Several cases have been reported in respect of community charge:

- *Crosby* v. *Wandsworth London Borough Council* [1991] Legal Action 3/91 – goods belonging to the son, Wayne Crosby, were seized and sold. He was awarded £310 compensation and the council was ordered to better supervise their bailiffs.
- *Rai & Rai* v. *Birmingham City Council* (1993) unreported: the detail of the judgment is discussed at 8.1.1 The deputy stipendiary magistrate, on finding a "threefold commission of irregular levy" ordered that the goods removed by the bailiffs be returned.
- *H* v. *Sandwell MBC* [1993] Legal Action August p.15: see 8.3.1 for details. On hearing the case the magistrates made an order declaring the attempted levy to be irregular, the walking possession charges unlawful and prohibiting further enforcement against the plaintiff.

If a complaint is dismissed, appeal may be by way of case stated (see 9.30.2).

9.25 Interpleader

9.25.1 Applicability

Interpleader is a process by which a person faced with competing claims for goods, and who may be sued by different people in respect of those claims, may start an action in court to settle the claims. It is a way of compelling claimants to pursue their claims, not for their benefit but for the relief of the person interpleading – who takes no further part in the case (*De La Rue* v. *Hernu, Peron & Stockwell Ltd* [1936] 2 KB

164). There are two forms of interpleader, but we shall only be concerned with execution interpleader which applies to sheriff's officers, county court bailiffs and bailiffs enforcing road traffic penalties. Before the process is examined, a number of observations on general principles may be made.

- *claimants*: claims to property seized from the debtor may be made by a wide range of individuals – for example, partners, spouses, relatives, friends, lodgers, trade suppliers, trustees or liquidators in insolvencies, mortgagees under bills of sale (*Usher* v. *Martin* [1889] 24 QBD 272) and hire or HP firms. These groups may all assert that the assets in question are owned by them. A claim does not need to be based solely on an assertion of absolute ownership. A person with an equitable interest in the goods, such as a lien or right of possession, may also make a claim. A debenture holder may thus make a claim. An assignee of a debt may not claim the proceeds of sale of an execution on a judgment for the debt (*Plant* v. *Collins* [1913] 1 KB 242). In all cases, the claimant should put their claim in writing.
- *goods:* relief can be given in respect of any debt, money, goods or chattels. This can include choses in action such as share certificates (*Robinson* v. *Jenkins* [1890] 24 QBD 275) and money paid out under protest to prevent execution (*Smith* v. *Critchfield* [1885] 14 QBD 873). A claimant may not be able to use interpleader to protect their goods if they have allowed the debtor to use them as their own – for instance, in the course of trade (*Engelbach* v. *Dixon* (1875) 10 CP 645). Application can be made in the High Court even if there is only an intention to seize though there has been no actual seizure and regardless of whether the bailiff is actually in possession (O.17 r.1 RSC; *Day* v. *Carr* (1852) 7 Exch 883). Alternatively, where the bailiff suspects that a claim may be likely to be made by a third party, no seizure has to be made. Instead a return of no goods may be made, thus avoiding the need to interplead, even though the debtor may have some interest in the goods eg: the equity of redemption in goods covered by a bill of sale (*Scarlett* v. *Hanson* [1883–84] 12 QB 213).
- *investigation:* the bailiff should inquire into the validity of the claims made as failure to do this may disentitle the bailiff to protection from court action.
- *delay*: allowing for the above investigations, it is nonetheless important for the bailiff to seek interpleader as quickly as possible. Delay may mean the court refuses any protection or penalises the bailiff with costs (*Cook* v. *Allen* [1833] 2 LJ Ex 199). The claimant may also be penalised for delay – for example it was held in *Watson* v. *Park Royal (Caterers) Ltd* [1961] 2 All ER 346 that the defendants failed to act with "reasonable promptitude" in starting interpleader three and a half months after becoming aware of the competing claims.

Interpleader is **not** applicable where:

- the bailiff is no longer in possession of the goods, either because they have been abandoned or released to the claimant or the bailiff has been withdrawn (*Lea* v. *Rossi* (1855) 11 Exch 13);
- the goods have been sold and the proceeds have been passed to the creditor; or,

- the claimant is the landlord seeking rent arrears. A special procedure applies (see 6.6.1).

9.25.2 Procedure

Application is under O.17 RSC for sheriff's officers and under ss.100–101 CCA and O.33 CCR for county court bailiffs and those enforcing road traffic debts (as applied to the latter by Enforcement of Road Traffic Debts Order 1993, though no deposit is required from the claimant in advance under s.100).

The bailiff seeks protection by initiating proceedings:

- to determine whether the property belongs to the debtor and thus may be seized or belongs to the claimant and is thus protected; and,
- to gain protection against other court actions arising out of any real and substantial grievance caused by his wrongful acts (see "damages" later). The bailiff will be protected in respect of actions which could result only in the award of nominal damages (*Cave* v. *Capel* [1954] 1 QB 367). Thus even though the sheriff may, by a honest mistake, have entered third party premises and seized a third party's goods, if there is "mere nominal trespass" the sheriff will be protected unless there is an aggravating factor, such as insolent or oppressive behaviour (*Smith* v. *Critchfield* [1885] 14 QBD 873).

The procedure will then follow the course described below.

Notice In the High Court the third party must give notice of the claim, including a full description of goods, to the sheriff, who must forthwith notify the execution creditor, sending a copy of the claim. It is better to enter into specifics about the items claimed, rather than relying on a general claim such as to "all goods and money seized under the warrant", unless perhaps the costs of listing all items would be disproportionate (*Richardson* v. *Wright* (1875) 10 Ex D 367). The creditor must then, within seven days, give notice whether or not the claim is admitted or disputed. If the creditor admits the claim, the sheriff withdraws. If the sheriff then fails to withdraw he may be liable to be sued and the court may refuse protection (*Sodeau* v. *Shorey* (1896) 74 LT 240). The creditor is only liable for fees incurred by the sheriff until the notice was sent. If the creditor disputes the claim or fails to reply, the sheriff can apply to the Court for protection against any proceedings relating to the seizure and should withdraw from possession of the goods claimed. Protection from proceedings will normally be granted as the sheriff is protected by s.138B(1) SCA but relief will not be granted where there is a substantial grievance against the sheriff which seems serious enough to override this immunity (see "damages" later). On withdrawal the goods cease to be in legal custody and may be distrained (*Cropper* v. *Warner* (1883) Cab & El 152), the execution creditor's remedy being against the deposit (*Wells* v. *Hughes* [1907] 2 KB 845). Even though the sheriff has withdrawn, the claimant may not remove the goods as this would be contempt.

In the county court the interpleader claimant serves notice on a county court district judge if the levying bailiff will not accept his/her claim. The district judge then notifies the creditor and requires a reply in four days. If notice is received within four days admitting the claim the bailiff is withdrawn and the creditor is only liable for fees incurred before the notice was served (O.33 r.2). The district judge may then seek an order from the Circuit Judge restraining any action being brought as a result of the disputed seizure. Normally the district judge will be protected under s.98 CCA but, as with the sheriff, this may be overridden (see later).

Application In the High Court, if the claim is disputed by the execution creditor the sheriff applies for "interpleader" on notice under CPR Part 23, serving it on the creditor and interpleader claimant. It is good practice at this point for the bailiff to supply all parties with a copy of the inventory taken – certainly the sheriff should act impartially as an officer of the court and not supply an inventory to one party only (*Fredericks & Pelhams Timber Buildings* v. *Wilkins* [1971] 1 WLR 1197). Within 14 days, the interpleader claimant must serve on the other parties an affidavit specifying goods and chattels claimed and the grounds for the claim. S/he can also claim damages and give details of any grievance against the sheriff. The court may order a deposit as security (O.17 r.5 and see below).

In the county court if no reply is received or the creditor refuses to return of the goods then an interpleader notice is issued on N88 to the parties and a hearing of the case is arranged (O.33 r.4).

The effect of the issue of interpleader proceedings is to stay enforcement of the debt by any means (*Re: Ford* [1886] 18 QBD 369). If there is any concern about the safety of seized goods, application will have to be made to court for leave to remove or otherwise protect them.

Security deposit The High Court may order payment of a deposit or the provision of security, and the county court **must** require this under O.33 r.1(2)(b) and s.100 CCA when accepting any interpleader claim. The security may be a solicitor's undertaking, a bond from a bank or insurance company or a guarantee from a person with two other sureties. The purpose of the deposit is to place in the court's control a sum equivalent to the value of the disputed goods and, if the interpleader claimant wishes the bailiff to withdraw, a sum representing the possession costs that the bailiff has incurred up until that date. This fund then becomes the subject matter of the dispute and the goods are released to the claimant and cannot be seized again by that creditor, even if the value is less than the debt due (*Haddow* v. *Morton* [1894] 1 QB 565). In the county court if no deposit is paid the goods must be sold and the proceeds paid into court to await the judge's decision (s.100(3) CCA) unless the judge decides otherwise in the circumstances. Such a sale will pass good title to the goods (*Goodlock* v. *Cousins* [1897] 1 QB 558 CA). If less than the value is deposited the bailiffs must not withdraw from possession and the court can order the bailiff to retake possession (*Miller* v. *Solomon* [1906] 2 KB 91). If the deposit does cover the debt and costs though not the value of the goods, the bailiff must not remain in possession after the date of the deposit and is not entitled to possession fees from then on (*Newsum Sons & Co Ltd* v. *James* [1909] 2 KB 364). If a second execution occurs on goods already the subject of interpleader proceedings, the existing deposit cannot be relied on in further proceedings and the claimant will have to provide a further sum of security (*Kotchie* v. *The Golden Sovereigns Ltd* [1898] 2 QB 164).

Sale of goods As an alternative to requiring the deposit the court may order sale of the goods and that the proceeds be applied as it thinks just (O.17 r.6 RSC). This may be done where:

- the goods are subject to a bill of sale;
- they are perishable;
- the safety of the goods is uncertain, for instance because the debtor will not agree to walking possession;
- it would be just and reasonable in order to save costs; or,
- as seen, where the interpleader claimant fails to provide the security required by the court.

The division of the proceeds is to be as the court sees fit, including interest at whatever rate and for whatever period is thought appropriate (*Forster* v. *Clowser* [1897] 2 QB 362). If money remains in the hands of the sheriff after sale, this may only be released to the interpleader claimant or debtor on order from the court, and until then the bailiff cannot be sued (*Discount Banking Company of England & Wales* v. *Lambarde* [1893] 2 QB 329). If the claim is then settled out of the proceeds, the claimant is not entitled to demand other sums from the sheriff not included in the original claim (see *Hockey* v. *Evans* [1887] 18 QBD 390 in which the holder of a bill of sale demanded interest and extra costs and charges that would have been recoverable from the debtor under the agreement). Another option for the court is appointment of a receiver and manager of the disputed property if it seems that forced sale would lose value and where, most probably, the items claimed are business assets that can continue to be used to earn money by the claimant whilst the case is pending (*Howell* v. *Dawson* [1884] 13 QBD 67).

Damages: in county court cases under O.33 r.5 the interpleader claimant may enter a claim for any damages s/he feels were incurred within eight days of receiving the summons. In the High Court any such claim for damages will be made in a separate action. If it is proved that there is the basis for a "substantial grievance" or that substantial injury has been suffered, damages should be awarded as it will not be just and reasonable to protect the bailiff. Factors to be taken into account when considering an award of damages will include:

- where there has been a sale at undervalue (*London, Chatham & Dover Railway Co Ltd* v. *Cable* [1899] 80 LT 119);
- where the bailiff has entered the premises of a stranger and seized goods in belief that they are the debtor's, he may be protected against an action for trespass if no substantial grievance has been done. Thus a bailiff may be protected from an action by a person whose premises were wrongly entered or wrongly seized – but only so long as there was no insolent or oppressive behaviour or other misconduct (*Smith* v. *Critchfield* [1885] 14 QBD 873). If only nominal damages could be recovered by the plaintiff, the bailiff should be protected (*Winter* v. *Bartholomew* (1856) 11 Exch 704). The bailiff is not protected where they are guilty of a moral fault and substantial grievance is caused (*De Coppet* v. *Barnet* [1901] 17 TLR 273); or

- where the claim arose from the bailiff's own wrongful actions – for instance, there has been forced entry or trespass against the person (*Cave* v. *Capel* [1954] 1 QB 367), goods were seized in the knowledge that they were not the debtor's (*Tufton* v. *Harding* (1859) 29 LJ Ch 225) or that they were already seized in distress (*Haythorn* v. *Bush* (1834) 2 Dowl 641).

Even if the bailiff acts mistakenly, he or she will not be protected where the circumstances aggravate the wrongs done. Damages can be awarded even though the goods have been sold and are no longer under the court's control (*Hills* v. *Renny* (1880) 5 Ex D 313). The fact that action is stayed against the bailiff will not prevent the claimant suing the purchaser – this cannot be stopped as part of interpleader proceedings (*Hills* v. *Renny, ante*). See also the discussion at 10.5.6 under "Title on sale".

A damages claim in the county court must be made before the hearing of the interpleader claim. If it is not, it will be too late afterwards as the decision on the matter by the county court under s.101 CCA is treated as final and conclusive (*West* v. *Automatic Salesman Ltd* [1937] 2 All ER 706). Section 101(3) requires that the judge "shall adjudicate on the claim" – this renders the matter effectively "res judicata" (*Death* v. *Harrison* (1871) 6 Exch 15). Whether the claimant forgets to claim or fails to particularise the claim, once the decision has been made the court is "*functus officio*" however good the claim for damages (*Kershaw* v. *Automatic Salesman Ltd* (1937) 4 LJCCR 60).

Hearing The court can summarily determine the matter when the sheriff applies, where all parties consent or one so requests or where the question at issue is one of law, not fact, and the case is thus straightforward and speed is important. Summary determination does not mean that no time will be given to gather evidence or to cross examine witnesses. A special hearing date should be set, discovery should be allowed etc (*PB Manufacturing* v. *Fahn* (1967) 1 WLR 1059). If, on the basis of the evidence in the claimant's affidavit, the issue appears to be a dispute as to the ownership, the court may direct it to be tried either before a High Court Judge or in the county court (O.17 r.5 RSC). Summary determination is not appropriate where the claimant's affidavit raises a serious claim to goods of an overall considerable value and the prospect of difficult points of law (*Fredericks & Pelhams Timber Buildings* v. *Wilkins* [1971] 3 All ER 545).

If the interpleader claimant fails to attend or fails to comply with the order made, the Court may bar him/her from any future claims. If the execution creditor does not appear the sheriff is ordered to withdraw from possession. The sheriff will of course be told to withdraw if the third party's claim is established. If the claimant only establishes title to some of the goods, he or she is entitled to be paid from the deposit a sum representing the value of those goods, though the execution creditor will receive the balance (*Tellus Super Vacuum Cleaners* v. *Ireland* (1938) LJNCCR 54). If the claimant fails to establish the title claimed, he is not normally precluded from relying on a different title that is found by the court. See *Peake* v. *Carter* [1916] 1 KB 652 in which the claimant asserted that goods were his sole property but which turned out to be joint property of a partnership with the judgment debtor and thus protected by s.23(1) Partnership Act 1890. Similar orders may be made in the county court.

Costs If the claimant fails, the bailiff can receive costs from the date of notice of claim or from the sale, which is earliest. If the claimant succeeds, the bailiff gets costs from the creditor from the time when the latter authorised interpleader proceedings. All costs are awarded at the judge's discretion under either O.17 r.8 RSC or CPR Part 47 *et seq.*

9.26 Interference with goods

Any misappropriation of goods should properly be referred to as wrongful interference with goods (under the Torts (Interference with Goods) Act 1977), which now comprehends and provides common remedies for a range of wrongs against personal property that were previously actionable separately and are encountered in the older case reports as trover, detinue and trespass. Wrongful interference may be defined in three ways (conversion, trespass and negligence), though the offences are not completely exclusive and a seizure may turn out to be both conversion and trespass.

The remedies available through the court are:

- an order for delivery of the goods and the payment of any consequential damages (s.3(2)(a) 1977 Act);
- an order for delivery with the alternative for the defendant to pay damages based on the value of the goods, with consequential damages in addition in either case (s.3(2)(b)); or,
- damages alone, based on the assessed value of the goods plus any consequential damages (s.3(2)(c));
- plus, if appropriate, an interlocutory injunction (s.4) for recovery of the goods.

An order for specific delivery alone is at the discretion of the court and is rare unless the item is of special significance or value to the plaintiff, or it may be impossible for the plaintiff to find a replacement, perhaps because they are no longer made (*Howard Perry & Co* v. *British Railways Board* [1980] 2 All ER 579). The plaintiff may choose between the other remedies, though in cases where the goods are no longer in the defendant's hands, whether through destruction or disposal, the latter is clearly the option to choose. The debtor can sue both the bailiff who commits the act and any person who is responsible for that action, e.g. a creditor who has authorised wrongful seizure.

9.26.1 Conversion

Conversion includes three different forms of wrongful interference that involve appropriating or altering another's goods or depriving that person of their use or possession. The gist of conversion is that there has been some wrongful act that interferes with, is inconsistent with, or deprives the owner of his/her proprietary rights over their goods. There need not be any intention to question or deny the plaintiff's rights, the conduct must simply be inconsistent with them by asserting rights that are contrary or negative them. Thus wrongfully taking goods into possession will be conversion (see *Tinkler* v. *Poole* (1770) 5 Burr 2657; *Shipwick* v. *Blanchard* (1795) 6

Term Rep 298), as will wrongfully receiving goods, wrongfully selling them, wrongfully retaining them or any other dealing that leads to the loss or destruction of the goods or which denies the plaintiff's title. Taking under duress, such as obtaining property under a wrongful threat of execution, can be conversion (*Grainger* v. *Hill* (1838) 4 Bing NC 212). The duress must be equivalent to forcible taking and thus we must assume that taking property as a result of a lawful threat is not conversion.

Conversion can apply to execution (*Garland* v. *Carlisle* (1873) 4 Cl & Fin 693) and distress (*Shipwick* v. *Blanchard* (1795) 6 TR 298; *Clowes* v. *Hughes* (1870) 5 Exch 160). Conversion will be more permanent than the possibly brief interference with possession that constitutes trespass. The three forms are:

- *wrongful dealing*: this is any dealing with or disposal of goods that is inconsistent with the owner's rights, whether in intentional or not. An illegal sale of goods is thus conversion (eg: *Neumann* v. *Bakeaway* later at 10.5.6). An auctioneer who knowingly receives illegally seized goods is also guilty of conversion by wrongful dealing.
- *wrongful detention*: this covers any detention of goods that consciously deprives a person of the use or possession of them. Thus a bailiff would be liable to an action if he refused to deliver up goods wrongly seized after being informed that this was the case or wrongfully impounded them after tender of the debt due (*Six Carpenters' Case* (1610) All ER 292). Refusal of tender after impounding is not conversion (*Singleton* v. *Williamson* (1862) 7 H&N 747) nor is levying for more than is due (*Whitworth* v. *Smith* (1832) 5 C&P 250). A mere threat to detain goods or prevent their removal by the rightful owner would not be conversion (*England* v. *Cowley* (1873) LR 8 Exch 126). Seizing exempt goods is conversion (*Keen* v. *Priest* (1859) 4 H&N 236). The plaintiff must make a demand for the goods which should be unconditional and specific and the refusal should also be unconditional. Unlawful keeping may also be implied if the defendant uses the goods in a manner inconsistent with the owner's rights. This could include "abuse" of distrained goods (see 10.4.2).
- *wrongful destruction*: this term refers to any loss or destruction of goods that a bailee like a bailiff in possession has allowed in breach of his duty to the owner.

The measure of general damages in conversion is the market value of the goods lost at the date of conversion (*Chubb Cash Ltd* v. *John Crilley & Son* (1983) 2 All ER 294 CA) plus any consequential or special damages incurred by the plaintiff provided that they are not too remote. If special damages are claimed there is no need to prove any financial loss in order to recover them. All such damages that are a natural and direct result of the conversion may be recovered, including damages for non-pecuniary losses such as inconvenience, distress and loss of enjoyment (*Harris* v. *Lombard New Zealand* [1974] 2 NZLR 161), loss of a purchaser, wasted expenses and standing charges, insurance excesses, lost no-claims bonuses, loss of use of a vehicle or cost of hire of a substitute and loss of profit from an income earning chattel. Losses such as loss of profits on a contract cannot be recovered as they are too remote unless the defendant could have foreseen them, for example, perhaps where tools of the trade are seized. Where the goods are on HP the measure is the market value or the sum still due under the agreement, which ever is the lesser. The best evidence of market value is the price obtained by sale at auction by the bailiff. If there is no market value, the cost of replacement should be used. If the value of the item has risen, this may be recoverable as consequential damages.

If goods are not lost but damaged the measure of damages is the reduction in their value (i.e. the reasonable costs of repairs to restore goods to their prior condition) plus loss of use until the repairs are done or the cost of hiring a replacement in the interim. These damages may be topped up if, despite the repairs, the market value of the goods is now permanently reduced. If it is cheaper to replace rather than repair goods, the replacement price will be awarded. It does not matter that the repairs have not yet, and may never be done. If other previous damage is also repaired, a lesser sum than the costs of the repairs will be awarded. The plaintiff may repair an item personally and recover any overheads or expenses incurred (*South Wales Electricity plc* v. *DMR Ltd* (1997) 4 CL 210), though if the repairs are excessively expensive the full sum will not be recoverable (*The Patoclus* (1857) Swa 173). If the repair betters the chattel, no deduction need be made from the damages recovered. No deduction from the damages may be made for the debt due (*Edmondson* v. *Nuttall* (1864) 17 CBNS 280). It is not a defence that sums illegally raised were applied to a debt legally due (*Attack* v. *Bramwell* (1863) B&S 528).

Aggravated damages may also be possible, such as damage to business or reputation: *Brewer* v. *Drew* (1843) 11 M&W 625 and *Smith* v. *Enright* (1893) 69 LT 724 support this, though *Dixon* v. *Calcraft* [1892] 1 QB 458 is to the contrary. For more discussion of aggravated damages see 7.5.1.

As for exemplary damages, it used to be maintained that such an award could only be made in cases of trespass not conversion. It is arguable that *Rookes* v. *Barnard* [1964] AC 1129 has widened the scope for such awards: certainly Widgery LJ inclined to this position in *Mafo* v. *Adams* [1970] 1 QB 548. An example of the potential level of an award for exemplary damages is *Bhatnagar & Elanrent* v. *Whitehall Investments* (1996) 5 CL 166. A landlord levied distress on the entire contents of a business premises after both re-entry and a judgment for the arrears in the High Court. It was held that the landlord's actions (an excessive as well as illegal levy and obstructiveness) indicated that they were motivated by a desire to make a profit and, in addition to an award of general damages of £54,500 for conversion based on the value of the goods seized, the court awarded exemplary damages to the plaintiffs of £12,500 – plus interest.

Exemplary damages arising from statute *do* have an application to conversion. The goods of service men and women are protected from seizure by Reserve & Auxiliary Forces (Protection of Civil Interests) Act 1953 (see 7.1). Section 13(2) of the Act allows the court to award exemplary damages against defendants for seizures in such cases (though Lord Kilbrandon in *Broome* v. *Cassell & Co* [1972] AC 1027 sought to interpret this as referring to aggravated damages, not exemplary awards).

If goods are redelivered and accepted by the defendant an action is not barred but the damages will be reduced or mitigated. The same applies where the goods are returned after the action is commenced. The plaintiff may get nominal damages for loss of possession, as the fact of conversion cannot be absolved (*Lamb* v. *Wall* (1859) 1 F&F 503), plus consequential damages and damages for any deterioration in goods. If there has been no substantial loss, the plaintiff may face the costs of the action. This is because, although the conversion vests a right of action, the recovery of the goods will be regarded as pro tanto satisfaction and will accordingly reduce the award (*Plevin* v. *Henshall* (1833) 10 Bing 24). The plaintiff may refuse to accept redelivery as the action is for the value of the goods, not the goods themselves. The court may however stay an action on the basis that the goods are handed over and/or grant an order for consequential damages only. The damages will also be reduced if the goods were never taken out of the debtor's use, such as the bailiff putting a man in possession (*Bayliss* v. *Fisher* (1830) 7 Bing 153).

Co-owners may maintain conversion against each other for wrongful disposal, destruction or sale of goods (s.10(1) 1977 Act). The sheriff is able to sue on this basis as seizure gives him a special property similar to co-ownership. The sheriff however cannot be sued by debtors for a sale they did not consent to as execution and distress are exempted from these provisions (s.10(2)).

Plaintiffs with a limited interest may sue a stranger with no interest in the goods for conversion, to the extent of the value of that limited interest (see *Chubb* v. *Crilley* above). Thus a bailee can sue a bailor to the extent of his interest e.g. the value of the pledge. He or she must however account to the actual owner for any surplus recovered over and above the value of their own interest.

9.26.2 Trespass to goods

Conversion is any interference (whether by detention or dealing, whether temporary or permanent) that denies or is inconsistent with the rights of the owner of goods, whether s/he has actual possession or an immediate right to possession. By contrast trespass concerns direct taking from the claimant's actual physical possession, thus a bailee in possession may sue whereas a bailor may not. Note that these same principlea apply to replevin – see for example *Smith* v. *Mulcahy* [1934] 1 KB 608 (in which the authority of *Templeman* v. *Case* (1711) on this point is doubted – see 9.28). Trespass to goods shares characteristics of both conversion and negligence (see 9.26.4). It is often possible for the plaintiff to sue for either trespass or conversion. The same rules apply to the assessment of damages (*The Mediana* [1900] AC 113).

As stated trespass to goods is direct, intentional or forcible interference that disturbs possession of goods. As trespass is a wrong concerned with the taking of goods it will arise when there is an illegal seizure or removal or any other unpermitted impact upon contact with them. This contact must be deliberate or direct though as the tort is actionable without proof of damage, only very minor damage or contact will suffice (*Fouldes* v. *Willoughby* (1841) 8 M&W 540). It can include moving goods on the debtor's premises, though they may be moved only a very short distance (*Kirk* v. *Gregory* (1876) 1 Exch 55). Trespass can also include direct acts causing damage to goods, but the onus of proof of such negligence will be on the claimant (the owner of the goods). The successful claimant is entitled as of right to recover general damages as there has been a trespass (as to land), but the award may also be exemplary or aggravated. Such trespass could arise if a bailiff seizes hire purchase goods (*Jones Bros (Holloway) Ltd* v. *Woodhouse* [1923] 2 KB 117).

The measure of damages for trespass are as in conversion if the claimant is deprived of the goods. Special damages can thus be claimed for loss of employment as well as loss of tools if the trade implements of a self employed person were taken, or for fall in value of stock that could not be sold, or the loss of hire of a chattel. If goods are damaged without possession being lost, damages for trespass will only be the loss actually suffered as a direct result of the trespass – that is, any depreciation plus any consequential losses.

Aggravated damages will be recoverable to compensate for mental distress or injury to feelings arising from the defendant's manner of committing the tort, or his/her conduct afterwards: for example, injury to the trader's reputation.

Exemplary damages have always been regarded as recoverable in trespass to goods (see for example *Owen & Smith* v. *Reo Motors* (1934) 151 LT 274). This award was treated more as an award of aggravated damages in *Rookes* v. *Barnard* [1964] AC 1129, and certainly any such award will now have to comply with the principles enunciated in that case (see 7.5.1).

9.26.3 Seizure of fixtures

The old common law rule on the severance of fixtures was that the plaintiff could sue for either trespass to land or for trover (conversion) for the value of the items severed. The choice depended on the relative values before and after severance. The same choice still applies today because of the difference in damages between trespass to land and trespass to goods under the Torts Act 1977. In the former the plaintiff may be entitled to claim not only general damages but a figure for aggravated damages if fixtures have been removed. In conversion, even if the value of thc item is greater as a fixture than as a chattel, that larger sum has not been allowed in actions for conversion. This is strictly correct as conversion concerns wrongful interference with goods and there is no such interference until fixtures have been severed and have already got a lower value. Actions for trespass to land are therefore probably preferable. See for example *Clarke* v. *Holford* (1848) 2 C&K 540; *Moore* v. *Drinkwater* (1858) 1 F&F 134; *Barff* v. *Probyn* (1895) 64 LJQB 557. In the latter action the measure of damages allowed was as in trespass, the figure being not a sum equivalent to the proceeds of sale of the severed fixtures but the amount that an incoming tenant would pay for them if they were in situ.

9.26.4 Negligence

This is any mishandling of goods leading to their damage, loss or destruction (see *Watson* v. *Murray & Co* [1955] 1 All ER 350). This could be at any stage during the levy, whether during seizure (*Anon* (14 Eliz) 3 Leon Rep 15) or during removal or sale. The claim is for the value of the goods lost. The plaintiff may also claim an injunction but where the goods are either lost or only partially damaged specific delivery or an order for delivery or the payment of damages based on the full value of the goods under s 3 of the 1977 Act is not appropriate. The payment of the damages will extinguish the plaintiff's claim to the remains of their goods (*Attack* v. *Bramwell* (1863) 3 B & S 520; *Keen* v. *Priest* (1859) 4 H & N 236). A bailiff is *not* negligent if damage is done by third parties (*Willis, Winder & Co* v. *Combe* [1884] 1 Cab & El 353).

9.27 Wrongful execution

Although illegal execution is trespass the levy remains good (*De Gondouin* v. *Lewis* (1839) 10 Ad & E 117). Thus goods seized after a tortious entry are still validly taken (*Percival* v. *Stamp* (1853) 9 Ex 167 at 171–2) i.e. illegal execution does not necessarily affect the validity of subsequent seizure or sale, but the person can sue. The remedy is for the debtor to apply for the execution to be set aside or amended or for restitution of the wrongfully seized goods to be ordered, if necessary (*Rhodes* v. *Hull* [1857] 26 LJ Ex 265). An application to the High Court for a restitution order will have to be on summons – see p.830 "Chitty's Archbolds Queens Bench Division Practice (14th edition)." There can be an action for damages if there is evidence of malice, bad faith or actual damage which can be proved or if the goods had been sold (*Perkins* v. *Plympton* (1831) 7 Bing 676). An example (if unusual) of damages for wrongful execution is where goods wrongfully seized by the sheriff were then seized from his custody by another bailiff in distress. The owner paid off the second debt and then sued the sheriff for the amount paid (*Keene* v. *Dilke* (1849) 4 Exch 388).

9.28 Replevin

Replevin is an historic remedy to obtain recovery of goods that have been illegally seized, whether by distress or by other means (*Mellor* v. *Leather* (1853) 1 E& B 619). It is used rarely because of its obscurity and cost and because interlocutory orders for the delivery up of goods under s.4 Torts (Interference with Goods) Act 1977 (see 9.26) are now a preferable means of achieving the same result. A right of possession is not enough upon which to found replevin (*Templeman* v. *Case* [1711] 10 MR 24), the claimant must have property in the goods, though a person with use or enjoyment of goods by the consent of the owner has enough special property to justify a replevy (*Fell* v. *Whittaker* [1871] 7 QB 120). Thus a bailor may not replevy goods taken from a bailee (*Mennie* v. *Blake* (1856) 6 E&B 842), though the bailee may do so (*Smith* v. *Mulcahy* [1934] 1 KB 608). An agent cannot replevy (2 Co Inst 146). If separate individuals' goods are taken in one levy, each must replevy separately, though joint owners may initiate one replevin. Executors may replevy a testator's goods taken whilst s/he was alive (*Arundell* v. *Trevell* (1662) 1 Sid 81).

Replevin is applicable to statutory distraint as well as to distress for rent (*Sabourin* v. *Marshall* (1832) 3 B & Ad 440, 110 ER 158; *Rhymney Railway Co* v. *Price* (1867) 16 LT 395 ; *London County Council* v. *Hackney Borough Council* [1928] 2 KB 588). It is not applicable to execution in the High Court (see *George* v. *Chambers* (1843) 11 M & W 149 or *Bradshawe's Case* [1597] Cro Eliz 570). However, the sheriff can be ordered to return wrongfully seized goods (see 9.27). Seizure under the order of an inferior court – i.e. either a county court or magistrates' court – cannot normally be replevied unless the warrant in question was issued in excess of or completely outside the court's jurisdiction (*George* v. *Chambers* above; *Wilson* v. *Weller* [1819] 3 Moore CP 294; *Fenton* v. *Boyle* [1807] 2 Bos & Pul NP 391). For instance in *Hannigan* v. *Burgess* [1888] 26 NBR 99 the court stated that replevin will not lie against distress for a fine as the conviction is conclusive and not questionable by replevin. To attempt to replevy a valid court warrant could be construed as contempt of court (*R.* v. *Burchet* [1723] 8 Mod Rep 208, 88 ER 209). At common law distress by the Crown could not be replevied (*Cawthorne* v. *Campbell* [1790] 1 Anst 205) but it would seem that since the Crown Proceedings Act 1947 s.21 the remedy is possible against Crown levies.

Replevin is not available where a distress is lawful but can be used in any case of trespass by illegal seizure, for instance, where there is no debt due, an illegal entry occurred or exempt goods were seized. It could also be used after a wrongful second distress (*Anon* (1702) 7 Mod Rep 118). The distress must be wholly illegal, therefore a replevin cannot be founded on a dispute over levy for a debt, part of which is admitted to be due (*White* v. *Greenish* (1861) 11 CBNS 209). The use of replevin bars other remedies for the same distress (*Prude* v. *Beke* (1310) Hil 4 Ed II) and is an alternative to an action for trespass to goods (*Solers* v. *Wotton* (1405) YB 7 Hen 4 fo 27 p.15). If replevin is commenced in error, an action may still be commenced (*Allen* v. *Sharp* [1848] 2 Exch 352). However the bailiff may still be sued for trespass to land, even after a replevy, as the remedy relates to wrongful taking of goods and not to torts relating to land (*Gibbs* v. *Cruickshank* [1873] LR 8 CP 454). Even if the goods are successfully replevied, they may be seized again by the same creditor for a debt that accrued subsequently (*Hefford* v. *Alger* (1808) 1 Taunt 218).

A person can replevy within six years of seizure if the goods are unsold (*Jacob* v. *King* [1814] 5 Taunt 451; *Griffiths* v. *Stephens* (1819) 1 Chitt 196). Action can be taken against the bailiff, the authorising person or both. It is begun in the county court for the district in which the goods were seized (*R.* v. *Raines* (1853) 1 E&B 855; *Fordham* v. *Akers* (1863) 4 B&S 578), the powers being found under s.144 and sch.1 CCA, and consists of two parts.

9.28.1 The replevy

The owner (the replevisor) presents a notice stating the facts, provides a replevin bond and gives an undertaking that an action will be commenced within four weeks within the county court or within a week in the High Court. The bond will either be a sum deposited in court, or a bond with securities, that the action will be commenced "with effect and without delay". The level of security required is set by the district judge at a figure considered sufficient to cover the probable costs of the action and the alleged debt. The security could be a solicitor's undertaking to pay. Any fees payable are at the discretion of the district judge within limits of the county court fees scale.

The term "with effect" means that the action must be pursued to a successful conclusion – if not, the security is forfeit (*Jackson* v. *Hanson* (1841) 8 M&W 477). Delay should be avoided as otherwise the action may be regarded as having been abandoned, in which case again the security may be forfeit for breach of the conditions (*Axford* v. *Perret* (1828) 4 Bing 586 – a delay of two years; *Morris* v. *Matthews* (1841) 2 QB 293; *Evans* v. *Bowen* (1850) 19 LJQB 8). The district judge is empowered under CCR O.50 r.9 to determine the terms and manner of the security, which must be accepted provided that it is adequate (*Young* v. *Broughton Waterworks Co* (1861) 31 LJQB 14). All forms will need to be drafted from precedents by the plaintiff as standard court forms do not presently exist. The district judge then instructs the court bailiff by warrant to deliver the goods to the replevisor. The replevisor must then begin the action without delay and undertake to return the goods if ordered. If the bailiff does dispose of the goods, despite notice of the replevy, he may be sued (*Mounsey* v. *Dawson* (1837) 6 A&E 752).

It is possible for the replevy to be challenged. The creditor may apply to set it aside (*Rhymney Railway Co* v. *Price* (1867) 16 LT 394) or to attach a court officer for contempt (*R.* v. *Monkhouse* (1743) 2 Stra 1184). This would normally occur where an unreplevisable distress has been the subject of court proceedings (see above).

9.28.2 The action

The action must then be commenced by summons, with particulars of claim filed in line with CCR O.6 r.1A or, in the High Court, a statement of claim claiming damages and costs as appropriate. A hearing follows with the bailiff (the seizor) as defendant.

If successful, the replevisor recovers the expenses of the replevy plus damages to be assessed as in an action for trespass (*Dixon* v. *Calcraft* [1892] 1 QB 458). As the goods will usually have been returned, these will normally be the value of the replevin bond itself, though if the goods are not recovered the full value of the goods plus damages for detention may be awarded. It used to be held that the joinder of other causes of action with an action for replevin was at common law illegal and irregular (*Mungean* v. *Wheatley* (1851) 6 Exch 88 at 97) and the county court rules included provisions requiring leave of court to join actions. However since *Smith* v. *Enright* (1893) 69 LT 724 it has been the practice to assess damages as in illegal distress and thus to allow inclusion of any consequential damages suffered by reason of the distress (*Gibbs* v. *Cruickshank* as above). Examples are *Brewer* v. *Dew* (1843) 11 M&W 625 in which damages for injury to credit and reputation were also awarded, *Sperry Inc* v. *CIBC* (1985) 17 DLR 236 in which the cost of maintaining a letter of credit as security for the goods was held to be a reasonable consequential loss and *Smith* v. *Enright* (1893) 63 LJQB 220 in which damages were held to be allowable for loss, annoyance and injury to a person's reputation. No further action could then be taken in respect of damages. If the seizor is unsuccessful, it is not usually possible to appeal the decision, even on payment of the costs. This is because it is generally seen as unfair to the sureties to renew their liability and to expose the plaintiff once more to the risk of paying full costs, whilst there is normally some other remedy available for the debt due (*Parry* v. *Duncan* (1831) 7 Bing 243; *Edgson* v. *Caldwell* (1873) 8 CP 647).

If the seizor (the bailiff) is successful, s/he is entitled to an order for the return of the goods. Though it is usual to recover the seizor's costs, a money judgment in lieu of the goods is not possible (*Jamieson* v. *Trevelyan* (1855) 10 Exch 748) unless for some reason it is impossible to recover the goods. If this is the case, damages for their value and for their detention may be awarded (*Ash* v. *Wood* (1587) Cro Eliz 59).

If the conditions of the replevin bond are not satisfied distrainors have two remedies. They may either :

- claim the sum secured by the bond (*Dix* v. *Groom* (1880) 5 Ex D 91); or,
- sue for the damages caused by the breach (*Waterman* v. *Yea* (1756) 2 Wils 41; *Turnor* v. *Turner* (1820) 2 Brod & Bing 107; *Tummons* v. *Ogle* (1856) 6 E&B 571). The action may be against all the sureties jointly or any one of them. Each surety or obligor is only liable for the amount of rent in arrear at the date of the distress and the costs of the distrainor (*Ward* v. *Henley* (1827) 1 Y&J 285). Their total liability cannot exceed the amount of the penalty on the bond and the costs of the action on the bond (*Hefford* v. *Alger* (1808) 1 Taunt 218). Any award of costs and any decision as to the basis upon which these are calculated is completely at the discretion of the court. Proceedings on the bond may be stayed by payment of the penalty and costs, even though the plaintiff's costs in the replevin action are bound to exceed the penalty (*Branscombe* v. *Scarborough* [1844] 6 QB 13) and if

the debt due is argued to be less than the sum secured, the court may rule on this (*Dix* v. *Groom* [1880] 5 Exch 91). The fact that the distrainor has obtained judgment for the rent due in the trial of the replevin action is no defence to an action on the bond (*Turnor* v. *Turner* (1820) 2 Brod & Bing 107).

Breach of the bond may occur, for instance, the claimant does not prosecute the case within a reasonable time, but the court will protect the claimant if the reason for delay has been delay by the seizor (*Evans* v. *Bowen* (1850) 19 LJQB 8) or simply the death of the replevisor (*Morris* v. *Matthews* [1841] 2 QB 293).

9.29 Restitution order

One further remedy applies only to Inner London. Under s.27 Metropolitan Police Courts Act 1839, a metropolitan stipendiary magistrate has the power to order the return of goods that have been unlawfully obtained. If goods have been wrongfully seized and then unlawfully deposited or sold, they may be recovered from any broker or dealer in whose possession they are to be found.

Complaint is made before the magistrate by the owner of the goods that they are being illegally detained within the Inner London area. The magistrate can issue a summons or warrant to that person, requiring the production of the goods and the appearance of the person accused. The magistrate may make an order for the return of the goods either absolutely or on terms as to payment of such sums at such times as the magistrate thinks fit. If the order is not complied with or if the goods are disposed of despite the order, the broker or dealer shall forfeit the full value of the goods as assessed by the magistrate. The broker or dealer may in turn take an action to recover any goods delivered up under this summary remedy provided that this is done within six months of the magistrate's order being made.

This remedy is clearly of limited applicability both in terms of the area and circumstances to which it applies, but it may be a relatively quick and inexpensive means of recovering goods if it is available to a client.

9.30 Rent remedies

A number of little used remedies apply to distress for rent for the protection of goods that have been wrongfully seized for one reason or another.

9.30.1 Exempt goods

A restitution order can be made where any of the tenant's clothing and bedding within the statutory exemption (s.4 LDAA 1888 and see 9.22.2) have been seized by the landlord. The court may order either restoration of the goods if not sold or a sum to be paid in compensation by the bailiff, the figure being assessed by the courts (s.4 LDAA 1895).

9.30.2 Lodger's or stranger's goods

If the property of any third parties such a strangers and lodgers (see 9.22.2) are removed by the landlord, despite service of written notice, application may be made to the magistrates' court for a declaration that the goods are exempt and for an order for their return. It has been held that as landlords' common law rights were altered by these provisions in favour of lodgers and sub-tenants in the LDAA 1908, the Act should be construed strictly and in landlords' favour (*Lawrence Chemical Co* v. *Rubinstein* [1982] 1 WLR 284).

These individuals must make a written declaration to the landlord in a set form accompanied by an inventory stating that items levied upon are theirs. It is an offence under the Perjury Act to make a false declaration (s.2 LDAA 1908). Such declarations can only be made within a reasonable time after distress – they are not effective against a distress which is not yet authorised or threatened (*Thwaites* v. *Wilding* [1883] 12 QBD 4). If the declaration fails to state that the goods are exempted from seizure by the 1908 Act, it is a fatal defect and the goods lose the protection given by s.1(c) (*Druce & Co Ltd* v. *Beaumont Property Trust Ltd* [1935] 2 KB 257). A declaration that includes an inventory of goods that is unsigned is not defective providing the declaration itself is signed (*Godlonton* v. *Fulham & Hampstead Property Co Ltd* [1905] 1 KB 431). A declaration made by a person without declaring their status (a lodger) or without stating whether rent was due to the landlord was sufficient as the Act requires no statement on the declarant's status and failure to make any assertion about rent due must be interpreted as implying that no rent was due (*ex parte Harris* [1885] 16 QBD 130). If the declaration is made by a company, it can be made by a duly authorised agent such as a solicitor as well as by a director or company secretary (*Lawrence Chemical Co Ltd* v. *Rubinstein* [1982] 1 WLR 284). If the declaration is made by a partnership there is no need for all partners to sign it; nor does it have to be in the form of a statutory declaration (*Rogers, Eungblutt & Co* v. *Martin* [1911] 1 KB 19).

The declaration must include a claim to the goods seized, plus a statement of the rent payable to the mesne landlord, and the periods for which it is due, plus an undertaking to pay this rent direct to the head landlord until the rent arrears of the mesne landlord are cleared (s.1). Additionally under s.6 of the 1908 Act the landlord may serve notice on a sub-tenant requiring direct payment of future rent. Such a notice is not a levy of distress, but has been described as a "statutory assignment of a chose in action" (Lord Greene MR at 84 in *Wallrock* v. *Equity & Law Life Assurance Society* [1942] 2 KB 82). Sub-tenants must then pay any rent direct to the landlord until the tenant's arrears are cleared. If the sub-tenant then fails to pay, distress may be levied upon them directly.

On receiving a declaration the landlord should return the goods and to continue to distrain would render it illegal. If this is not done the person may apply before two JPs or one stipendiary magistrate for a restoration order, which should be granted if the court is satisfied that the applicant is entitled after enquiry into the truth of their declaration and inventory. In either case if the bailiff does not comply, he faces committal or daily penalties until the goods are returned.

Whilst if any goods belonging to a stranger are seized by the landlord the owner can be reimbursed for their value by the tenant owing the rent (*Exall* v. *Partridge* (1799) 8 Term Rep 308 – and see 9.32 later), it does not seem that there is any implied indemnity for the rent by the mesne landlord to the sub-tenant upon which the latter may sue (*Schlenker* v. *Moxsy* (1825) 3 B&C 789; *Baber* v. *Harris* (1839) 9 Ad & El 532). A lodger may sue the landlord and bailiff for selling even if s/he has not served the declaration described earlier (*Sharpe* v. *Fowle* [1884] 12 QBD 385). The claimant to the goods has the option also to sue for illegal distress (*Lowe* v. *Dorling*

[1905] 2 KB 501; affirmed on appeal [1906] 2 KB 772 CA). The Court of Appeal held that the summary means of restitution before the justices does not prejudice the right to sue for the tort, or replevy (though the summary remedy supplements the right to replevy, which is hampered by the need for security). If the landlord does continue to distrain after notice from the lodger, an action for illegal distress lies against him/her but not against the bailiff (*Page* v. *Vallis* (1903) 19 TLR 393).

9.30.3 Exempt beasts

At common law plough beasts were not seizable in distress for rent if other sufficient goods were available, and this rule was confirmed by the Statute of Exchequer (Hen 3 date uncertain). If a levy occurs that is illegal in this respect the tenant may rescue the beasts or may sue on the statute, there being no action at common law (*Porphrey* v. *Legingham* (1666) 2 Keble 290). This is for trespass against the provisions of the statute. It is for the defendant to allege that there was no distress available for seizure at the time of the levy (*Dawson* v. *Alford* (1572) 3 Dyer 312a): an action on the statute thus reverses the normal burden of proof (per Lord Campbell CJ in *Nargett* v. *Nias* (1859) 1 E&E 437). Even though the tenant may pay or tender the rent claimed in order to release their beasts, this will not prevent them suing for violation of the statute (see Coke's commentary in 2 Inst).

9.30.4 Double damages

In the case of a distress that was illegal because no rent was due, the owner of the goods (whether that is the tenant or third party) has a right by statute (s.4 DRA 1689), to recover double the value of goods taken and sold by an action of trespass or upon the case (*Chancellor* v. *Webster* (1893) 9 TLR 568). This procedure is similar to the exemplary damages that might be recoverable in cases of unjustified statutory distraint. The offence is not complete unless actual sale occurs. This is an additional remedy to those discussed earlier. Nothing less than double damages may be awarded (*Masters* v. *Farris* [1845] 1 CB 715).

9.30.5 Agricultural Holdings

Wrongful distress against an agricultural holding attracts extra remedies for the tenant under s.19 Agricultural Holdings Act 1986. If there is any dispute as to:

- whether any levy of distress for rent complies with the 1986 Act;
- ownership of stock or the cost of feeding agisted beasts (see 9.22.1); or,
- any other related question,

a county court or magistrates' court may determine it. The court may order return of any stock or things unlawfully distrained, declare the price of feed, or make any other order justice requires.

9.31 Criminal Remedies

9.31.1 Criminal damage by clamping

It has been suggested (see *Tibber* (1991) 135 SJ 408 or 8 WRTLB 53) that clamping may be criminal damage by the bailiff under s.1 Criminal Damage Act 1971. Under this provision it is an offence punishable by fine or imprisonment if a person destroys or damages another's property without lawful excuse, or is reckless as to whether their actions will cause such damage. It is also an offence to threaten criminal damage, which, it has been suggested, could apply to the making of threats to clamp cars on signs in private car parks. Certainly criminal damage of goods seized cannot be justified by a distress (*Bromhall* v. *Norton* (1690) 2 Jo 193 – burning turves seized damage feasant).

The key to this argument is the definition of damage that has emerged from the case law. To be guilty of the offence, the defendant must have caused damage, however slight and however negligible its value (*Gayford* v. *Chouler* [1898] 1 QB 316). Damage is not just physical interference which breaks an item: it can be displacing an engine so that trifling damage is caused, even though the engine still works (*R.* v. *Foster* (1852) 6 Cox CC 25); it can be displacing parts and interfering with an engine's running so that it temporarily does not work (*R.* v. *Fisher* (1865) LR 1 CCR 7); or it can be by taking out and removing a part so that a machine does not work – though the part is easily removable and on replacement, the machine would be in perfect order again (*R.* v. *Tacey* (1821) Russ & Ry 452). By analogy to the last case, it may be arguable that adding a part to a machine, although that may be done without damage and it may be easily removable, leaving the machine in its original state, would also be damage.

A defence to such a claim may be that the addition of a clamp, though inconvenient, is not a serious enough interference to constitute criminal damage – see *Roe* v. *Kingerlee* (1986) *Crim Law Review* 735 in which the Court of Appeal held that what constitutes damage is a matter of fact and degree and that it is for magistrates, applying their common sense, to decide whether what has occurred is damage or not. It may of course be that the justices are reluctant to treat enforcement of a court order as a criminal act.

9.31.2 Case stated

Any party to proceedings who is aggrieved by any order, determination or other proceedings in a magistrates' court may question them on the grounds that they are wrong in law or in excess of jurisdiction by way of a procedure known as "case stated" (s.111 MCA). Thus unreasonable use of discretion by the court could be challenged by the debtor e.g. the court's use of its discretion to issue distress (*R.* v. *Clacton JJ ex parte Customs & Excise* (1987) 152 JP 129), as could refusal of an appeal against a levy made under local tax or child support regulations (*Evans* v. *South Ribble Borough Council* [1992] 2 All ER 695).

9.32 Pay and sue

It would be open to a third party owner of goods to simply pay the debt due and then sue the debtor, as it is a principle of law that where one person's goods are taken to satisfy another's debts, the owner shall have a remedy against the debtor for an indemnity (*In Re: Button ex parte Haviside* [1907] 2 KB 180; *Edmunds* v. *Wallingford* [1885] 14 QBD 811). This will be encountered in the older case reports as an action for "assumpsit" (e.g. *Exall* v. *Partridge* (1799) 8 TR 308). The action would be either for the sum paid out to the bailiff or the value of the goods if they have been sold

(*Groom* v. *Bluck* (1841) 2 Man & G 567; *Lampleigh* v. *Braithwaite* (1620) Hobart 106; *Dering* v. *Winchelsea* (1787) Coa 318). An exception may be made by the courts where the claimant is personally liable to the debtor or where she/he has left goods at the debtor's property for his/her own convenience and could have removed them to avoid seizure (*England* v. *Marsden* (1866) 1 CP 529).

If the debtor denies the validity of the seizure or feels exempt goods have been seized, it is also open to him/her to pay off the debt and costs to the bailiff and then sue to recover those sums from the creditor. Although payment under protest in such circumstances is not the only option open to the debtor to alleviate an alleged unlawful interference with his/her property (replevin and the like are arguably more apposite), any such payment is involuntary, being made under coercion, and an action may be commenced to recover it (*Kanhaya Lal* v. *National Bank of India* (1913) 29 TLR 314). For the use of this remedy to recover disputed fees, see 11.3.2.

If an agent of the debtor pays off a bailiff without the debtor's authority, s/he may be sued to recover those sums by the debtor (*Sweet* v. *Turner* [1871] 7 QB 310).

Chapter Ten

CONCLUDING LEVIES: REMOVAL AND SALE

10.1 Conduct after seizure

Once goods have been seized, the bailiff cannot remain an unreasonable time upon the debtor's premises (*Cartwright* v. *Comber* cited in *Griffin* v. *Scott* (1727) @ 2 Ld (1809) Raym 1427; *Cooke* v. *Birt* (1814) 5 Taunt 765; *Winterbourne* v. *Morgan* (1774) 11 East 395). In the latter case a bailiff stayed fifteen days on the premises and was held to be a trespasser for remaining too long and disturbing the plaintiff's possession. In *Aitkenhead* v. *Blades* (1813) 5 Taunt 198 unreasonable possession by the sheriff was held to render the execution trespass *ab initio*. The sheriff entered into the property on April 10th and remained 12 hours. This was repeated on diverse days thereafter until May 6th. Sale of the seized goods was held on the premises, without the debtor's consent, on April 26th, but the sheriff remained constantly on the premises for a further ten days even though the goods could have been sold and removed in only a few hours. This major disturbance of the debtor's possession was held to be wholly illegal (see also *Ash* v. *Dawnay* (1852) 8 Exch 237; *Lee* v. *Dangar & Co* [1892] 1 QB 231). It may not, though, be trespass *ab initio* in most forms of distraint (*Smith* v. *Egginton* (1837) 7 A&E 167) though the sheriff remaining in possession for nearly six months was held to be trespass *ab initio* (*Reed* v. *Harrison* (1778) 2 Wm Bl 1218). The common law position is altered for distress for rent by s.10 Distress for Rent Act 1737, which requires removal and sale after a minimum of five days (*Griffin* v. *Scott* (1726) 2 Ld Raym 1424, Stra 717). It is trespass to expel the occupant after entry (*Bissett* v. *Caldwell* (1791) Peake 50). Conversely, it amounts to trespass for the debtor to exclude the bailiff (see 7.5).

10.2 Notice of Seizure

Having completed the seizure the bailiff will commonly leave the debtor with a notice of seizure confirming what has occurred. Notices will generally include the following information:

- the debt due and costs incurred so far;
- an inventory of the goods seized, and;
- often, a walking possession agreement. Though strictly speaking this is a separate document, it is often incorporated in to the notice of seizure for convenience.

Other information may also be required to be left by statute: for example the Distress for Rent Rules 1988 contain a prescribed form for use in rent and road traffic distress. It would not appear that the seizure or impounding can be invalidated just because the debtor refuses to accept the notice or inventory (*R.* v. *Butterfield* (1893) 17 Cox CC 598).

10.2.1 Notice

No notice of distress at all is required from the magistrates' bailiff, Inland Revenue or Customs and Excise – though the latter both do provide one as a matter of good practice. Where notices must be provided, the contents are usually prescribed, for example:

- *High Court execution* On a first levy the sheriff will leave a prescribed notice of seizure at the premises or hand it to the debtor. This has been introduced under O.45 r.2 and draws the debtor's attention to his/her right to seek interpleader if it is felt that certain goods should be treated as exempt from seizure.
- *distress for rent* Under r.12(2)DRR the distrainor must present a signed notice in prescribed form setting out the amounts levied for – arrears plus authorised costs, and also give an inventory of goods seized (*Tancred* v. *Leyland* (1851) 16 QB 669). A bailiff must give details of the certificate held and the right of replevin. The notice should be left at "the chiefe mansion house or other most notorious place on the premises" (s.1 DRA 1689), though it is usually handed to the tenant or owner of the goods. To sell without serving such a notice is irregular (*Trent* v. *Hunt* (1853) 9 Exch 14). Also details of costs of removal should be left with the tenant using Form 9, DRR. It may be difficult to prove the facts if the notice is simply left at the premises, and a witness to prove the regularity of the distress may be necessary (*Walter* v. *Rumbal* (1695) 1 Ld Raym 53). If and when removal occurs, the goods should not be removed from the county in which they were seized. The landlord or bailiff may be subject to a penalty if this is wrongfully done (Chapter 4, Statute of Marlborough 1267).
- *local tax distraint* After seizure, the bailiff must hand to the debtor, or leave at the premises, a copy of the relevant sections of the appropriate enforcement regulations, a copy of the schedule to those regulations showing permissible costs, a copy of any possession agreement that the debtor has signed and a memorandum setting out the sums due (reg. 45(5) CT; reg. 14(5) NNDR). Alternative documentation will not be acceptable.
- *county court execution* O.26 r.12 CCR requires the bailiff to deliver or send to the debtor a sufficient inventory of the goods seized. The form, N332, can be handed or posted to the debtor at his/her home or premises where the goods were seized.
- *CSA distraint* On completing a CSA levy the bailiff should hand to the debtor or leave at the premises copies of regs. 30, 31 and sch. 2, which contains the charge scale, a memorandum setting out the sums due, a memorandum setting out any possession agreement made at the time of the levy in accordance with para. 2(3) of sch. 2 and a memorandum detailing the debtor's appeal rights (reg. 30(2)).

Certain errors on notices will **not** invalidate them – in the name of the debtor (*Wootley* v. *Gregory* (1828) Y&J 536), in the date the debt fell due (*Gambrell* v. *Earl of Falmouth* (1835) 4 Ad & El 73) or in not including the date at all (*Moss* v.

Gallimore (1779) 1 Doug KB 279). Generally minor mistakes that neither prejudice nor mislead the debtor will be ignored (*Rutherford* v. *Lord Advocate* (1931) 16 Tax Cases 145). The fact that exempt items are included in the list does not give an aggrieved person a right to sue as an intention to sell is not a cause of action (*Beck* v. *Denbigh* (1860) 29 LJCP 273).

A notice does not have to be presented personally to the debtor in distress for rent or local taxes, but if it is some flexibilty in contents may be allowed (*Chesterfield* v. *Farringdon* (1713) 11 Ann CB per Trevor CJ).

10.2.2 Inventories

No inventory need be given in distress for income tax, VAT or local taxes. Where a notice is mandatory, failure to provide one or provision of an inadequate notice will make the distress irregular (see later at 10.8). The CSA require that all items seized should be listed in duplicate on an inventory attached to the walking possession agreement. All reasonable steps should be taken to verify ownership and an estimated sale value should be endorsed on the inventory.

Case law has established that where an inventory is supplied, it must make it clear what goods have been seized. In *Davies* v. *Property & Reversionary Co Ltd* [1929] 2 KB 222 it was held that a notice should either:

- list and identify each item seized; or,
- imply that all goods on the premises have been seized.

The court reached this decision by reference to earlier authority. In *Wakeman* v. *Lindsay* [1850] 14 QB 625 a notice mentioning certain goods "and any others on the premises" was held not to be illegal, though it was perhaps excessive. It was also, arguably, so vague that any walking possession agreement founded on it would be a void contract because of simple uncertainty and would thus be of no effect on the debtor. By contrast in *Kerby* v. *Harding* (1851) 6 Exch 234 a list of "all goods on the premises that may be required" was held to be too vague. Neither the debtor, nor later bailiffs attending to levy, could with certainty identify the goods intended. Most bailiffs opt for the phraseology approved in *Wakeman* v. *Lindsay*.

10.3 Tender and payment

As suggested before, the purpose of distress is to provoke payment through the threat of goods' sale and removal rather than those steps actually being taken. Consequently the bailiff aims either to either receive a lump sum or to agree instalment payment. The latter is the most common result of the bailiffs' call. For example it seems that, for sheriff's officers, about 90 per cent of levies lead to instalments being arranged.

10.3.1 Instalment arrangements

Difficulties may arise for both parties when an affordable payment cannot be agreed. This is often because of the timescales for recovery laid down by creditors. Local authorities may, in respect of local taxes, be happy to see instalments accepted, but will often want them only to run for two or three months. Magistrates' courts and local authorities collecting road traffic penalties do not tend to accept instalments. In either case if the debtor is on low income the options open to the bailiff may be limited.

Bailiffs in the civil courts can be made to accept instalments and withdraw if the court consents to suspending the execution on terms (see 3.1.1 & 3.1.2). The terms of such suspensions can be quite low offers over extended periods. In other forms of distress there is no option for the debtor to make application to the court and s/he will have to rely on negotiation with the bailiff or creditor.

10.3.2 Tender or payment before seizure

Over and above any contractual requirement imposed on the bailiff regarding payments, there are both common law and statutory restrictions as to how payment may be made by the debtor, when it must be accepted by the bailiff or creditor and the impact thereof. Reference is often made in the regulations to "tender" of payment of a debt and costs. It is required that tender should be accepted and that this should end the levy process. For example if the sums due to the CSA are paid or tendered to the Secretary of State or bailiff before seizure, the payment should be accepted (reg. 30(4)). If the amount of local tax due is paid or tendered before distraint, then goods cannot be levied (reg. 45(3) CT; reg. 14(3) NNDR).

Tender may be defined as an unconditional offer to pay, whether by means of cash or a banker's draft or building society cheque, and the money should be produced at the time of making such an offer. If there is no actual tender, the debtor's mere presence on the premises will not prevent a levy taking place (*Horne* v. *Lewin* (1700) 1 Ld Raym 639). Equally the readiness to pay must have continued until the moment of seizure (*Cranley* v. *Kingswell* (1617) Hob 207). Tender must be of the full sum of debt and costs, though less than the full sum due may be accepted without prejudice to the right to pursue the outstanding balance (*Finch* v. *Miller* (1848) 5 CB 428). Tender may be to the creditor or bailiff (*Smith* v. *Goodwin* (1833) 4 B & Ad 413; *Hatch* v. *Hale* [1850] 15 QB 10) and either should accept. The bailiff can receive the rent and cannot be told to refuse it by the landlord (*Hatch* v. *Hale* [1850] 15 QB 10), but a man in possession cannot receive a tender (*Boulton* v. *Reynolds* [1859] 2 E&E 369). In execution it seems tender should be to the sheriff or the creditor (*Taylor* v. *Bekon* [1878] 2 Lev 203). In *D'Jan* v. *Bond St Estates* [1993] NPC 36 the Court of Appeal held that a landlord is not entitled to reject a tender by banker's draft either because it is less than the full amount claimed or because the s/he feels that a large sum should be paid in cash.

A tender under protest, reserving the right to dispute the sum claimed later, is good tender provided that no conditions are imposed on the creditor (*Manning* v. *Lunn* (1845) 2 C&K 13; *Greenwood* v. *Sutcliffe* [1892] 1 Ch 1). The creditor should not refuse the tender, simply because the payer preserves the right to take legal action later (*Scott* v. *Uxbridge & Rickmansworth Railway Co* (1866) 1 CP 596). Where the sum due is disputed, a request for a receipt is not such a condition as will invalidate a tender (*Richardson* v. *Jackson* (1849) 8 M&W 298), unless the receipt is requested to specify that it covers rent for a certain period and the periods for which rent is due are disputed (*Finch* v. *Miller* (1848) 5 CB 428). Tender by a third party who is neither co-debtor (*Smith* v. *Egginton* (1855) 10 Exch 845) nor co-tenant (*Smith* v. *Cox* [1940] 2 KB 558) is only acceptable if they act as agent for the debtor – whether their agency has prior authorisation or later ratification. In *Smith* v. *Cox* an action for illegal distress for rent by the plaintiff failed when he admitted that payment of the rent had been made by a stranger without his knowledge or consent.

Offering a current account cheque or other means of payment does not qualify as valid tender, though of course the bailiff or creditor may accept such a method of settling a debt and may suspend enforcement until the cheque is cleared, rather than withdrawing the levy altogether. Payment by instalments is handled in the same way as payment by cheque. It is not valid tender with the consequences that flow from that, but enforcement may be stayed whilst payments are maintained. Where a landlord did accept a bill of exchange from a tenant for rent due, it was held to be evidence of an agreement to suspend the remedy of distress during the currency of the bill (*Palmer* v. *Bramley* [1895] 2 QB 405). The tenant was therefore entitled to replevy his goods (see 9.28). Equally the ordinary rule is that acceptance of a cheque is not absolute satisfaction of a debt but conditional payment and operates to suspend a creditor's remedies until it is either met or dishonoured. The creditor would have the choice, if the cheque was dishonoured, of either suing on the cheque or pursuing the debt as normal (*Re: Romer & Haslam* [1893] 2 QB 286; *Gunn* v. *Bolckow, Vaughan & Co* (1875) 10 Ch App 491). Thus in *Bolt & Nut Co (Tipton) Ltd* v. *Rowlands, Nicholls & Co* [1964] 2 QB 10, a judgment entered after receipt of a cheque to settle the claim was set aside as irregular. The court however suggested that, if judgment had been entered before the cheque was taken, it would could have been argued that a better course of action for the creditor might be to levy execution rather than sue on the cheque. The court also noted that the situation is different in distress for rent. The acceptance of a cheque or bill in such cases is not conditional payment and until it is met by the bank the landlord may still pursue the debt by distress, his "better remedy" of seizure of goods not being suspended (*Davis* v. *Gyde* (1835) 2 A&E 623; *Belshaw* v. *Bush* (1851) 11 CB 191; *Henderson* v. *Arthur* [1907] 1 KB 10 per Farwell J at 13). Note also that payment by tender of a cheque that later is dishonoured has been held not to be obtaining pecuniary advantage by deception under s.16 Theft Act 1968 (*R.* v. *Locker* [1971] 2 QB 321).

If tender of the full sum due is made before seizure, the levy is illegal (*Branscomb* v. *Bridges* (1823) 1 B&C 145). No costs need be included in the tender as none can be recovered before the levy (*Bennet* v. *Bayes* (1860) 5 H&N 391). Refusal of a valid tender gives the debtor the right of rescue (*Bevill's Case* (1585) 4 Co Rep 6a and see 6.3), to sue in trespass (*Bennet* v. *Bayes* (1860) 5 H&N 391), to replevy (see YB (1347) 21 EIII 56b pl7 and 9.27) or to sue in conversion (*Smith* v. *Goodwin* (1833) 4 B & Ad 413). The time for valid tender in such cases may be extended by bringing replevin in order to establish the validity of the distress (YB (1333) 7 EIII 28a pl 20).

In the magistrates' court distraint or sale cannot proceed if the person pays or tenders the fine on the warrant (plus costs) to the distrainor (r.54(11) MCR). The same applies if the defendant tenders to the bailiff a receipt for the correct sum from the Clerk of the Court (r.54(11)). Sometimes courts refuse to accept payment from the defendant when the warrant is with the bailiff. This is justified by r.55(1) MCR. However this provision deals with payment in the circumstances laid out in s.79(2) MCA which applies only when a period of committal has also been imposed by the magistrates. This is unlikely to apply in the case of most warrants being enforced by bailiffs and the debtor should therefore be free to pay whoever is most convenient to them, which may often be the bailiff.

10.3.3 Tender or payment after seizure

If tender is made between seizure and impounding, it would be illegal for the bailiff to proceed to impound. After seizure, but before removal, if the debt and costs are tendered any removal or retention of the seized goods is illegal (*Loring* v. *Warburton* (1858) EB&E 507). Tender of the rent and costs after seizure and before impounding makes possession and removal wrongful (*Vertue* v. *Beasley* (1831) 1 Mood & R 21; *Evans* v. *Elliot* (1836) 5 Ad & El 142).

If the tender is made after the goods have been impounded, it is too late for the levy to be rendered wrongful (*Six Carpenters' Case* (1610) 77 ER 695). After removal but before sale tender of the debt and costs renders any sale irregular (*Johnson* v. *Upham* (1859) 2 E&E 250). If tender is made any goods removed must be returned, otherwise the debtor could sue for conversion, though the continuing possession is not trespass (*West* v. *Nibbs* (1847) 4 CB 172). Tender after impounding does not render it wrongful (*Six Carpenters' Case* (1610) 8 Co Rep 146) as such a tender of rent and costs is invalid at common law (*Tennant* v. *Field* (1857) 8 E&B 336; *Firth* v. *Purvis* (1793) 5 D&E 432). A tender after impounding but within the five day period for replevin would make a sale irregular and the tenant may sue on the "equity" of the DRA 1689 (*Johnson* v. *Upham* (1859) 2 E&E 250). If the distress were to be continued the tenant could apply to the county court for an order returning the goods. The sheriff can receive the debt due and therefore if payment or tender is made, he must withdraw from possession. If the debtor tenders or pays the debt, execution is discharged and the sheriff may not then sell (*Taylor* v. *Baker* (1677) 3 Keb 788/2 Lev 203; *R.* v. *Bird* (1679) 2 Show 87; *Brun* v. *Hutchinson* (1844) 2 D&L 43).

There are provisions for payment in such circumstances in statutory distraint. If the sums of child support maintenance due are paid or tendered to the Secretary of State or bailiff before sale, the payment should be accepted and the distraint will not proceed, any sale being cancelled and the goods being made available for collection by the debtor (reg. 30(5) CS (C & G) Regulation). If, after seizure, the sums of local taxes due are paid or tendered, the billing authority must accept the amount and the goods cannot be sold. The debtor can then collect them (reg. 45(4) CT; reg. 14(4) NNDR). If the respondent pays or tenders the road traffic penalty due on the warrant plus the fees, or any sum that will be accepted as satisfying the debt, to either the local authority or the bailiff, the distraint is terminated and any seized goods must be released (art. 7(2)). This repeats s.87 CCA, which also applies. Payment cannot be made to the court (O.48B r.5(5) CCR).

For fines it has been held that if goods are seized, bailiffs are not liable on payment of the penalty to return them until they are demanded by the debtor nor are they liable for any damage to the goods (*Hutchings* v. *Morris* (1827) 6 B & C 464). If the bailiff is paid, or receives sale proceeds, the sums must be passed to the clerk of the court (r.54(3) MCR) and it is an offence punishable by a fine up to level one (£200) for the bailiff to fail to do this by wilfully retaining improper fees (s.78(5) MCA).

10.3.4 Distress damage feasant payment

In distress damage feasant, because of the nature of the remedy, no demand for amends need be made before the seizure, but afterwards tender of amends must be accepted (*Browne* v. *Powell* (1827) 4 Bing 230). It is for the owner of the trespassing goods to assess the damage and to offer sufficient sums. Distress may be levied for even a very nominal amount but as soon as a reasonable tender is made, the distrainor's duty is to release the chattel. If a large sum is then demanded by the distrainor without any justification, the owner may pay under protest and then sue for the sum extorted as money had and received (*Green* v. *Ducket* [1883] 11 QBD 275). If tender is made and refused, the rest of the distress becomes illegal. The owner could pay sums into court and then sue for wrongful interference, or replevy and recover any sums paid as special damages (*Anscomb* v. *Shore* [1808] 1 Camp 285). There is no need for tender if the sum demanded is exorbitant, and tender of the proper sum would have been refused. In such a case the owner may simply sue (*Sorrell* v. *Paget* [1949] 2 All ER 609). The owner may sue for the difference between the fair sum and the excessive demand (*Ashowle* v. *Wainwright* (1842) 2 QB 837).

Commentary

The rules on the validity of tender before and after seizure are curious and inequitable. The courts have clearly sensed the injustice in the doctrine, and sought ways around the problem – such as the judgment in *Johnson* v. *Upham* cited above. For a detailed explanation and analysis of this "modern muddle" see Professor Glanville Williams (1936).

10.4 Removal and Storage

Removal and sale is a last resort where acceptable payments cannot be agreed or maintained. As an indication of the frequency with which it is used, it is understood that sheriff's officers remove in only five per cent of cases; CIPFA states that only three per cent of warrants lead to actual removal of goods; the CBA estimate that only two per cent lead to sale and the Lord Chancellor's Department states that less than two thousand of the million and a half warrants issued annually actually lead to auction.

In most cases where goods are to be sold, they will be removed from the debtor's premises and stored before disposal at an auction room. Very little is laid down in law as to how this should be done, despite the regularity with which it occurs.

10.4.1 Removal

This will not usually happen until at least five days after seizure, not including the day of the levy (*Robinson* v. *Waddington* [1849] 13 QB 753). This timescale is set by statute for some bailiffs, but has merely been adopted as good practice by others.

The bailiff may, following a valid seizure (see chapter 8), force entry on returning to a property, but only if the debtor is deliberately excluding them (*Khazanchi* v. *Faircharm Investments* and *McLeod* v. *Butterwick* [1998] 2 All ER 901 CA). The Court of Appeal overruled both the previous decision made on this point in *McLeod* v. *Butterwick* ([1996] 3 All ER 236) and the longstanding view on the matter, deciding that there was no general common law power, either in distress for rent or in execution, for a bailiff to force re-entry to premises in order to remove seized goods. On a review of the case law it was held that the right of forced re-entry only applied after forced exclusion (see also 7.3.4). If the debtor is unaware of the bailiffs' intended return, a locked door may not be treated as a deliberate exclusion. It will therefore be necessary for the bailiffs to give prior notice of a date and possibly time for their return (see also *Aga Kurboolie Mahomed* v. *The Queen* (1843) Moo PC 239 on the need for prior demand for entry). It may be possible for bailiffs in certain circumstances to get round this need to make prior appointments by including some general clause in their walking possession agreements permitting forced re-entry at any time (see Morritt LJ in *Khazanchi* at 911b and *Lavell* v. *O'Leary* [1933] 2 KB 200) though there may be questions about the validity of such agreements made under duress and such amendments will not be possible for the walking possession agreements prescribed for distress for rent, road traffic penalties and execution. County court bailiffs require the permission of a district judge, even an indemnity from the plaintiff, before such entry. If the county court bailiff feels that the are goods of insufficient value to justify the expense of removal and sale, but the creditor insists upon it, the bailiff can refuse to proceed until the creditor has indemnified the court for any costs that might not be recovered.

On return only what was previously seized may be removed (*Smith* v. *Torr* (1862) 3 F&F 505). If extra goods are discovered after the seizure and notice was presented, they cannot be included in the levy and to remove them would be trespass (*Bishop* v. *Bryant* (1834) 6 C&P 484).

In distress for rent several procedural requirements apply at the removal stage. First a detailed breakdown of the costs should be left by handing it to the tenant using Form 9 (r.12(3) DRR). This details the number of vehicles used, the number of men employed, the number and type of special removal machines, the time spent at the property and loading and unloading the vans and the basic charge for each item. This form also applies to road traffic distraint (r.12(3) & sch. 2).

Secondly under s.9 DRA 1737 notice of where the goods are lodged or deposited shall be given to the tenant or left at the house within one week of the lodging or deposit of those items (the week does include the day of removal). Furthermore, under c4 Statute of Marlborough 1267 goods should not be removed outside the county in which they were seized. The statute provides that the landlord will be "grievously punished by amerciament". What this exactly means today is not clear, but it is probable that the tenant will be able to sue upon the statute for penal (aggravated) damages.

Finally for rent under s.10 DRA 1737 "*it shall be lawful for any persons whatever to come and go from such a place where any distress for rent be impounded and secured . . . , in order to view, appraise and buy, and also in order to carry off and remove on account of purchase thereof*". This applies specifically to the right of prospective buyers to attend a sale at the tenant's home if the goods are impounded there, but more generally to their right to attend auction houses and confirms the general right of the bailiff to re-enter to remove goods for sale.

The bailiff must take care when removing and storing goods otherwise an action for negligence could be brought by the debtor (see 9.26). If the goods are stored at an auction house, the auctioneer must exercise ordinary care and diligence in keeping them and is liable for any damage or loss arising from default or negligence. Equally the auctioneer's possession gives an interest in the goods which entitles him/her to sue for any trespass or conversion of the goods, so, if a debtor sought to rescue the goods, the auctioneer could take action.

10.4.2 Abuse of Distress

The bailiff may not use items distrained for his own purposes but may use items if necessary for their preservation and for the benefit of the owner e.g. milking cows (per Powis J to the contrary in *Vaspor* v. *Edwards* (1702) 12 MR 658 is doubted in "Halsbury's Laws" vol. 13 para. 315 note 1). In *Bagshaw* v. *Goward* (1607) Yelv 96 a defendant seized a stray horse and rode it. The court held such use to be a misdemeanour as seizure gives only a custody and no property in the items. Consequently the seizure was wrong from the beginning and the plaintiff was entitled to damages for the value of the item. In *Chamberlayn's Case* (1590) 74 ER 202 the court held that cattle etc should be made available to the owner to feed during impounding.

If impounded items are damaged or lost as a result of the neglect of the impounder, the owner may sue for their value (*Perkins* v. *Butterfield* (1627) Het 75 – though note that in this case in a dissenting judgment Hitcham J felt that trespass did lie for such mistreatment and that loss of goods seized could render the levy trespass *ab initio*). More modern examples might include the fact that a bailiff may not drive a motor vehicle seized from a debtor but may be entitled to periodically operate certain equipment that would otherwise deteriorate if not regularly used.

10.5 Sale

The conclusion of the process of distress is sale, though there must of course be a valid seizure to entitle the bailiff to sell (*In Re: Townsend* (1880) 14 Ch D 132). Both execution and statutory distraint are defined by the fact that the purpose of seizure is to sell (Lord Wright in *Potts* v. *Hickman* [1941] AC 212) – though the real purpose of distress is to compel payment, not to sell goods. Thus in execution if the debtor fails to pay, the bailiff must proceed at once to prepare for a sale. The goods cannot be handed over to the creditor (*Thomson* v. *Clark* [1596] 78 ER 754) but both the creditor and the debtor can buy them at the sale (*Re: Rogers ex parte Villars* (1874) 9 Ch App 432 or *Stratford* v. *Twynan* (1822) Jac 418). A sheriff also cannot retain the goods and pay the debt with his own money (*Waller* v. *Weedale* (1604) Noy 107).

NB in distress damage feasant there is **no** right to sell the seized chattels (*Pledall* v. *Knapp* (1581) 123 ER 356). If goods are sold, it will be trespass *ab initio* (*Dorton* v. *Pickup* (1736) Selw NP 670). At the same time there is no limit on the period during which seized goods may be held (*Anon* [1314] YB 8 E2).

10.5.1 Timing

In most cases except High Court and local taxes statute requires that there is a delay of at least five days between seizure and sale of goods (e.g. s.93 CCA, which also applies to road traffic penalties under art. 4(1) ERTDO; r.65(4) for VAT; s.61(4) TMA). In magistrates' courts r.54(5) MCR sets limits upon when the sale may occur. The goods cannot be sold earlier than six days after the levy unless a person gives written consent. Further if a period for sale is not specified on the warrant, sale should be no later than fourteen days after levy. There is no set delay in local taxes (*McCreagh* v. *Cox & Ford* (1923) 92 LJKB 855) but the five day period tends to be followed. Sale may take place earlier than the statutory period if the goods are perishable or the debtor consents in writing.

In any event, the sale should be conducted within a reasonable time unless there is good cause (*Jacobs* v. *Humphrey* (1834) 2 Cr & M 413; *Ayshford* v. *Murray* (1870) 23 LT 470) and the bailiff will be liable in damages for an unreasonable delay (*Aireton* v. *Davis* (1833) 9 Bing 740). If the goods are left an unreasonable time on the premises before sale they may have been abandoned, in which case the bailiff will be a trespasser if he tries to collect them (*Griffin* v. *Scott* (1726) 1 Barn KB 3). Equally if a sale is attempted on the premises of goods impounded there, after a reasonable time has elapsed, the bailiff will also be a trespasser (*Winterbourne* v. *Morgan* (1809) 11 East 395). Ten days has been held to be reasonable period of time to prepare (*Re: Finch* (1891) 65 LT 466).

In distress for rent, although the DRA 1689 gives the power to sell, the landlord is under no obligation to sell (*Hudd* v. *Ravenor* (1821) 2 Brod & Bing 662). However after five days from, but not including, the date of the distress, if the arrears remain unpaid or replevin has not been commenced, he may sell for the "best price that may be gotten" (s.1 1689 Act) and pass good title (*Harper* v. *Taswell* [1833] 6 C & P 166). This period of five days can be extended to fifteen at the tenant's request, in order to allow replevin (s.6 LDAA 1888). Sale before the five day "waiting period" mentioned above has elapsed is an irregularity.

10.5.2 Appraisement

There is generally no requirement to set a reserve price before sale (for example in the High Court see *Bealy* v. *Sampson* (1688) 2 Vent 93) except for taxes (s.61(5) TMA – the collector will have this done by an auctioneer or some other qualified person such a private bailiff). In most cases "appraisement" can be requested by the debtor, at his/her own expense. For example in distress for rent the tenant can in writing request that competent persons carry out an appraisement of the goods (s.5 LDAA 1888), but s/he must meet the costs (*Pitt* v. *Shew* [1821] 4 B & Ald 206). In distress for rent it has been held that appraisers need not be professionals (*Roden* v. *Eyton* (1848) 6 CB 427), but they should be impartial (*Westwood* v. *Cowne* [1816] 1 Stark 172), so it is irregular for the bailiff to be both appraiser and broker (*Lyon* v. *Weldon* (1824) 2 Bing 334; *Andrews* v. *Russel* [1786] BNP 81d). If there is loss due to failure to (properly) appraise, the debtor can sue for special damages based on the value of the goods less any sums due (*Knotts* v. *Curtis* (1832) 5 C&P 322; *Whitworth* v. *Maden* (1847) 2 C&K 517). Even though there may have been an appraisement, the resulting valuation is not conclusive proof of the goods' value (*Cook* v. *Corbett* (1875) 24 WR 181 CA). Appraisers may buy the goods at their own valuation price.

10.5.3 Mode and conduct

Sale is normally by public auction. Sometimes this is the only method permitted by the regulations (e.g. VAT reg 65(5); road traffic penalties art 13 ERTDO; s.61 TMA). Sometimes other modes of sale are possible:

- *in magistrates' courts* the sale shall be by public auction unless the person consents in writing to some other method (r.54(6)MCR);
- *in High Court execution*, unless the court orders otherwise, under s.138A(1) SCA if the debt and expenses exceed £20 the sale must be by public auction which should be advertised for three days beforehand (*Re: Crook ex parte Southampton Sheriff* (1894) 63 LJQB 756) but the sheriff should allow reasonable time before

sale to allow claims for interpleader. Another mode of sale can be employed by order of court on application under CPR Part 23 from any of the concerned parties (O.47 r.6 RSC). If the sheriff has notice of other executions, for example (it would appear) a warrant for a road traffic penalty, an application to sell privately cannot be considered by the court until the other creditors have been served notice of the application (SCA s.138A(2)). The sale can be on the debtor's premises with his/her consent. If a sale is by any means other than public auction, without leave of court having been obtained first, it is valid until it is set aside by the court (*Crawshaw* v. *Harrison* [1894] 1 QB 79). The court can set aside a sale under a fi fa if the sheriff did not take reasonable care to advertise it, leading to a sale at undervalue (*Edge* v. *Kavanagh* (1884) 24 LR Ir 1). A sale is unlawful if the sheriff sells part of the goods without the authority of the execution creditor in order to recover possession money, fees and expenses (*Sneary* v. *Abdy* [1876] 1 Ex D 299);

- *in distress for rent* there are no regulations as to the mode of sale, but an expensive method should only be employed when a better price can be expected. There is not a set order for sale – in other words, there is no need to sell all unprivileged items before conditionally privileged goods. In *Jenner* v. *Yolland* (1818) 6 Price 3, a landlord took cattle, inter alia, but after the sale it transpired that there would have been enough to cover the rent and costs without needing any goods with qualified privilege. The distress was not illegal as there had been reasonable grounds for supposing (after qualified appraisement) that there would not have been sufficient otherwise. The sale can take place at the tenant's home (s.10 DRA 1737), but if s/he requests transfer in writing and is prepared to cover the costs and any damages, it can be transferred to an auction room or other suitable place (s.5 LDAA 1888). Irregular sale will make the landlord liable to account for the proceeds and the value of the goods and the tenant will be entitled to recover the full value less the rent and costs; and,
- *in county court execution* sale should be advertised for three days previously and is by public auction unless the court orders otherwise. Under O.26 r.12 CCR the debtor must have four days' notice of the time and place of the auction on N333. Private sale cannot be ordered where the debt is less than £20 but otherwise the court can order this on application from the creditor, debtor or District Judge (s.97). Any other creditor enforcing against the debtor should be given four days notice of the hearing and can attend to make representations (O.26 r.15).

Only in the county court is the debtor actually entitled to notice of when and where the sale will occur (though if goods are removed for sale the CSA code requires that the debtor must be informed by the bailiff of the date, time and location of the sale). If goods seized under the same warrant are sold over several days, it will be treated by the court as one sale (*In Re: Rogers ex parte Villars* (1874) 9 Ch App 432). If the goods are of a specialist nature, it is the bailiff's duty to obtain advice on the mode of sale – for instance advertising in specialist press to encourage bids by creating "an excitement or an opposition" (*American Express* v. *Hurley* [1985] 3 All ER 564). The best price possible should be obtained (*Ridgway* v. *Lord Stafford* (1851) 6 Exch 404). Restrictive conditions should not be laid down that will effect the sum raised (*Ridgway* v. *Lord Stafford* (1851) as above; *Hawkins* v. *Walrond* (1876) 1 CPD 280).

Any conditions preventing the best price being achieved are illegal. The best price is not necessarily that offered by the highest bidder if this is still greatly under the item's value and no reasonable price can be obtained (*Keightley* v. *Birch* (1814) 3 Camp 521). If the goods have been appraised but do not reach the reserve price, the sale may proceed for the best price that can be obtained. It may be necessary for several attempts to be made to reach the appraised price at successive auctions before sale for a lesser sum is reasonable (Vin Abr vol 9).

An action can be taken for not selling at the best price, giving evidence of mismanagement in connection with the handling of the goods at the sale (e.g. in *Poynter* v. *Buckley* (1833) 5 C&P 512 the goods were left in the rain and inadequately lotted). Improper lotting and hurrying the sale was held to invalidate it (*Wright* v. *Child* (1866) LR 1 Exch 358). Care should be taken to properly advertise the sale (*Edge* v. *Kavanagh* (1884) 24 LR Ir 1). If a bailiff is to be sued for being negligent in the conduct of a sale only nominal damages will be recoverable unless actual loss and damage can be shown (*Bales* v. *Wingfield* (1843) 4 A&E 580).

10.5.4 Amount

A bailiff acts wrongfully by seizing and selling more than is "reasonably sufficient" to cover the debt and costs (*Gawler* v. *Chaplin* (1848) 2 Exch 503; *Cook* v. *Palmer* (1827) 6 B & C 739), though obviously there must be a margin for error and a reasonable amount may be seized in the first place. The bailiff should closely monitor a sale to make sure that too much is not sold (*Batchelor* v. *Vyse* (1834) 4 Moo & S 552).

If goods are sold for greatly under their value the debtor can be assumed to have a substantial grievance upon which an action for damages in conversion could be based. However the onus is on the claimant to show that there was substantial difference between the price realised and the value at the date of sale. In the absence of such proof the bailiff will be protected from proceedings. The auction price is not conclusive proof of the value of the goods (*Neumann* v. *Bakeaway* [1983] 1 WLR 1016) but, as confirmed by Morritt LJ in *Khazanchi* v. *Faircharm Investments* [1998] 2 All ER 901 at 920f "*The price realised at auction is not necessarily the best evidence of value at any particular date but if there is no evidence . . . to the effect that the auction had not been properly advertised or conducted it is evidence a judge is entitled to accept*". It was also confirmed that evidence as to prices fetched for goods on the second hand market may be acceptable, but in the absence of such indications of worth, the price of goods if bought new could not be relied upon as evidence as to the value of seized items sold some years later (Millett J at 919). The judgment also contains useful guidance on the matter of accounting for VAT in the course of assessing the price obtained (Millett J at 921b&c).

If several items, each worth more than the debt due, are seized and all are sold, this is clearly trespass (*Wooddye* v. *Coles* (1595) Noy 59, 74 ER 1027). Thus in a case where the sale was extended over two days, where enough was sold by the sheriff on the first day, it was trespass to continue with the sale on the second day, even if there was a fear that actual delivery of the goods might somehow be prevented by loss or accident (*Aldred* v. *Constable* (1844) 6 QB 370).

If the sale is irregular, damages can be claimed. If the sale is wholly void there is no basis for an action in damages (*Owen* v. *Leigh* (1820) 3 B & Ald 470). Presumably if goods were sold in such circumstances an action for money had and received by the debtor might be possible (see 9.32).

10.5.5 Proceeds and surplus

The proceeds should be paid over to the creditor promptly and the debtor is then entitled to receive any surplus and any goods that remain unsold – see for instance s.1 DRA 1689; VAT reg. 65 or TMA s.61(5), and *E. India Co* v. *Skinne*r (1695) 90 ER 516. In *Lyon* v. *Tomkies* (1836) 1 M&W 603 it was held that if no overplus is passed on, it may be a ground on which to question the reasonability of fees. The balance of the proceeds, after satisfying any debt and costs, constitutes a debt from the bailiff to the debtor (*Harrison* v. *Paynter* (1840) 6 M&W 387). The sheriff may retain any surplus until it is demanded by the debtor – there is no need for the sheriff to search for him/her (*Wooddye* v. *Coles* (1595) Noy 59) or pay the amount into court (*Wooddye* v. *Coles* (1595) Noy 59). A landlord who sells enough to clear the debt should leave any surplus with the sheriff and return any surplus goods to where they were seized or leave them at a more convenient location, details of which will be notified to the tenant, for collection (s.1 DRA 1689; *Evans* v. *Wright* (1857) 2 H&N 527). If money is paid direct to the tenant, his/her receipt of it is not necessarily acceptance in satisfaction and s/he may still question any fees charged etc. (*Lyon* v. *Tomkies* (1836) 1 M&W 603). If the landlord fails to leave an overplus with the sheriff as required by DRA 1689, the tenant should sue for breach of the statute, rather than money had and received (*Yates* v. *Eastwood* (1851) 6 Exch 805).

10.5.6 Title on Sale

How good title is passed depends partly on the form of distress involved but some general observations can be made before examining the assorted forms.

Sale by a bailiff is recognised as passing good title even though it is not sale in market overt. However (except for distress for rent) if the goods are on hire or HP even sale under an execution cannot pass absolute title if the debtor does not possess it. Such a sale is conversion (*Lancs Waggon Co Ltd* v. *Fitzhugh* (1861) 6 H&N 502). In other cases a true sale, however irregular, passes title to the purchaser in distress (*Lyon* v. *Weldon* [1824] 2 Bing 334) and in execution (*Jeanes* v. *Wilkins* (1749) 1 Ves Sen 195). If, however, the levy is void, good title cannot be passed (see below).

Execution If goods are sold under an execution good title will generally be passed and the officer will be protected from any action against them for selling goods or paying over the proceeds, provided that no third party claim to them has been made (s.138B SCA; s.98 CCA; art. 14 ERTDO). However if the sale occurs before a person has had any chance to make a claim to them, the sale will not pass good title (*Crane & Sons* v. *Ormerod* [1903] 2 KB 37) but contrast this with *Goodlock* v. *Cousins* [1897] 1 QB 558 CA where goods sold in default of a claimant complying with the conditions laid down in interpleader procedure were held to pass good title.

The protection for a bailiff selling under an execution is not available if there is a "real or substantial grievance" against the bailiff e.g. he was insolent or oppressive or the goods were sold at undervalue. See *Neumann* v. *Bakeaway Ltd* [1983] 1 WLR 1016 in which an interpleader (see 9.25) was begun after wrongful seizure and sale by the bailiff, though with no misconduct on the sheriff's part. Good title will also not be passed if it can be shown that notice of a third party claim was received or that on "reasonable enquiry" the sheriff should have ascertained that the goods were not the property of the judgment debtor. See for instance *Pilling* v. *Teleconstruction Co Ltd*

(1961) 111 L J 424 in which the defendants were held liable for damages in trespass and costs. They were judgment debtors at whose rented premises the plaintiffs left industrial machinery. The equipment was seized by a county court bailiff and sold. As bailees the defendants should have notified the bailiffs and the court of the situation, whilst the court did all it could to try to establish the facts. Compare this with *Observer Ltd* v. *Gordon* [1983] 1 WLR 1008 in which interpleader protection was granted to a sheriff as the defendants had failed to show a "fairly arguable" case that the sheriff was liable in conversion. The defendant had repaired pianos, which were seized and sold for a judgment creditor. The owners made claims and the sheriff was protected by the court. He was entitled to defend the action unless he had notice of ownership or it would have been reasonable for him to make enquiries. In this case, in the absence of notice as to ownership despite repeated visits to the shop, because it was not unreasonable of him not to enquire (removal and sale occurred after the judgment debtor's death so goods were removed from an unoccupied shop) and, even if he had made enquiries, the true facts would not have been revealed in a reasonable period of time, the sale was valid. Sale in the county court passes good title and creditors making claims against the debtor cannot recover any sums for the sale of the goods unless the court had notice of their claims or "reasonable enquiry" would have shown that the goods were not the judgment debtor's (CCA s.98). In such cases the owner may be entitled to sue the bailiff and the execution creditor who has received the proceeds for money had and received (*Curtis* v. *Maloney* [1951] 1 KB 736) and anyone who converted the goods before sale (*Farrant* v. *Thompson* (1822) 2 Dow & Ry KB 1).

The protection granted in execution is also subject to the right of any person (e.g. a hirer or HP company) to any remedy against any party other than the bailiff or county court district judge (for instance the purchaser) to which they may be entitled if they can prove good title at the time of the sale (s.138B(2) SCA/s.98(2) CCA). If the execution is regular the buyer is protected by statute, even if s/he had notice of some defect in title (*Dyal Singh* v. *Kenyan Insurance Ltd* [1954] AC 287 – the appellant secured good title to a car purchased at auction and subject to a chattels mortgage, the registration of which was deemed to have given all parties notice).

If the execution is irregular for some reason (see 5.2), for example the sheriff deals wrongly with the proceeds, the execution creditor is not entitled to seize the goods again in order to recover the judgment debt once they have been sold as a bona fide buyer's title is secure (*Smallcomb* v. *Cross & Buckingham* (1697) 1 Ld Raym 252). A purchaser in good faith is entitled to protection against other executions which should have had priority (*Imray* v. *Magnay* (1843) 11 M&W 267), even if the writ itself is void through fraud unless s/he was aware of or party to this (*Bessey* v. *Windham* (1844) 6 QB 166; *Shattock* v. *Craden* (1851) 6 Exch 725). The title of a purchaser, even though s/he acted in good faith, is not secure if the irregularity made the execution altogether void (*Jeanes* v. *Wilkins* (1749) 1 Ves Sen 194; *Bushell* v. *Timson* [1934] 2 KB 79): for instance the levy is trespass *ab initio* (see for example *Lee* v. *Gansel* (1774) 1 Cowp 1) or the goods seized were not those of the execution debtor (*Hoe's Case* (1600) 5 Co Rep 89b). In the latter case the owner may recover the value of the goods from the purchaser (*Tancred* v. *Allgood* (1859) 4 H&N 438). In *Bushell* v. *Timson* execution was issued without the necessary leave – the sheriff was held liable for damages.

Distress for rent For title to pass by means of a sale under a distress for rent there must be actual sale to a third party. The landlord is guilty of conversion if s/he purchases the goods or takes them in satisfaction (*King* v. *England* (1864) 4 B & S 782). In *Plas-y-Coed Collieries Co Ltd* v. *Partridge Jones & Co* [1912] 2 KB 345 it was confirmed that a landlord purporting to buy does not get good title, even after an appraisement. The sale will be invalid and the tenant will be able to sue for wrongful interference. This will render the distress irregular and the measure of the tenant's special damages will be the full value of the goods. Sale will also be irregular even if the form of an auction is gone through – in *Moore, Nettlefold & Co* v. *Singer Manufacturing Co Ltd* [1904] 1 KB 820 it was emphasised that an auctioneer, as the landlord's agent, is not an independent vendor. It may be noted that the tenant may agree to cede goods to a landlord in full or part satisfaction (*King* v. *England* above).

10.6 Accounts

There is almost no regulation on the provision of information to the debtor on the sums raised and the fees deducted by bailiffs. In the county court and magistrates' court the debtor is entitled, after sale, to a statement of the proceeds raised, the costs charged and the proportion of the debt cleared, though in the magistrates' court the debtor must attend the court themselves to inspect this within one month of the levy at a reasonable time to be set by the court (r.54(10)). In no other form of distress is there such an entitlement, though under the CSA code of practice after the sale the bailiff must notify the debtor of the buyers' names and prices paid for each item.

Sheriff's returns Special provisions apply in execution to the information to be supplied at the conclusion of the process. A writ of fieri facias contains a direction that it should be endorsed after execution with a statement of the manner of execution and that a copy of this "return" should be sent to the creditor. A similar procedure also applies in the county court. There are three main forms of sheriff's return:

- *fieri feci* – goods were seized and sold, the debt being satisfied and paid to the creditor. A return of partial execution is commonly made;
- *nulla bona* – no goods or proceeds insufficient to cover the levy costs or prior writs were found. There must have been an attempted seizure for such a return to be made (*Doker* v. *Hader* [1825] 2 Bing 479). If there are goods on the premises, but they cannot be seized due to prior insolvency, this return is appropriate (*Milner* v. *Rawlings* (1867) 2 Exch 249) as would also be the case where rent is due, exceeding the value of the goods seizable (*Dennis* v. *Whetham* (1874) 9 QB 345); and,
- *unsold for want of buyers* – no bid or satisfactory offer was made. The sheriff's valuation of the seized goods must be attached to the return and the sheriff should await an instruction to sell for the best price possible in the circumstances, known as "venditioni exponas" (*Keightley* v. *Birch* (1814) 3 Camp 521).

If a debtor (or a creditor) is dissatisfied with the sheriff's action in an execution, s/he may give notice requiring a return to the writ (RSC O.46 r.9 – "*Any party . . . against whom a writ of execution was issued may serve notice on the sheriff . . .*

requiring him, within such time as may be specified . . . to indorse on the writ a statement of the manner in which he has executed it and to send that party a copy of the statement . . . If the sheriff fails to comply, he may apply to court for an order"). The debtor may only request this after execution (*Richardson* v. *Tuttle* (1860) 8 CBNS 474). If, in making the return, the sheriff discloses a breach of duty on his part the return is bad and the sheriff is liable to an action (*Mildmay* v. *Smith* (1671) 2 Wms Saund 343; *Stockdale* v. *Hansard* (1840) 11 A&E 297; *R.* v. *Sheriff of Leicestershire* (1850) 9 CB 659). If by the return the sheriff discharges himself, the aggrieved person may still sue for a false return or for any alleged misconduct during the levy. A mere false return where there has been no breach of duty is not actionable (*Stimson* v. *Farnham* (1871) 7 QB 175).

10.7 Repeat levies

The frequently stated rule is that a second levy cannot be conducted. In fact this principle deals with two issues under the same heading. A bailiff cannot distrain again for the same debt after a completed levy. This is because the second levy is rendered illegal by the fact that no debt is any longer due. Secondly the bailiff may not split the demand and try more than once under the same warrant because he realises he has not seized enough the first time around. There is an exception to the second instance for execution (and statutory distraint too, if one argues on the basis of the execution/distraint analogy) as repeat levies can be made in any circumstances where any portion of the debt is outstanding.

10.7.1 Second levies

The following principles on second levies of distress may be derived from the case law. A bailiff cannot levy more than once – even though the levies are only separated by a few hours (*Wallis* v. *Savill* [1701] 2 Lut 493) – if:

- *it is for the same debt* after a complete levy has satisfied it already (*Wotton* v. *Shirt* [1600] Cro Eliz 742; *Owens* v. *Wynne* [1855] 4 E&B 579 *ex parte Shuttleworth & Hancock: In Re Deane* (1832) 1 Deac & Ch 223);
- *the bailiff has levied for too little* previously (*Dawson* v. *Cropp* (1845) 1 CB 961) and simply failed to get enough through his "own folly" (*Wallis* v. *Savill* (1701) 2 Lut 493; *Anon* (1550) Moore 7, pl. 26 Distress);
- *the bailiff has abandoned seized goods* (see 8.4.1). In *Bagge* v. *Mawby* (1853) 8 Exch 641 a landlord withdrew after receiving a notice that another creditor intended to petition for the tenant's bankruptcy. After the order he distrained again. It was held that if there was no lawful cause for not following the levy through, he should have continued. The notice from the creditor was not a good cause or excuse, rather it was a mere idle threat from a stranger with no right to interfere in the distress. The landlord ought to have proceeded and could not levy again. The same would appear to apply in execution (*Castle* v. *Ruttan* (1854) 4 CP 252). This may also happen where the bailiff is withdrawn by the creditor on reaching an arrangement with the debtor. A new warrant would be needed (*Shaw* v. *Kirby* [1888] 52 J.P. 182);

- *if seizable goods are lost to the creditor* either because the goods that were seized were of inadequate value when the bailiff had a fair opportunity to levy for more or because those goods that have been levied upon have been lost through negligence on the part of the bailiff. This applies to landlords in distress for rent but does not seem to apply to execution. Here the bailiff may levy again, but may be liable to be sued by the parties to the execution;
- *the total debt due is split* between separate warrants to give a series of small levies (*Forster* v. *Baker* [1910] 2 KB 636; *Rothschild* v. *Fisher* [1920] 2 KB 243). Of course separate rents may be distrained for separately (*Sheppard's Touchstone of Common Assurances* 81) as may separate instalments of rent (*Anon* (1550) Moore 7, pl. 26 Distress; *Gambrell* v. *Earl of Falmouth* (1835) 4 A&E 73). This may be in any order, and does not have to be in the sequence in which the sums fell due (*Palmer* v. *Stanage* (1661) 1 Lev 43) but multiple levies must be avoided (*Holt* v. *Sambach* (1627) Cro Car 103; *Hunt* v. *Braines* (1694) (6 W & M) 4 MR 402);
- *in distress damage feasant* there can be no second distress once possession has been given up and chattels have been left with their owner. This is because the right to distrain is associated with a specific incident of trespass, which, once terminated, removes the right to seize.

A wrongful second levy could be resisted by the means described in 3.3. However second levies of distress and execution are permissible where:

- *there were insufficient goods* on a first visit upon which to levy execution (*Anon* (1585) Cro Eliz 13; *Jordan* v. *Binckes* (1849) 13 QB 757; *R.* v. *Sheriff of Essex* (1839) 8 Dowl PC 5). Writs of execution remain in force until the whole sum due has been collected – they are a continuing power to seize any goods that become available until such time as the debt is clear. In the former case above it was held permissible to complete the levy some eleven years after the first seizure. Thus a further levy may be permitted because on the first levy it was found that all the goods then available had been seized by another bailiff (*Edmunds* v. *Ross* (1821) 9 Price 5; *Drear* v. *Warren* (1833) 10 Bing 341) or because more effects are discovered at a later date (*Hopkins* v. *Adcock* [1772] 2 Dick 443). The bailiffs may make a partial levy but are entitled to wait until the levy can be completed rather than make a return of no goods. Bailiffs may also distrain in "instalments" where they are concerned to avoid an excessive levy (*Hudd* v. *Ravenor* (1821) 2 Brod & Bing 662). This ability to make successive moderate levies is endorsed by both Gilbert and Bradby as to the advantage of the debtor, as otherwise items of great value may have to be seized on the first visit. Thus a further levy is legal if on the first occassion the bailiff acts out of "moderation or tenderness" and does not levy for full value (*Hutchins* v. *Chambers* (1758) 1 Burr 580);
- *the bailiff made a reasonable mistake* because of the uncertain or illusory value of the items (*Hutchins* v. *Chambers* (1758) 1 Burr 579);
- *the levy has been obstructed.* This may be because the debtor obstructed or attacked the bailiff or refused entry (*Lee* v. *Cooke* (1858) 3 H & N 203). On such a second levy the bailiff need not confine himself to goods seized on the previous occasion

(*Gislason* v. *Rural Municipality of Foam Lake* [1929] 2 DLR 386). Equally a second levy may be justified if circumstances at the auction prevented the best price being obtained. See for example *Rawlence & Squarey* v. *Spicer* [1935] 1 KB 412 where demonstrations and threats by the debtor prevented a sale or *R.* v. *Judge Clements ex parte Ferridge* [1932] 2 KB 535 where a crowd prevented the sale by attending the auction, harassing bidders and making ridiculous offers;

- *seized cattle died in the pound* by an act of God (*Anon* (1568) 3 Dyer 280 pl 14; *Anon* (1700) 12 MR 397; *Vaspor* v. *Edwards* (1702) 12 Mod Rep 658). We may assume that if the bailiffs' warehouse were to be burnt down following a lightning strike, this would provide a more likely modern reason for a further levy. The right to relevy in such cases does not apply to distress damage feasant;
- *the first attempted levy was trespass* and thus void *ab initio* (*Grunnell* v. *Welch* [1906] 2 KB 555). This could be where a levy on goods was made, but it transpires that none of the goods were the judgment debtor's (*Re: A Debtor ex parte Smith* [1902] 2 KB 260);
- *the first distress is withdrawn*, at the request of the tenant. This may be because the debtor simply asks the creditor to "forbear now and postpone the distress" (*Bagge* v. *Mawby* above) or because instalments are agreed (*Thwaites* v. *Wilding* (1883) 12 QBD 4). If the arranged payments are not made, the bailiff can distrain again; and,
- *the debtor goes bankrupt* so that the first levy is withdrawn, but the bankruptcy is later annulled (*Crew* v. *Terry* (1877) 2 CPD 403).

10.7.2 Second Warrants

The previous section dealt with repeat levies under the same warrant. Various regulations on statutory distraint permit repeat warrants to be issued, as many times as are necessary, for the same debt (e.g. reg. 52(3) CT(A&E) Regulations). That this is permissible in these cases strengthens the analogy between statutory distraint and execution, as it is accepted in respect of the latter that an execution creditor may issue further or simultaneous warrants (*Lee* v. *Dangar, Grant & Co* (1892) 2 QB 337). A second warrant should not be issued whilst the first is still in the bailiff's hands (*Chapman* v. *Bowlby* (1841) 8 M&W 249) even if the levy has been abandoned (*Miller* v. *Parnell* (1815) 5 Taunt 370). If the bailiff is withdrawn on the instructions of the creditor, following an arrangement between debtor and creditor, a new warrant will have to be issued to permit the bailiff to return (*Shaw* v. *Kirby* (1888) 52 JP 182). A new warrant can be issued if the first was inoperative due to prior seizure and assignment of goods to a third party (*Dicas* v. *Warne* [1833] 10 Bing 341). A second warrant cannot issue whilst interpleader proceedings are pending the first (*In Re: Follows ex parte Follows* [1895] 2 QB 521).

10.8 Remedies for errors in removal or sale

10.8.1 Illegal and irregular distress

At common law there was no distinction between an illegality and an irregularity in the conduct of a levy (see *Six Carpenters' Case* (1610) 8 Co Rep 146). Both made the process void and trespass *ab initio*. Statute intervened, initially for the benefit of landlords (s.19 DRA – to avoid the "very great hardship upon landlords" that distresses should be rendered void by "mistake or inadvertency" during a levy), but the differentiation of illegality and irregularity has been extended to other regimes as well – for details see 10.8.2 below. The result is that:

- removal and sale will still be lawful despite an irregularity in any other aspect of the levy ;
- an irregular sale will still pass good title (*Wallace* v. *King* (1788) 1 H Bl 13), therefore the debtor cannot sue for conversion;
- if the plaintiff fails to show any loss, s/he is not entitled to nominal damages (see *Rodgers* v. *Parker* (1856) 18 CB 112); and,
- the normal measure of damages is the value of the goods less any sum actually due (by analogy from s.19 DRA). See for example *Bygus* v. *Goode* (1832) 2 Cr & J 364 or *Rocke* v. *Hills* (1887) 3 TLR 298. It will be possible to recover any consequential losses as well.

Readers should note that independent acts unconnected with the conduct of the levy are not effected by the provisions on irregularities and will still be illegal (for example, a wrongful eviction of the tenant – *Etherton* v. *Popplewell* (1800) 1 East 139). Equally in those forms of distress where such provision is not made, any wrongful act continues to be a potential illegality. These forms are:

- *execution by the sheriff* (see *Aitkenhead* v. *Blades* (1813) 5 Taunt 198). Execution follows the basic common law principle that anything not within the authority of the writ is illegal and therefore trespass or conversion. Irregularities tend to be treated as breaches of duty by the sheriff for which any actual damage can be recovered (see earlier);
- *distraint for income tax and VAT*; and,
- *distress damage feasant.*

For an irregular act to be an illegality it is going to have to be a "positive" irregularity, rather than a "negative" one – that is, the bailiff must do something wrong rather than fail to take an action he should have taken. For example, an irregularly conducted sale may be illegal where as a failure to give a prescribed notice of distress is unlikely to be regarded as unlawful. See Lord Coke in *Six Carpenters' Case* (1610) 8 Co Rep 146 – "not doing is no trespass".

10.8.2 Irregular distress

The following regimes contain a provision distinguishing illegal from irregular distress:

- *distress for rent*, as already stated, s.19 DRA 1737 gave the tenant the right to sue for special damages for any irregularity either by an action for trespass or on the case. The successful plaintiff is entitled to recover his/her full costs, but if the landlord tenders amends before the action is commenced, any award of damages is barred (s.20 DRA 1737). Payment into court is thus unnecessary (*Jones* v. *Gooday* (1842) 9 M&W 736) and the landlord is provided with a complete defence.

- *local taxes*: under reg. 45(7) CT(A&E) Regulations and reg. 14(7) NDR(A&E) (LL) Regulations a bailiff shall not be treated as a trespasser from the beginning because of any subsequent irregularity in distress, but the debtor sustaining special damages from such an irregularity can recover full satisfaction for the special damages (and no more) by proceedings in trespass or otherwise;
- *county court*: no officer trespasses because of any irregularity or informality in either any proceedings on which the validity of a warrant depends, or the form of the warrant or mode of execution (s.125 CCA). However any person aggrieved may sue for any special damages sustained, though no costs will be awarded if the damages do not exceed £2. In an action for wrongful execution on goods, the owner need only show that the warrant did not authorise the officer to levy execution to the value of the goods in fact seized – see *Moore* v. *Lambeth County Court Registrar* [1970] 1 All ER 980/1 QB 560 which demonstrated that execution is excessive if the warrant does not authorise it, even in the absence of malice on the part of the bailiff.
- *distraint for road traffic penalties* (s.125 CCA is applied by art. 4(1) ERTDO);
- *magistrates' court*: if there is any irregularity in execution of a magistrates' warrant, the bailiff shall not be held a trespasser as a result (s.78(2) MCA), but the debtor could claim special damages (s.78(3));
- child support maintenance: s.35(5) provides the bailiff is not a trespasser *ab initio* because of any subsequent irregularity in the levy, though special damages may be recoverable (s.35(6)).

The bailiff may be sued and the creditor can be included in a claim if he or she authorised the distress, though not the irregular act, as the creditor's duty is to ensure proper execution. The debtor can only recover what "special damages" can be proved and any action for trespass or conversion would be barred (*Wallace* v. *King* (1788) 1 H Bl 13; *Whitworth* v. *Smith* (1832) 5 C&P 250). The damages are based on the actual damage suffered, which is often said to be the full value of any goods lost or injury sustained less the debt and costs. In the absence of proof of special damages, the plaintiff cannot even get a nominal sum (*Rodgers* v. *Parker* (1856) 18 CB 112). Special damages need to be proved if, for instance, the bailiff sells within five days (*Lucas* v. *Tarleton* (1858) 3 H & N 116), sells without appraising (*Biggins* v. *Goode* (1832) 2 C & J 364) or sells without notice of distraint (*Whitworth* v. *Maden* (1847) 2 Car & Kir 517). Any consequential losses such as for detention after tender of the sums due or for sale after tender is made but before the time for replevin has expired may also be recovered.

10.8.3 Excessive distress

An excessive distress has always been treated as wrongful at common law, and an action will lie. The common law position was confirmed and codified by two successive medieval statutes which remain in force. Capitula 4 Statute of Marlborough 1267 requires that distresses are reasonable and not too great: anyone levying an unreasonable distress will be "grievously amerced" for the excess. This necessity for distresses to be reasonable and not outrageous is repeated by the Statute of Exchequer (date uncertain). Despite the reference to "amercements" it is not an offence to levy in an excessive manner and no information or indictment can be laid (*R.* v. *Ledgingham* (1670) 1 Vent 104). Viner's "Abridgment" terms it a "private offence" and rather than prosecution the remedy for excessive distress is an action in case founded on the statute. It will be conducted as for irregular distress above, the measure of damages being the excess. It is accepted that the above mentioned statutes deal generally with levies of distress for rent (see remedies at 7.8), but Bradby at p. 275 cites Coke (2 Inst 107) to the effect that the operation of the statutes regarding excessive levies is general and applies to all cases of distress whatsoever (see for example 42 Ed III 26; 8 Hen IV 16). Readers should recall that execution is subject to separate rules (see 5.2).

If an excessive levy has taken place the plaintiff cannot sue for trespass (*Hutchins* v. *Chambers* (1758) 1 Burr 580; *Lynne* v. *Moody* (1729) 2 Stra 851; *Woodcroft* v. *Thompson* (1682) 3 Lev 48), unless perhaps goods of very great value are taken for a very small debt (*Moir* v. *Munday* (1755) at 1 Burr 590; *Crowther* v. *Ramsbottom* (1798) 7 TR 654). Baron Gilbert in his analysis of *Moir* v. *Munday* notes that the seizure was of gold and silver – assets of known worth – and that this serves to distinguish this decision from any distress on goods of "arbitrary and uncertain value" (Gilbert at p.60). Recovery of damages in a replevin will bar any action for excessive distress (*Phillips* v. *Berryman* (1783) 3 Doug 286; *White* v. *Wallis* (1759) 2 Wils 87; *Pease* v. *Chaytor* (1863) 1 B&S 658). This is because replevin is founded upon the distress being illegal, whereas an action for excessive distress is founded upon there being a cause for the distress. However an agreement between landlord and tenant to prevent sale will not prevent a later action for an excessive seizure (*Willoughby* v. *Backhouse* (1824) 2 B&C 821).

There is no need to prove malice in the action but the excess will have to be disproportionate rather than trifling. There is no cause of action if the value of the goods taken is less than the sum actually due (*Tancred* v. *Leyland* (1851) 16 QB 669). No special damage need in fact be shown for the plaintiff to succeed (*Chandler* v. *Doulton* (1865) 3 H&C 553), but if the plaintiff only establishes an entitlement to nominal damages s/he may be deprived of the costs of the action (*Crowder* v. *Self* [1839] 2 Mood & Ry 190). The price realised at sale by auction, rather than in the normal course of the plaintiff's business, is prima facie evidence of the item's value (*Rapley* v. *Taylor & Smith* (1883) Cab & El 150; *Wells* v. *Moody* [1835] 7 C & P 59) and will be the measure of damages. Again the debt and costs due will be deducted from the amount awarded (*Knotts* v. *Curtis* (1832) 5 C&P 322). An action can be begun even when the goods are not yet sold (*Hooper* v. *Annis* (1838) 2 JP 695) the measure of damages then being the loss and inconvenience to the debtor occasioned by the goods' removal, though this may be nominal (*Chandler* v. *Doulton* (1865) 3 H&C 553; *Mudhun Mohun Doss* v. *Gokul Doss* (1866) 10 Moo Ind App 563). It may include excessive sums paid to prevent removal (*Fell* v. *Whittaker* (1871) 7 QB 120). Consequential losses, such as for loss of use and enjoyment are also recoverable (*Piggott* v. *Birtles* (1836) 1 M&W 441). If the person had to replevy in order to recover seized goods, the costs of replevying the excessive sum are also claimable as consequential damages (*Piggott* v. *Birtles* at 451) unless these costs have already been taxed in the replevin action (*Grace* v. *Morgan* (1836) 2 Bing NC 534). If there is no inconvenience as in a case where the bailiff took walking possession, no aggravated damages may be awarded (*Watson* v. *Murray & Co* [1955] 1 All ER 350). In this latter case the sheriff's officers had attended at the plaintiff's shop and said they must take charge of everything there. The plaintiff signed a walking possession agreement under protest and then sued. The court held the seizure to have been valid, if excessive. The excessive seizure caused no damage as the trader was able to carry on dealing with the stock in the course of business. If the distress is both irregular and excessive, damages can be substantial (*Smith* v. *Ashforth* [1860] above). In an action for an excessive levy any bailiff should not appear as a witness for the creditor unless released from their agency (*Field* v. *Mitchell* (1806) 6 Esp 71).

If an excessive amount of growing crops are seized, the measure of damages is not their value but the inconvenience and expense to the farmer of being deprived of the management of them, or the value of the farmer's replevin sureties. As growing crops can be levied under DRA 1689, they are covered by the common law principles of excessive distress under 52 H3 c4 (*Piggott* v. *Birtles* (1836) 1 M&W 441).

Chapter Eleven

CONCLUDING LEVIES: CHARGES

11.1 Charge Scales

The costs chargeable by most bailiffs are regulated by scales found in the various statutes and statutory instruments. The purpose of the scales is to regulate what is charged to debtors and to prevent the "extortion" of "helpless debtors" (per Lord Coleridge CJ in *Roe* v. *Hammond* (1877) 2 CPD 300) by the levying of any "unfairly large sum" (*Phillips & Another* v. *Rees* (1889) 24 QBD 17).

11.1.1 Elements of charge scales

The charges allowable are found in schedules or appendices to the regulations, for example sch. 5 CT(A&E) Regulations; sch. 3 NDR(A&E)(LL) Regulations; Appendix 1 DRR; sch. 1 CS (C&E) Regulations; sch. 1 ERTD(CB) Regulations. The broad outline of each of these is the same, but readers are referred to the text of each as the specific wording and effect differs from scale to scale. The following paragraphs consider a few significant features, but the main focus of this chapter will be abuses of the charging system and the remedies available to the debtor.

Typical elements within the scales are fixed or set daily fees for certain activities such as visits to the debtors property, "reasonable" costs for activities like removal and storage and fees for levies and auctions based on a percentage of the debt due. The local tax and child support scale charges include VAT, whereas they are additional to charges for distress for rent and taxes. As stated there is now a standard format of fee scale across most forms of statutory distraint, but there are a few major exceptions to this considered in the following sections.

11.1.2 Magistrates' courts

The charge scale will be negotiated between the bailiffs and the court, but will typically follow the broad outlines of the statutory charge scales and include elements to cover initial administrative costs on the issue of the warrant, attendance and levy charges and charges for removal – particularly of vehicles. Note that these costs are not added on to the sum if it remains unpaid and the matter returns to the court for committal proceedings. This because the penalty due only includes court costs (*Cook* v. *Plaskett* [1882] 47 JP 265) and the court has no liability for any charges, even in cases where the levy is unsuccessful, as only the defaulter can be made to pay. Although the fees are the subject of a private contract, a request to the court or the bailiffs' firm involved will normally elicit a copy.

11.1.3 High Court Execution

The sheriff is entitled by statute to fees and costs for enforcing writs, unless the debt is below £600 (O.47 r.4), and the writ instructs him to levy for these and all legal incidental costs. A formal seizure must be made first (*Barker* v. *Dynes* (1832) 1 Dowl 169; *Nash* v. *Dickenson* (1867) LR 2 CP 252). The sheriff can take the poundage and fees out of the proceeds of sale of the property seized (*Curtis* v. *Mayne* (1842) 2 Dowl. NS 37). The sheriff cannot include the cost of previous abortive executions as these are only payable out of proceeds of that execution and may not be carried over to another: the execution debtor is under no personal liability for them (*Re: W M Long & Co ex parte Cuddeford* (1888) 20 QBD 316).

If the creditor loses the right to enforce, the sheriff cannot sell goods for fees (*Sneary* v. *Abdy* (1876) 1 Ex D 299). By the same token, if the creditor authorises release of the goods in possession, the sheriff cannot then seize them in respect of his fees, as such a release is treated as a release consented to by the sheriff as well and if the execution creditor's right to the goods is ended, so is the sheriff's (*Goode* v. *Langley* (1827) 7 B&C 26).Whenever execution is withdrawn, satisfied, stopped or fails, the sheriff is entitled to the same fees from the creditor as if the execution had been completed (*Mortimer* v. *Cragg* [1878] 3 CPD 216). If insolvency occurs between seizure and sale, the sheriff can claim expenses for possession and preparing for sale, but not poundage (*Re Craycraft* (1878) 8 ChD 596 and *Re Thomas* (1899) 1 QB 460). It is up to the court to decide, when awarding damages for illegal execution, whether a sheriff should be allowed the costs of selling the goods wrongfully seized (*Clarke* v. *Nicholson* [1835] 4 LJNS Exch 66).

Expenses not covered by the rules should not be incurred unless either the execution debtor or creditor has authorised them and agreed to pay for them (*Re: Woodham ex parte Conder* (1888) 20 QBD 40). It is unlikely that the courts will support extra fees demanded from defendants. Expenses incurred without consent, even though they may be of benefit for a party, cannot be charged as part of the costs of an execution (*Buckle* v. *Bewes* (1825) 4 B & C 154; *Joynson* v. *Oldfield* (1847) 8 LTOS 468).

Under s.20(2) Sheriff's Act 1887 and Sheriff's Fees Order (1920/No 1250) as amended, the sheriff is entitled to the following:

- *set allowances* for actions taken, such as mileage at a statutory rate for one journey to seize and one to remove goods; set seizure fees; charges for enquiring into claims on seized goods by landlords and third parties; daily fees for close and walking possession. Possession money is chargeable between seizure and removal (*Howes* v. *Young* (1876) 1 Ex D 146). The fees are only payable for a reasonable period (*Davies* v. *Edmunds* (1843) 12 M&W 31).
- *incidental expenses* of removal, storage, etc.
- *auctioneer's fees and advertising costs,* based upon a percentage of sums received and recovered. These are deducted by the sheriff to cover the reasonable out of pocket expenses of an auctioneer. If there is no sale the auctioneer still gets flat rate commission based on the value of the goods.
- "*poundage*" calculated as a percentage of the amount recovered. Poundage is only payable on sums which the bailiffs "levy and deliver in execution" – this means getting payment under compulsion of the writ, however that may come about: there does not have to be a sale (*Mortimer* v. *Cragg* [1878] 3 CPD 216). A levy is not complete until the goods are turned into money i.e. until after the sale (*Miles* v.

Harris (1862) 12 CB 550) or payment (*Re: Ludmore* (1884) 13 QBD 415). Without any seizure at all there can be no poundage (*Nash* v. *Dickenson* (1867) 2 CP 252) so even though the money may be paid or tendered after the writ is delivered to him for execution no poundage can be charged upon it (*Brun* v. *Hutchinson* [1844] 2 D&L 43), and any poundage claimed in such circumstances and paid under protest by the defendant to prevent seizure may be recovered by action (*Colls* v. *Coates* (1840) 11 Ad & El 826). If the money is paid after seizure but before sale, poundage can be claimed (*R.* v. *Jetherell* [1757] Park 176). The same applies if a compromise (i.e. instalment payments) is reached after seizure (*Alchin* v. *Wells* [1793] 5 Term Rep 470). If a settlement for *less* than the judgment debt is reached, poundage is only chargeable on the lesser sum (*R.* v. *Robinson* (1835) 2 C, M&R 334).

The sheriff is entitled to poundage if the execution is later withdrawn, satisfied, stopped or stayed (*Union Bank of Manchester* v. *Grundy* [1924] 1 KB 833) but the claim is made against the person issuing execution or the person at whose instance the sale is stopped (e.g. the trustee or Official Receiver). Poundage cannot be recovered if the judgment is set aside after seizure but before sale (*Miles* v. *Harris* as above). In all other cases, if judgment is set aside poundage and fees can be recovered (*Bullen* v. *Ansley & Smith* (1807) 6 Esp 111). Poundage is *not* recoverable on irregular executions (*Anon* Loyt 253).

- *VAT* is payable in addition

11.1.4 County court costs

Costs are recoverable under O.26 r.9 CCR. Figures are set by the County Court Fees Order 1982 and updated periodically. They are much lower than any other fees that will be encountered. For example there is a flat rate issue fee for a warrant of execution of £20 for a debt of under £125, and of £40 for any sum in excess of that figure. Other charges are then only made if a sale has to take place.

11.1.5 Liability

Charges should only be made for steps actually and necessarily taken by the bailiff. This is a specific provision in distress for rent under rr.10 & 12(2) DRR and see *Day* v. *Davies* [1938] 2 KB 74. This rule also applies to road traffic distraint (reg. 4 ERTD (CB) Regulations). As stated at 11.1.3, in execution case law confirms that the same principle applies and steps must actually be taken to permit a charge (*Holmes* v. *Sparks & Nicholas* (1852) 12 CB 242; *Cohen* v. *Das Rivas* (1891) 64 LT 661). It seems from *Re: H K Stinton* (1900) 109 LT Jo 427 that the full fee is not chargeable unless each item on the scale is fully performed but that a lesser amount may be allowable. It is suggested that a similar principle is likely to be applicable to other forms of distraint, as discussed below.

In *A.W. Ltd* v. *Cooper & Hall Ltd* [1925] 2 KB 816 during the course of his judgment Salter J observed "*In the absence of any special bargain [*between bailiff and creditor*], the rights of the bailiff to his fees are purely statutory. He may in some cases have contractual rights to fees arising by bargain . . .* ". As there was no bargain in this case, the bailiff could only claim the sums set in the relevant statutory scale. The statutory scales apply to both the creditor and the debtor, but, except in distress for rent, there is nothing in the legislation specifically precluding special agreements for extra remuneration, even though these may be contrary to the provisions of the law (*Robson* v. *Biggar* [1907] 1 KB 690). However it will become clear that, whilst special arrangements with a creditor may be conscienced by the court, there will be great reluctance to endorse similar arrangements with debtors due to their weak bargaining position.

If a debt is paid, without the costs, before any seizure has occurred the right to distrain ceases (*Bennett* v. *Bayes* (1860) 5 H&N 391; *Branscomb* v. *Bridges* (1823) 1 B&C 145) and a levy for the costs alone would be illegal (*Cotton* v. *Kaldwell* (1833) 2 Nev & M 391). If the debt is paid to the creditor and the bailiff is instructed to withdraw, the bailiff would not be able to proceed to recover any costs by sale as it would be conversion and would not pass good title (*Harding* v. *Hall* [1866] 14 LT 410). Tender of the debt and costs similarly removes the right to sell (*R.* v. *Bird* [1679] 2 Show KB 87). If the creditor instructs the bailiff to withdraw any authority to sell is lost as the bailiff is acting as the creditor's agent. If the creditor loses the right to enforce, the bailiff cannot sell goods for fees (*Sneary* v. *Abdy* [1876] 1 Ex D 299). Whenever a levy is withdrawn, satisfied, stopped or fails, the principle in execution law is that the bailiff is entitled to the same fees from the creditor as if the execution had been completed (*Mortimer* v. *Cragg* [1879) 3 CPD 216). The costs of previous unsuccessful levies should not be included in later levies as these are only payable out of proceeds of the first and may not be carried over to another: the debtor is under no personal liability for them (*Re: W M Long & Co ex parte Cuddeford* [1888] 20 QBD 316).

In local tax levies, where any proceeds are produced as a result of the use of distraint which total less than the full sum due, whether they are proceeds of sale or payment by the debtor, they are applied first to the bailiff's permissible charges under the relevant schedule, the balance (if any) then going to the liability due to the local authority (reg. 52(4) CT(A&E) Regulations; reg. 19(3) NDR(A&E)(LL) Regulations). It is finally interesting to note that this order of distribution of proceeds provided for local taxes refers to the deduction of charges under the relevant schedule. From this it would appear that, even if "non-statutory" charges *are* permissible (see 11.3 later), they could only be paid after the sums due to the local authority had been cleared in full.

11.2 Disputed bills

Introduction

Of all the areas for dispute that will be encountered, the issue of charges is probably the most common and one of the most difficult. Money diverted into fees to which bailiffs are not entitled is money not discharging the debtor's liability so it unnecessarily extends repayment periods. However there are considerable pressures on bailiffs to try to raise such additional fees. In *Phillips* v. *Another* v. *Rees* (1889) 24 QBD 17 the Court of Appeal held that when a bailiff and creditor enter into the relationship of principal and agent, an implied contract is created, a term of which is that the bailiff should receive reasonable remuneration for his services. By custom, this had been set at five per cent of the sum due. The aim of legislation regulating fees was to set a tariff for what charges could reasonably be passed on to debtors by deduction from proceeds. The scales did not seek to regulate the implied contract between creditor and bailiff and if extra costs were incurred, it was clearly the expectation of the Court of Appeal in this case that these extra sums would be the subject of an arrangement between bailiff and creditor and that the latter would reimburse reasonable amounts. However recently the phenomenon of the "nil tender" has emerged. Local authorities receive tenders from bailiff's firms whereby their enforcement will be undertaken at no cost to the authority. This arrangement is naturally very attractive to cash starved councils, but the true result is that the charges not levied upon them are simply passed on to their debtors.

To quote Coleridge J in *Roe* v. *Hammond* (1877) 2 CPD 300, "*Although the sums in dispute are small, yet the matter is of some importance*" as vulnerable debtors need protection from possible exploitation. The amounts that debtors are often wrongfully required to pay are not, in absolute terms, large, but in relation to their overall debts and (often) to their incomes, they are significant extra amounts. It is perhaps to be regretted that, as these sums are often under £3000, any proceedings related to them are not eligible for civil legal aid and as a consequence the legal profession has applied little attention to the abuses that occur and the justifications advanced for these. The following sections will seek to highlight these issues to readers.

If fees are to be challenged, it may be done on the basis of three general principles, whether the matter is being heard by taxation or by some other means.

11.2.1 Reasonable charges

The court can consider if the sums billed are a fair charge for the work done. In deciding this question the court must take into account the following factors.

- *the ratio between charges and sum due*: disproportionate charges will be disallowed (*ex parte Arnison* (1868) LR 3 Exch 56);
- *the work involved*: for example, if one levy is conducted for several warrants simultaneously, charges may be restricted to those allowable for one levy (*Glasbrook* v. *David & Vaux* [1905] 1 KB 615; *Frisch* v. *Gateshead MBC* (1992) 25 Adviser 17). It is implicit in the local tax scales (Head B(i)) that less than a multiple of the percentage levy fee may be considered reasonable if multiple warrants are levied at once. The courts have held that multiple fees will only be allowed where there are separate seizures and one levy is not for the benefit of all creditors. If the same goods are taken to satisfy several warrants, only one possession fee is possible. If different goods are taken under several warrants, even though they are all seized on the same premises and are held in possession simultaneously by one person under the several warrants, the bailiff is entitled to possession money under each warrant (*Re: Morgan* [1904] 1 KB 68). However see *Throssell* v. *Leeds City Council* (1993) 41 Adviser 22 in which a county court allowed only one visit charge for an attempt to levy three warrants simultaneously. Although it was also argued that the scale sum is still only a maximum and that the reasonable figure the court might allow could be less, the court felt that the effort involved by the bailiff in preparation, travel, attendance and follow up reports meant that the sum in the scale *was* reasonable;
- *expense to the bailiff*: In *Flanagan* v. *Crilley* (1987) unreported a van charge was taxed down on the basis that the bailiffs' firm could not justify a charge several times in excess of the commercial hire rate when the van was part of a fleet

operated by them and any individual visit it made would also be combined with other visits to other debtor's homes.

- *the period for which charges are made*: in *Re: Finch ex parte Sheriff of Essex* [1891] 65 LT 466 a sheriff remained in possession an unreasonable time without the debtor's consent. The court held that he could not charge beyond a reasonable period (held to be 10 days). However where debtor and creditor agree a longer time, higher charges can be made, for example for up to 15 months (*Re: Beeston* [1899] 1 QB 626; *Re: Hurley* (1893) 1 WR 653).

11.2.2 Appropriate charges

The court may consider if the charges are reasonable in the context of the stage that the bailiff has reached in the levy process. A frequently encountered example is the correct point for charging vehicle fees, as there is a tendency for bailiffs' firms to seek to recover these as early in the levy process as possible, especially in local tax distraint. Firms will often charge for a vehicle at the same time as a levy (and some even charge for a vehicle used when attending to visit, where entry is not gained).

In the local taxation regulations the relevant provision states that a reasonable charge may be made "for one attendance with a vehicle with a view to the removal of goods (where, following the levy, goods are not removed)" (Head C, sch. 5 CT(A&E) Regulations; sch. 3 NDR(A&E)(LL) Regulations). It is undoubted that the wording is ambiguous. It seems clear that no charge can be made before initial entry and seizure have occurred, as the charge is expressed to arise after a levy (for a definition of which, see Appendix Two). It also seems obvious that only one charge per warrant is possible, though multiple vehicle fees and fees for pre-entry vehicle use will be encountered. The wording does however allow various interpretations as to when a vehicle may then be allowed, and in other regimes similar wording is used for the same sort of purpose, for example in road traffic penalty distraint "for removing, or attending to remove . . ." (Paragraph 6, sch 1, ERTD(CB) Regulations) or "For other expenses incurred in connection with a proposed sale . . . " (Head G, sch. 2, CS(C&E) Regulations). It is important in every case to examine the client's bill and check the circumstances of the levy.

In every case the principle of "actual and necessary" expenses must be applicable. Other considerations that the court may take into account in respect of disputed van charges include:

- what was seized – what sort of vehicle was necessary?
- was walking possession taken? Was there evidence of any real intention to seek to remove at the time of seizure, bearing in mind the great costs and inconvenience for the bailiff?
- what sort of vehicle, if any, did attend, and is the charge reasonable for it?

11.2.3 Permissible extra charge?

The final and most important issue is the charging of additional, non-statutory fees. There are essentially two categories of these. There are those which are for activities permitted by the scale, but which are being charged wrongly – for example, multiple vehicle fees or levy fees, walking possession fees when there has been no agreement or higher daily fees than those permitted or levy fees when there has been nothing more than a visit to the premises. Then there are those extra fees which simply do not appear on the charge scales at all (see below).

There are numerous cases illustrating the court's attitude to the charging of fees extra to the scale figures allowable. Examples include *Usher* v. *Walters* (1843) 4 QB 553, *Jenkins* v. *Biddulph* (1827) 4 Bing 160 and *Braithwaite* v. *Marriott* (1862) 1 H&C 591: these were all sheriff's cases and show the sheriff facing action to recover the wrongful overcharges. It is clear that in most cases the courts have felt that the statutory bar on extra fees should have been final and that there was exasperation that the rule was regularly flouted, with the result that the courts were still being called upon repeatedly to consider *"complaints against auctioneers, bailiffs and all those locusts who prey upon the estates of necessitous defendants . . ."* Grose J in *Woodgate* v. *Knatchbull* [1787] 2 Term Rep 148.

What extras are charged? It is normal for bailiffs to charge for activities such as writing to the debtor prior to levy, setting up and administering an instalment payment scheme, writing to the debtor when an instalment scheme fails, or where a cheque bounces, making and receiving phone calls and negotiating with a client. It is at least arguable that charges made by the bailiff that would have been incurred by the debtor if the levy had not occurred, may be legal (see *R.* v. *Smith ex parte Porter* [1927] 1 KB 478: the bailiffs charged a range of extra fees not permitted by the scales but including the expenses of feeding the horse seized. It was not argued that this was irrecoverable, perhaps because it would have been a cost met by Porter anyway.)

Letters and negotiation are specifically allowed for (within limits) in distress for rent. Beyond these limited provisions permitting charges for some peripheral work and forbidding fees other than those authorised by the rules, there is no clear authority on whether extra charges may be made, for instance, in statutory distraint. As a result they continue to be added to bills and to be justified in various ways:

- as being allowed as "*such other terms as may be agreed*" (para. 2 sch. 5 CT (A&E) Regulations) as part of a walking possession agreement. This provision could be read as enabling the bailiff to negotiate different scales and extra fees; or,
- as being subject to an entirely separate agreement made by the bailiff with the debtor.

In order to decide whether there is a legal basis for such fees, the following issues must be considered.

Is there a statutory prohibition? Many of the regulations dealing with statutory distraint state that the creditor may levy distraint for an appropriate amount, which is defined as the debt plus "*a sum determined* [as prescribed] *in respect of charges connected with distress*". The charges are then determined by reference to the appropriate charges scale. The schedule will contain a list of permitted charges, and is often headed "charges connected with distress". See for example reg. 45(2)(b) CT(A&E) Regulations, reg. 14(2)(b) NDR (A&E) (LL) Regulations 1989 or s.35(2) CSA and reg. 32 CS(C&E) Regulations 1992. On the basis of this wording alone, it may be argued that additional charges are simply not possible.

In *Day* v. *Davies* [1938] 1 All ER 686 the Court of Appeal reviewed the permissible charges a bailiff could make under the Distress for Rent Rules 1920. As under the current r.10 DRR the bailiff could not charge fees for " *for doing any act in relation [*to a levy*], other than those specified and authorised*" by the rules. On this basis the court held that any charge for actions related to distress **not** covered by the rules was directly prohibited, and as the charge being made by the plaintiff was not in the rules, it could not be recovered. The principle of this case still seems applicable, despite slightly differing wording in some of the current regulations, and appears to represent a complete bar on extra charges. Other cases reinforcing the conclusion that extra charges are unlawful in respect of distraint are *Megson* v. *Mapleton* (1884) 49 LT 744; *R.* v. *Smith & Others ex parte Porter* [1927] 1 KB 478 and *Headland* v. *Coster* [1905] 1 KB 219 (confirmed on appeal [1906] AC 286 HL).

Although there is limited case law on the legality of extra charges in distraint, there is extensive authority in respect of sheriffs' officers levying execution. Scales have been provided for their charges since the reign of Henry VI (and see 2 Co Inst on Statute of Westminster I c.26). It is clear that, whatever the reason, charges not in accordance with the scale are not permissible. This is the case whether:

- *the bailiff has been put to extra trouble or expense*: this will include extra costs of keeping possession, whether with extra bailiffs or for an extended period (*Davies* v. *Edmonds* (1843) 12 M&W 31; *Jones* v. *Robinson* (1843) 11 M&W 758; *R.* v. *Fereday* (1817) 4 Price 131; *Halliwell* v. *Heywood* (1862) 10 WR 780), or other extra expenses arising from inconvenience (*Lane* v. *Sewell* (1819) 1 Chit 175; *Slater* v. *Hames* (1841) 7 M&W 413);
- *the extra fee is not excessive*: however reasonable a fee may be, if it is contrary to law it cannot be allowed (Abbott CJ at 566 in *Dew* v. *Parsons* (1819) 2 B&A 562);
- *it has become customary to make additional charges:* usage and custom cannot be claimed as a defence however reasonable the extra fee may be (*Dew* v. *Parsons* (1819) 2 B&A 562). See also *Gill* v. *Jose* (1856) 6 E&B 718 where charging double the allowed mileage, as was the local practice, was deemed illegal; or,
- *the fees are illegal*: if there is no statutory authorisation for a fee it cannot be recovered as at common law the sheriff is entitled to no compensation (Best J at 568 in *Dew* v. *Parsons* (1819) 2 B&A 562). See also *R.* v. *Palmer* (1802) 2 East 411.

In all the cases the sheriff was ordered to repay the excess plus costs.

Is there a separate contract? If the argument for statutory bar on extra charges is wrong, consideration must be given to bailiffs' commonly advanced proposition that a "separate contract" has been made with the debtor for the recovery of such sums. Separate must be understood to mean separate from the process of distress and irrecoverable under that distress. Is such a contract is permissible, is it a genuine agreement and is it valid? It is worth also noting that the Court of Appeal in *Day* v. *Davies* (above) stated "*As for special agreements, where a prohibition under statute is absolute, it cannot be waived by the party for whose benefit it is made. If an act is prohibited, it cannot be the subject of a valid contract. No special agreement as to charges for an act of distress, other than those permitted by the rules, can be made* *and the agreement relied upon to justify a [*non-statutory charge*] cannot be enforced*". From this, it would seem that the separate contract idea fails for the reasons already given. However attention should be paid to two cases that seem to reach different conclusions.

In *Robson* v. *Biggar* [1907] 1 KB 690 the court held that it was permissible for a person and bailiff to agree to pay fees extra to the statutory scale as long as each party consented. However the case concerned a landlord making the agreement and the statute in question, the Distress (Costs) Act 1817, was aimed primarily at preventing the "great oppression of poor tenants". From this it would appear that the court may well not have upheld an agreement for extra fees by a debtor because of the risk of oppression, excessive charges and an unfair bargaining position. Creditors are in a different position as they can always refuse, negotiate or employ a different bailiff if they are unhappy with the service. See also the dissenting judgment of Darling J which is discussed later.

Further in *Lumsden* v. *Burnett* [1898] 2 QB 177 CA, in a dispute about possession charges, it was suggested by Chitty LJ at 186 that the court may sanction an agreement by the debtor to pay for a man in walking possession, which was then not allowable and therefore a wrongful charge, if such a charge was getting rid of the unnecessary inconvenience of man in possession and was therefore to the debtor's benefit. The learned Judge remarked that there is nothing in the statute to stop a debtor contracting out of the protection given to them if it would be to their advantage to agree to constructive rather than actual possession (and to pay for it). However this remark is obiter to the substance of the appeal so that the decision is not a clear authority. It must be contrasted with *Phillips* v. *Viscount Canterbury* (1843) 11 M&W 619, a sheriff's case, in which it was explicitly decided that a charge not permitted by the scale is not recoverable, even though the action in question – private sale by bill of sale – was more advantageous to the parties than sale at auction. It is certain, though, that charges not to the debtor's benefit would still not be condoned by the court.

Separate agreements are often justified by provisions in charges scales that prescribe the contents of a possession agreement, but which are "*(without prejudice to such other terms as may be agreed)*". Examples are para. 2(2)(c) sch. 5 CT(A&E) Regulations or para. 2(3) sch. 2 CS(C&E) Regulations. This phrase, it has been suggested, justify arrangements to pay extra sums. It is questionable if this was actually Parliament's intention. A glance at the prescribed form of walking possession to be found in the DRR suggests what other terms may have actually been intended – an agreement to inform the bailiff if other bailiffs call, an agreement to inform that latter bailiff that distress has already been levied. Agreements to make additional charges are therefore probably not intended, and, in any event, are not properly part of a walking possession agreement.

Can an agreement for extra charges made in these circumstances be valid? The argument may be analysed as follows:

- the bailiff is collecting the tax due as agent for a local authority etc. An agent's powers are limited to those of the principal (see 12.1). Hence, bailiffs as agents can only charge what the local authority can charge. On this basis extra charges are questionable;

- if the debtor consents to pay an extra amount, what is the bailiff's consideration? What the bailiff offers is forbearance of their statutory and contractual duties – i.e. removal of goods is postponed. The power to collect certain debts by either seizing goods or money is given by Parliament. In giving time to pay under threat of distress the bailiff as agent is doing no more than exercising discretion in the application of the principal's statutory powers. Performing one's duty as an officer of the law certainly was not regarded as consideration in the earliest cases (*Bridge* v. *Cage* (1605) Cro Jac 103; *Darlye's Case* (1631) 124 ER 433). More recently it has become acceptable to pay for performance of legal duties in some contexts (e.g. paying witnesses) as long as this is not against public policy. The cases already quoted suggest that the courts could still feel that public policy considerations (namely, preventing the exploitation of debtors) would be an objection against extra charges by bailiffs. However agreeing to perform an act over and above one's legal duty has been held in contract law cases to be good consideration. In other words doing more than the bare minimum required by the law entitles the officer in question to require extra payment. Despite this general principal though, it will be noted that in the numerous sheriff's cases that could be cited that the courts have consistently felt that in the context of execution going to extra trouble was a cost the sheriff would have to carry, and that it could not be passed on. Thus forbearing to do one's statutory duty (or more than the minimum) does not seem to be genuine consideration;
- even if giving time to pay is valid consideration from the bailiff, another principle of agency law is that an agent may not make a private profit from the agency. It would therefore not be unreasonable for the court to wish to be satisfied that any charge being made solely reflects the cost incurred by the bailiff firm, and includes no element of profit (see also 12.1.2);
- the decision in *Foakes* v. *Beer* (1884) 9 App Cas 610 HL has bearing in this matter as it was held that allowing a debtor to pay a judgment by instalments was not a valid agreement that prevented enforcement of the debt. The creditor's "forbearance and indulgence" in giving time to pay an obligation that is already fully due is not consideration that constitutes a binding contract with the debtor – it is a "nudum pactum" without legal consideration (see also *Williams* v. *Stern* [1879] 5 QB 409). Again it appears that the only extra charges that may be allowable would be those for identifiable extra expenses incurred by the bailiff, but not liaison and negotiation with the creditor;
- is a contract made in the context of seizure of goods valid simply because of the inequality of bargaining power between the two parties? Under the purported threat of distress (though in fact their remedy would be to sue in the county court) the bailiffs require the debtor to make extra payments. Agreements made under such duress could well be invalid, if not criminal. In a dissenting judgment in *Robson* v. *Biggar* (1907) 1 KB 690 Darling J held that separate bargains are outlawed by statute, which sets the maxima that can be charged, in order to protect the debtor "*who [is] in too bad a position to be able to resist exorbitant demands*".
- finally, these "separate" agreements are never actually separate. The charges are never part of a contract distinct from the walking possession agreement. They are

mixed in with the permissible scale charges and seem to all be enforceable by distress. There is never any suggestion that the bailiff would sue separately for them, which is of course their only real remedy for non-payment. See also 12.1.2 on this matter in the context of agency law.

11.3 Remedies for disputed charges

Generally specific remedies will have to be employed for challenging disputed charges. It will probably not be possible to sue for trespass or illegal distress, as an overcharge alone is not such a tort as to render a distress unlawful (*Shorland* v. *Govett* (1826) 108 ER 181, 5 B&C 485), though it should be noted that the court in *Hickman* v. *Maisey* [1900] 1 QB 752 observed that the decision in Shorland might have been otherwise had the facts been slightly different. The sheriff left as soon as the full sum, including the wrongful costs, had been paid. It is conceivable that remaining in possession solely to receive the unlawful charges might have caused the court to view the bailiff's presence as no longer legitimate or reasonable, and hence trespass.

11.3.1 Taxation

Taxation may be used to challenge all the aspects of a bailiff's bill as discussed in 11.2. Any of the scale costs in distress are open to taxation by a county court and usually the regulations or rules will refer to this right – see for example r.11(1) DRR or para. 3(2) sch. 5 CT(A&E) Regulations.

Procedure A debtor may apply for taxation within three months of the receipt of the bill under O.38 r.22(1) CCR. This rule permits the court to tax any costs, fees or expenses under "any Act or statutory instrument". The notable exception from these powers is magistrates' court distraint. This is because the charges are set by the contract between bailiff and court, and are not laid down in regulations.

Application is under CPR Part 8 "alternative claims procedure" to the county court or on request to the Sitting Master's clerk in the High Court, without any summons or order, in respect of sheriff's fees. The court may allow a "reasonable amount in respect of all costs reasonably incurred" with any doubts as to the reasonability being resolved in favour of the paying party. The court can allow the bailiff the costs of the taxation (*Butler* v. *Smith* (1895) 39 SJ 406) or allow costs to a debtor who is successful in opposing the fees. A person cannot appeal sums decided by taxation (*Townsend* v. *Sheriff of Yorkshire* (1890) 24 QBD 612), but the principles of the taxation can be appealed (*Re: Beeston* (1899) 1 QB 626).

Note that there is a link between certification and overcharging. Under r.11(3) DRR if at the end of a taxation under the DRR a district judge feels overcharging has occurred of such magnitude that the bailiff's fitness to hold a certificate has been called into question, and the court where the taxation took place is not the court where the certificate was granted, a copy of the taxed bill endorsed with the district judge's opinion is sent to the relevant court and acts like a certification complaint (see 6.2.10).

11.3.2 Pay and sue

An alternative civil remedy for an aggrieved debtor would be to sue for money "had and received". A number of cases illustrate the application of this remedy in the case of charges and confirm that there would be grounds for an action against a bailiff.

The debtor's course of action is to pay the disputed debt under protest and then start an action to recover any sums wrongfully paid on the grounds that they were paid under duress. This is technically known as an action for money "had and received" by the bailiff and is found as such in the older case reports. The debtor sues for money paid to the bailiff but which rightfully belongs to him/her. Such an action is not an action for damages: the defendant's liability to the plaintiff is that s/he has unjustly benefitted from the plaintiff's money. The debtor may sue not only the bailiff but, in the case of High Court execution, the sheriff – even though there may be no evidence of the unlawful fees coming into his hands from the sheriff's officer (*Jons* v. *Perchard* (1797) 2 Esp 507); and, in the case of distress and distraint, the principal who instructed the bailiff (*Dawe* v. *Cloud & Dunning* (1849) 14 LTOS 155).

Payment under duress in the context of distress means compulsion under which a person pays money to a bailiff through fear for their property (or the property of a close family or household member) being wrongfully seized or detained. The distress in question may be threatened or actual. The payment must not be voluntary, defining which can be difficult, but the debtor should be expected to have made it clear that they were paying the sum claimed under protest (*Atlee* v. *Backhouse* (1838) 3 M&W 633). Ideally the fact that payment was being made under protest should have been conveyed by unambiguous words or in writing, but the court may find that the circumstances of payment or the plaintiff's conduct are sufficient indication of their intention. Establishing that payment was made under protest is important to the plaintiff because the general rule is that seizure in a legal distress is **not** illegal pressure and any payment made by the debtor to release goods is simply submission to that form of legal process. Money paid to release goods in the custody of the law is thus not paid under duress and cannot be recovered (*Liverpool Marine Credit* v. *Hunter* (1868) LR 3 Ch App 479). Consequently there must be some wrongful element in the levy and the debtor, in paying, would have to make clear that this was not seen as an end to the matter but simply a way of retaining use of the goods rather than being deprived of them during lengthy litigation over the alleged illegality (*Green* v. *Duckett* (1883) 11 QBD 275).

There is some uncertainty whether the remedy applies to all forms of distraint. The authorities are as follows:

- *execution* It is clear that the debtor could sue in this way to recover excess fees charged in cases of execution (*Blake* v. *Newburn* (1848) 17 LJQB 216). If a public officer such as a sheriff demands an illegal or excessive fee for performing his legal duties it is extortion "colore officii" and the fee or excess is recoverable (*Dew* v. *Parsons* (1819) 2 B&Ald 562).
- *statutory distraint* In *R.* v. *Judge Philbrick & Morey ex parte Edwards* (1905) 2 KT 108 a bailiff distrained for rates on a gold watch and brooch, sold them and retained a sum for costs amounting to six times the debt and reputedly covering removal, storage, possession, delivery to sale yard and haulage. Edwards began a county court action claiming the sums were unreasonable, which the judge refused to hear. On appeal it was confirmed that there was indeed a right of action as noted

in *Nott* v. *Bound* (1866) LR 1 QB 405 – the bailiff "*might be liable to be made to refund by an action in the county court charges which were unnecessary or not strictly lawful*" (even if they had been charged in error for acts that had been done and were not excessive). See also *Maskell* v. *Horner* [1915] 3 KB 106.

- *distress for rent* It may be harder to make a successful claim in cases of distress for rent (*Glynn* v. *Thomas* (1856) 11 Exch 870; *Yates* v. *Eastwood* (1852) 6 Exch 805; *Skeate* v. *Beale* (1840) 11 Ad & El 983). These actions were often begun in cases of illegal or irregular distress and were rejected on the grounds that such bailiffs' offences attract their own remedies such as replevin or an action for trespass and therefore, in such cases, payment by the tenant is to be deemed voluntary. It is more likely that an action would succeed where there has been excessive distress, where the measure of the money had and been received is the excessive sum sought by the creditor (*Loring* v. *Warburton* (1858) EB & E 507 or *Fell* v. *Whittaker* [1871] LR 7 QB 120), or where the goods have been sold so that replevin is impossible. See also *Hills* v. *Street* [1828] 5 Bing 37 in which a tenant requested a broker not to proceed with the sale of his goods on payment of his charges. A dispute however arose over the charges and Best CJ held that he would "*allow the legal expenses of the distress and inventory but the other charges were made (and paid) improperly and the plaintiff was entitled to recovery*" by an action for money had and received. The action is certainly appropriate where bailiff's fees are at issue and especially where an element of fraud could be shown in the purported contract between bailiff and debtor (*Clarke* v. *Dickenson* [1858] EB&E 148).

This remedy would be pursued by the debtor commencing an action for a liquidated sum which the defendant must have received. There can be no action where the defendant has received goods instead of money (*Leery* v. *Goodson* [1792] 4 Term Rep 687) unless the goods in question can easily be converted to money (e.g. securities). Electing to sue this way extinguishes any right to damages on the part of the debtor, although it is possible for a plaintiff to sue for trespass or money had and received on the same summons.

11.3.3 Magistrates' court remedies

There are several remedies for overcharging possible through the magistrates' court.

Prosecution of the bailiff under the Theft Act 1968 for either:

- *deception* – under s.15 a person who by any deception dishonestly obtains property (including money) belonging to another with the intention of permanently depriving the other of it, shall on conviction on indictment be liable to imprisonment for a term not exceeding 10 years; or,

- *blackmail* – a person is guilty of blackmail under s.21 if, with a view to gain for himself or another or with an intent to cause loss (monetary or property) to another, he or she makes (either verbal or written) any unwarranted demand with menaces. Menaces include any threats of action detrimental to or unpleasant to the person addressed. Words or conduct are menaces if they are likely to operate on the mind of a person of ordinary courage or firmness so as to make him/her accede unwillingly to the demand. A defence could be that the bailiff acted in the belief that there were reasonable grounds for the demand or the use of menaces was the proper means of re-enforcing the demand. On conviction the person is liable to up to fourteen years imprisonment.

Complaint under the Magistrates Court Rules against the court's own bailiff. From the proceeds of sale the magistrates' bailiff may retain their charges and should return any balance to the owner of the goods after clearing the sum due (r.54(9)). A bailiff can be fined up to £200 for exacting high or improper costs (s.78(5) MCA). It is not possible for a defendant to seek taxation of charges made in the levy of magistrates' distraint as there is no statutory provision providing a scale of charges, but this provides an alternative remedy.

11.3.4 Complaint under the Sheriff's Act

It is an offence under s.29(2) Sheriffs Act 1887 to breach any terms of the Act (see 5.4.1). The sheriff may be sued by the complainant for a penalty plus damages, or action may be taken to punish the officer for a misdemeanour or for contempt. Under s.20(2) of the Act the officer "may demand, take, and receive such fees as may from time to time be fixed". As stated at 11.1.3 the current fees are fixed by the Sheriff's Fees Order 1920. Any overcharge is therefore an offence though this remedy cannot be used where the charges made had been imposed without malice or with reasonable or probable cause. Thus an innocent mistake may be excused where there is no culpability (*Lee* v. *Dangar, Grant & Co* (1892) 2 QB 337) or there has been a clerical error (*Shoppee* v. *Nathan & Co* (1891) 1 QB 245). An unintentional overcharge is not misconduct by the sheriff but an action can be taken for excessive fees (*Blake* v. *Newburn* (1848) 17 LJQB 216). However see *Braithwaite* v. *Marriott* (1862) 1 H&C 591 in which a sheriff was successfully sued for an overcharge and for contempt.

PART FOUR – GENERAL REMEDIES & CONCLUSIONS

Chapter Twelve

COMPLAINTS TO CREDITORS AND BAILIFFS

12.1 Contracts

In most cases there will be a written contract between creditor and bailiff. Contracts are the norm where local authorities are the creditors, and the Lord Chancellor's Department has recently recommended that magistrates' courts should adopt contractual relationships with their bailiffs, rather than the more informal "non-binding agreements" that have been preferred in the past.

12.1.1 Contractual terms

The bailiff's power to levy derives from the warrant that is issued. The purpose of the contract is to regulate the general administration of enforcement by distress and to ensure that distress is conducted in an acceptable manner. Contracts will normally be for a fixed period of time. Typical terms in a contract will cover such issues as timescales for enforcement (the period of time which is to be allowed for a bailiff to execute a warrant and the number of visits that should be made to try to do that), the charges to be made, cash handling (the frequency with which monies should be remitted to the creditor), monitoring of the bailiffs' activities and the conduct of levies themselves (this latter issue is normally governed by a code of practice – see 12.2).

It will of course not be possible to get access to the detailed contract between bailiff and creditor, but elements relevant to the treatment of debtors will often be revealed by either the creditor or the bailiff, and codes of practice are normally circulated freely.

12.1.2 Agency

Regardless of the detailed terms of the contract, the effect of it will be to make the bailiff the agent of the creditor so that, besides all the explicit terms of any agreement, there will be certain terms implicit as a result of the relationship of principal and agent. One is that the agent has the powers of the principal, but cannot exceed those powers. Thus, where statute gives a local authority the power to levy distraint in a certain way, the bailiff may exercise those same powers, but may not go beyond them. There is an implied authority to do all subordinate acts necessary or incidental to the exercise of that authority – though these may be restricted by codes of practice and the like (see later). Where an agreement is vague, an agent acts in good faith if s/he uses discretion, places a reasonable construction on the principal's authority and seeks to act in the best possible manner for the principal. If the agreement is clear, there is no right to exercise discretion. Authority cannot be given to act illegally and the agent cannot seek reimbursement from the principal for performing any illegal act.

Secondly, as the agency relationship is a fiduciary one, there is an implicit term that the agent must not acquire any profit or benefit from the agency not contemplated by the principal at the time of making the contract. To receive such sums is a breach of duty (*Rogier* v. *Campbell* [1939] Ch 766). This duty is combined with the requirement that the agent should not put their agency in conflict with their own interests and therefore must not enter into any transaction likely to produce that result (*Phipps* v. *Boardman* [1965] Ch 992), unless it has been fully disclosed to the principal and consented to by him/her. Any profit must be accounted for to the principal and the whole benefit paid over less any commission and expenses – it cannot be pocketed by the agent (*De Busscher* v. *Alt* (1878) 8 Ch D 286). This appears to have implications for separate agreements with debtors over the payment of "non-statutory" fees as discussed in chapter 11. Note *Erskine, Oxenford & Co* v. *Sachs* [1901] 2 KB 504 in which it was held that such a "secret" profit made out of a share deal should be accounted for to the creditor – and also that failing to separate private and agency elements in the deal and treating it all as one transaction to the benefit of the agent made the agents liable to make payment to the principal. The agent cannot defend such a claim on the basis that in acting for the principal, the agent incurred a possibility of loss (*Williams* v. *Stevens* (1866) 1 PC 352).

Generally the principal will be responsible for those acts of the agent that are expressly authorised or procured or are within the scope of the agent's apparent or implied authority. Thus if the agent exceeds that authority, the principal may become responsible for acts of illegal distress and may be sued along with or instead of the bailiff (*Megson* v. *Mapleton* (1884) 49 LT 744; *Re: Caidan* [1942] Ch 90). The principal will be liable whether the bailiff's wrongful act is deliberate or arises from carelessness, provided that it was in execution of the warrant and for the benefit of the principal (*Dawe* v. *Cloud & Dunning* (1849) 14 LTOS 155). If the act in question is completely outside the agent's authority, there can be no joint and several liability (*Richards* v. *W. Middlesex Waterworks Co* (1885) 15 QBD 660 – in which the company was not liable for an assault committed by a bailiff executing a warrant in their name as such an excessive action was not within the fair scope of the bailiff's duty). But contrast this decision to that in *Dyer* v. *Munday & Price* [1895] 1 QB 742, in which a manager was held liable for an assault committed by an employee repossessing furniture on HP. It was held that the assault was in "furtherance of his employment" and that the employer was therefore liable. In addition the fact that the employee had been convicted did not affect or release the matter's liability in tort. The principal is also liable for any acts of the agent that are ratified. S/he then becomes liable for any tortious act as well. For examples of acceptance of illegal distraint see *Carter* v. *St Mary Abbot's Vestry* (1900) 64 JP 548 or *Whitehead* v. *Taylor* (1837) 10 A&E 210. Ratification must be a clear adoption of the acts in full knowledge of the facts (*Green* v. *Wroe* (1877) WN 130). Thus receipt of proceeds of sale of wrongfully seized fixtures without knowing the source of the money is not ratification (*Freeman* v. *Rosher* (1849) 13 QB 780; *Lewis* v. *Read* (1845) 13 M&W 834; *Haselar*

v. *Lemoyne* (1858) 5 CBNS 530), nor is offering to compromise an action (*Roe* v. *Birkenhead Railway* (1851) 7 Exch 36). However keeping goods illegally seized with knowledge of the illegality is evidence of ratification (*Becker* v. *Riebold* (1913) 30 TLR 142). Ratification relates back so an action done without authority becomes legal if it is later authorised – for example, a bailiff distrains without authority but later receives it and thus ceases to be liable (*Potter* v. *North* [1669] 1 Wms Saund 347(c); *Hull* v. *Pickersgill* (1819) 1 Brod & Bing 282). The principal will also be liable for acts that are a breach of his/her personal duty as principal and, of course, for acts jointly undertaken with the agent.

Otherwise the agent is personally liable for any wrongful act or ommission done on behalf of the principal as if it was done on his/her own behalf. Examples of such liability include:

- the bailiff signed a distress warrant and then after issue refused a tender of rent. The agent was personally liable for the illegal distress (*Bennett* v. *Bayes* (1860) 5 H&N 391);
- the bailiff illegally seized a lodger's goods and was liable under s.2 LDAA 1908 (*Lowe* v. *Dorling* [1906] 2 KB 772);
- an agent converted third party goods to the principal's use and was liable to the true owner for the full value (*Stephens* v. *Elwall* (1815) 4 M&S 259);

The issue of the bailiff's authority as agent is linked to the next section on codes of practice. Where an agent purports to do anything as agent of the principal s/he is deemed to warrant that s/he has, in fact, received authority from the principal to act in that way. If there is no such authority the agent may be sued by the third party for "breach of warranty of authority". Thus if a bailiff acts outside a code of practice, even though those actions may not amount to wrongful distress, those actions may still form the basis for an action for damages by the debtor or other aggrieved individual.

The damages that may be obtained in an action for breach of warranty of authority are the losses engendered by the absence of authority. The measure is based on what normally applies in cases of breach of contract, i.e. any fair and reasonable loss actually sustained as the natural or probable consequence of the breach. These damages reflect the position that the plaintiff would have been in had the representation been true and the position the person is in because it is untrue.

Finally if the agent makes wilfully false statements about his/her authority an alternative course of action is for the debtor to sue for deceit or to consider prosecution for obtaining pecuniary advantage by deception (see 11.3.3).

12.2 Codes of Practice

It is now normal practice for local authorities and central government agencies to impose codes of practice on bailiffs as part of the contract agreed between them. Magistrates' courts will not do this, relying instead on the firm itself having its own internal code, though the agreement made with the firm may well specify certain items that typically would be part of a code – for instance, those classes of debtors who should not face distraint, the information that should be given to a debtor when levying or the form and content of any standard letters to be used.

The formulation and publication of codes has at various times been recommended for local authorities by central government (DoE Practice Notes on council tax), by professional bodies – for example the Institute of Rating, Revenues and Valuation has drafted and promoted a model code for use by all revenues departments – and by representative bodies such as the Association of District Councils (guidance on distress for rent) and the Local Government Association (best practice recommendations on distraint for local taxes). Many codes are well-drafted and offer considerable additional protection, both by exempting vulnerable groups and by expanding upon the present legislation or clarifying or defining the law where it is either unclear or even absent. However criticisms may be made of some codes. In many local authorities codes are regarded as internal only, part of the private contracts between local authority and bailiff that may not be published. They are thus of little use either to the debtor or, indeed, to the creditor as a means of verifiable monitoring of bailiffs' activities. Furthermore in several cases known to the author codes have endorsed practice by bailiffs that were either illegal or of dubious legality. Whatever the contents of any contract or code between bailiff and creditor, it cannot authorise illegal acts and with the bailiff acting as agent for the creditor, both will be liable for any wrongful act.

Typical terms in codes include:

- *contact with the debtor:* the information and proof of identity that should be provided when contact is made with the debtor, the acceptable times of visits, guidance on means of entry and those with whom the debt being collected should be discussed;
- *vulnerable groups:* the exemption from distress of groups such as the recently bereaved or long term sick and disabled (and/or the need to report back to the creditor before further steps are taken against such individuals);
- *exempt goods:* comprehensive lists of goods which should be regarded as exempt from seizure (eg: children's toys or facilities for the disabled);
- *levies:* the proper procedure upon removal of goods and general guidance on the bailiffs' conduct – demeanour, appearance etc.

A notable example of detailed and comprehensive code that has been repeatedly referred to in the text is that drawn up by CSA.

12.3 Ombudsmen

Another (indirect) sanction may arise where there has been maladministration by a local authority by a local or central government department which has used a bailiff's services. A final informal remedy for the aggrieved debtor could be to complain to the relevant ombudsman eg: the Commission for Local Administration for local authorities or the Revenue Adjudicator for the Inland Revenue and Customs and Excise. Although the Revenue Adjudicator deals with most complaints regarding the Revenue and C&E, the other means of taking up a complaint would be through the Parliamentary Ombudsman. This service will certainly have a role in handling complaints about the CSA (see also 12.6). A person must complain within twelve months of the alleged injustice caused by maladministration by a government department or agency and must complain through their MP.

The maladministration that would form the basis of any complaint to an ombudsman includes error, ultra vires acts and failure to act eg: neglect and delay, failure to follow proper procedures or giving misleading (or inadequate) information. If a complaint is upheld following investigation by the ombudsman it is usual to recommend review of and improvements in administration and the award of compensation to the individual. Bailiff related problems fairly frequently form the basis of complaints to the Local Government Ombudsman, typically arising from poor communications between the council and bailiffs and failure to keep adequate records and accounts.

12.4 Judicial review

The scope for the use of judicial review against ultra vires or otherwise wrongful decisions by government bodies in respect of their use of the power of distress is generally little explored. There appear to be grounds upon which judicial review could be employed: for instance to review a decision to use distress in circumstances when it was unlawful; to review an unreasonable use of the remedy, particularly where there has been a mistake as to the facts, or to review an improper policy, such as a code of practice, in its application to the individual client. It will be up to practitioners to explore the possibilities of the remedy, but one major restriction will be the expectation that other avenues of appeal will have been tried first. The existence of replevin and actions for illegal distress and the like will inevitably limit the scope for judicial review. There is little authority on its use, but there is one nineteenth century authority to the effect that the court will not grant prohibition against a magistrates' court issuing a warrant unless it has done so in excess of its jurisdiction (*Ricardo* v. *Maidenhead Board of Health* (1857) 27 LJMC 73).

12.5 Damages actions

12.5.1 Misfeasance in public office

Even if an unlawful action is quashed by judicial review, there is not as a consequence any liability in tort. There is however a developing area of tort, misfeasance in public office, upon which an aggrieved person may rely to recover damages for any loss, injury or damage resulting from an administrative action known by the relevant authority or officer to be unlawful or done maliciously. It is a new area of tort and little explored (see *Bourgoin SA* v. *Ministry of Agriculture* [1986] 1 QB 716; also *Jones* v. *Swansea City Council* [1989] 3 All ER 162).

The key elements of the tort of misfeasance are an abuse of power leading to damage, whether financial or loss of reputation and the like. There are two ways in which the tort may arise. Those actions motivated by malice are clearly misfeasance. Malice renders an action both ultra vires and tortious. However if it can be shown that the defendant knew his/ her actions to be illegal and likely to cause loss to the plaintiff there may also be the basis for a claim in misfeasance (*Three Rivers DC* v. *Governor & Company of the Bank of England* [1996] 3 All ER 558). In the second instance it must be shown that the officers knew their actions were unlawful, or were reckless about whether they were acting within their powers or whether damage would be caused. Recklessness may be proved by showing that the officer suspected that they were behaving in an ultra vires fashion, but failed to take reasonable steps to check the true position. The quantum of damages will include compensation for the plaintiff's losses, but may also include an exemplary element.

Any public authority may be sued, as may any individual officer. The action lies for both abuse of the individual's and the authority's power. The authority is not liable for the officer's action if the person behaved in a way that s/he knew to be deliberately unlawful and beyond his/ her powers.

The application of misfeasance to the area of distraint has only been examined in one case, that of *R.* v. *Hampstead Magistrates Court & another ex parte St Marylebone Property Company* (1995) Legal Action, September 1996 p.21 or Lexis, which was a judicial review case. In his judgment Carnwath J acknowledged that, despite the lack of proper pleadings or evidence on the matter, there were reasons for imputing to the local authority, Camden Borough Council, knowledge that their acts were unlawful: "*..one would have thought it possible to infer, in the absence of evidence to the contrary, that those responsible for rates were aware of something as basic as the ordinary requirements for service*" of demand notices for NNDR. However, the problem was that the levy of distress in question naturally rested upon a liability order from the magistrates' court. The validity of the order had not been challenged, therefore the council was entitled to rely upon it and regard the distraint as lawful. As knowledge of the illegality of one's acts is an important element in proving misfeasance, the judge did not find the claim proved in this case. From this it may be suggested that levies based on some form of court order or judgment are unlikely to be susceptible to challenge by this route. Those warrants issued by public officers without prior recourse to court (eg income tax and VAT) may still be.

12.5.2 Negligence

An alternative means of bringing the matter to court may be by means of an action for damages for negligence on the part of the Crown department or local authority, as they will be vicariously liable for the torts of their servants. Taking action for negligence may be preferable simply because there is no need to prove malice or deliberate illegality. It would also be possible to sue a bailiff's employer for negligent acts associated with the person's conduct of their job or to sue the principal instructing the enforcement agent. In such cases there would be joint liability on the part of bailiff and employer.

Where an operational task is carried out negligently or in excess of statutory power, there may be liability for negligence. Negligence can arise where a public body uses its powers in such a way that care is not taken to avoid foreseeable and proximate damage or it fails to act fairly, reasonably or with justice. The duty of care must be established, but a person is entitled to assume that a public body will comply with statutory regulations and seek to avoid any probable harm that could arise from their activities. As negligence is concerned with the defendant's conduct, it may be possible to claim for damages for both negligence and for another tort committed at the same time, for instance, trespass. There is no duty of care if a body is acting within a statutory discretion. Any matter of policy concerned with the exercise of discretion is not actionable – so an authority cannot be sued for choosing to use distress as against another remedy, but it may be sued for the manner in which distress was levied.

The plaintiff can sue only for such actual damage as can be proved. There is no right for nominal damages. The court may of course feel that no duty of care is owed in the exercise of certain statutory powers and duties, in the context of the statutory framework or if alternative remedies exist (such as replevin). An authority's defence may be that they were acting in good faith in a reasonable manner within their statutory powers. The defence may also be that the action complained of was outside the authority given to an employee and outside the scope of their employment.

12.6 Internal complaints

All creditors and most bailiffs' firms will operate some sort of internal complaints procedure which will obviously in most cases be the first stage in any effort to resolve a dispute. For instance the Child Support Agency has a customer services manager at each local child support centre to whom complaints should be addressed. If the complainant is not satisfied with their handling of the matter, the person can then take the matter to the Chief Executive of the CSA. If they are still not satisfied with the result of the investigation, they may take the matter to the independent complaints examiner. This procedure covers all matters that fall within the discretion of the CSA, such as the use of a particular recovery remedy or the rate of arrears repayment being demanded. In all cases the overriding consideration is the welfare of any children involved (s.2 CSA). This may involve striking a balance between the needs of the children for whom maintenance is being collected and any children of the absent parents' present relationship. The other remedy is to complaint to the Parliamentary Ombudsman (see 12.3).

12.7 Trade bodies

All the professional/ trade associations representing bailiffs have training programmes for members plus disciplinary codes and complaints procedures.

12.7.1 Sheriffs' Officers Association

The Sheriffs' Officers Association exists to regulate its members, maintain professional standards and lobby government. It bases its membership exams on the its handbook "Execution of Sheriff's Warrants" (see Appendix 3). It has an internal disciplinary procedure for dealing with complaints against members which deals with five or six complaints each year. Complaints about members of the Association are handled by a disciplinary committee which will seek the officer's comments and examine his records. They then seek to mediate between the parties. It is possible for an award of compensation to be made and for an officer to be expelled from the Association if the complaint is of sufficient gravity. The Under Sheriffs' Association can also investigate and arbitrate on disputes. They may be contacted c/o 6 Chapel Street, Preston, PR1 8AN.

12.7.2 Certificated Bailiffs' Association

The Certificated Bailiffs' Association (CBA) exists to represent both individual certificated bailiffs and firms. Those seeking membership must pass the Association's examination with marks in excess of 74 per cent and must have two referees supporting ther application. The CBA lobbies government, provides support and assistance to members and offers a professional qualification and has its own code of practice and disciplinary procedure.

Under the rules of the Association, the annually elected committee may investigate any accusation or complaint made against a member to the effect that he or she has acted illegally or brought the profession into disrepute. There are several stages to this.

- All complaints should be in writing and addressed to the Secretary. The Secretary can request information from the member which must be supplied within 14 days. Other members of the CBA can give advice on any legal points raised.
- A complaint with merit or otherwise deserving of the committee's attention is reported to it. The committee may consider the complaint on the basis of documents alone and, if the grievance is upheld, may recommend that certain penalties may be imposed. The member may be fined (with all or part suspended), suspended from the CBA, excluded from membership completely or given a "conditional discharge" i.e. no sanction will be imposed provided that there are no further complaints about the individual or firm.
- either the complainant or the member may ask for the complaint to go to the independent complaints assessors panel. The members of the panel are not bailiffs but are experienced in bailiff's law. Three assessors will consider the complaint either by studying documents or by hearing. The panel may impose a penalty as described above for the committee. The decision is ratified and enforced by the committee, unless the member appeals it as being inappropriately harsh, in which case a lesser penalty may be imposed. This in turn may be appealed to a general meeting if the CBA.

The major weakness in this procedure is any lack of direct compensation for the complainant.

The CBA also operates a code of practice which clearly is linked with the above disciplinary procedure. It seeks to promote high standards of ethics and business practice. Its major concerns are the handling of client money and proper, legal conduct by members.

12.2.3 Association of Civil Enforcement Agencies

The Association of Civil Enforcement Agencies (ACEA) exists to represent the larger firms operating nationally, lobbying on their behalf with government and other policy makers. It also aims to raise standards generally in the industry, the first element in this being the establishment of its complaint procedure.

The full member firms who subscribe to the Association and to the complaints procedure are: Madagans plc, John Crilleys Ltd, Jefferies & Pennicott, Drakes, Gaults, Rayner Ferrar & Co, Rossendales CB Ltd and Professional Recovery Services

Ltd. All Association members have undertaken to abide by the decisions reached at any stage in the complaints procedure and comply with whatever recommendation may be made.

The procedure works as follows. If a complaint is received by a member firm it will initially be handled internally. The complaint will be acknowledged immediately and will be responded to in writing within 14 days. That reply will be accompanied by the ACEA's leaflet explaining how the Association may become involved to reconsider the matter if the complainant is not satisfied with the firm's response.

Certain matters cannot be handled. These are:

- complaints about the amount of the debt/ penalty being collected. This sum was set by the creditor or court and is of course beyond the control of the bailiff firm. Fees are not excluded by this proviso;
- allegations of violence – which should be referred to the police;
- cases already subject to court proceedings. If the complainant has sued, issued replevin or commenced interpleader (see chapter 9), ACEA will not intervene.

If a complainant is unhappy with the firm's response s/he may then write to the Secretary of the ACEA at 16, Connaught St, London W2 2AF. This letter should include details of the complaint, proof of any financial loss suffered and a copy of the firm's reply. This will be acknowledged within three days of receipt and will be sent to three of the Association's directors for their consideration. They will not be connected to the member firm in question. The directors will meet to consider the complaint and may seek further information from the member firm as to its handling of the matter. If it is felt that the problem was not dealt with appropriately a remedy will be proposed (e.g. the return or remission of fees) and the firm will be asked to reconsider its decision. Both parties will be notified of this decision no later than 28 days after the complaint was received.

If the complainant is still not satisfied, s/he may ask that the matter be referred to a panel of independent complaints adjudicators. The panel members are drawn from the likes of local authorities, CABx and magistrates' courts. Three will be asked to sit as a panel to consider the complaint, and the aggrieved individual may attend in person to present their case. The offending bailiff or a representative of the firm will also be invited to be present. The ACEA has decided that it will be possible for parties to take along an adviser or other "McKenziefriend" to assist or support them.

If the panel is convinced that the individual's complaint is justified, it may recommend remission, reduction or refund of fees; payment of compensation based on the panel's assessment of the complainant's actual losses or both. Presumably it would also be expected for the member firm in question to issue a formal apology at the same time as any pecuniary restitution.

Notice of the decision is sent to the parties. If compensation is being recommended, it will be necessary for the complainant to confirm in writing that s/he accepts this in full and final settlement of the matter. The firm will then be obliged to pay as instructed.

The panel's decision is final. If the complainant still is not happy with the result, s/he will have to turn to the other remedies described earlier in the text.

The ACEA procedure is a welcome innovation. Few complaints seem to get to the panel stage and the rest have been resolved by the member firms themselves. Whether the low numbers so far dealt with reflect a lack of problems or a lack of awareness of the scheme is open to question. The ACEA complaints leaflet must be supplied by the firm itself, and obviously failure to do this would undermine the whole procedure (there is some evidence of difficulties with this). Secondly the strength of the scheme must depend on the member's own internal complaints handling procedures. The ACEA has not laid down any minimum standards for these. Consequently how well a matter is responded to (if at all) depends very much on the individuals concerned.

Conclusions

Enforcement law is a neglected but important area. Upon the successful enforcement of debts rests much central and local government revenue. Also the credibility of justice rests upon the ability of the successful party to put their judgment or order into effect. Thus, although the individual sums may be small, their recovery is vital. This economic need nevertheless must be balanced again a concern of society to deal fairly and sensitively with individuals in difficulty. The law of distress and execution sits uneasily with this as the bailiff depends upon his ability to be able to seize and sell personal possessions. In addition it is a remedy that operates almost entirely outside the courts and in the debtor's own premises. The fact that it concerns private difficulties and is conducted in the privacy of the debtor's home means that many problems remain hidden. There is potential for abuse and oppression in many ways. This is compounded by the archaic nature of many of the statutes and authorities. Whilst reform is essential, in the meantime practitioners need to monitor the enforcement process both to protect the vulnerable from illegal acts and in order to inform the review process as to the shortcomings and strengths of the present law.

FURTHER READING

Bradby, J. Law of Distress – London, 1828.

Buller Jr., Frances, An Introduction to the Laws regarding Trials at Nisi Prius, 7th ed., London, 1817.

Certificated Bailiffs Association – forthcoming 1999 – chapter by author on development of bailiffs law since 1601.

Coke, Sir Edward – on Littleton, First Part of Institutes – Second Part of Institutes of Laws of England, London, 1794.

Enever, F.A. A History of the Law of Distress, Routledge, 1931.

Espinasse, Isaac, Digest of law of actions and trials at Nisi Prius, 4th edn, London, 1812.

Feldman, Law Relating to Entry, Search and Seizure" (Butterworths 1986).

Fitzherbert, Anthony, The New Nativa Brevium, 9th edn, London, 1794.

G. Gilbert, Law & Practice of Distresses & Replevin – Impey, 1794

Halsbury's Laws of England: volume 13 (distress); volume 17 (execution).

Keith, Podevin & Sandbrook, Execution of Sheriff's Warrants – Barry Rose Ltd, 1996.

Kruse, J., Impounding by private bailiffs in distraint – Civil Justice Quarterly, v. 17, 1998.

— The Spoils of Law – an essay on the language of the early English and Celtic laws of distraint – Pontypridd, 1998.

— Civil Justice Quarterly, vol. 18 p.58, 1999.

Law Commission, Distress for Rent – Working Paper No.97, HMSO 1986.

Law Commission, Landlord & Tenant, Distress for Rent – Report No.97, HMSO 1991.

Lord Chancellor's Dept., A Review of the Organisation & Management of Civil Enforcement Agents: Consultation Paper – HMSO, August 1992.

Magor, Distress for Rent & Local Taxes – IRRV 1995.

Noy W., A Treatise of the Principal Grounds and Maxims of the Laws of the Kingdom, London, 1641.

Wigan & Maston, Mather on Sheriff & Execution Law – Gaunt & Sons, 1990.

Williams Prof. Glanville, "A Strange Offspring of Trespass Ab Initio" in *Law Quarterly Review* 1936, No. 52, p. 106, 1936.

— Liability for Animals, Cambridge, 1939.

INDEX

abandonment of goods 2, 33-5, 128-9, 203, 209
  impounding 122-7, 128-9, 130-1, 137-8
  interpleader 176
  re-entry rights 104
Abbott CJ 223
abuse of distrained goods 31, 182, 202
accounts 208-9
administration orders 47, 48, 58, 61
advertising sale 73, 203-4, 205, 217
agency contracts 231-3
aggravated damages 175, 185, 201, 215
  conversion 183
  trespass 108-9, 111, 184-5
agistment 166, 191
agricultural holdings 52, 86, 146-7, 156-7, 191
  distress for rent 166, 169, 171, 172-3
  exempt goods 169, 171, 172-3
  floating charges 164-5
aircraft 157
Allen CJ, Sir John 125
annexation of fixtures 142-4, 146, 152
antiques 139, 142
apparent possession 120, 125
appeals 23, 24, 25, 27, 136, 195
  drainage rates 7
  magistrates' court 113, 175
  resisting distress 30, 31, 37
  staying enforcement 14-17
appraisement 203, 204-5, 208, 213
armed forces 95, 183
arrest 12, 72, 78, 114
  entry rights 99, 102, 103, 106
  resisting distress 30, 33
art works 139
assault 74, 114, 128, 232
  entry rights 102, 105
  exemption of personal items 150
  resisting distress 28-32
  trespass to person 110-11
Association of Civil Enforcement Agencies (ACEA) 238-9
assumpsit 192
Atkin LJ 107

Bacon CJ 51, 120
bailiffs 1-5, 11-12, 13, 70-1, 81, 82-5, 90-1, 116, 242
  accounts 208
  cars 154
  certification 2, 3, 82-5, 226, 238
  charges 216-29
  common law distress 8-10
  competing claims 89-93
  complaints 113, 231-40
  concealing or removing goods 35
  criminal remedies 114, 191
  deceased debtors 151
  distrainor 80-5
  entry rights 99-106
  exempt goods 149-50, 169
  failed levies 37-8
  farming stock 156-7
  final warnings 93-4
  financial assets 140-1
  fixtures 144, 145
  floating charges 163-5
  identification 105
  impounding 119-38
  injunctions 112
  insolvency 45-9, 52-63
  interference with goods 181-5
  interpleader 176-81
  liable persons 95
  notice of seizure 194-6
  pay and sue 192-3
  place of execution 97-8
  preconditions 86
  protecting goods from seizure 31-5
  refusal of entry 28-30
  remedies 174-5, 213, 215
  rent remedies 189-91
  repeat levies 209-11
  replevin 187, 188
  resistance to distress for rent 38-9
  road traffic penalties 24-5
  sale 202-7
  saleable goods 139
  seizure procedure 117-19
  statutory distraint 6-8, 9
  staying enforcement 16, 17
  storage 200-2
  sums leviable 86
  tender and payment 196-9
  third party goods 157-8, 160-2
  time of execution 96
  transfers to third parties 39-44

bailiffs (*cont*):
  trespass 107-10
  VAT 23
  warrants 77, 79
  wrongful distress 65-7, 70-1, 72-4, 76
  wrongful execution 186
bankruptcy 45, 46-7, 48, 52, 53-4, 72
  competing claims 90
  distress for rent 49-58
  exempt goods 147, 149
  farming stock 156
  fixtures 146
  impounding 120, 124, 126
  incomplete executions 54-8
  leave to proceed 58-61
  repeat levies 209, 211
  resisting distress 37, 38
  security 62-3
  staying enforcement 14
  three month rule 63
  transfers to third parties 40, 424
  warrants 79
Beck J 9
bedding 73, 147, 148, 149
Best CJ 223, 228
bills of exchange 140-1
bills of sale 19, 41-4, 117-19, 139, 162
  charges 224
  exempt goods 169
  fixtures 145
  impounding 120, 125, 126
  insolvency 50, 55
  interpleader 176, 179
  resisting distress 36-7
  transfers to third parties 39, 40-4
binding effect of warrants 79-80
Bingham MR, Sir Thomas 136
Blackburn J 165
blackmail 228-9
Bowen LJ 1, 104
Bramwell LJ 117, 242
Bray J 10
breach of the peace 31-2, 114, 150, 173
  entry rights 103, 105, 106
Brown LJ, Simon 66, 116, 129, 132
Brown P, Sir Stephen 17
business assets 155-7

Campbell, LCJ 96, 191
Carnwath J 236
cars 5, 97, 139, 143, 152-4, 173-4, 202
  bills of sale 162
  charges 216, 221-2
  clamping 9, 133-5, 136-7, 153, 191-2
  exempt goods 147-8, 149, 153, 155
  title on sale 207
Certificated Bailiffs' Association (CBA) 200, 238
charges, costs and fees 2, 3, 7, 116, 181, 216-29
  accounts 208
  armed forces 95
  competing claims 91-2
  complaints 239
  contracts 231, 232
  conversion 183, 219
  disputed bills 219-29
  distrainor 83-4
  distress for rent 39, 165, 173, 216, 218-19, 222, 228
  excessive 2, 228-9
  farming stock 157
  final warnings 93
  financial assets 141
  illegal or improper 73, 83, 175, 199, 227
  impounding 121-4, 126, 127, 130, 131
  injunctions for trespass 112
  insolvency 56-7, 61, 217
  interpleader 176, 177-9, 181
  liability for sums claimed 20
  local taxes 27, 216, 219-21, 224
  notice of seizure 194, 195
  pay and sue 193
  possession warrants 11
  remedies 212-15
  removal and storage 201
  replevin 186-8, 228
  road traffic penalties 3, 24-5, 218, 221
  sale 203-7
  saleable goods 139
  scales 216-19
  seizure 117, 118, 119
  staying enforcement 15, 17
  sums leviable 85-6
  tender and payment 197, 198, 199
  third party goods 161
  treble for poundbreach 33
  wrongful distress 1, 66, 67, 73, 75
  see also possession fees
cheques 19, 140, 198, 222
Child Support Agency (CSA) 8, 25, 82, 140, 204
  accounts 208
  code of practice 234
  complaints 235, 237
  exempt goods 149, 150
  final warnings 93
  notice of seizure 195, 196
  place of execution 97
  tender and payment 197
  time of execution 96
child support maintenance 8, 25, 140, 192, 199, 213

charges 216
complaints 113
entry rights 105
impounding 130, 131
insolvency 47
preconditions 87
staying enforcement 16
wrongful distress 75, 174
children's goods 158
Chisholm J 118
Chitty LJ 12, 224
choses in action 140-1, 176, 190
clamping 9, 133-5, 136-7, 153, 191-2
close possession 121-2, 217
impounding 120, 121-2, 131, 134
see also possession man
clothes and apparel 73, 133, 150-1, 189
exempt goods 147-9, 150-1, 167
Cockburn CJ 67
Coleridge LCJ 216, 220
Collector of Income Tax 7, 23
Commission for Local Administration 234
community charge 3, 113, 123, 129, 174, 175
company administration 45, 48, 63
Company Administration Orders 48, 63
competing claims 89-93
complaints 4, 113, 174-5, 231-40
bailiffs' certificates 83-4
magistrates' courts 113, 123-4, 174-5, 229, 231
maintenance orders 87
concealing or removing goods 35-7
consequential damages 215
conversion 182-4
replevin 188
trespass 108, 110, 185
constructive possession 34, 40, 125-7, 128, 130-2
constructive seizure 118, 130-1, 144
contempt 12, 30, 73, 114, 229
insolvency 45
replevin 186, 187
continued possession 51-2
contracts 231-3
conversion 33, 35, 181-4, 185, 201, 212-13
charges 183, 219
impounding 120
insolvency 45, 51, 54, 55
sale 205-8
tender and payment 198, 199
third party goods 160, 161
transfers to third parties 41, 43
wrongful distress 65, 72, 75
Cooke J 127
costs *see* charges, costs and fees
council tax 3, 6, 26-7, 81, 234
counter levies 135-6
county court 4, 6, 8, 70-1, 73-4, 81, 86
accounts 208
business assets 155, 156
competing claims 89, 91, 93
costs 218, 220, 225, 226, 228
death of parties 85
distrainor 80, 81, 82, 83-4
entry rights 102, 103, 104
exempt goods 149, 150, 167
final warnings 94
financial assets 140
floating charges 165
impounding 122, 127, 135
injunctions for trespass 111
insolvency 45, 47, 53, 57, 61
interpleader 176-80
liability for sums claimed 22-4
notice of seizure 195
place of execution 97
preconditions 88
remedies 174, 191, 213
removal and storage 201
replevin 186-8
resisting distress 28, 30, 33, 38
sale 204, 207
staying enforcement 13, 15-16
tender and payment 199
warrants 78, 79
wrongful distress 67, 70-1, 73-4, 75
criminal remedies 114, 191-2
crops 9, 42, 156-7, 164, 215
distress for rent 166, 167, 172-3
Crown 10, 37, 47, 92, 152, 156-7
exempt goods 148, 168
replevin 186
warrants 78-80
Customs and Excise (C&E) 5, 7, 9, 52, 82, 133
competing claims 92
complaints 234-5
notice of seizure 195
VAT 3, 7, 23, 87

damage to impounded goods 182, 202
damages 107-9, 117, 174-5, 179-80, 191, 212-15, 235-7
abuse of distress 202
armed forces 95
charges 217, 227, 228, 229
clamping 136-7
complaints 233, 235-7
conversion 35, 51, 55, 160, 182-3, 205
crops 173
distrainor 84
distress damage feasant 9, 17-18
distress for rent 22, 38

damages (*cont*):
  double for fraudulent removal 1, 37
  double for wrongful distress 1, 191
  entry rights 99
  farming stock 157
  forced entry 117
  impounding 132, 136-7
  interference with goods 181, 182-5
  interpleader 177, 179-80
  replevin 188
  sale 203, 205, 207
  statutory distraint 7
  third party goods 157
  time of execution 96
  treble for poundbreach 1-2, 33-5
  treble for rescue 32, 35
  trespass 107-9, 110-12, 132, 184-5
  warrants 77
  wrongful distress 1, 65-75, 170, 191
  wrongful execution 186
  see also aggravated damages; consequential damages; exemplary damages; general damages; nominal damages; special damages
Danckwerts J 126
Darling J 224, 225
Davies LJ 122
death 21, 85, 95, 151-2, 189, 207
  insolvency 45
  partnerships 154
debentures 42, 155, 163-4, 176
deception 102, 228, 233
delay 89, 176, 187
  re-entry 103-4
  sale 202, 203
  wrongful distress 70, 72, 73, 75
delivery warrants 11
Denning, Lord 3
Denniston JA 153
diplomatic staff 95, 97
distrainor 80-5
distraint 1-3, 5, 6-8, 80-5, 115, 117-18, 174-5, 212-13
  abuse of goods 182
  charges 218-19, 221-3, 226-7, 229
  codes of practice 234
  competing claims 89-93
  contracts 231, 233
  damages 236
  death of parties 85
  defined 242
  distress damage feasant 174
  distress for rent 165-70, 173
  entry rights 99-107
  exempt goods 147-50
  final warnings 94
  financial assets 140
  floating charges 163-5
  impounding 119, 121, 124-6, 130-1, 134
  insolvency 46-53, 58-9, 61-3
  interpleader 177
  jointly owned goods 141
  liability for sums claimed 17-22, 23, 26
  mortgages 43-4
  notice of seizure 194, 195
  place of execution 97-8
  preconditions 86-9
  preventing seizure 31-4, 36
  prior levies 152
  rates 9-11
  repeat levies 209-11
  saleable goods 139
  staying enforcement 16-17
  storage 201-2
  sums leviable 85-6
  taxes 10-11
  tender and payment 197-9
  time of execution 96-7
  trespass 107, 108
  warrants 77, 79
  wrongful distress 65, 67, 75, 76
  see also statutory distraint
distress damage feasant 1, 9, 35, 98, 136-7, 173-4, 199-200, 212
  armed forces 95
  clamping 134, 136-7
  criminal damage 192
  entry rights 104
  excessive 66
  fresh pursuit 98
  impounding 18, 132, 134, 136-7
  liability for sums claimed 17-18
  protecting goods from seizure 31, 35
  repeat levies 210-11
  sale 202
  time of execution 96
  trespass 9, 17-18, 110, 174, 199, 202, 210
distress for rent 1-3, 8, 116, 165-73, 189-91, 212-14, 228, 242
  armed forces 95
  bills of sale 44
  business assets 156
  case-law 9-11
  charges 39, 165, 173, 216, 218-19, 222, 228
  codes of practice 234
  competing claims 89-92
  death of parties 85
  distrainor 80-1, 82-5
  entry rights 102, 105
  excessive 66-7
  exempt goods 20, 148, 165-73
  final warnings 93

financial assets 140
fixtures 141
floating charges 165
hire purchase 161
hired goods 160
impounding 121, 124, 125-6, 130, 131, 134
injunctions 112
insolvency 46-8, 49-58, 61
interpleader 177
liability for sums claimed 18-22
notice of seizure 20-1, 194-6
partnerships 155, 172
place of execution 97-8
preconditions 88-9
prior levies 152
removal and storage 200-1
repeat levies 210
replevin 22, 172, 186, 188-9
reservation of title clauses 162
resistance 32-3, 35-7, 38-9
sale 202-3, 204, 206, 208
statutory remedies 115
sums leviable 85-6
tender and payment 197-9
time of execution 96-7
trespass 21, 110, 112
warrants 79
wrongful 66-7, 71
dogs 29
Donaldson, Lord 106
doorstep levies 132-3
drainage rates 7
du Parcq LJ 144
duty of care 29, 117, 132, 154, 174
complaints 236-7
wrongful destruction 182

Ellenborough LCJ 90
enclosing 38-9
entry 99-107
failure 37, 106
illegal 28, 84
refusal 28-31, 37, 101-2
see also forced entry; re-entry
equitable interests 139-40
errors 30, 210, 211-15
charges 229
complaints 235
irregular execution 69-70, 74, 75-6
notice of seizure 195-6
time of execution 96
trespass 107-8
warrants 77
Esher MR, Lord 99
eviction 11-12, 16, 121
excessive distress 1, 65, 66-7, 71, 76, 213-15
charges 228
injunctions 112
inventory 196
remedies 175, 212-15
repeat levies 210
exemplary damages 191
conversion 183
trespass 109, 111, 184-5
exempt goods 2, 3, 117, 147-50, 166-71, 174, 189-91
armed forces 95, 183
business assets 155, 157
cars 147-8, 149, 153, 155
codes of practice 234
conversion 182, 183
distress damage feasant 173-4
distress for rent 20, 148, 165-73
farming stock 157
fixtures 157
hired 160
impounding 133
injunctions 112
interpleader 148, 150, 195
notice of seizure 150, 195-6
pay and sue 193
personal items 150-1
qualified 166, 204
replevin 186
sale 204
trespass 110, 112
wrongful distress 65, 73

false imprisonment 29, 72, 110
Farwell J 198
fees *see* charges, costs and fees
financial assets 140-1
fines 1, 7, 10, 75
entry rights 103
fraudulent removal 37
impounding 134
insolvency 47
liability to pay sums claimed 27
preconditions 87
replevin 186
rescue 33
tender and payment 199
warrants 77
Fitzgibbon HHJ 148
fixtures 43, 141-7, 167, 185, 232
heirlooms 152
third party goods 157-8
floating charges 61, 163-5
forced entry 28-9, 35, 37, 99-101, 103-5, 106, 117
criminal remedies 114
interpleader 180

forced entry (*cont*):
removal and storage 200-1
seizure of cars 153, 154
third party premises 98
trespass 99-101, 104, 108, 110
warrants 11, 12
wrongful distress 65, 69, 74
forestalling 38
Fraser J 10
fraud and fraudulent removal 1, 35-7
charges 228
competing claims 91
impounding 130
insolvency 55, 58, 61
title on sale 207
transfers to third parties 39, 44
wrongful distress 67
fresh pursuit 98, 115
furniture 42, 44, 126, 159, 232
exempt goods 148, 149, 168
heirlooms 152
saleable goods 139

garnishee order 5
general damages 107-8, 175
complaints 113
conversion 182, 183
interference with goods 182-5
trespass 107-8, 111, 184
gifts 39-41, 42, 44, 80, 159
children's goods 158
deceased debtors 151
goods subject to prior levies 152, 167
Greene MR, Lord 190
Grose J 222

Hanworth MR, Lord 32, 125
harbour rates and dues 5, 10
Hardwick CJ 100
heirlooms 152
High Court 5-6, 175, 216-18
business assets 155
charges 216-18, 226, 227
competing claims 89, 92
complaints 113
conversion 183
counter levies 135
exempt goods 150
insolvency 48, 62
interpleader 176, 177-8, 179, 180
liability to pay sums claimed 22-3
notice of seizure 195
partnerships 155
possession warrants 11
replevin 186-8
resisting distress 33
sale 202, 203
saleable goods 140
staying enforcement 13-15, 16
warrants 78
wrongful distress 65, 73, 75
wrongful execution 186
hire purchase 141, 143-4, 161, 167, 169-70, 172
bills of sale 162
cars 154
complaints 232
delivery warrants 11
interference with goods 182-3, 184
interpleader 161, 176
title on sale 206, 207
hired goods 118, 141, 160-1, 167, 169, 170, 171
interpleader 160, 176
resisting distress 34
title on sale 206, 207
warrants 80
Hirst LJ 136-7
Hitcham J 202
Holt J 10

illegal distress 1, 22, 65, 66, 71, 138
charges 226, 228
complaints 113, 232, 233, 235
conversion 183
entry rights 102-3, 106
exempt goods 170
notice of seizure 196
prior levies 152
remedies 174-5, 183, 186-8, 191, 211-12
replevin 186-7, 188
tender and payment 198, 199, 200
time of execution 96
trespass 107, 112
warrants 77
impounding 2, 119-38, 242
abuse of goods 31, 182
cars 153
competing claims 90, 91
criminal remedies 114
crops 172
death of cattle 210
distress damage feasant 18, 132, 134, 136-7
insolvency 50, 62
interference with goods 182
levies procedure 116-38
problems 128-38
re-entry 103, 128-9, 137
rescue 32-5
sale 203
storage 201, 202
tender and payment 199

inability to pay 13-14
income tax 7, 23, 43, 89, 94, 141, 174, 212
  competing claims 92
  complaints 236
  distrainor 82
  entry rights 103
  exempt goods 148
  financial assets 140
  insolvency 47
  inventories 196
  see also Inland Revenue
incomplete executions 54-6
indemnity 151, 157
Individual Voluntary Arrangements (IVAs) 45, 46, 47, 48, 62
injunctions 111-12, 135, 181, 185
Inland Revenue 9, 52, 82
  complaints 234-5
  entry rights 102, 103
  hire purchase 161
  jointly owned goods 141
  notice of seizure 195
  see also income tax
insolvency 45-63, 208
  charges 56-7, 61, 217
  interpleader 48, 55-6, 57, 176
  wrongful distress 69, 70
instalment payments 54, 86, 129, 196-7, 198, 211
  bills of sale 42-3
  charges 218, 222, 225
  competing claims 92-3
  preconditions 87, 89
  staying enforcement 13-16
  local taxes 26
Institute of Rating, Revenues and Valuation 234
insurance premium tax 7
interest 25, 42, 67, 179, 183
interference with goods 28, 65, 181-5, 200, 208
  clamping 135
  transfers to third parties 39, 44
  trespass 108, 110, 181-3, 184-5
interim orders 46, 47, 62
interpleader 6, 175-81
  complaints 239
  exempt goods 148, 150, 195
  floating charges 163
  hire purchase 161, 176
  hired goods 160, 176
  impounding 127, 137
  insolvency 48, 55-6, 57, 176
  notice of seizure 177-8, 195
  partnerships 155, 176, 180
  sale 179, 204, 206, 207
  saleable goods 139
  second warrants 211
  spouses' goods 159, 176
  transfers to third parties 39, 41, 43
  trespass 112, 177, 180
  wrongful distress 68, 71
inventories 66-7, 116, 118-19, 170, 190, 194-5, 196
  bills of sale 42-3
  charges 228
  impounding 119, 121, 124, 126, 130, 133
  interpleader 178
irregular distress 1, 65, 66, 175, 211-13, 214-15
  charges 228
  complaints 113
  notice of seizure 196
  poundage 218
  prior levies 152
  sale 207, 208
  tender and payment 198, 199
  time of execution 96-7

Jacob, Sir Jack 3
Jessell, Sir George 48
jewellery and watches 132-3, 139, 159, 227
  doorstep levies 132-3
  exempt goods 149, 150, 167
joint debt 50, 95
jointly owned goods 141, 157, 172
  conversion 184
  interpleader 180
  replevin 186
  spouses 159-60, 169
Jones, Sir W M 98
judicial review 16, 67, 235, 236
  counter levies 136

keys 84, 101
Kilbrandon, Lord 183

landfill tax 7
landlords 1, 89-92, 118-19, 189-91, 212-14
  business assets 156-7
  charges 217, 224
  clamping 134
  conversion 183
  death of tenant 85
  distress for rates 10
  distress for rent 1-3, 8-10, 18-22, 80-1, 84, 88, 166-7, 170-3
  entry rights 101, 104
  fixtures 145, 146, 147
  floating charges 164
  impounding 2, 121, 126-7, 134
  injunctions 112
  insolvency 49-52, 53, 63
  interpleader 177

landlords (*cont*):
  notice of seizure 195
  place of execution 97-8
  prior levies 152
  repeat levies 209-10
  resisting distress 33-9
  sale 203, 204, 206, 208
  statutory remedies 115
  storage 201
  sums leviable 85-6
  tender and payment 197-8
  third party goods 158, 161
  time of execution 96
  transfers to third parties 39, 44
  warrants 79
  wrongful distress 66-7, 72
legal aid 84
liability orders 7, 46, 47, 67, 75, 123
  warrants 77, 78
liability for sums claimed 17-28, 95-6
life assurance policies 141
Lindley LJ 9
Littleton J 69
local authorities 6-8, 81, 174
  charges 219-20, 224
  codes of practice 233-4
  complaints 231, 233-4, 236-7, 239-40
  contracts 231
  entry rights 103
  impounding 129
  insolvency 47
  instalment payments 196
  local taxes 26
  road traffic penalties 24
Local Government Association 234
Local Government Ombudsman 235
local taxes 6, 26-7, 81, 86, 123-4, 174, 213
  armed forces 95
  charges 27, 216, 219-21, 224
  codes of practice 234
  complaints 113
  criminal remedies 192
  distrainor 81, 82, 84
  entry rights 103, 105
  failed levy 38
  financial assets 140
  impounding 122, 123-4, 130-1, 133
  insolvency 47, 52
  liability to pay sums claimed 25, 26-7
  mortgaged goods 43
  notice of seizure 195, 196
  place of execution 97
  sale 202
  sums leviable 85
  tender and payment 196-7, 199
  trespass 110
  warrants 78
  wrongful distress 67, 75
  see also rates
locksmiths 100
London 8, 189
Lopes J 73
Lord Chancellor's Department 2, 3, 4, 16, 149, 200
  certification 84
  contracts 231
Lush J 10, 120

Macnaghten J 123
magistrates' courts 4, 7, 27-8, 74-5, 87-8, 117, 213
  accounts 208
  business assets 156
  charges 216, 226, 228-9
  codes of practice 233-4
  complaints 113, 123-4, 174-5, 229, 231
  contracts 231
  criminal remedies 114, 192
  distrainor 82
  entry rights 103, 104
  exempt goods 147-8, 172
  final warnings 94
  financial assets 140
  impounding 129
  insolvency 46, 47, 48
  judicial review 235
  liability to pay sums claimed 25, 26, 27-8
  mortgaged goods 43
  notice of seizure 195
  preconditions 86, 87-8
  rent remedies 189-91
  replevin 186
  resisting distress 37
  restitution orders 189
  sale 202, 203
  staying enforcement 16-17
  tender and payment 197, 198
  warrants 77, 78, 79
  wrongful distress 71, 74-6
mailed goods 168
malice 68-9, 76, 96, 186, 213, 214
  charges 229
  complaints 235-6
  criminal remedies 114
  trespass 108, 109, 111
Mansfield LCJ 10, 101
market tolls and stallages 5
Maule J 125
McCarlie J 11
Mellish J 118, 120
Millett J 205
misfeasance in public office 235-6

misrepresentation 72, 93-4, 102, 128, 130
money 140, 167
money had and received 205-7, 226-7, 228
Morritt LJ 107, 116, 127, 201, 205
mortgages 42-4, 62, 80, 120, 157, 176
  fixtures 144-5

national non-domestic rates (NNDR) 6-7, 27
negligence or neglect 33, 157, 185, 210, 236-7
  interference with goods 181, 184, 185
  removal and storage 201, 202
  sale 205
  wrongful distress 65, 67, 71-5
nil or "no goods" returns 37-8, 55, 106, 113, 139, 176
  repeat levies 210
nominal damages 205, 212, 214, 237
  conversion 183
  interpleader 177, 179
  trespass 111
notice 53-4, 66, 194-6, 204
  competing claims 90
  distress for rent 20-1, 194-6
  exempt goods 150, 195-6
  failure to give 212, 213
  farming stock 156
  final warnings 93-4
  impounding 125-6, 129, 131-2
  insolvency 53-4, 56, 57-8, 62
  interpleader 177-8, 195
  re-entry 201
  replevy 187, 195
  seizure of cars 153
  third party goods 161
  warrants 79
nulla bona 208

ombudsmen 234-5, 237
ovens and ranges 144, 146, 167

Palace of Westminster 97
parking 8, 9, 24
  clamping 133, 136-7
partnerships 48-9, 95, 154-5, 157, 190
  distress for rent 155, 172
  fixtures 144
  insolvency 45, 48-9, 53
  interpleader 155, 176, 180
patents 141, 149, 166
pawnbrokers 161-2, 168
pay and sue 192-3, 226-7
payment under protest 197, 200, 227
  interpleader 176
  wrongful distress 67, 71, 72
personal representatives 151-2
Phillimore J 165
place of levy 1, 20, 31, 96, 97-8
  entry rights 99-100
  highway 115
  impounding 129, 132
  sale 204
  statutory remedies 115
  wrongful distress 68, 71
pledges and liens 161-2
police 7, 28, 37, 72, 75-6, 82, 114
  clamping 133
  forced entry 103, 104-5, 106
  violence 105-6, 239
  warrants 77, 78
possession fees 57, 91
possession man 67, 118-19, 121-2
  charges 224
  clamping 134
  conversion 184
  floating charges 164
  impounding 120, 121-2, 124, 126, 128, 131, 134
possession warrants 11-12
poundage 56, 57, 117, 217-18
poundbreach 32-5, 50, 127, 152
  clamping 135
  preventing seizure 31-5
  treble damages 1-2, 33-5
Powis J 202
previous distress 92-3
prior levies 152, 167, 180
privileged goods *see* exempt goods

racial or sexual abuse 93
railways 155-6
rates 6-7, 9-11, 27, 119, 132, 227, 236
  exempt goods 148
  floating charges 164-5
  insolvency 48, 52, 59
  place of execution 97
  resisting distress 28, 31
  trespass 108, 110
  wrongful distress 67, 75
  see also local taxes
recaption 31-3, 115, 135
re-entry 28-9, 102, 103-4, 200-1
  conversion 183
  impounding 103, 128-9, 137
refusal of tender of payment 69
rent seck 18
repeat levies 209-11
replevy and replevin 10, 186-9
  charges 186-8, 228
  clamping 135
  competing claims 91
  complaints 235, 237, 239
  distress damage feasant 18

replevy and replevin (*cont*):
  distress for rent 22, 172, 186, 188-9
  impounding 126, 135
  income tax 23
  injunction 112
  insolvency 51
  notice 187, 195
  pay and sue 193
  place of execution 98
  remedies 115, 174, 184, 186-9, 191, 213-15
  sale 203
  tender and payment 198, 199, 200
  trespass 109, 112, 186-7, 188
  wrongful distress 71, 75
reputation damage 108, 113, 235
  wrongful seizure 175, 185, 188
rescous 1, 32
rescue 31, 32-5, 98, 198, 201
  stranger's cattle 173
reservation of title clauses 155, 162-3
restitution orders 186, 189
restoration orders 170
Revenue Adjudicator 234-5
reversion 19, 21-2
road traffic penalties 3, 8, 24-5, 81, 194, 201, 213
  cars 154
  charges 3, 24-5, 218, 221
  competing claims 89, 93
  death of parties 85
  distrainor 81, 82, 84
  entry rights 105
  exempt goods 147, 150
  final warnings 93
  financial assets 140
  impounding 131, 134
  interpleader 176, 177
  partnerships 155
  place of execution 97
  sale 202-4
  tender and payment 197, 199
  warrants 79
Romalpa clauses 162
Roskill LJ 78
royal residences 97

sale of goods procedure 5-6, 202-8
  best price 204-5, 208, 211
  interpleader 179, 204, 206, 207
  undervalue 66, 73, 179, 204-6
saleable goods 139-40
Salter J 218
Scotland 3
security 62-3, 120, 178, 179
  replevin 187, 188-9
seisin 38
seizure of goods prevention 13-44
seizure of goods procedure 116-19
  remedies for wrongful 174-93
self-employed persons 25, 86, 153, 184
sheriffs and sheriffs' officers 67-8, 71-3, 81, 117-18, 174, 212, 215
  charges 2, 25, 216-18, 221-7, 229
  competing claims 90, 91-2
  conversion 184
  criminal contempt 114
  defined 242
  distrainor 81, 82
  distress for rent 166
  entry rights 102-5
  execution 5-6
  exempt goods 150
  farming stock 156-7
  financial assets 140-1
  fixtures 145, 146
  floating charges 165
  hired goods 160
  impounding 120, 122-4, 126-8, 132, 137
  insolvency 49-50, 53-9
  interpleader 176, 177-80
  liens and pledges 161-2
  notice of seizure 194-5
  place of execution 97-8
  replevin 186
  resisting distress 29-30, 35, 38
  returns 208-9
  sale 202, 204, 205-7
  saleable goods 139
  staying enforcement 13-14
  storage 200
  tender and payment 196, 197, 199
  trade bodies 237
  trespass 107, 110, 112
  warrants 11, 79, 80
  wrongful distress 65, 67-8, 69-74
  wrongful execution 186
Sheriffs' Officers Association 237
ships 157
Smith J 74
special damages 65, 77, 113, 175, 200, 212-14
  conversion 182
  entry rights 99
  sale 203, 208
  trespass 108, 184
spouses 21, 44, 50, 158-60, 167, 169, 171
  gifts 40-1
  interpleader 159, 176
  walking possession agreement 123-4, 131-2
statutory distraint 1, 6-8, 52, 53, 61, 119, 141
  charges 216, 218, 222, 227-8
  compared with common law distraint 9-11
  deceased debtors 151

exempt goods 148-50, 165
hired goods 160
impounding 122, 131
partnerships 155
place of execution 97
rent remedies 191
repeat levies 209, 211
replevin 186
sale 202
tender and payment 199
time of execution 96-7
stays of proceedings 46-9, 58-61
conversion 184
interpleader 178, 180
replevy 188
tender and payment 198
wrongful distress 69, 73
storage 200-2, 216
subletting and subtenants 19, 21-2, 190
competing claims 89
exempt goods 170-1, 172
Sundays 12, 20, 69, 96
suspension of execution 197-8
suspension of warrants 11, 17

taxation of fees 83, 215, 220-1, 226, 229
taxes 10-11, 78, 152, 165, 216
sale 202, 203, 206
see also council tax; income tax; local taxes
tenants 2, 115, 118, 145-6, 190-1, 212, 214
business assets 156-7
charges 224, 228
competing claims 89-91
death 855
distrainor 81
distress for rent 18-22, 165-73
entry rights 101, 102
fixtures 143-4, 145-6, 147
floating charges 164
impounding 121, 123, 125, 126, 130
injunctions 112
insolvency 49-52
liability for sums claimed 18-22
notice of seizure 195
place of execution 97-8
preconditions 88
removal and storage 201
repeat levies 211
resisting distress 34-9
sale 203, 204, 206, 208
sums leviable 85-6
tender and payment 197-8, 199
warrants 11, 79
wrongful distress 67
tender and payment 196-200
third party goods 2, 157-65, 170-1, 189-91
competing claims 91
complaints 233
distress for rent 22, 165-6, 169, 170-1, 172
insolvency 50, 51
interpleader 176, 177, 179, 180
prior levies 152
sale 206-7
transfers 39-44
trespass 110
wrongful distress 65, 67-8, 72
third party premises 98, 104, 177, 179
three month rule 46, 63
time 96-7, 129, 221, 234
entry rights 103
sale 202-3
warrants 78
wrongful distress 65, 69
Tindal CJ 71, 125
title on sale 206-8, 212, 219
tools of the trade 20, 73, 167
cars 153-4
exempt goods 147-8, 149, 155, 165-6, 167, 173
interference with goods 182, 184
trade bodies 4, 237-40
trading businesses 124-5
transfers of goods to third parties 39-44
trespass 107-12, 114, 115, 117, 174-5, 184-5, 212-14
after seizure 194
charges 226, 228
clamping 134-6
competing claims 91
complaints 113, 237
distrainor 81, 82
distress damage feasant 9, 17-18, 110, 174, 199, 202, 210
distress for rent 21, 110, 112
entry rights 99-101, 104, 108, 110
farming stock 156
fixtures 144
hired goods 160
impounding 120-1, 127, 132, 134-6
interference with goods 108, 110, 181-3, 184-5
interpleader 112, 177, 180
place of execution 98
removal and storage 201, 202
rent remedies 191
repeat levies 210, 211
replevin 109, 112, 186-7, 188
resisting distress 28-9, 32-3, 38
sale 202, 203, 205, 207
tender and payment 198, 199
time of execution 96
warrants 77

trespass (*cont*):
  wrongful distress 65-75
  wrongful execution 185
trespass *ab initio* 109-10, 111, 212-13
  clamping 135
  conduct after seizure 194
  distress damage feasant 202
  loss of goods seized 202
  repeat levies 211
  sale 202, 207
  wrongful distress 65, 68
trespass to goods 65, 71, 109, 110, 184-5, 187
trespass to person 71, 109, 110-11
Trevor CJ 196
trustees of bankruptcy 37, 40, 45, 49-58, 62-3
  farming stock 156
  fixtures 146
  impounding 120, 124
  wrongful distress 72
trusts 39, 41, 42, 151

under-sheriffs 6, 73, 81
Under-Sheriffs' Association 237
unfair dealing 58, 61
unlawful wounding 114
unsold goods for want of buyers 208
utility fittings 157-8, 167

value added tax (VAT) 7, 23, 33, 86-7, 141, 212
  charges 216, 218
  competing claims 92
  complaints 236
  entry rights 102
  exempt goods 3, 148
  insolvency 47, 52
  inventories 196
  sale 202, 203, 205, 206
  time of execution 96
  warrants 77
venditioni exponas 208
violence 28-30, 34, 93, 114, 239
  entry rights 103, 105-6
  trespass to person 110-11

waiver 66, 70, 96, 102, 130
  exempt goods 150
  prior levies 152
walking possession 2, 7, 116, 122, 123-7, 175, 215
  cars 153
  charges 217, 221-2, 224, 225
  complaints 113
  impounding 120-1, 122, 123-7, 128-35, 137-8
  insolvency 62-3
  interpleader 179
  inventories 196
  notice of seizure 194, 196
  removal and storage 201
  resisting distress 33-5
warrants 2, 6, 7-8, 11-12, 77-80
  staying enforcement 13-17
  suspension 11, 17
white goods 139, 144, 148, 149
Wightman J 104, 116
Wills J 168
Windeyer J 3, 106
windings up 48-9, 51, 52, 53, 56-7, 63
  leave to proceed 58-61
windows 100, 101, 130
Woolf reforms 6
Wright LJ 111, 202
writ of *fieri facias* (fi fa) 10, 30, 67, 72, 94, 132
  accounts 208
  insolvency 56
  sale 204
  warrants 79
wrongful execution 67-71, 185-6
wrongful interference *see* interference with goods